MARX AND THE MISSING LINK:
"HUMAN NATURE"

Also by W. Peter Archibald

SOCIAL PSYCHOLOGY AS POLITICAL ECONOMY

Marx and the Missing Link: "Human Nature"

W. Peter Archibald

Associate Professor of Sociology
McMaster University, Hamilton, Ontario

MACMILLAN

First published 1989

Published by
THE MACMILLAN PRESS LTD
Houndmills, Basingstoke, Hampshire RG21 2XS
and London
Companies and representatives
throughout the world

British Library Cataloguing in Publication Data
Archibald, W. Peter
Marx and the missing link: human nature'.
1. Man. Nature, Theories of Marx, Karl,
1818–1883
I. Title
128' .4
ISBN 978-1-349-09186-7   ISBN 978-1-349-09184-3 (eBook)
DOI 10.1007/978-1-349-09184-3

For Marx, Lindsey, and Emma

Acknowledgments

Perhaps no one was more adamant than Marx that any human project, no matter how individual and esoteric it might seem, is the product of much collective effort, and this one is clearly no exception.

Thus it was a comment by Martin Silverman on an earlier work of mine, where I had compared the actions of individuals in different cultures, which led me to explore what, for me, was a whole new side of Marx's theorizing. The comment was, "Yes, but what is an '*individual*'?"; the other side was the theories of 'individuation' and 'agency'. Similarly, my attempts to rectify the apparent absence of a 'general human nature' in Marx floundered until my students – especially Sara Erskine – asked me when I was going to stop simply reviewing Freudian, existential, and symbolic interactionist neo-Marxisms and tell them what *I* thought Marx and contemporary human beings were up to.

Since taking that fateful step I have benefitted from the encouragement and constructive criticism of more friends, colleagues, and students than I could ever hope to acknowledge here. However, special thanks should go to Jim Rinehart, who set me straight after a vague first draft, and to Jim Peterson, that Renaissance man who, while jogging with me on the Niagara escarpment, gave me instantaneous feedback on most of the arguments set out in the book. (If only my knees had lasted as long as his have!) Others who have criticized various parts of the book and/or suggested references include Roy Broadbent, Tom Langford, Bhula Bhadra, Michael Michie, Bob Storey, and Richard Bourhis.

Special mention should also be made of the various people who helped make a half-year sabbatical in Europe in 1982 possible and so stimulating. To McMaster University, and Dean Peter George in particular, many thanks, and the same to the Social Science and Humanities Research Council of Canada (contract #410-81-0761) for travel and living expenses, and typing and word processing resources for the early stages of this research. My stay in England would not have been so commodious and profitable without the hospitality and patience of the philosopher Gerry Cohen, who assured me that what is general need not be either unimportant or uninteresting; the sociologists Huw Beynon, Theo Nichols, Anna Pollert, John Torrance and Paul Willis; and the psychologists Michael Billig, Rupert Brown, Colin Fraser, and

John Turner. I hope they will forgive me for continuing to try to force their work into my own mould, and for 'picking their brains' and then not following up many of the leads.

Finally, I would like to acknowledge the specifically 'womanual' labour which has gone into this project. Until I mechanized my own labour with a word processor, the typing and word processing of Jackie Tucker, Amy Stott, and Shirley McGill (and transferal work of George Stewart) was indispensable. After I mechanized, I was fortunately kept in touch with the realities of human nature by the love and support of my wife, Lindsey George, and the demands and smile of our daughter Emma, who arrived, complete with 'colic', just when I had promised Mr Farmiloe, the publisher, I would finally send him a completed manuscript! (My thanks to him for *his* patience.) The finishing of this book has undoubtedly modified Lindsey's and Emma's nature as well as mine. I can only hope they have shared in some of the pleasure and excitement I have experienced along the way. As for the pain and drudgery, if someone invents a machine that will find and type footnotes rather than simply move them around and renumber them, I might even write another book!

Contents

Introduction   1

Part I: Re-reading Marx for the Individual and the Psyche

1 New Grundrisse for the Levels of Analysis Problem   13

Part II: "Human Nature as Modified in each Historical
       Epoch"

*2 Community and Individuality: the Theory of
   "Individuation"*   45

*3 The Role of "The Individual" in History: the Theory of
   "Agency"*   61

Part III: "Human Nature in General"

Introduction   79

4 Needs and Wants   83

5 Responses to Gratification and Deprivation   97

6 Knowledge   113

7 A General Psychology of Intergroup Relations   133

Part IV: Evaluating Marx's Theories of Human Nature
       "Empirically"

Introduction   165

8 Individuation and Agency Revisited   181

9 How "General" is "Human Nature"?   235

10 Conclusion   299

Index   302

Introduction

We have just now emerged from a period of theorizing by Marxists where individual human beings have often been discounted as epiphenomenal. Their psychic characteristics have been conceived as nearly totally derivative of social relations, ideology, or social formations as a whole, and as having little impact upon social structuration and change. To the extent that such characteristics have any role at all in this mode of theorizing, they have usually done so only passively. For example, because human individuals have an expanding coterie of needs the production of commodities is also said to expand (automatically). That such individuals are also the conscious and active producers of their own social relations and ideology, who *demand* that (certain of) their needs be met and (sometimes) become *agents* of social change when these needs are *not* met, has often been lost in the fray.

These "crimes against humanity", so to speak, have been especially evident among French structuralists and their sympathizers,[1] but they have recurred cyclicly throughout the history of Marxist theorizing. Nor has the problem simply been the appropriation of mechanistic models from the natural sciences, as is alleged to have occurred with Engels and, later, orthodox Marxists in the Stalinist period, since a remarkably similar discounting of individual and psychic processes can be found in the early critical work of Georg Lukács, who insisted that class consciousness "is identical with neither the psychological consciousness of individual members of the proletariat, nor with the (mass-psychological) consciousness of the proletariat as a whole", and as such is very distinct "from the empirically given, and from the psychologically describable and explicable ideas which men form from their situation in life."[2]

It is difficult to avoid the conclusion that such anti-psychologistic stances have been motivated by the requirements of particular political praxes, and often highly sectarian ones. Lukács was concerned with the complacency of German social democrats, which he felt derived from their methodological individualism: if too few workers are conscious of their true class interests, they maintained, one should simply wait until political–economic conditions change and (automatically) change enough individual workers' consciousness.[3] Similarly, Althusser himself has expressed his concern that "humanist" interpretations of Marx have been used to criticize Eastern Communism as well as Western Capitalism.[4]

1

However, to reduce the problem to "ideological police work"[5] is also to fail to understand the spread and depth of its roots. The facts of the matter are that the vast majority of Marx's interpreters, whether sympathizers or critics, have been profoundly anti-psychological. Furthermore, although there is anything but a dearth of treatises on Marx and "the" human individual, the bulk of these can be lumped into two categories: those whose authors expound mainly upon the more abstract and philosophical of Marx's conceptions of individuals, which are alleged to provide the ethical and methodological foundations for his work as a whole, and/or those whose authors have a genuine interest in psychology, but who have approached Marx with their own sectarian interests in modern psychology (for example, Freudian) and pronounced him to have either lacked a psychology or possessed an inappropriate (for example, naively rationalistic) one.[6]

My purpose here is to attempt to set the record straight, especially with regard to Marx himself, with the hope that by understanding his own psychologizing better we can both evaluate and revise his and our own theorizing more adequately than we have in the past. My own reading and presentation of Marx's psychological anthropology or social psychology has four premises.

First, Marx had an elaborate conception of "human nature" – an anthropology – which was not simply philosophical and sociological, but psychological. He was concerned to specify not only human individuals" abstract capacities and "objective", "empirically" observable demographic and other characteristics, such as their age and sex, social activities, and freedom and individuality, but also their "internal", covert thoughts, emotions, needs and other predispositions to act which we usually think of as psychic and unanalyzable without a psychologic.

Second, the psychic processes with which he was concerned were those he believed to be common to individuals in all periods of history as well as those specific to only certain periods. That this has been so little appreciated may lie with common misconceptions of Marx's methodology. That individuals can only be analyzed within their "given social connection" does not mean that they are not engaged in psychic processes which occur in all social connections.[7] I suspect that those who have hitherto argued for Marx's interest in "human nature in general" have been less than completely persuasive because they have not followed Marx's own method for concluding what such general processes are.[8]

Third, and contrary to many of those who can rightly claim awareness of Marx's method of abstraction, these psychic processes common to individuals in all periods of history do not simply constitute an abstract "shell" which has little explanatory import. They are by no means restricted to either bio-physical characteristics[9] or simply those psychic characteristics which make all human producers architects rather than bees. Rather, they include the complicated structures such as need hierarchies and processes such as social comparison and "frustration–aggression" which we more typically associate with Freud and modern mainstream psychology.

Fourthly and finally, the explanatory importance of such general psychic processes is by no means restricted to the level of the individual; to, for example, the emotional withdrawal from labour which is one aspect of Marx's account of alienation, and the frustration which leads to individualistic acts of sabotage. To the contrary, such individual-level processes are inexcisable, albeit not always explicit, components of Marx's explanations for most of the structured social processes with which he was concerned, from the seeming independence of the capitalist political economy from the "consciousness and wills of individuals" to the class-conscious revolt which is supposed to bring social relations under the control of the individuals who participate in them.

The latter claim raises the spectre of "methodological individualism", even "psychological reductionism", and is therefore likely to be most strongly resisted by Marxists and non-Marxists alike. This is understandable, but unwarranted. Although Dumont, Tucker, and Elster have recently argued that Marx was, and/or should have been, both a methodological individualist and a psychological reductionist,[10] this is far from the general point I would like to make here. Marx was never *only* an individualist and psychological reductionist, even when he was explaining phenomena on the level of individuals. For Marx *neither* social *nor* individual phenomena were completely reducible to a psychologic. But this by no means precludes psychic processes playing a crucial, even decisive role in social processes, as I believe they often did in Marx's own theorizing.

Given the centrality of the latter problems of levels of analysis, we shall examine them and lay out a framework for analyzing the nature and role of individuals before moving on to discuss the specifics of Marx's psychological anthropology or social psychology. When we arrive at the latter we shall proceed in keeping with Marx's own professed methodology, beginning with his descriptions of individuals in each historical epoch, and only after doing so abstracting the psychic characteristics he appears to have assumed individuals in all such epochs have in common. Having thus examined "human nature in general and human nature as modified in each historical epoch", we shall discuss the utility of Marx's psychology in light of empirical work in the social sciences since his own time.

The conclusions I have drawn in the latter parts of the book are too numerous and complex to be summarized very adequately in this brief introduction. Nevertheless, I shall try to give the reader some idea of where he or she is being taken.

One conclusion, already implied above, is that the psychology which underlies much of Marx's theorizing is far less different from that which one finds in contemporary social science than has usually been assumed; Marx's Hegelian, utopian socialist, and other seemingly esoteric roots notwithstanding. Specifically, he too relied heavily upon assumptions about needs and their hierarchical organization, about processes of "social comparison", "relative deprivation", and "frustration–aggression".

Another conclusion is that although Marx himself avoided many of the pitfalls which often accompany the use of such psychologics, he by no means avoided *all* of them, and the hitherto failure of some of his predictions for the future of capitalism can be partly lain at the feet of these misconceptions about human nature. Nor are these misconceptions necessarily those most commonly attributed to Marx. For example, it can be argued that Marx's problem was less that he had a naively rationalistic conception of human nature than that some of his other assumptions about how individuals respond to deprivation are faulty. For instance, human individuals often tolerate much more deprivation and frustration than Marx believed they can and will.

On the other hand, when measured against the yardstick of modern social psychology much of Marx's psychologizing about "human nature in general" turns out to be sound. In these cases the failure of some of Marx's expectations appears to lie only in the fact that the historically specific "initial conditions" which set off certain psychic processes rather than others have often failed to materialize. Perhaps most importantly, both the experience of deprivation and one's responses to it tend to be very different depending upon whether one functions highly individually or as part of a group in conflict with another. However, most workers have been far less likely to function collectively, at least on a class-wide and long-term basis, than Marx expected them to.

Part of the latter problem may lie with Marx's predilection for *post hoc* analyses of social movements of workers who were unusually highly organized – emigré German artisans, Parisian workers in the late 1840s, and so on. But it may also have to do with the peculiar strengths and weaknesses of his theory of alienation.

To wit, Marx's expectation that the circumstances most workers face most of the time – fragmented ties and competition with each other – combine with their general human nature to produce indifference, even hostility, toward each other, turns out to be all too correct and to work against the alternative process of class organization. On the other hand, the effects of other circumstances which are supposed to goad workers to organize themselves in spite of their alienation from each other were often exaggerated by Marx.

Thus, while psychic alienation from labour is in fact rife, it often does not have the effect of drawing workers together and increasing their sense of collective deprivation and injustice. Rather, either or both of two other results are at least as frequent: on the job, workers organize on a very local basis and develop ways, often highly innovative, of making their work more meaningful and less alienating; off the job, they often avoid both their work and each other. The former is then likely to counteract their sense of deprivation and injustice; the latter their tendency to organize against deprivation and injustice even when they do experience them.

Marx's psychology differs most from those currently popular in psychology and sociology – indeed, in anthropology and history, often whether Marxist or otherwise – in both its methodology for arriving at what is specific and general and in its stress upon the ubiquity and importance of the historically specific. Here he was concerned to emphasize on the one hand the changing parameters of, and resources and constraints upon, individuals – especially how distinct and autonomous they are from each other – and on the other with the specific form and content their "inner" psychic processes, particularly their needs and experiences, take in different communities, historical epochs, and classes. Contrary to Althusserian structuralists, the former theories of "individuation" and "agency" owe a great deal to Hegel's *Philosophy of History*, but contrary to Hegelian humanists they were not intended as simply neat schemes from deriving one concept from another. However, as we shall see in Chapter 8, the Hegelian scenario of a dialectical transformation from individuals completely immersed in, and dominated by, the community to those apparently, and eventually actually, developed in their distinctiveness and autonomy is in fact *too* neat as a characterization of human history. Indeed, I suspect that there is more empirical support for Marx's theories of "human nature in general", which overlap most with contemporary social psychology, than for his theories of "human nature as modified in each historical epoch", which his followers have been most concerned to flog. Nevertheless, the latter not only raise questions which no others have, but provide or point to many interesting and accurate answers.

Having outlined my major arguments, I would like to comment upon two critical queries I have often received from colleagues and friends about this kind of enterprise. One, most often from fellow Marxists, is this: "While you *claim* to be presenting and critiquing *Marx*'s psychology, how can we be sure this is what you have given us? Is there not in fact *at least as much* of Peter Archibald's as Marx's psychologizing here?" The other, more typical of neo- and non-Marxists, is this one: "Why are you still so concerned with what Marx 'really meant'? Shouldn't we dispense with this ultimately unanswerable, and even uninteresting, question and instead concentrate upon what is going on now and how *we* can best explain it?"

On the first problem, I confess to having brought my own experiences to this project, but since, as Marx himself noted, we are all prisoners of our own milieu, how could it have been otherwise? I think we should ve leery of those of Marx's interpreters who either insinuate that they have no "biases" or that their having them has made little difference.

To illustrate the problem with the latter strategy, consider the highly useful but sometimes misleading account of Marx's conception of human nature by Bertell Ollman.[11] He begins by suggesting that "Marx must be allowed sufficient time unimpeded by constant interruptions to establish his views."[12] Marx is then portrayed as having made "rational man" the centrepiece of his conception of human nature in general,[13] and subsequently criticized for allegedly having been naive in this respect.[14] Then, and only then, do we learn that Ollman is a neo-Freudian of the Reichian variety who feels that Marx should have stressed, or at least that we should now stress, the role of sexuality, character structure, and others of the "irrational" aspects of the human psyche.

By way of contrast, John Plamenatz[15] and Melvin Rader[16] began their interpretations of Marx on human nature by explicitly noting that they were liberals with serious misgivings about much of Marx's theorizing. However, among the various psychic processes utilized by Marx the more "irrational", "lashing out" processes of "frustration-aggression" and the like are stressed at least as much as the rational.[17] The irony here is that, as we shall see below, these latter two presentations of Marx's psychologizing are probably much closer to the truth of what Marx himself intended than is Ollman's.

Why a Freudian, for whom processes of frustration–aggression are central, should overlook these aspects of Marx's psychologizing while two "enlightenment" liberals, for whom rationality is central, should not, is difficult to fathom. But hopefully I have illustrated my point: whether or not there is a clear, one-to-one relationship between one's own starting point and the conclusions one is likely to draw about Marx's conception of human nature, there is little assurance of objectivity. The long-term interests of science as a whole may therefore be better served by a variety of different readings than a single, allegedly definitive reading of Marx.

To my own way of thinking, if the present work helps others to better understand and critique Marx's psychologizing it will not be because I have been more objective than others, but because I have brought to Marx a background which has hitherto not been. This is my training in mainstream sociology and psychology and familiarity with both the "levels of analysis" problem in general and various theoretical trends in contemporary social psychology. Just as G.A. Cohen has recently used analytic philosophy to great advantage in drawing out and critiquing the formal logic of Marx's explanations,[18] so I would like to believe that my training in social psychology has allowed me to discover and critique various aspects of Marx's psychologizing that others have missed. Obviously, however, the reader must decide this for him or herself.

As to the second charge, that Marx's theorizing should not be our major object of study in the first place, I hope to show in Part IV that this has in effect not been the case in this project after all; that much of Marx's psychologic has not in fact been peculiar to him. Certainly, when a Genovese (or even a Finley) analyzes slavery, a Hilton feudalism, or a Thompson the early stages of capitalism, he employs much the same reasoning, and the same can be said for many other well-known contemporary analysts who have not been so avowedly Marxist. To evaluate Marx's social psychology, therefore, is to evaluate the worth of much of the received wisdom in contemporary social science.

How fair I have been to Marx and others is something the reader will also have to judge for him or herself. I have at least devoted much more space to an "empirical" assessment of these conceptions of human nature than any other analyst of whom I am aware. The reasons for this lie not only with my mainstream background, which is admittedly a somewhat peculiar one for a "Marxist" (although this has been changing of late), but with my relative disinterest in "what Marx really said or meant" and concern to get on with the task of finding the best means for understanding and changing reality.

NOTES

1. Louis Althusser, *For Marx* (Harmondsworth: Penguin, 1969) pp. 10–11, 221–3, 231. (With E. Balibar) *Reading Capital* (London: New Left Books (Verso), 1979) pp. 111–12. See also Victor Molina, "Notes on Marx and the problem of individuality", pp. 230–58 in Centre for Contemporary Cultural Studies, *On Ideology* (London: Hutchinson, 1978) pp. 232, 236, 243.
2. Georg Lukács, *History and Class Consciousness* (Cambridge, Mass.: MIT Press, 1971) pp. 73, 51.
3. Lukács, op. cit., p. 77.
4. Althusser, 1979, op. cit., pp. 51–2.
5. E. P. Thompson, *The Poverty of Theory* (New York: Monthly Review Press, 1978) p. 131.
6. In the first category I would place such works as Adam Schaff's *Marxism and the Human Individual* (New York: McGraw-Hill, 1970) and István Mészáros's *Marx's Theory of Alienation* (New York: Harper and Row, 1972); in the second, Bertell Ollman's *Alienation* (Cambridge: Cambridge University Press, 1971).
7. As, for example, Molina (op. cit.) wrongly implies. See the next chapter.
8. Ollman, op. cit. John McMurtry, *The Structure of Marx's World View* (Princeton: Princeton University Press, 1978). Norman Geras, *Marx and Human Nature: Refutation of a Legend* (London: New Left Books (Verso), 1983).
9. As is implied, for example, by Agnes Heller, *The Theory of Need in Marx* (London: Allison and Busby, 1978) pp. 32, 43.
10. Louis Dumont, *From Mandeville to Marx: The Genesis and Triumph of Economic Ideology* (Chicago: University of Chicago Press, 1977). D. F. B. Tucker, *Marxism and Individualism* (Oxford: Blackwell, 1980). Jon Elster, "Marxism, functionalism, and game theory: The case for methodological individualism", *Theory and Society*, vol. 11, 1982, (July), pp. 453–82.
11. Ollman, op. cit.
12. Ibid., p. xvi.
13. Ibid., p. 114.
14. Ibid., pp. 238–9.
15. John Plamenatz, *Karl Marx's Philosophy of Man* (Oxford: Oxford University (Clarendon), 1976) p. x.
16. Melvin Rader, *Marx's Interpretation of History* (New York: Oxford University Press, 1979) p. vi.

17. Plamenatz, pp. 97–8, 124, 142; Rader, pp. 18–27.
18. G. A. Cohen, *Karl Marx's Theory of History: A Defence* (Princeton: Princeton University Press, 1978).

Part I
Re-reading Marx for the Individual and the Psyche

1 New Grundrisse for the Levels of Analysis Problem

For many of his interpreters, Marx was both a "methodological holist" and a "sociological reductionist"; that is, his only units of analysis were collective "totalities" such as entire communities and classes, and he regarded such collective phenomena as not only "independent of the consciousness and wills" of individuals, but themselves the only (or by far the most important) *sources* of the latter. For some such interpreters, most notably Lukács and Althusser, this was as it should be;[1] for others such as E. P. Thompson, Jean Cohen, and Jon Elster, such thinking is a misguided hypostatization of society and reification of individuals, an "objective teleology" which, in Marx's case, represented a regression to the Hegelianism of his youth and/or an obsession with bourgeois political economy and its stress on the market.[2] Astoundingly, for still others, especially Louis Dumont,[3] Marx was *both* a methodological individualist *and* a *psychological* reductionist! Here too he is alleged to have been unable to escape the quagmire of political economy, only now the major carryover was *homo economicus* rather than a self-regulating market. Finally, for a fourth category of commentators, including Joachim Israel and D. F. B. Tucker, Marx was a methodological individualist in order to avoid an objective teleology, but he did not in fact resort to psychological reductionism either.[4]

These are the issues we shall try to unravel in this chapter. They are highly complex; they are also overly convoluted in the literature. For a start, one can be a methodological holist without also being a sociological reductionist, or, as Israel has noted, a methodological individualist and not be a psychological reductionist. For this reason I have tried to separate the two sets of issues here. However, as we shall soon see, Marx's theorizing does not appear to fit into *any* of the above boxes.

METHODOLOGICAL INDIVIDUALISM, "INDIVIDUALITY" AND "AGENCY"

In the *German Ideology* Marx wrote of the need to analyze "real", "living" "individuals" and their seemingly inherently individual characteristics; their "corporeal" features such as "needs", deprivation, "suffering", and so on.[5] Yet he also stressed that by "real" he meant individuals who exist in "given social connections" or "relations".[6] To analyze individuals separately from the latter relations, as had left Hegelians such as Feuerbach as well as the bourgeois political economists before them, is to employ a highly inappropriate methodology.[7] In the *Ideology* such relations and the wider "totalities" of which they are parts are labelled and analyzed in various ways: as analytically separate relations such as the division of labour, exchange and property; collectively as "forms of intercourse" and institutions; periods and epochs of history, and so on.

In both his outline of historical materialism in the *Poverty of Philosophy* and methodological introduction to the *Grundrisse*, Marx strongly cautioned against analyzing collectivities and systems as simply aggregates of individuals. His own starting point, he wrote, was not "the population" and other such aggregative concepts but the "*social individual*", which he defined as the individual who, as with *all* human individuals, must, and does, belong to a community and/or sub-community such as a social class and produce "in society".[8] Furthermore, the social relations with which Marx appeared to have been concerned in most of his analyses are not "interpersonal" relations among independent and unique "individuals", but in effect "role" relationships where, to the extent that individuals are unique to begin with, which they may well not be, as we shall see in a moment, individuals' "individual" (distinct, unique) characteristics are excluded from analysis.[9] Put otherwise, "individuals" as we usually think of them are only "partially included" in the analysis.[10]

These strictures suggest a fundamental asymmetry in Marx's conceptualization of the relationship between "the" individual and society: all individuals, and presumably all of each individual, are included in the community, but all of the community – and the social relations of which it is composed – is not included in the population of individuals who are its members. If this conclusion is correct, we should presumably also conclude that Marx's *primary* unit of analysis was *not* in fact "the" individual, but the community as a whole and/or the social relations which form its core. Certainly Marx stressed that "the" individual is a highly variable phenomenon historically, so much so that in the beginning of human "history" in the weak sense of the term (more of this in a minute) such a creature (that is, a distinct and autonomous one) did not even *exist*.

"The more deeply we go back into history", Marx wrote in the *Grundrisse*, "the more does the individual, and hence the producing individual, appear as dependent, as belonging to a greater whole . . . . Only in the eighteenth century, in 'civil society', do the various forms of social connectedness confront the individual as a mere means toward his private purposes, as external necessity."[11] Furthermore, he was later to write that the problem with which he was most concerned was not how separate producers came to relate to each other and their equally separate means of production, labour and particular products, as they do in bourgeois society, but how these separations occurred in the first place.[12] Finally, in the *Grundrisse* the vast bulk of Marx's analyses of "individuals" concern the process whereby they became "individuated" from the community, particular exploiters of labour power, the land and distinct means of production; "individuation" here referring to both quantitative and qualitative differences in "freedom" or autonomy, and "individuality" or distinctiveness.[13]

According to Marx, in the earliest human communities "individuals" were in fact so little characterized by freedom and individuality that one can think of them as "species-beings" or "herd animals" who were in a sense possess*ions*, rather than possess*ors*, of their own community.[14] As social act*ors* they were by definition act*ive*, but they were "agents" only in the weakest sense of the term; that is, they thought of themselves and acted as representatives of the community as a whole rather than as "free agents" with "self-interests".[15] Certainly, believing as they did that their community had a divine origin, and ruled as they often were by despots who were believed to be representatives of the deity, they can hardly be thought of as agents in the sense of the (intentional) "makers" of "history".[16] Even in those early communities whose members had some interests in property which partially separated them from each other, as was the case in Greece and Rome in classical antiquity, communal took precedence over individual interests, and as such even the establishment of city states, in part for the protection of property interests, can be seen as only "*partly* historic" events.[17]

We shall return to the saga of individuation through history in the next chapter, but hopefully the reader has gotten enough of the flavour of Marx's account of the changing parameters of individuality and agency to see that a straightforward interpretation of Marx as strictly a methodological holist *or* individualist is highly problematic.

The truth to the individualist label is that Marx often did describe the actions and internal psychic states of biologically distinct human individuals, even where he believed them to lack any significant amount of psychic distinctiveness or autonomy to express or develop it. Furthermore, to anticipate the next section of this chapter, the beliefs and motives of such "individuals" were important aspects of his *explanations* for various collective as well as individual phenomena in such communities. Thus in those described above, individuals' allegiance to the community as a whole rather than themselves figures prominently.

On the other hand, precisely because individuals thought of themselves and acted as part of a collectivity rather than as self-interested individuals, any legitimate analysis must start with the nature of the community and the immersion or separation of its individual members from it. Members may indeed be individuated to the point where rational calculation of self-interest is a reasonable, partial explanation for their thoughts and actions, but this cannot simply be assumed to be universal, as is the case with bourgeois political economy, or with Elster, who suggests that we should all become "game theorists".[18] Similarly, as Perry Anderson has pointed out so well,[19] members *may* be organized and knowledgeable enough to be historic rather than simply free (albeit largely deluded) agents, in opposition to the Althusserian conception of them as *necessarily* duped "personifications" of their economic roles in bourgeois society[20] and in support of critics such as Thompson, but one cannot simply assume them to *necessarily* be so organized and knowledgeable either, as Thompson and others often do.[21]

This is the curious thing about Marx's would-be defenders and critics: whether "structuralist" *or* "humanist", most have failed to fully appreciate his own comparative historical methodology, a methodology he used both to identify and critique the ideological biases of bourgeois political economy and German idealism and to make his own discoveries and construct his own theories. This methodology should be no deep secret: rather than presuming, *a priori*, that the particular features of individuals in any one social formation, such as bourgeois society, are common to all individuals in all social formations, one must first study and compare individuals in *different* societies and classes. When an Althusserian such as Molina takes the split between the "class" and "personal" individual, or individuals' "indifference to each other's individuality", to be universal, he has violated Marx's own methods, but the same is true of a humanist like Ollman who universalizes the same split and then proclaims Marx to have presumed all human individuals to be rational.[22]

Yet for all this, *Marx himself did not deny the validity of inducing features common to human individuals in different, and even all, social circumstances*, providing it is done with such a comparative historical method and not through introspection or some other speculative method such as those employed by the "German ideologists". In support of this position I offer the following "facts".

First, Marx's method for abstracting "human nature in general" from "human nature as modified in each particular epoch"[23] – for example, the needs all human individuals share in common – is no different from that he used to abstract the general features of the processes of "cooperation" and "human labour" from those in particular modes of production.[24]

Second, for Marx the major problem with *both* bourgeois political economists *and* Young Hegelians such as Feuerbach is *not* that they employed conceptions of human nature in general, but that they (a) generalized from observations of individuals in only one social formation, nation, class or stratum – indeed, as with Max Stirner, the penniless and solitary (and therefore also hungry and sexually frustrated) schoolteacher, sometimes from *themselves* alone,[25] and (b) therefore came up with *particular* presumptions about what is common to human nature which are simply wrong.[26]

The first "fact" is in fact an extrapolation, but a highly reasonable one, and the second was explicitly asserted by Marx himself.[27] This being the case, one might well wonder why structuralists and most others who claim to have dissected Marx's methods have failed to distinguish between legitimately (and illegitimately) derived conceptions of human nature in general. As suggested earlier, I believe that much of the problem lies with blinding sectarian passions against either "humanism" and psychologism in general or particular psychologies. However, were these the only problems, a great many psychologically non-aligned humanists should have arrived at Marx's psychological conceptions of human nature in general.

I suspect that ignorance of social psychology more generally may be part of the problem. Certainly, most humanist accounts have been so concerned with the highly abstract qualities and "potentialities" of humans that they have seldom descended to earth to describe "real", "corporeal" individuals, at least in a manner which would allow us to explain their actions. The latter tendency is probably related to the reason most obvious to the reading empirical mind: a propensity to confuse the relationship between the specific and the general in *Marx's* mind. Put more concretely, although Marx believed human individuals in different social formations and modes of production have many characteristics in common, he did not consider these characteristics to either *pre*-exist or exist *outside* of specific historical circumstances. Put otherwise, Marx's conception of human nature in general was not an "ontology" in the strict sense of the term.[28]

If there was a substantial change in Marx's thinking from his Hegelian youth to his scientific maturity, it was much less a matter of his having dispensed with his belief in the importance of a general human nature and such psychic phenomena as alienation than in a new concern to study them more empirically and comparatively in the manner broadly outlined above. Yet his humanist interpreters still spend an inordinate amount of time and effort agonizing over the precise nature of his alleged ontology and little if any on the concrete, psychological aspects of his theorizing. Lukácsian Hegelians like István Mészáros are among the worst offenders (although Gyorgy Márkus is much better),[29] but they are not alone. If I may again "pick on" Ollman, I refer the reader to a qualification he makes to his otherwise helpful characterization of Marx's method for studying human nature in general as the search for "what is common to all men at all times". The qualification is that what is common is that which characterizes "man 'outside of history' "![30]

Even more surprising are recent accounts whose authors have made liberal use of English translations of the *Grundrisse* and Marx's theories of individuation and agency. Thus given that she explicitly attributes an ontology to Marx, it is perhaps not so surprising that the individuals in Carol Gould's rendition always possess individuality, seldom suffer, and never even *attempt* to make history.[31] Similarly, in clear contradiction to Marx's own disclaimers that he was interested in the movements among "mere concepts", Roslyn Bologh proclaims that "Marx does not do an empirical history, but using empirical illustrations, he formulates the possibility of capital in terms of the possible forms that are *analytically* prior to capitalism – unity as analytically prior to separation. Thus the stages [of individuation] are not empirical events in history, but analytic formulations."[32] Incidentally, this same un-Marxian anti-empiricism is a feature common to almost all of the Marxacologists we have been discussing here.[33]

PSYCHOLOGICAL EXPLANATION AND REDUCTIONISM

It is very easy to establish that Marx often explained the thoughts, feelings and actions of *individuals psycho*logically. As an example, take one of the best-known phenomena associated with his theorizing: alienation. The medieval craftsman, Marx suggested, was far more involved in his work than the modern wage labourer – in fact, he was "completely absorbed in it" – because of two antecedent conditions: he anticipated becoming a master, which required that he become "proficient in the whole of his craft", and becoming proficient entailed at least a modicum of artistic, and therefore also self, expression.[34] Indeed, such self-expression even distinguishes the shepherd in earlier, pastoral modes of production from the modern wage labourer.[35]

Having done so, however, it would be much more difficult to demonstrate that (a) such psychological explanations for individuals' actions are "complete" and "closed"; that is, that they contain enough assumptions to fully explain the phenomena in question, and that even if they do, that none of these assumptions themselves depend upon other, for example, *socio*logical assumptions which are not explicitly employed in the original explanation;[36] and (b) that such psychological processes can also explain *social*, and particularly socially organized or *structured*, processes, and especially can do so completely and closedly.

The latter two conditions define a strictly psychologically reductionistic explanation. By these criteria, even Marx's explanations for psychic alienation are not psychologically reductionistic. Thus neither the craftsman's belief that he will become a master nor his capacity to express himself are ultimately reducible to his own psychic makeup. Rather, these conditions also result from a number of socially structured circumstances which themselves cannot simply be reduced to the psychic characteristics of the individuals who are affected by them,[37] even though these individuals contribute to the existence of these structured circumstances in the first place, as Marx himself often pointed out.[38]

However, having said this, I would like to serve notice that I shall eventually argue that Marx, good dialectician that he was, was in fact *both* a *partial socio*logical *and* a *partial psycho*logical reductionist. The necessity for such an interpretation has already been hinted at in the example we have just examined,[39] but I shall reserve fuller discussion until we have reviewed some of the vast and perplexing literature on these problems of levels of analysis.

For the purpose of this review I shall follow the practice of most other writers on the topic and simply distinguish between two levels and types of analysis: the individual level, where analysts tend to emphasize "social action", "human agency" and "internal" psychic processes in their explanations, and the level of "collective behaviour", and especially social organization, where explanations tend instead to be "systemic", "functionalist", and otherwise supra-individualistic.[40] As I see it, at least four relationships between these two levels and types of analyses have been suggested.

(1) The two types of analyses are contradictory

This thesis has recently been provocatively presented by Alan Dawe.[41] Systemic type analyses, the argument goes, preclude an adequate account of human agency; conversely, an adequate account of the latter obviates the need for the usual type of systemic analysis. Dawe does not opt for complete methodological individualism and psychologial reductionism, but he rejects systemic analyses which are not closely derived from analyses of social action.

Such an assumption has long served as an interpretation of Marx's theorizing. For example, after having forcefully argued that Marx was able successfully to transcend "the classic dichotomy between subject and object", Shlomo Avineri went on to note an apparently contradictory element in Marx's theorizing: under present circumstances, those in a developed capitalist formation, individuals cannot in fact practise this new epistemology and are therefore much more the objects than the subjects of their society.[42] As we saw earlier, since then a host of critics have accused Marx of having pushed this claim too far.

Perhaps the first thing which should be said of these charges is that they are largely true. Thus as Elster as well as Thompson has shown, Marx in fact often not only employed systemic analyses, but systemic analyses of the most vulgar functionalist variety: capitalism as a whole or its representative, the state, is portrayed as an "organic system" which not only regulates itself, but appears to do so for its *own* purposes and through its *own* actions.[43] On the other hand, it is by no means obvious why Marx employed such analyses, precisely how he intended us to interpret them, and how much weight they were meant to carry in his overall theoretical effort. The rest of the material in this chapter is in effect designed to try to answer these questions. My approach is a "valued-added" one.

A first approximation I would endorse is that (a) the two types of analyses in Marx's theorizing *are* in fact often contradictory and that (b) Marx himself was often not aware of this fact. He often wrote for vastly different audiences, even only himself, and he seldom took the time and effort to resolve contradictions among these different accounts.

But there is a second and equally reasonable possibility which seems to have escaped serious consideration by most interpreters: that Marx was sometimes not only *aware* that the two types of analyses in his work are contradictory, but that he *intended* them to be. Here Barry Smart's critique of Dawe and Giddens is useful, in that he suggests, reasonably, that the antimony of structure versus subject or agent is not in fact a mistaken perception of social reality, but an inherent feature of that reality whose absence would obviate the need for sociology.[44] Thus the facts of the *matter* are that all individuals' subjective experiences of reality are mediated by socially organized social processes, and the very existence of such mediation, whether or not it occurs in a capitalist formation, is likely to limit individuals' agency, and therefore also to produce a minimum amount of psychic alienation, as Marx himself was careful to note.[45]

This latter suggestion flies in the face of a vast literature whose authors proclaim alienation to be restricted to capitalism, but it appears to be both an accurate interpretation of Marx and an inescapable assumption for any but the most vulgar Marxist. But to leave matters there is to leave out an equally important point of Marx's: although there are minimum amounts of social structuring and alienation in all societies, the very degree to which social processes are structured, and certainly the degree to which even structured social processes alienate the individual members of a society, varies a very great deal.[46]

This is one of the points to be demonstrated in Chapter 3 below. According to Marx, human individuals in early Asiatic communities were in fact heavily dominated by their social relations, and anything but free or historical agents. Agency in the latter senses emerges only gradually with subsequent social and individual change, but then sinks to new depths with the systematization of the capitalist mode of production. In communist society there is the highest possible amount of free and historic agency, but only precisely because (a) individuals are then free and distinct; that is, truly individuals, and (b) as such they transform their social relations to be "inter*personal*", "informal", and even bordering on the anarchistic; for example, the state is allowed to "wither away".

But this proposition that social relations can be more or less structured, and therefore more or less alienating, is still only part of the story Marx wished to tell. Social organizations are initially designed, selected and/or reproduced largely because they aid community members in adapting to their environment, both natural and social.[47]

In societies where particular classes dominate, most of the benefits of social organization may accrue to a small proportion of the community, but even here the benefits may outweigh the disadvantages for most members. The socialization and technical modification of labour may provide the basis for the mass production of a wide variety of goods and services, the reduction of necessary manual labour and an increase in leisure time, and so on.[48]

To fail to recognize that *more* structure can, and under certain conditions does, permit a *freer* agency than does less structure would be to fall into much the same trap as have laissez-faire bourgeois theorists, who see mere association as necessarily interfering with the activities and rights of self-interested, and allegedly largely self-sufficient, individuals, and, therefore, as at best a necessary evil.

The latter proviso suggests there are limits to how far Marx saw, and we should see, structure as precluding agency and agency, structure. If social organizations are not consciously designed and controlled by the majority of community members, their disadvantages may outweigh their benefits. But this need not always be the case, and under opposite conditions Marx expected the reverse outcome: a highly organized political economy would permit the freest possible agency. As Marx himself put it, "Only within the community has each individual the means of cultivating his gifts in all directions; hence personal freedom becomes possible only within the community."[49]

(2) The two types of analyses apply only to different levels and/or phenomena on each level

One can distinguish two versions of this thesis. One, the strong version, is that whereas analyses of individuals may or may not be psychological, analyses of *social* processes can *only* be *socio*logical, and often systemic or functionalist to boot. The other, the weak version is that while neither type of analysis is restricted to one or another level, certain phenomena on each are more amenable to one type of analysis than the other.

If the point is simply that many social phenomena have qualities which cannot be reduced to psychic processes in individuals, one must agree wholeheartedly. Durkheim made this point well, as early as the turn of the century, by demonstrating that rates of suicide for occupational and other groupings, as well as societies as a whole, often relate more closely to each other than to many simultaneous phenomena on the level of individuals; for example, whether or not, and to what extent, individual members are "mentally ill".[50] The reverse assumption – that social trends are simply aggregates of individual-level trends – has become known as the "ecological fallacy", and its fallacious nature has been demonstrated across a wide variety of social phenomena.[51]

This fact, that many social phenomena cannot simply be reduced to the psyches of the individuals who participate in them, is the important truth to the strong version of the thesis in question. However, Parsonian "structural functionalists" and Althusserian "structural Marxists" alike have often taken this argument for the necessity of uniquely sociological explanations to its illogical extreme by maintaining that collective entities not only have a logic of their own, but, in effect, *purposes* of their own. *This* fallacy, that of assuming a supra-individual, or "objective teleology", has been well-documented and critiqued for both the Parsonian and Althusserian camps and need not detain us here.[52] That one can do a uniquely sociological, Marxian analysis without committing this latter fallacy has been shown by G. A. Cohen. Interestingly, furthermore, to anticipate argument 4 below, while Cohen often employs models of natural or chance selection to fill the explanatory gap, he nevertheless argues that such functionalist explanations require "elaborations" which in turn usually contain the intentions of individuals.[53]

In practice the weaker version usually amounts to Robert Merton's distinction between analyses, albeit both allegedly "functionalist", of social structurings which are intended ("manifest") and those which are unintended ("latent").[54] Here too the argument applies to Marx, who stressed that the systematization of the capitalist mode of production is heavily conditioned by (a) the continual *repetition* of the same interaction and relations, presumably as both effect and cause of the habits of individual capitalists and workers, and (b) the reproduction of capitalist relations over several *generations* of wage labourers. These conditions in turn help make it very difficult for any one aggregate or group of labourers to control their social relations objectively, because their immediate relationships are now mediated by the relationships of a large number of distant others, and subjectively, because they no longer recognize the structuring process as human-made, on-going, and therefore also transformable.[55] On the other hand, from Marx's point of view it would be wrong to simply identify sociological explanations with unintended collective, and psychological with intended individual phenomena, since the former are very much dependent upon the lack of knowledge and *particular* intentions of individuals. This point is elaborated upon in a subsequent subsection of this chapter.

A final argument for recognizing a division of labour between the two types of analyses, not *between* levels but *within each*, might be constructed around the distinctions between "social organization" and "social change", but especially that between "institutions" and "collective behaviour" and/or "social movements", in that the usual distinctions drawn between them have to do with these phenomena's relative routinization, legitimation, and therefore stability or changeability.

Thus Marx himself distinguished periods of relative social disorganization between dominant modes of production where there is greater scope for at least free, and to a lesser extent historic, agency. Two examples which come to mind are the "golden age for labour", which occurred "in the period of the decline and fall of the feudal system, but where it still struggles internally – as in England in the fourteenth and first half of the fifteenth centuries", and that which occurred under the frontier conditions of North America up through Marx's own time.[56] Similarly, although, as with modern sociologists, Marx was well aware that even the most primitive forms of working class resistance are – and soon will become even more so – organized, some of them, for example, individual acts of sabotage, are not *very* organized. Finally, revolutionary periods themselves usually involve spontaneous strikes, riots and other incidences of "collective behaviour" for which overly systemic analyses are simply inadequate.[57]

In these latter cases, it seems to me Marx's analyses can often be legitimately regarded as social activist rather than simply systemic. Thesis (2) above, it appears, is *also* correct, and therefore both adds to our understanding of Marx's theorizing and legitimates our looking for psycho-analyses therein.

(3) The two types are complementary means for analyzing the same phenomena

This is another way of conceiving the relationship between the two types of analyses. If one assumes that (a) *all* social phenomena involve *both* the social organization *of* social actors *and* social organizing *by* social actors, and therefore also (b) that social organization and social action presuppose each other, then one must presumably also conclude that (c) models of systemic and action processes are equally necessary metaphors for the social analyst. One may also go further and conclude that (d) since the two models are only metaphors for getting at the *same* elusive social reality, it is perfectly legitimate to translate the terms of one (for example, the systemic) into those of the other (the action).

However, the reality of academic discourse is that certain disciplines and/or sects within each proclaim one or another metaphor to accurately represent social reality and the other to be *epiphenomenal*, *merely* metaphorical. Thus for structural Marxists, systems are real and individual agents illusory, an artifact of bourgeois ideology and the egocentric manner in which we experience reality.[58] For many of their critics, whether Marxist or otherwise, only individual agents are real. That many of us often believe otherwise is also a consequence of ideologies – for example, the same bourgeois ideology which "hails us" as individual free agents portrays us as subject to either or both an innate animal nature and an equally ubiquitous, but conveniently "invisible", "hand of the market"; and to egocentric motives – for example, "bad faith".[59] Marx himself is then divided into two persons: the naive young man who only recognized individual agents and the mature adult who became a systems theorist (the structuralist version); or the enlightened historical materialist who emphasized human agency and the unhealthy old man who had become obsessed with the very systemic models he had set out to demolish (the humanist version).[60]

Here the footing to and through Marx himself is much less sure than was the case with the previous theses we have examined. However, I do think there are good grounds for rejecting the stronger version, regardless of whether the content is structuralist or humanist. Specifically, it is highly questionable that the mature Marx denied a reality *sui generis* to either social systems or human agents. At the very minimum, he believed in the existence of such equilibrium processes as markets and falling rates of profit, but also that such processes are anything but independent of the social activities of individuals.

Various of Marx's methodological formulae have been garnered to justify one or another side of the strong position, but none of them has an unambiguous meaning, and a close examination of the relevant passages can usually just as likely support the opposite point of view.

Structuralists have made a fetish of the Sixth Thesis on Feuerbach and asserted that it demonstrates how Marx collapsed phenomena on the individual level and absorbed them into the structural (that is, "the ensemble of the social relations"). However, it is far from clear that this is what Marx meant here, especially since he immediately went on to refer to Feuerbach's "religious sentiment" as "itself a social product" rather than an epi-phenomenon.[61] Were they to employ Marx's statement that "circumstances make men", they should acknowledge that it continues with "just as much as men make circumstances",[62] and that the Third Thesis is anything but more supportive of an exclusively structuralist reading. Thus "the changing of circumstances and of human activity" are clearly analytically separate, and "it is men who change circumstances" through "revolutionizing practice".[63]

Humanists have typically appealed to two other formulae. One is that "social relations are just as much produced by men as linen, flax, etc.", and that "to draw up the real, profane history of men in every century" is "to present these men as both the authors and the actors of their own drama".[64] The other is that "Men make their own history, but they do not make it just as they please; . . ."[65] The problem here, of course, is that the dramaturgical metaphor can easily be interpreted as meaning that the authors and actors are different rather than the same individuals; but even if not, that as actors all individuals, even if they had originally authored the play, do, perhaps even must, stick to the script.

This idea that the circumstances which prevent human individuals from making history just as they please are structured rather than simply aggregates of what other individuals are doing is clearly suggested by the rest of the second formula: ". . . they do not make it under circumstances chosen by themselves, but under circumstances directly encountered, given and transmitted from the past. The tradition of all the dead generations weighs like a nightmare on the brain of the living." Then, incidentally, these circumstances – organized traditions – are likened to language: individuals may "seem engaged in revolutionizing themselves and things, in creating something that has never yet existed", but they may instead be using a "borrowed language", just as someone beginning to learn a new language "always translates it back into his mother tongue".[66]

To recapitulate, Marx's methodological formulae simply do not support the notion that he believed his models of either structure or social action to be nothing but convenient *fictions* for understanding the same social phenomena. One can argue that he believed all social phenomena to be a complex totality of structured social action, such that one requires *both* types of models to fully understand reality, but this need not entail collapsing one aspect of that reality into the other.

This, the weaker interpretation, seems even more reasonable if one moves beyond Marx's general methodological statements to those in analyses of particular social phenomena, for there he often qualified one form of explanation by referring to the other if not explicitly, as he sometimes did, then at least by restating his explanation of one type in the language of the other. I reiterate that this process of translation goes *both* ways: systemic explanations are rendered more action-like and action explanations made more systemic. We have already seen examples of the latter in our discussion of Marx's methodological individualism, as, for example, when Marx referred to his analyses of production as beginning not with *isolated* individuals, but individuals producing "*within society*".[67] Such examples could be expanded upon, but since my major purpose here is to "carve out" a place for psycho-analyses I shall concentrate instead upon Marx's qualifications and translations in the opposite direction.

For example, at one point in the *Grundrisse*, a work often cited for containing inappropriately functionalist explanations, we find Marx characterizing "the system of bourgeois economy" and "bourgeois society in the long view and as a whole" as "merely a moment, a vanishing moment" in a general historical trend which contains its own negation. However, this characterization is immediately qualified with the statement that the "only subjects" of this movement "are the individuals, but individuals in mutual relationships, which they equally reproduce and produce anew". It is "The constant process of their *own* movement, in which they renew themselves even as they renew the world of wealth they create."[68]

At another point we find Marx suggesting that "it is an inherent property of money to fulfill its own purposes by simultaneously negating them; to achieve independence from commodities; to become a means which becomes an end; to realize the exchange value of commodities by separating them from it; to facilitate exchange by splitting it; to overcome the difficulties of the direct exchange of commodities by generalizing them; to make exchange independent of the producers in the same measure as the producers become dependent on exchange". However, *immediately* after this reference to *money* fulfilling its *own* purposes we find this qualification: "(It will be necessary later, before this question is dropped, to correct the idealist manner of the presentation, which makes it seem as if it were merely a matter of conceptual determinations and of the dialectic of these concepts.)".[69]

Thompson singles out two other explanations of Marx's which are vulgarly functionalist, but these too can be translated into social action terms in spite of the fact that in these particular cases Marx himself did not stop to do so.

Thus when Marx referred to bourgeois society as an "organic system" which, as "with every organic system", proceeds by "subordinating all elements of society to itself" and "creating out of it the organs which it still lacks", he seems to have meant that when capital*ists* confront conditions not sufficiently developed for full-fledged capitalism – for example, access to land by independent producers, who therefore refuse to become wage labourers – they have to, and do, change these conditions. In this case they have tended "artificially" to make land too expensive for such producers.[70]

Similarly, when Marx wrote that capital "proceeds from itself to create the conditions for its maintenance and growth", his point is surely that whereas initially the primitive accumulation which allowed an individual to become a capitalist could occur "perhaps by means of savings garnered from products and values created by his own labour" by "hoarding", (a) this individual could not actually become a capitalist unless he went on to exploit labour, and (b) once the exploitation of labour requires large amounts of fixed capital, saving and hoarding by single individuals is no longer sufficient.[71]

A final example from the *Grundrisse* may be especially helpful here because it illustrates Marx's general model that while the whole of the "movement" of circulation is "neither located in their consciousness" nor "subsumed under" the community of individuals "as a whole", "the individual moments of this movement arise from the conscious will and particular purposes of individuals", and that "the totality of the process" *also* arises "from the mutual influence of conscious individuals on one another".[72]

Here is how Marx himself concretized this influence of individuals at another point:

. . . since the general bond and all-round interdependence in production and consumption increase together with the independence and indifference of the consumers and producers to one another; since this contradiction leads to crises, etc., hence, together with the development of this alienation, and on the same basis, efforts are made to overcome it; institutions emerge whereby each individual can acquire information about the activity of all others and attempt to adjust to his own accordingly, e.g. lists of current prices, rates of exchange . . . This means, that although the total supply and demand are independent of the actions of each individual, everyone attempts to inform himself about them, and this knowledge then reacts back in practice on the total supply and demand. Although, on the given standpoint, alienation is not overcome by these means, nevertheless, relations and connections are introduced thereby which include the possibility of suspending the old standpoint.[73]

Capital is the other major work where Marx is alleged to have regressed to the "objective teleology" of Hegel and/or the bourgeois political economists, but it is no less open to translation. If the individual therein is characterized as not *individually* "responsible for relations whose creature he socially remains, however much he may subjectively raise himself above them",[74] this occurs not because "economic categories" have lives of their own, or even because the individual members of bourgeois society are only "personifications of economic categories, embodiments of particular class-relations and class-interests", but for the reasons mentioned above.

To see that this is the case, let us examine two of the major analyses in the first volume: the determination of value, and the determination of the sequence in which capitalists have employed various means for increasing surplus value.

In a capitalist economy the law of value operates for the most part "behind the backs" of individual producers and consumers. It even has many of the qualities of laws in the natural sciences.[75] However, that it operates in this way is a function of a history "made" by human individuals rather than "nature" or the purposes of a supernatural being.

In truly primitive societies the division of labour and exchange of different products may not be explicitly designed to serve the conscious economizing purposes of individuals. That there be *some* division of labour, and *some* concern that those products which are exchanged are not totally lacking in equivalence, is a "functional prerequisite" which could well be fulfilled by the processes of natural or other forms of selection about which Cohen has written, rather than *directly* by the *intended* actions of individual members of the community. Nevertheless, no analysis of the determination of value in any society would be complete without an analysis not only of the actions of individual members, but of their intentions in acting. That Marx himself often completed his analyses of value in this way is relatively easy to demonstrate.

The "naturalness" of the relative absence of universal equivalents in the most primitive of societies does not lie just in the nature of the economy as a whole, but in the particular needs and activities of individual members. Specifically, when individuals are satisfying most of their needs directly through their own labour there is not much exchange to begin with, and what is exchanged tends to be surplus production. Because of this, individuals do not need to be overly concerned with equivalence, and can and do exchange in kind.[76]

Although the individual members of such societies may not be very *aware* of what they do and why they do it, given the direct relationship between their needs and activities and the exceptional nature of their exchange activities, they nonetheless exercise a considerable degree of control over their economy, as can become evident to both us and them when ruling classes emerge and attempt to subvert this control. Hence, for example, popular pressure twice prevented the Roman ruling class from legally instituting payments in cash, and failure to heed such desires for majority control is supposed to have been one of the most important provocations for the revolt of the French peasantry in 1789.[77]

If we now skip ahead and analyze the process of value determination in bourgeois society, we find that new objective conditions have emerged which we might well expect to enlighten most individuals about the process; specifically, "the great mass of the produce of labour takes the form of commodities" and has therefore allowed "the notion of human equality" to have "acquired the fixity of popular prejudice".[78] However, now the other objective conditions which allowed more primitive peoples to control their economy in spite of their ignorance no longer exist. Individuals no longer labour independently in order to directly satisfy their own needs. Decisions about the allocation of labour time and the "price" of products are not made directly by most producers, indeed, not even by individual capitalist employers. In good part because of this, knowledge of the determination of value is still difficult to come by and is only approximate under the best of circumstances bourgeois society has to offer; that is, in analyses by bourgeois political economists.[79]

The second problem of which strategies capitalists use to extract surplus value can also be analyzed functionally, as Marx himself does. Thus theoretically the capitalist can increase the surplus value available to him by (a) employing more labourers, (b) extending the length of their work day, (c) intensifying their labour, and/or (d) otherwise making their labour more productive (for example, by mechanizing it and making it more efficient).[80] However, at any one time a host of objective and subjective conditions constrain him from using many of them. In the early stages of capitalism, his workers are likely to be craftspeople who jealously maintain their traditional methods of work and work habits, and/or small farmers who retain subsistence plots upon which they can rely if work becomes too onerous. If the period is a later one the capitalist may have successfully lowered wages, extended the working day, and employed cheaper labourers. However, by then workers are likely to have organized politically and successfully pressured states to legislate firm limits on how far their employers could go in these particular directions.[81]

It was these very circumstances, and not some mythical purpose of capital as a whole, which subsequently led capitalists to "militarize" and mechanize labour. With earlier strategies largely closed off to them this was a "rational choice", but of course rational choices were likely to have been far from the only means through which innovations in the labour process were initiated or continued: one *had* to mechanize to remain competitive, but someone starting an enterprise might well simply begin with the then traditional "state of the art" without necessarily considering other possible organizations of the labour process. And, of course, the mere fact that remaining competitive "required" innovations hardly assured that this or that capitalist would in fact remain competitive. Many did not, and therefore no longer remained capitalists.[82] This may well be "natural selection", but it is anything but independent of the purposeful actions of individuals.

(4) Each type is a necessary, but only partial, explanation for all social phenomena

To recapitulate, all three of the previously discussed, possible relationships between structural and action analyses appear to apply to Marx.

Specifically, at least under certain, but also common, conditions, where social relations are highly structured there are stringent limits upon human agency, and vice versa: where most individuals are highly active agents their relations are likely to be much less systematic. But matters are also much more complicated than this. For one thing, Marx's systemic and action analyses sometimes apply to somewhat *different* phenomena, even on the supra-individual level, with, for example, the systemic applying more to the "normal" operation of the capitalist political economy and the action to working class resistance and revolt. Yet for another, the two types of analyses are sometimes simply different ways of looking at the *same* social phenomena: all social phenomena are both socially organized and involve, not just the actions of individuals, but the often *consciously intended* actions of individuals, even if systemic processes themselves are often not consciously intended.

Here we examine an aspect of the relationship between structural and action analyses which is still more radical, but again no less applicable to Marx and necessary for adequate analyses of most social phenomena. The argument builds upon the immediately preceding one. To wit, if all social phenomena involve both social organization and social action, then a full explanation for all such phenomena must include *both* structural *and* action analyses.

Earlier I stressed my belief that systemic phenomena are no less real than action phenomena.[83] Although any given social phenomenon involves both processes of action and the structuring of that action, one can often distinguish between the two, certainly analytically, but often empirically as well. But the empirically observable or otherwise analyzable differences between the two types of phenomena may be more or less independent of each other. Some structured processes presuppose not simply some social action, but certain specific social activities, and vice versa. This means that many systemic analyses themselves are partly reducible to action analyses, and, again, vice versa.[84]

Of the various phenomena we might use to illustrate Marx's use of such reductions, perhaps the best is that of needs, for here we have processes which are clearly intra- as well as inter-individual, and which Marx himself included in his analyses of structured social processes. Most of Marx's own outlines of his historical materialism give a prominent role to the needs of human individuals.

In the *German Ideology* Marx's first premises are that all history presupposes the gratification of certain basic human needs – that "the first historical act is thus the production of the means to satisfy these needs" – and that the subsequent development of both social organization (for example, the division of labour) and individuals (for example, new needs) depends upon the extent and manner in which the initial, most basic needs are gratified. Indeed, both the fact that humans must socially produce their life and the fact that "they must produce it moreover in a certain way . . . is determined by their physical organization".[85]

Although the outline in the *Poverty of Philosophy* is often interpreted as indicating a narrow technological determinism on Marx's part, a full rendering of that statement does not justify such an interpretation: "When, consequently, in order to save principles as much as to save history, we ask ourselves why a particular principle was manifested in the eleventh or in the eighteenth century rather than in any other, we are necessarily forced to examine minutely *what men were like* in the eleventh century, what they were like in the eighteenth, what were their respective *needs*, their productive forces, their mode of production, the raw materials of their production – in short, what were the relations between man and man which resulted from all these conditions of existence."[86]

True, needs are not included in the formulae of the *Preface*,[87] but only a year earlier Marx felt he needed to remind himself that "These questions about the *system of needs* and *system of labours* – at what point is this to be dealt with? Will be seen in due course."[88] Like so many other important concepts in his theorizing, including class, needs never were to receive their full due from Marx, but with the aid of interpreters such as Agnes Heller and Kate Soper[89] we can now fill in some of the gaps for ourselves. For example, throughout the *Grundrisse* Marx emphasizes that an increase in the number and variety of needs and wants is an important prerequisite for the emergence and subsequent growth of commodity production.[90] Furthermore, the value of the specific commodity, labour power, is heavily determined by the needs of individual workers; needs which, to be sure, only have this effect when they are averaged over the working class as a whole and can be fashioned into effective demands within the capitalist circulation process, but the needs of individual workers nonetheless.[91]

In recognizing that processes of effective demand intervene between individuals' needs and their gratification, we are also tacitly acknowledging that the effect of needs upon structured social processes is not simply one of passive determination, of capitalists being free to gratify only those of workers' needs related to their mere physical subsistence. However, it is nevertheless true that individuals may not be aware of many of their own needs, even those which make up effective demand, and it may be for this reason that even Althusser can acknowledge the role of needs in the determination of the value of labour power without altering his claims regarding the agency of individuals.[92]

Given the latter consideration, let us move on to psychic processes "in" individuals, which are more directly related to agency, to their beliefs about and attitudes toward others, their own labour, products, themselves, and so on. The importance of such orientations of individuals become especially evident when one examines Marx's own explanations for why capitalist relations of production in particular are "independent of the will and consciousness of individuals". Indeed, we shall soon see that Marx's characterization of the capitalist system in this way is highly misleading.

In the *Ideology* Marx clearly stated that if the division of labour is "above us, growing out of our control, thwarting our expectations, bringing to naught our calculations", it is because it appears to the individuals who reproduce and develop it "as an alien force existing outside them, of the origin and goal of which they are ignorant, *which they thus are no longer able to control*". Both the objective difficulty in controlling their relations and subjective perceptions of these relations and their own power to control them are then related to the fact that (a) the division of labour has developed "naturally" or "spontaneously" rather than "voluntarily" according to a conscious, collective plan,[93] and that (b) there are conflicts of interest which lead workers to compete among themselves rather than combine on a class-wide basis.[94]

These psychic prerequisites for the systemic features of capitalism are put even more explicitly, albeit with somewhat different emphasis, in the *Grundrisse*. There the narrow interests of atomized or sectoralized workers and their competition are claimed to lead less to "hostility" than to "indifference". Marx could hardly have been clearer about his belief that the relative independence of the capitalist system depends upon this relative independence and indifference: the fact that "this material and mental metabolism" "is independent of the knowing and willing of individuals", he wrote, "*presupposes* their reciprocal independence and indifference"; the "subordination" of individuals "to relations which subsist independently of them" is not a natural fact of all societies, but one which depends upon the additional fact that these relations "*arise out of* collisions between mutually indifferent individuals."[95]

By the time he came to write *Capital* Marx appears to have taken these psychic prerequisites enough for granted that he felt he could just mention them in passing, but he was no less emphatic about their importance. "In the form of society now under consideration", he wrote, "the behaviour of men in the social process of production is purely atomic. *Hence*", he continued, "their relations to each other in production assume a material character independent of their control and conscious individual action."[96] It is also in *Capital* that Marx is most explicit about another psychic prerequisite which had been treated only obliquely in his earlier critiques of bourgeois political economists and their claims for the naturalness and inevitability of the invisible hand of the market.

The psychic orientations in question are those of individual workers toward their own labour and its products: they tend to treat them as (a) relatively independent of their own person, and (b) commodities *by nature*. As a consequence the only "meaning" they have for individual workers is a means for the narrow end of physical survival. If these arguments are only implicit and oblique in *Wage Labour and Capital* and the *Grundrisse*,[97] they are far from so in *Capital*, where Marx simply stated that "labour-power can appear upon the market as a commodity, only if, and so far as, its possessor, the individual whose labour-power it is, *offers* it for sale, or sells it, as a commodity", or even more pointedly, that "The capitalist epoch is therefore *characterized* by this, that labour power takes *in the eyes of the labourer himself* the form of a commodity which is his property; his labour consequently becomes wage-labour. On the other hand, it is only from this moment that the product of labour universally becomes a commodity."[98]

I also take this to be the meaning of his later account of "the servitude of the labourer" which was "the starting point of the development that gave rise to the wage-labourer as well as the capitalist". Initially this was accomplished largely through force, often by the state, but eventually the normal functioning of the capitalist system depends much more on the fact that "The advance of capitalist production develops a working-class, which by education, tradition, habit, looks upon the conditions of that mode of production as self-evident laws of nature."[99] Presumably the collective and individual experience of alternative forms of labour was eventually lost, and individuals' orientations toward their labour subsequently became merely "instrumental" or "alienated", and that toward their material and social products one of believing that they are neither their own nor capable of being brought under their control.

If we stop and reflect upon this latter material we can now see how misleading Marx's references to the capitalist system being "independent of the knowing and willing of individuals" really are. In fact, of course, we have just observed him argue that this relative independence is itself dependent upon individuals' ignorance of the system and where it has come from, and of the relatively small number and variety of demands they make upon it. *What* most individuals do and do not know and *what* they do and do not will, are therefore anything but irrelevant to the nature of the system.

One must be cautious here and avoid *completely* reducing the independence of the system to the beliefs and attitudes of individuals. Marx's point appears to be that such beliefs and attitudes among a majority of workers are often *sufficient* conditions for the independence of the system, but not *necessary* conditions for the same.

As we have just noted, Marx himself stressed that capitalist relations of production initially became systematized largely through force. He also claimed that this was necessary because potential wage labourers continued to aspire to be independent producers,[100] and that the process of systematization occurred in spite of this fact that the majority of individuals were unwilling. Furthermore, Marx emphasized time and again that as long as workers have not organized themselves on a class-wide basis, such that they are objectively in a position to control their relations, they can know and will whatever they like subjectively and still not successfully exercise such control.[101]

Nevertheless, the reverse also holds: all possible material conditions can be present, but if the necessary knowledge and will are not, workers *also* cannot control their relations. Marx himself said so in as many words,[102] and most of his various outlines of the conditions for a successful proletarian revolution include not only two major objective, structural conditions – a huge growth in the productivity of labour and a "naturally" organized or "socialized" labour force – but the two subjective, individual conditions we have been discussing: the knowledge and will of individual workers. They must have developed needs and wants which cannot be gratified within the system, they must *know* that they have these needs and wants and that their deprivation is the fault of the system, and so on.[103] (More of this later.)

All of this is not to suggest that Marx had, or that we should endorse, an explanation for proletarian revolution which simply postulates parallel psychic states "in" all individual workers which then somehow converge and eventuate in revolution. Such vulgarly psychologically reductionistic accounts have been rejected by enlightened psychologists as well as historians and sociologists,[104] and, as we shall see in Chapter 7, were far from what Marx himself had in mind. On the other hand, as these same enlightened thinkers were equally as concerned to point out, that individuals experience needs and wants, deprivation and frustration within an intergroup context rather than an individual vacuum does not make them any less psychic beings whose psyches must still be analyzed if we are to understand what they think and do, collectively as well as individually.[105]

NOTES

1. See the Introduction, Notes 1 and 2.
2. Thompson, op. cit., pp. 55–70. Jean Cohen, *Class and Civil Society: The limits of Marxian critical theory* (Amherst: University of Massachusetts Press, 1982). Elster, op. cit.
3. Dumont, op. cit.
4. Joachim Israel, "The principle of methodological individualism and Marxian epistemology", *ACTA Sociologica*, vol. 14, 1971, pp. 145–50. Tucker, op. cit.
5. *German Ideology* in Karl Marx and Friedrich Engels, *Collected Works*, vol. 5 (New York: International Publishers, 1976) pp. 31, 41–2.
6. Ibid., pp. 31–2, 35–7.
7. Ibid., pp. 29, 39, 55–7, 235. See also the "Theses on Feuerbach", *Collected Works*, vol. 5, pp. 4–5.
8. *Grundrisse* (Harmondsworth: Penguin, 1973) pp. 83–5, 100–1.
9. *The Poverty of Philosophy* Collected Works, vol. 6, p. 159. *Grundrisse*, p. 265. *Capital, 1* (Moscow: Progress Publishers, no date) pp. 20–1.
10. I think this concept is Floyd Allport's. I suspect I picked it up from Arnold Tannenbaum of the University of Michigan, Ann Arbor.
11. *Grundrisse*, p. 84. See also p. 472.
12. Ibid., p. 489.
13. Ibid., pp. 84, 496. The appropriateness of distinguishing between the relative autonomy of the individual (from nature, and perhaps others) and his or her distinctiveness is suggested by Marx's references to "free individuality" (ibid., p. 158).
14. *Grundrisse*, pp. 495–6.
15. Ibid., p. 485. For representative agency with regard to exchange in particular, see pp. 204, 740 and 873. Also *Capital 1*, pp. 83–4, 91.
16. *Grundrisse*, pp. 472–6. The distinctions I have drawn here among "representative", "free" and "historic" agency were partly inspired by Perry Anderson in his *Arguments within English Marxism* (London: New Left Books (Verso), 1980) pp. 15–20.
17. *Grundrisse*, pp. 474–5, 483.
18. Op. cit.
19. See Note 16, above.
20. Althusser, op. cit.
21. For example, at one point Thompson (op. cit., p. 87) corrects Engels for reiterating Marx's claim that the relative independence of capitalist relations lies with the atomization and ignorance of workers, arguing that one should instead recognize that the consciousness and wills of individuals are always *grouped*. Yet Marx and Engels' point that the independence which exists does so precisely because workers are often more *individualized* than grouped is probably more accurate than Thompson's. Either way, one cannot simply assume that workers are *always* grouped.
22. Molina, op. cit.; Ollman, op. cit.
23. The reference to "human nature in general", etc., is in *Capital 1*, p. 571 (footnote). For one application to needs, see the *Grundrisse*, p. 92. On

the parallel between Marx's treatment of needs and that of other phenomena not so directly related to individuals, see Kate Soper's *On Human Needs* (Sussex: Harvester Press, 1981) pp. 14–15.

24. See *Capital 1*, pp. 313, 174.
25. For example, "Adam Smith . . . has only the slaves of capital in mind" (*Grundrisse*, p. 612). For mistaken generalizing by Max Stirner and other Young Hegelians, see, respectively, the *German Ideology*, pp. 255–6, and Note 7, p. 37.
26. For example, Smith wrongly presumed human individuals require tranquillity more than activity (*Grundrisse*, p. 611); Feuerbach wrongly presumed they always feel powerless and religious ("Theses on Feuerbach", pp. 4–5).
27. "Bruno Bauer, for example, is mightily shocked by the heresy with which Feuerbach transforms the holy trinity of reason, love and will into something that 'is in individuals and over individuals', as though, in our own day, every inclination, every impulse, every need did not assert itself as a force 'in the individual and over the individual', whenever circumstances hinder their satisfaction. If the holy father Bruno experiences hunger, for example, without the means of appeasing it, then even his stomach will become a force 'in him and over him', *Feuerbach's mistake is not that he stated this fact* but that in idealistic fashion he endowed it with independence instead of regarding it as the product of a definite and surmountable stage of historical development." (*German Ideology*, p. 102. I have removed Marx's emphases and added my own.)
28. Note, for example, Marx's derogatory references to Feuerbach's use of the distinction between "being" and "essence" in the *Ideology* (p. 58).
29. Mészáros, op. cit., p. 43. See also his "Contingent and necessary class consciousness", pp. 85–127 in *Aspects of History and Class Consciousness* (London: Routledge and Kegan Paul, 1971). Gyorgy Márkus, *Marxism and Anthropology* (Essen: Van Gorcum, 1978) pp. 40–1.
30. Op. cit., pp. 76, 124–6.
31. *Marx's Social Ontology* (Cambridge: MIT Press, 1978). On the problem of individuality, see pp. 17, 146–8, 156–7.
32. *Dialectical Phenomenology: Marx's method* (London: Routledge and Kegan Paul, 1979) p. 104.
33. I have already quoted Lukács to this effect. For other Lukácsians' avoidance of the empirically inevitable, see Mészáros' *Aspects* . . ., op. cit. For Althusser, see especially *Reading Capital* (op. cit.) Ollman (op. cit., pp. 232, 244–5) manages to both ridicule any kind of systematic empirical analysis *and* proclaim Marx's theory of alienation to have already been proven. Thompson and Anderson (op. cit.) are important exceptions to this anti- "empiricism".
34. *Ideology*, p. 66.
35. *Grundrisse*, p. 611.
36. See my "Psychology, Sociology and Social Psychology: Bad fences make bad neighbours", *British Journal of Sociology*, vol. 27, 1976 (June), pp. 115–29.
37. Ibid.
38. See point 4, p. 31.

39. See Archibald, op.cit., for a rationale for doing so in general. For Marx in particular, see my "Psychic alienation in Marx: The missing link?", *Praxis International*, vol. 3, 1983 (April), pp. 73–81, and point 4, p. 31.

40. In fact, one could argue that there is a third level of relatively unstructured, usually face-to-face interaction, which has properties different from either individuals considered singly or large-scale social organizations. See Archibald, "Psychology . . .", op. cit. However, not everyone agrees with such a distinction. For example, see Anthony Giddens, *Central Problems in Social Theory* (London: Macmillan, 1979) p. 77.

41. Alan Dawe, "Theories of social action" pp. 362–417 in Tom Bottomore and Robert Nisbet (eds), *A History of Sociological Analysis* (London: Heinemann, 1979).

42. *The Social and Political Thought of Karl Marx* (Cambridge: Cambridge University Press, 1968) p. 61.

43. For example, in addition to the passages cited by Elster (op. cit.), see the *Grundrisse*, pp. 278 and 460. However, see p. 24 for an alternative interpretation of these passages.

44. "Foucault, sociology, and the problem of human agency" *Theory and Society*, vol. 11, 1982 (March), pp. 121–41.

45. "this division of labour [in manufacture] is a particular sort of co-operation, and many of its disadvantages [e.g., "each workman becomes exclusively assigned to a partial function, and . . . for the rest of his life, his labour-power is turned into the organ of this detail function."] spring from the general character of co-operation, and not from this particular form of it." (*Capital 1*, p. 320).

46. This appears to be part of Anderson's point in attempting to find a middle path between Althusser and Thompson.

47. This is implied, for example, in the *Ideology*, pp. 31, 41–2.

48. See Chapter 2 below.

49. *Ideology*, p. 78.

50. Emile Durkheim, *Suicide* (New York: Free Press, 1966).

51. Archibald, "Psychology . . .", op. cit. For a more comprehensive review of this particular problem, see Michael T. Hannan, "Problems of aggregation" pp. 473–508 in H. M. Blalock (ed.), *Causal Models in the Social Sciences* (Chicago: Aldine/Atherton, 1971).

52. For one of the recent and most virulent of such critiques, see Thompson, op. cit.

53. G. A. Cohen, *Karl Marx's Theory of History*, pp. 185–90. This does not mean I would necessarily endorse all aspects of Cohen's analyses.

54. Robert Merton, *Social Theory and Social Structure* (New York: Free Press, 1957).

55. On the role of repetition, see especially *Capital 3*, p. 793 (also p. 830); of generations, the *Ideology*, p. 54, and *The Eighteenth Brumaire of Louis Bonaparte (Collected Works, 11)*, p. 103. For the importance of individuals' knowledge about their social relations, see 4, p. 31.

56. *Grundrisse*, p. 510; *Capital 1*, p. 458.

57. *Manifesto of the Communist Party (Collected Works, 6)*, p. 492; *The Class Struggles in France (Collected Works, 10)*. G. A. Cohen distinguishes between Marx's largely systemic explanations for the "normal"

functioning of capitalism and his more "strategic" analyses of class struggle. See his "Reply to Elster on 'Marxism, functionalism and game theory' " (*Theory and Society*, vol. 11, 1982 (July), pp. 483–95.)

58. Althusser, op. cit. See also his "Ideology and ideological state apparatuses" and "Freud and Lacan" in *Lenin and Philosophy* (New York: Monthly Review Press, 1971). For other structuralists, see the previously cited reviews by Anderson and Giddens.

59. Thompson, op. cit.; Jean Cohen, *Class and Civil Society*, op. cit.

60. Althusser, *For Marx*, op. cit.; Thompson, op. cit.

61. Marx, *Theses* . . . . See also Norman Geras (*Marx and Human Nature: Refutation of a Legend* (London: New Left Books (Verso), 1983), who devotes a whole chapter to unravelling various possible meanings of the Sixth Thesis alone.

62. *Ideology*, p. 54.

63. *Theses*, p. 7.

64. *Poverty of Philosophy*, p. 165.

65. *Eighteenth Brumaire*, p. 103.

66. Whether or not language is an *appropriate* model for structure, and/or speech for agency, is another matter. Again, see Anderson and Giddens.

67. *Grundrisse*, p. 87.

68. Ibid., p. 712 (my emphasis). Giddens (op. cit., p. 53) also appears to endorse a social action reading of this passage.

69. *Grundrisse*, p. 151.

70. Ibid, p. 278.

71. Ibid., pp. 459–62.

72. Ibid., pp. 196–7.

73. Ibid., p. 161.

74. *Capital 1*, pp. 20–1.

75. Ibid., plus pp. 51–2, 78–81.

76. Ibid., pp. 83, 91.

77. Ibid., p. 140.

78. Ibid., p. 65.

79. Ibid., pp. 164–5. See also the *Grundrisse*, pp. 463–5. However, the bourgeois political economists themselves had not even "once asked the question why labour is represented by the value of product and labour-time by the magnitude of that value" (*Capital 1*, p. 85), and capitalists themselves only begin to recognize that they exist on surplus value when their employees remove their labour-power by striking (ibid., p. 200).

80. *Capital 1*, p.288.

81. For the first stage, see the *Grundrisse*, p. 510, and *Capital 1*, pp. 318–20; for the latter, the *Grundrisse*, pp. 736, 769–70, and *Capital 1*, pp. 252–7.

82. *Capital 1*, pp. 448, 585–9.

83. See also Giddens, op. cit., p. 66.

84. Archibald, "Psychology . . .", op. cit.

85. *Ideology*, pp. 42–3.

86. *Ideology*, p. 170. My emphases.

87. *Preface to A Contribution to the Critique of Political Economy* in *Selected Works* (Moscow: Progress, 1968).

88. *Grundrisse*, p. 528.

New Grundrisse for the Levels of Analysis Problem   41

89. Op. cit.
90. Ibid., pp. 199, 287, 325, 419, 527–8.
91. *Wage Labour and Capital (Collected Works, 9)* pp. 205–10; *Capital 1*, pp. 167–8. See also Heller, op. cit., pp. 30–4.
92. *Reading Capital*, op. cit., pp. 165–7.
93. *Ideology*, pp. 47–8, my emphasis. See also p. 83.
94. Ibid., pp. 75, 77, 86.
95. *Grundrisse*, p. 161; p. 157 (my emphases). Molina (op. cit.) quotes from the first statement but (conveniently) leaves out the qualifying clause.
96. *Capital 1*, p. 96 (my emphasis).
97. *Wage Labour and Capital*, pp. 202–3; *Grundrisse*, pp. 310, 470.
98. *Capital 1*, pp. 164–5, 167. All emphases are mine. I interpret "characterized" to mean "presupposes", even "requires". However, Lukács (op. cit., p. 87) assigned only the reverse causal direction to the relationship, as does Ollman (op. cit., p. 173).
99. *Capital 1*, pp. 669, 689.
100. Ibid. See also the *Grundrisse*, pp. 507, 736, 769–70.
101. See especially the *Ideology*, p. 75.
102. "The English have all the material requisites necessary for the social revolution. What they lack is the spirit of generalization and revolutionary ardour." Marx to Kugelmann, March 28, 1870. *Letters to Kugelmann* (New York: International Publishers, 1934) p. 107.
103. *Ideology*, pp. 48–9, 51–2, 54, 79–80, 87–8; *Manifesto*, pp. 485–96.
104. E.g., Ralph Turner, "Collective behavior", pp. 382–425 in Robert E. L. Faris (ed.), *Handbook of Modern Sociology* (Chicago: Rand McNally, 1964). Michael Billig, *Social Psychology and Intergroup Relations* (New York: Academic Press, 1976). Philip Abrams, *Historical Sociology* (Somerset: Open Books, 1982).
105. For example, "It is not that frustration is a negligible factor in mass social violence, but that a crude application of the concept is unsatisfactory to account for large-scale phenomena" (Billig, op. cit., p. 151). Similarly, Abrams (op. cit.) suggests that fully adequate explanations for collective events such as revolutions must not only get away from a false dualism between society and the individual (p. 227), but should include at least "the typical dispositions of typical actors in typical relationships" (p. 215), and may well legitimately include even an appeal to "innate human nature" (p. 223). Parenthetically, those Lukácsians and Althusserians who dispute this usually bring in psychological notions "through the back door" anyway. Some of these notions are reasonable ones suggested by Marx himself, but many of them are highly questionable. Thus Lukács himself referred to bureaucrats "adjusting" their way of life to their working conditions, and capitalists "repressing" from consciousness information which goes against their class interest (op. cit., pp. 63–4, 98), and Mészáros alleges "an 'inner need'" in man for "being active and finding fulfillment for the powers inherent in him" (*Alienation*, op. cit., pp. 91–2). In the structuralist camp, Althusser himself makes the surprisingly un-Marxian claims that man is an *ideological* creature by nature, but that this ideology is "stamped into" him ("Ideology . . .", op. cit.)! Similarly, John Mepham

("The theory of ideology in 'Capital' ", *Working Papers in Cultural Studies*, 1974, No. 6, pp. 98–123) disputes suggestions that Marx saw any psychic mechanisms behind workers' acceptance of bourgeois ideology, but then goes on to suggest that their acceptance is in fact pragmatic, because such ideological notions as the wage contract "work". Finally, Molina (op. cit., p. 255) wrongly dismisses any suggestion of absolute immiseration in Marx, and then endorses the importance of *relative* deprivation.

Part II

"Human Nature as Modified in each Historical Epoch"

2 Community and Individuality: The Theory of "Individuation"

Here we go back to the account of individuation begun in the previous chapter.

One should keep in mind that what is presented here is only part of Marx's story of the changing nature of the human individual. We examine the changing circumstances which both constrain and/or liberate individuals and affect their very nature as individuals – the degree to which they are distinct and autonomous, or individuated. But for the moment we are not concerned with how these various circumstances arose and have changed. The latter problem is taken up in the next chapter on agency.

In presenting Marx's account of individuation we are faced with another "chicken-and-egg" problem arising from the dialectical nature of his theorizing. Specifically, it is difficult, and certainly inefficient, to present details about the changing nature of individuals in a purely descriptive way and then induce the "historical" changes in circumstances which Marx employed to explain them.

In fact, of course, any such account must, of necessity, be deductive as well as inductive. Although a theory may originally be formulated for the most part inductively, it is subsequently used as a guide for what phenomena to look for and how to organize them, and Marx's own practices appear to have been little different.[1] Assuming this to have been the case, I have extrapolated a general model of individuation from Marx's various accounts of individuation and used this model to help me select and organize the specifics presented here. In most cases, deciding what Marx regarded as the most central and general sources of individuation has been relatively straightforward, since Marx himself often made general statements about such sources. Where he did not, I have tried to indicate, usually in the notes, why I have made a particular extrapolation.

THE GENERAL MODEL OF INDIVIDUATION

Recall from the previous chapter that individuation is defined as both the degree to which individuals are distinct and autonomous from nature and each other and the process whereby various degrees and kinds of distinctiveness and autonomy occur. What needs explaining, therefore, is why individuals are immersed in their communities, or why they are relatively distinct and autonomous from them.

The source of immersion or individuation which is described most by Marx is the form of ownership of the means of production. Specifically, where the individual is alleged to be most immersed in the community, land is owned communally and merely possessed by the individual families which work it. Under these conditions individuals do not have private property interests which set them off from the community.[2]

A second source is the division of labour. When it is low, individuals are not likely to be very distinctive in terms of the type of labour they perform and the skills with which they perform it.[3]

Third is the related process of exchange. If most individual families are producing similar goods for their own subsistence there is likely to be little to exchange.[4] Furthermore, whereas under some conditions – specifically, the production and ownership of relatively unique goods and services by separate individuals – exchange provides individuals with an incentive and opportunity to interact as relatively "free agents", under the present conditions of a low division of labour and communal ownership, exchange typically takes the form of entire communities exchanging occasional surpluses with other communities. "Individuals" obviously do the exchanging, but according to Marx they do so only as agents for the community as a whole.[5]

Fourth, the degree to which individuals are distinct and free agents depends upon the form of "political" control they exercise over each other. When there is very little division of labour and exchange, individuals are not very "objectively" dependent upon each other.[6] If their major aim is to reproduce their own community, they must therefore also reproduce themselves as dependent upon each other in other ways. According to Marx, the other way tends to be the political control of an agent representing the entire community over his or her "subjects".

Here as well as with the second point above we can see important similarities with Emile Durkheim's "mechanical solidarity".[7] Indeed, Marx stated the proposition as if political control were a "functional requirement": "The less social power the medium of exchange possesses . . . the greater must be the power of the community which binds the community together, the patriarchal relation, the community of antiquity, feudalism, and the guild-system."[8]

Finally, although by no means because it is the least important source, mention must be made of the forces of production and the level of surplus. When labour is very inefficient because the level of technology as well as the division of labour are low, such that most individuals must spend a great deal of time producing the means for their own subsistence, or where that surplus which is produced is absorbed by someone else who exercises political control over them, individuals will have little time and technical resources to develop distinctive characteristics. The exception, of course, is the person who exploits others' labour, although his own character will also be limited by the technology and products available to him when he pursues whatever activities he pursues.[9]

Having sketched Marx's general theory of individuation, let us fill in some of the details of the process as Marx recounted it.

THREE EARLY, COMMUNAL MODES: THE ASIATIC, CLASSICAL ANTIQUITY, AND THE GERMANIC

According to Marx, the paradigmatic, non-individuated individual was to be found in ancient China and India and in Slavonia, or what is now Rumania and the surrounding area. There individual families merely possessed rather than owned the land they worked, labour was not very divided, and there was little exchange, especially among individual families. Individuals "owed" the community a great deal of communal labour, which was usually initiated, supervised, and absorbed by an individual ruler in the name of the community as a whole, his or her rule being more or less despotic, depending upon a number of more specific conditions.[10]

Social relations in "classical antiquity" – ancient Greece and Rome – are also supposed to have been highly communal, although there was considerably more individuation than in the early Asiatic and Slavonic communities. Individual families were required to contribute to the production and defence of communal property in the form of aqueducts, baths, forums, fortifications, and so on, but these families owned and worked their own agricultural land away from the above communal property, which was located in the city-state.[11]

The separation of town from country itself necessitated a higher division of labour and more exchange,[12] and probably also permitted less political control over individuals than was the case in the early Asian communities. However, the form of political control was different to begin with, since this occurred through relatively equal, private-landed proprietors coming together publicly as formally equal citizens of the state and, often, relatively democratically formulating and enforcing legislation pertaining to the governing of the community as a whole as well as the protection of their own private property.[13]

Eventually, of course, this initial equality was to break down. Indeed, the very legislation which set a minimum on the amount of agricultural land an individual could own before he could become a citizen became a fetter upon the reproduction of the original community, for when population increased there was simply not enough land to go around.[14] This led to a whole series of changes which furthered individuation.

For one thing, it meant the exclusion of some members of the community from land ownership, and therefore also citizenship, which in turn often meant their relegation to urban crafts or trading occupations which increased their participation in a division of labour and exchange. Both because of this and because their exchange relations were often with aliens, they became less susceptible to control by the community.[15] For another, it meant the conquest and enslavement of foreign peoples, which permitted the concentration of property, extraction of higher levels of surplus labour, and therefore also greater leisure time for the personal development of more individual members of the community.[16]

Marx wrote much less about what he considered to be the third great communal form of appropriation the "Germanic", which is supposed to have characterized the Germanic tribes of the Middle Ages.

He did imply that the community was less solidary there than in classical antiquity, for basically two reasons. One, there was still less communal property. While there was some hunting, grazing, and timber land in common, this "*ager publicus* appears rather merely as a complement to individual property, and figures as property only to the extent that it is defended militarily as the common property of one tribe against a hostile tribe."[17] Two, members of the community lived not in the same locale but in many families or clans scattered in different parts of the forest. "For the commune to come into real existence, the free landed proprietors have to hold a *meeting*, whereas e.g. in Rome it *exists* even apart from these assemblies in the existence of the *city itself* and of the officials presiding over it etc."[18]

With less community solidarity one might well expect more individuation as compared with antiquity. However, other conditions may have mitigated this. Thus smaller production organizations may have meant lower surpluses and less leisure time for self-development, and less of a division of labour into crafts and trading. Certainly, according to Marx there was less of the latter, with "manufactures" having been "purely" a "domestic secondary task for women".[19]

From these three communal forms, where in spite of the above-mentioned differences individuals in a sense remained possessions of the entire community,[20] and aimed primarily to reproduce themselves as members of that community rather than as separate individuals,[21] Marx moved on to describe three modes in which most producing individuals were possessed, albeit to varying degrees, by particular other individuals who exploited their labour and imposed their own purposes upon the producers, although again to varying degrees.

"PERSONALIZED" EXPLOITATION: SLAVERY, FEUDALISM, AND THE GUILD-SYSTEM

Of the three, slaves are most possessed and circumscribed – in this case by individual landowners who treat them as "objective conditions of production"; that is, as if they were land itself or beasts of burden.[22] They also do not work independently of the owner or his representative,[23] but are instead his "labouring machine".[24] For all of these reasons, Marx implied, the slave is not free to "relate as subject to his particular expenditure of force, nor to the act of living labour".[25]

In the feudal mode of production the serf formally belongs to the land rather than the lord. While this makes him "an appendage of the soil, exactly like draught-cattle,"[26] it also mediates the relationship between the lord and himself and limits the domination and exploitation of the latter by the former. Often, for example in the case of "labour rent", the serf and his family work independently for their own subsistence on a plot of land he himself formally possesses, as well as for a certain number of days on the lord's land under his supervision.[27] In some cases serfs were actually able to purchase the land they possessed, and/or to exchange surpluses with travelling merchants or town dwellers. These then provided incentives for individuality in productivity as well as opportunities for some degree of individual agency.

The journeyman in the guild was under the control of a particular master, but here the relationship between exploiter and producer was mediated by the latter's close individual relationship to the instruments of production.

Most importantly, the instruments of the craft were not simply passed on by inheritance, but were earned by the individual producer through demonstration of his skill as an individual.[28] Indeed, these instruments were often *made* by him. Even the master was expected to have achieved and to maintain the highest level of skill, and to continue to work.[29] Although the methods of work and nature of the product were in part prescribed by tradition and the demands of the other guilds with whom one bartered, the work itself was at least "half-artistic, half end-in-itself",[30] and as such could, to a considerable degree, be a vehicle for the expression and development of one's own individuality.[31]

On the other hand, the same traditions of production limited the extent to which an individual master could exploit the journeyman and thereby limit his freedom and individuality. For example, because of the emphasis upon the skill of the individual workman, the master was not free to combine labour on a mass scale,[32] nor to further mechanize it, since, for instance, the number of looms a single individual could operate was fixed by tradition.[33] Nor was he free to sacrifice the quality of the product in order to produce it on a mass scale.[34]

IMPERSONAL EXPLOITATION: THE CAPITALIST MODE

The bourgeois revolutions which usually preceded industrial capitalism eradicated the direct, political-legal control of particular exploiters over particular producers. Producers were then permitted to purchase land or other means of production, to labour in the employ of whomever they chose to, and to purchase whichever goods and services they could afford.[35] In these commodity exchange relations even the sellers of their own labour became formally equal to the buyer, in that they could not be forced to work for him, and were seemingly assured that the return for their labour would be equivalent to its market value.[36]

The upshot of this new freedom and equality was the freeing of the individual from the control of the community or its traditional agents, and the replacing of the interests of the community as a whole or an exploitative class with the self-interests of individuals. Apparently, individuals were now free to do and possess whatever they wanted to, depending only upon their personal qualities, interests, efforts, and the demands of others for the goods and services which they could provide. Freedom and equality of opportunity therefore seemed to permit individuality.

Or *did* they? Most typically, of course, Marx's interpreters have assumed that these changes were merely the self-serving claims of the bourgeoisie. Individuals may have begun to *feel* and *think* of themselves as free and unique, but this was anything but objectively true. Indeed, it was less true than it was for producers in the guild-system.[37] Unfortunately, this standard interpretation misses at least two important subtleties in Marx's account of individuation. One is his assumption that there was indeed a genuine increase in freedom and individuality – "a golden age for labour" as he called it – "in the period of the decline and fall of the feudal system, but where it still struggles internally – as in England in the 14th and first half of the 15th centuries".[38] Another is his assumption that the subjective experience of individuation is itself anything but epi-phenomenal, but instead an important "material" source for social change, as we shall see later.

Nevertheless, there is no question that Marx regarded most of these initial changes to have been short-lived, and for the long-run, therefore largely "illusory".[39] The exceptions are the isolation of the individual from the community and the predominance of self-interest. For the rest, there is at best a replacement of earlier forms of control and exploitation by newer and different forms.

In the first place, even the freedom from direct political control by a class of exploiters was short-lived. Thus when large landowners wanted all of their land for sheep grazing and other pursuits, peasants were herded from their small landholdings. This "mass of living labour powers" became "dependent on the sale of its labour capacity or on begging, vagabondage and robbery as its only source of income. It is a matter of historic record that they tried the latter first, but were driven off this road by gallows, stocks and whippings, onto the narrow path to the labour market".[40] Later the ascendent bourgeoisie were able to pass legislation not only prohibiting loafing, but limiting wages and maximizing hours of work, and still later, preventing workers from combining against their capitalist employers.[41]

Secondly, whereas the use of such brute political force has now typically receded into the background, it has simply been replaced by indirect economic control. Specifically, those producers whose means of production had not already been forcibly expropriated (for example, spinners and weavers) were induced by the merchant middlemen with whom they dealt to give up subsistence farming and their own raw materials and instruments of production.[42] Although not dependent upon a *particular* employer, the propertyless became dependent upon the *class* of employers as a whole. Their relationships with others therefore became more "impersonal".[43]

Producers' subjection to employers was increased by their impersonal relationships with each other. Forced to compete with each other for employment and wages, and coming together not through their own initiative but only through the mediation of the employer, they became hostile and/or indifferent to each other, and thereby less capable of resisting domination and exploitation by the employer.[44]

If producers, therefore, were no longer free, neither were they equal to their employers. We have already seen this with regard to political and economic power. And, of course, Marx held this to be true for material wealth. It is not simply a case of a lack of equal opportunity, but the fact that what is exchanged in the capitalist labour process is not a fixed quantity of labour for its market value in wages, but the extended use of labour power for close to the mere cost of reproducing the labourers themselves.

The surplus value produced accrues to the capitalist who legally owns the means of production and the finished product.[45] The capitalist uses this surplus value to employ overseers and purchase machinery which either replaces labourers altogether, or further divides and indirectly controls their labour. In the process, individual producers' knowledge, skill, strength, and virtuosity become superfluous and "every connection of the product with the direct need of the producer" is destroyed."[46]

If a lack of individuality, as well as freedom and equality, therefore comes to characterize the capitalist production process with its high division of labour and mechanization, the same is true of the circulation process with its formal characteristics of freedom and equality. There, class position predominates over individuality, in that one's interest in, and control over, others depends mainly upon whether or not one owns the means of production. Aside from class position, one's own value as a person becomes equivalent to the value of the commodities one can exchange or purchase in the market; to one's possessions and income. Under these conditions "The individual carries his social power, as well as his bond with society, in his pocket,"[47] and "is merely the individuation of money".[48]

Now, whether Marx intended us to take the latter claim literally is difficult to say. In fact, there is reason to believe that he may have gotten "carried away".

For one thing, elsewhere he distinguished one's "juridical" or formal-legal personality from one's "natural individuality",[49] the implication being not only that in the sphere of circulation as compared with that of production there is somewhat more, if also somewhat "arbitrary", freedom,[50] but that outside of exchange relations, individuals remain at least somewhat distinct.[51]

For another, the logic of Marx's theory of agency and history – which I will take up in the next chapter – requires that workers retain, if not a great deal of objective individuality, at least some aspirations for it, as an incentive to change capitalist relations of production. We can see hints of this logic in Marx's earlier writing, where, for example, workers are portrayed as attempting to escape into leisure activities where, because they exercise more choice and express more of their individuality, they feel more like their true selves.[52]

However, we must be careful here.

In the first place, as noted in the previous chapter, the distinction between the "juridical" "person" and the "natural" "individual" is itself an historically-emergent phenomenon. In order to have "public" versus "private" and related distinctions for *individuals*, one must also have such distinctions between social activities and *relations*. Yet, Marx implied, such distinctions do not pre-date classical antiquity, and only become especially marked in bourgeois society.[53] To the extent, therefore, that individuals remain distinct "outside" of relations of production and circulation in the capitalist mode, they do so because considerable individuation had already occurred prior to the systematization of capitalist relations, and not because individuals naturally are, and have always been, very distinct from each other.

Secondly, however, free and distinct individuals in bourgeois society are in their own "private", "social" as compared to their "public", "economic", and "political" relations, Marx claimed that this freedom and distinctiveness would *also* attenuate; that commodity exchange relations come to contaminate even the former.

Thus courtship and love relationships become commodity exchanges.[54] The bourgeois family becomes dominated by the father's property; the working-class family by over-employment of both parents, and perhaps also the children, and the tendency for the father in particular to take out the frustrations of wage labour upon those closest to him.[55] Workers' leisure activities, while not more restricted legally, are restricted by the small amount of "free" time and low level of income available to them, and by their desire to escape into intoxication.[56]

BOTH COMMUNITY AND INDIVIDUALITY:
THE COMMUNIST MODE

In some respects, communist society incorporates the large degree of community of the earliest forms of society, with, among other characteristics, its communal ownership; but only dialectically in a new synthesis with the individuation which succeeded, and, as we shall see shortly, contributed to the transformation of this same large degree of community. This combination of community and individuality[57] is supposed to be made possible by a number of new circumstances which, so to speak, "grow in the womb of" bourgeois society. In very general terms, the material and social constraints upon community and individuality are overcome, and the latter then facilitate each other.

The major material, or better, physical constraint that is overcome is the low productivitiy of labour. The major means by which this is overcome is automation, although this had been preceded by the other progressive, if one-sidedly so, innovations in the preceding mode: the division of labour and direct disciplining of the labour force.[58] (These innovations increase individuals' alienation from their labour.)

One effect of this development of the forces of production is a drastic reduction in socially necessary labour time. This means that "even though production is now calculated for the wealth of all, *disposable time* will grow for all."[59] This allows for "the free development of individualities", since it "then corresponds to the artistic, scientific etc. development of the individuals in the time set free, and with the means created, for all of them."[60]

But the quality as well as the quantity of socially necessary labour is changed. Indeed, with automation:

> Labour no longer appears so much to be included within the production process; rather, the human being comes to relate more as watchman and regulator to the production process instead of being its chief actor. In this transformation, it is neither the direct human labour he himself performs, nor the time during which he works, but rather the appropriation of his own general productive power, his understanding of nature and his mastery over it by virtue of his presence as a social body – it is, in a word, the development of the social individual which appears as the great foundation-stone of production and of wealth.[61]

Carol Gould interprets Marx as also having argued that this

transformation in the quality of labour greatly decreases individuals' objective dependence upon each other. Specifically, automation reverses the earlier trend for the production of a single product to require a complex division of human labours. Being objectively independent – that is, because most necessary "labour" is performed by machinery – individuals are therefore free to become subjectively dependent upon whomever they choose on the basis of truly "*interpersonal*" attraction.[62]

This interesting suggestion may be accurate,[63] but I suspect that two other arguments are more central to Marx's claims regarding the beneficial effects of automation for "free individuality".

One – in the present list, our third general argument – is that automation permits an abundance of goods and services in spite of a drastic decrease in the necessity for individuals to labour. This means that individuals are no longer forced to compete with each other, directly for subsistence, or indirectly for labour, which previously was the major means for subsisting. Were this abundance lacking, individuals would not be inclined to communally own and share the little that was available, and to treat each other as free individuals. As Marx himself put it, "in general, people cannot be liberated as long as they are unable to obtain food and drink, housing and clothing in adequate quality and quantity."[64] If they were competing for these things, "the old filthy business" would occur all over again.[65]

Another, final argument with regard to the forces of production is that their development greatly increases the *variety* of goods and services available to individuals. This "universal development of individuals", of the "human productive capacity" of "the social individual", as Marx variously put it, allows separate individuals to develop their own individualities, since the various goods and services now available to them permit them to develop and gratify a wide and unique variety of needs. In Marx's own words, there are now "all-round needs".[66]

Of course, all of this presupposes certain relations of production. Were the means of production not owned communally, production would be geared to private profit rather than the needs of free individuals, and labour time would remain high for most individuals.[67] Were production still subject to a division of labour by class, with one class doing the planning and expropriating and another the executing and "alienating", then free time, the most pleasurable necessary tasks, and the many and various goods and services would all be distributed unequally.

On the other hand, needless to say, Marx assumed that the means of production would be owned and operated communally and that the community would not be divided by class. Furthermore, various other traditional social barriers would already have been broken down by the capitalist mode of production. Thus the capitalist division of labour will have broken down traditional divisions based upon skill, age, sex, and race and ethnicity.[68] Similarly, commodity exchange relations will have transformed the traditional divisions between town and country and nation and nation. As Marx put it, there will be "universal relations" or "universal intercourse".[69] This removal of traditional social barriers between individuals allows them to treat each other not simply "universalistically" rather than "particularistically", but now also individualistically rather than abstractly in terms of their exchange value on the labour market and their material possessions.

These various arguments about communism – indeed, much of the entire theory of individuation – are summarized well by Marx himself:

> Relations of personal dependence (entirely spontaneous at the outset) are the first social forms, in which human productive capacity develops only to a slight extent and at isolated points. Personal independence founded on *objective* dependence is the second great form, in which a system of general social metabolism, of universal relations, of all-round needs and universal capacities is formed for the first time. Free individuality, based on the universal development of individuals and on their subordination of their communal, social productivity as their social wealth, is the third stage. The second stage creates the conditions for the third.[70]

NOTES

1.   Lloyd Easton, for example, argues that while Marx often appears to have aspired to be purely inductive, he usually also employed either or both an Hegelian or hypothetico-deductive methodology. See "Alienation and empiricism in Marx's thought" *Social Research*, 1970 (Autumn), pp. 402–27.
2.   *Grundrisse*, p. 472. For example, "to exchange the land, their residence, to pawn it to alien communes, would be treason" (p. 740). (*Please note: Unless specified otherwise, all subsequent page references will be to this work, the Grundrisse.*)
3.   Of course, to claim that an initial division of labour fosters differences among individuals over and above those related to their biological and

other "natural" conditions, as Marx appears to have done (*Economic and Philosophic Manuscripts*, in *Collected Works*, vol. 3, pp. 320–2; *Poverty of Philosophy*, op. cit., p. 180; *Grundrisse*, pp. 199, 242), is *not* necessarily to claim either that (a) the individuals thus differentiated remain or become equal, or that (b) increasing differentiation necessarily means that individuals continue to acquire distinctive new knowledge and skills. To the contrary, whereas the latter are implied in Émile Durkheim's analysis of *The Division of Labour in Society* (New York: Free Press, 1964), Marx claimed the opposite. Thus the eventual separation of mental from manual labour gives some classes of individuals intellectual advantages as well as socio-political power over others (*German Ideology*, op. cit., p. 45; *Capital 1*, op. cit., pp. 341–2). Either way, individuals eventually become confined to a particular occupation (*German Ideology*, p. 47), and especially in the capitalist mode of production, labour becomes a commodity which is divided and mechanized (made "abstract") to the point where individuals and occupations become almost interchangeable (see below).

4. Pp. 158, 199, and 242–3.
5. ". . . it is not private individuals but families, tribes, etc., that meet on an independent footing'. (*Capital 1*, p. 332) One does not find "individual exchange" within a community until later, when there are class antagonisms (*Poverty of Philosophy*, p. 180). For other references to the communal aspects of the original forms of exchange, see the *Grundrisse*, pp. 204, 740 and 873, and *Capital 1*, pp. 83–4 and 91.
6. P. 158.
7. Durkheim, op. cit.
8. P. 157.
9. Pp. 701, 706–8.
10. Pp. 472–4.
11. Pp. 474–5.
12. *German Ideology*, p. 64; *Capital 1*, p. 332.
13. Pp. 465–6.
14. Pp. 493–4.
15. Pp. 494–5.
16. P. 494.
17. Pp. 483–4.
18. P. 483.
19. P. 484.
20. P. 495.
21. P. 485.
22. P. 495.
23. *Capital 3*, p. 791. (Moscow: Progress, 1971).
24. P. 465.
25. P. 464.
26. P. 465.
27. *Capital 3*, p. 792.
28. Pp. 497, 499.
29. Pp. 497, 586.
30. P. 497.

31.   P. 529.
32.   Pp. 511, 529.
33.   P. 505.
34.   P. 587.
35.   Pp. 283, 464–5.
36.   Pp. 283, 464–5.
37.   Pp. 464–5, 243.
38.   P. 510. See also Carol Gould, *Marx's Social Ontology* (Boston: MIT Press, 1978) p. 119, on this point.
39.   Pp. 163–4, 464, 649–52.
40.   P. 507.
41.   Pp. 736, 769–70.
42.   P. 510.
43.   *Wage Labour and Capital*, p. 203. *Grundrisse*, pp. 158, 464. However, Marx noted that pre-capitalist relations are not actually "personal" in the sense of participants recognizing each other as individuals having unique personalities and needs: " . . . the individuals in such a society, although their relations appear to be more personal, enter into connection with one another only as individuals imprisoned within a certain definition, as feudal lord and vassal, landlord and serf, etc., or as members of a caste, etc. or as members of an estate, etc." (p. 163). What Marx appears to have meant by "personal" in the original reference was what Talcott Parsons refers to as "particularistic": individuals do not regard and treat each other in terms of general rules pertaining to themselves as equal "individuals", but in terms of traditional role relationships of authority, in-group/out-group, and so on. See T. Parsons and E. A. Shils (eds), *Toward a General Theory of Action* (New York: Harper and Row (Torchbook), 1962) p. 82.
44.   Pp. 196–7, 585.
45.   Pp. 509–10, 673–4.
46.   Pp. 692–4.
47.   P. 157. See also pp. 241–6.
48.   P. 247.
49.   Pp. 245–6.
50.   Pp. 464–5.
51.   See especially pp. 241–2. This is also Gould's interpretation (op. cit., pp. 17, 146–8, 156–7).
52.   *Manuscripts*, op. cit., pp. 274–5.
53.   Pp. 245–6. See also the *Ideology*, p. 78.
54.   *Poverty of Philosophy*, p. 113.
55.   *Manifesto of the Communist Party*, p. 501. "Peuchet: On Suicide" in *Collected Works*, vol. 4, p. 605.
56.   *German Ideology*, p. 418.
57.   On this point see Gould, op. cit., pp. xii–xiii, 25–6.
58.   On the latter point, see p.325; on the former, pp. 701, 705–8.
59.   P. 708.
60.   P. 706.
61.   P. 705.
62.   Gould, op. cit., pp. 24–6.

63. However, I have not been able to find passages in Marx where he explicitly made this argument.
64. *German Ideology*, p. 38.
65. Ibid., p. 49.
66. *Manifesto*, op. cit., pp. 488, 491.
67. Pp. 708–9.
68. *German Ideology*, p. 49; *Grundrisse*, p. 158.
69. *German Ideology*, p. 64; *Grundrisse*, p. 158.
70. P. 158.

3 The Role of "The Individual" in History: The Theory of "Agency"

As suggested previously, a discussion of the relative autonomy and distinctiveness of individuals and the changing circumstances which affect them is an incomplete account of "human nature as modified in each historical epoch". Among the missing elements are answers to these questions: how do circumstances themselves change, and to what extent do they change because individuals themselves consciously intend to, and do, change them? How do individuals *feel* about their social relations and themselves, what is their experience of, and *knowledge* about them, and how do these affect the reproduction or change of the circumstances they encounter?

Again, it is helpful to begin by abstracting a baseline from which one can then compare various kinds and degrees of agency.

THE GENERAL MODEL OF AGENCY

Marx took as given that almost all of the circumstances humans face are produced and reproduced by men and women themselves. This applies to "nature" in the usual sense of the term, as well as to those circumstances which we more typically think of as "man-made", since, through industry, the human species "humanizes" inorganic matter and other animal species as well as itself.[1] Only "individuals" produce. They do so in order to satisfy their own needs, and in the process they produce, or at least reproduce, not only the social relations and principles within which they produce, but themselves. For example, in the process of gratifying their needs they develop new ones, and this appears to have been important enough to Marx to have referred to this process as the first truly historical act.[2]

However, Marx was equally adamant that production is seldom, if ever, a truly individualistic process. Individuals only produce as individuals within existing social relations of production, using raw materials and technologies already at hand. This is even true of such seemingly solitary labour as that of the single natural scientist in his or her laboratory.[3]

On the other hand, the social and individual circumstances under which individuals produce the circumstances which affect them vary a great deal.

In the first place, although all production by humans is of necessity social, the *degree* to which it is social is highly variable historically. For example, a high degree of "alienation" from others notwithstanding, labour in the capitalist mode is much more highly socialized than most labour in previous modes,[4] and, as we have already seen, this is itself a crucial prerequisite for the ultimate development of free individuality.

Secondly, although only individuals produce their social relations and themselves, and although all such production is of necessity to some degree social, the individuals who do the producing may or may not be very *aware* of these facts.[5] For example, as in most religions, they may regard their relations and themselves as created and maintained mainly by a supernatural being, or as in bourgeois economics, by overly natural individuals constrained only by "the invisible hand of the market".[6]

Thirdly, whether or not and to what extent individuals change their social relations and themselves depends upon a number of circumstances. For one thing, they must be *objectively* capable of doing so: material and social circumstances must be suitable. For example, in order to be able to establish communist relations of production, workers must be organized enough as a class to be able to defeat the bourgeoisie and have a large amount of wealth to redistribute.[7] For another, they must be *subjectively* prepared to make such changes: they must recognize that only they are the producers of their social relations and themselves, such that they themselves can change them, and they must have an interest in, and *want* to make, these changes.[8]

Fourthly and finally, the collective organization and awareness required for planned – i.e. truly historical – social change develop in a complicated dialectical relationship to each other.

The basis for Marx's accounts appears to have been Hegel's account of the slave, who, because the master dominates the labour process and expropriates the product without contributing anything essential to either, comes to experience the master–slave relation as frustrating and illegitimate. Until he has the latter experience, his typical responses to the frustration of his physical needs and desire for individual expression are to simply strike out at the product, and, if possible, his own master, without attempting to change the master–slave relation itself.[9]

Among Marx's modifications of this model is the suggestion that such an awareness comes only with a collective revolutionary praxis; which, by definition, presupposes that the slave labours collectively with others, and, while collectively struggling to adapt to it, shares experiences of the master–slave relation with these others and learns something new in the process. This something is the possibility of collectively changing the relation itself as well as its true nature.[10]

This model of the development of consciousness through collective attempts to overcome barriers to need gratification applies whether or not there are close relations of domination and exploitation. For example, at one point Marx suggested that the earliest humans were overawed as well as dominated by nature, conceiving of the Universe and themselves in terms of "natural religion", and only beginning to modify this conception after having successfully altered nature through collective action.[11] Nevertheless, the implication of Marx's account of history is that class relations, by concentrating power and wealth in the hands of a minority, both make social relations more frustrating and increase the likelihood that they will eventually be organized against and experienced as illegitimate.[12]

Three matters here are especially important and deserve being underlined and expanded upon.

One is that individuals' subjective conceptions of their social relations as human-made rather than natural or supernatural, and themselves as agents of history, are clearly prerequisites for fully historic change. In this respect Marx's theory of agency is probably not as different from other theories as has often been claimed.[13]

A second is that these subjective conceptions stand in no simple relationship to objective circumstances. It may well be that we are unlikely to set ourselves the task of ending history, or better, "pre-history", until we have accumulated a great deal of material wealth and organized ourselves as a class,[14] but our conception of ourselves as pawns or agents is mediated by a number of other important social processes, and one of the most important of these would appear to be individuation.

Specifically, unless individuals at least distinguish themselves from their social relations, activities, instruments of production, and products to begin with, they are not likely either to see themselves as having produced them or to become dissatisfied enough with them to want to change them.[15] Certainly, as Marx himself noted, dissatisfaction with oneself alone rather than dissatisfaction with one's social relations is a vastly insufficient condition for revolution.[16] One of the major thrusts of the theory of individuation is that the successive separation of the individual from the community, from particular exploiters, instruments of production and particular products, while likely to be experienced as painful, is also enlightening: individuals gain knowledge about social reality and themselves which will redound to their long-term benefit. Furthermore, in order to *want* to change their social relations – to experience them as dominating and exploitative, as illegitimate and deserving of change – individuals must presumably have some sense of having their own interests which are not well served by these relations.

The third and final point is this: it is not enough that individuals come to experience themselves as *individuals*, with interests separate from those of the community as a whole. Rather, they must come to see themselves as members of a separate subcommunity within the community as a whole, a *class*, who have interests in common which are opposed to those of another sector(s), but which are nevertheless coincident with the true interests of the community as a whole.

Marx appears to have appreciated the difficulty workers would have in organizing themselves as, and thinking of themselves primarily as, a class rather than as separate individuals and groups of workers. But he nevertheless remained optimistic because, as we shall eventually see, he believed that a combination of changing objective circumstances and a relatively unchanging core of their nature as humans would force workers to organize. He also believed that even though workers' initial motives for organizing are for the most part to protect and enhance their material standard of living, in the process of struggling together they will indeed develop truly interpersonal relationships and themselves as (individuated) individuals[17] – at least to the point where they will have enough aspirations for, and skills to acquire, the kinds of community and individuality required for communism as Marx himself conceived of it. However, let us first examine Marx's account of individuals' changing experiences of themselves as agents and how these and other "subjective" characteristics of individuals figure in social and historical change more generally.

THE EARLY COMMUNAL MODES, II

According to Marx, there was very little social change of any kind in societies with an Asiatic mode of production. To be sure, there were few truly *historic* changes. Marx explicitly attributed this absence of change to a low degree of individuation. "This is due," he wrote, "to its [the Asiatic mode's] presupposition that the individual does not become independent *vis-à-vis* the commune . . ."[18]

This is not to suggest that it was individuals' lack of a subjective sense of themselves as historic agents which Marx went on to stress. On the contrary, it was the more indirect consequences of a lack of individuation which got first mention. Specifically, the amount of surplus and technological innovation produced in such a society tends to be low because (a) with manufacturing developing in balance with, rather than in opposition to, agriculture there is little demand for higher productivity,[19] and (b) with individuals not owning the means of production with which they labour and having any surplus production appropriated by representatives of the community as a whole anyway, there would be little incentive for such a demand, should it exist, to be fulfilled.

On the other hand, Marx does go on to argue that this same immersion in the community makes it unlikely that individuals will experience themselves as producers of their own community. For example, shepherding and other pastoral pursuits do not require modification of the land or sophisticated tools which would give producers a sense of their own agency, and labour is not highly and consciously divided, but based on (supposedly) natural age and sexual divisions.

Partly as a consequence of these conditions, Marx claimed, the community is seen as having a supernatural rather than human origin. It is therefore not regarded as changeable. On the other hand, its individual members are not motivated to change it anyway. The surplus labour absorbed by the despot is regarded not as an illegitimate expropriation, but as something which "belongs to the higher community", which is given as a "tribute" to, and "exaltation" of, the community in the form of a person who represents it. This person, as it happens, is not simply "the imagined clan-being, the god", but "the real despot" who represents him, who is therefore also regarded as deserving producers' surplus labour.[20]

Conditions were considerably different in ancient Greece and Rome, for there the community had a "more active, historic" origin as a "created seat (centre) of the rural population (owners of land)", and producers' contributions to the community were partly motivated by a concern to protect their own private interests in property.[21]

The acts of migration and quasi-voluntarily contributing to the community gave individuals, more individuated to begin with than those in Asiatic and Slavonic communities, a greater sense of their having produced their own community. However, this sense was a restricted one: "The commune, although already a product of history here, not only in fact but also *known as such*, and therefore possessing an origin, is the presupposition of property in land and soil – i.e. of the relation of the working subject to the natural presuppositions of labour as belonging to him – but this belonging [is] mediated by his being a member of the state, by the being of the state – hence by a presupposition regarded as a divine etc."[22] Similarly, the act of migration meant new "conditions of labour" which developed "the energy of the individual more", and helped more individuals become private proprietors, who, in labouring "personally" and being responsible for their own subsistence, would also have been motivated to produce more. Nevertheless, Marx stressed, individuals were much more concerned to reproduce themselves as members of the community than to acquire wealth as such.[23]

As mentioned earlier, Marx saw the initial changes in the Greek and Roman communities as coming about not through design, but as unintended consequences of the attempts of citizens to reproduce themselves as members of the community under drastically different circumstances. Specifically, by continuing to require that citizens own a minimum amount of property in the face of large increases in population, these citizens excluded some individuals from the community altogether and forced others to migrate still further. These unintended consequences of their actions had still other unintended consequences, such as the development of slavery, which eventually changed the nature of the entire society and helped lead to its demise.

Although in the meantime slave-owning members of the ruling class in particular had greatly developed themselves as individuals, this development was restricted in degree by the material means available to them, and in numbers by the class structure, and was never a goal for all members of the community.[24]

Marx told us very little about social change in the *Germanic mode*. Since the community was much more a product of the conscious actions of its individual members than was the case in Asia and classical antiquity, it would presumably have been more subject to historic change. However, as noted earlier, other conditions may have limited the degree of individuation. Furthermore, the relative isolation and independence of groups of individual members might well have made overall communal change difficult, and the relative absence of class domination and exploitation would have provided little in the way of an incentive for such changes.

Perhaps for these reasons, Marx implied that social change came more from without, as these independent families were unable to compete with urban productive organizations.[25]

"PERSONALIZED" EXPLOITATION, II

The general model of agency discussed above suggests that slaves are highly likely to become aware that they are dominated and exploited and, eventually, to consciously attempt to change slave relations of production. In two passages Marx can be interpreted as going still further to claim that such revolts were also often successful.[26] However, such a prognosis is not the only one which follows from Marx's few accounts of slavery. Thus Marx himself stressed the absence of opportunities for slaves to develop, express, and act upon their individuality, and therefore also to aspire to, and become aware of, individuation and free and historic agency. Consequently, at a minimum the latter should take a long time, and considerable class organization and struggle, to develop. However, Marx also claimed that circumstances seldom favoured the latter either, since slaves were divided among different owners and, usually, closely supervised. Some also had highly paternalistic relationships with their owners.[27] At any rate, the latter interpretation is more in line with Marx's analyses of changes in other "personal" relations of production than is the imputation of successful, class-conscious rebellion by slaves themselves.

Having to labour for the lord over and above that required for their own subsistence, and/or being highly taxed, serfs were well-aware that they were exploited.[28] However, their segregation in different locations in the countryside meant that in spite of the fact that "The great risings of the Middle Ages all radiated from the country", they "remained totally ineffective." The more typical fate of serfs was simply a *freer* agency: they escaped separately to the towns and became journeymen or even members of the petty bourgeoisie.[29]

Because they produced their own means of production, journeymen began with a greater subjective sense of agency – of having produced their own community as a whole – than either slaves or serfs.[30] They were also often aware that they were exploited, and as a consequence often committed "acts of insubordination". Nevertheless, not only were the relationships between masters and journeymen highly paternalistic, and those between journeymen fragmented among separate shops and guilds, but most journeymen expected to become masters. The aforementioned acts of insubordination therefore tended to be "small" and "within separate guilds".[31]

The demise of these modes appears to have come not from their class-conscious overthrow by the producers most exploited and otherwise affected by them, but through more indirect processes. True, the relatively class-conscious revolutions by the *bourgeoisie* were crucial here. Being small in numbers and living close together in towns and cities, being literate and capable of organizing themselves through the written word, the bourgeoisie were able to provoke and lead the assault upon the feudal and guild-systems. However, the decline of the latter came about as much because of the bourgeoisie's construction of more efficient production organizations with which the guilds (and slave and feudal organizations) could not compete, as because of the political and legal changes they were able to deliberately produce through their revolutions.[32]

On the other hand, one should not assume that the absence of historical agency on the part of slaves, serfs, and journeymen means that Marx believed individual and psychic conditions played no important part in the stability and change of these modes.

Serf labour replaced slave labour because it was more productive, and much of its greater productiveness lay with the greater individuation of producers. Unlike many serfs, slaves were excluded from processes of exchange, and therefore had relatively few, or at least ineffective, needs.[33] This may have meant that they were less frustrated by their social relations than were serfs, even though their working and living conditions were often objectively worse.[34] On the other hand, according to Marx it was their own predilection to destroy implements which made their owners reluctant to introduce technological innovations.[35]

Over and above the aforementioned objective lack of organization on a class-wide basis, the journeyman was not very prone to revolt against his master because his very individuation made him "completely absorbed in his work, to which he had a complacent servile relationship".[36] Moreover, work in the guild-system was in effect considered a career, such that "journeymen were bound to the existing order even by their interest in becoming masters themselves".[37]

IMPERSONAL EXPLOITATION, II

Clearly, Marx believed the bourgeois revolutions to have involved a great deal of historic agency on the part of individuals of that class, and certainly much more than was the case with most previous social changes. Furthermore, the bourgeoisie is portrayed as continuing its revolutionary role for some time after achieving formal political and legal freedom and equality for itself relative to the former ruling classes, if not in fact for all members of the community, as proclaimed in its own rhetoric.

Many of these changes were expressly intended to serve their own class interest. For example, the bourgeoisie not only congregated producers in the same place, but deliberately wrested control over the process of production itself from these producers in order to dominate and exploit them more effectively.[38] As we saw in the previous chapter, this was often initiated and/or supported by explicit political and legal changes. Other changes were less intended, as when, in employing the cheapest producers available or seeking the widest possible markets for produce, the bourgeoisie unwittingly broke down national as well as traditional age, sex, racial-ethnic, and local barriers among producers.[39]

Either way, Marx maintained that this relatively high degree of agency on the part of the bourgeoisie would decelerate markedly, to the point where they would become so circumscribed that no matter how free and unique their subjective experiences of themselves, they would in fact be much more actors than authors of their own drama.[40] Thus, being *private* owners of capital, individual members of the bourgeoisie insist that the minute planning they engage in within their own factories and offices stop at the gate. Instead of collectively planning the economy as a whole, capitalists compete with each other, often to the point of driving each other out of business, if not always intentionally, then inadvertently by paying their own workers so little that they cannot be "good" consumers of other workers' products.[41]

Furthermore, of course, capitalists encounter resistance from workers. Having closed off most alternative forms of employment, they discover that their workers engage in sabotage and other "guerilla actions".[42] The same concentration of workers in a single workplace, which increases the amount of labour power for them to exploit, increases the likelihood that workers will organize and resist being dominated and exploited.[43] Employing cheaper and less well organized labourers, and extending the length of the working day, leads workers to organize politically and force the passage of legislation limiting such practices.[44] Alternatively, maintaining a long working day after introducing labour-saving technology leads workers to demand shorter working hours.[45] The same crises which arise from the bourgeoisie's refusal to exercise representative agency in the true interests of the community as a whole, lead workers to become dissatisfied with, and question the legitimacy of, capitalist relations of production and a state dominated by the bourgeoisie.[46]

It is only after the bourgeoisie has already largely lost control over the capitalist system that the working class emerges as the major collective agent, as an historic agency which also represents the true interests of the community as a whole (a "universal class").[47] Yet the emergence of workers as agents in these respects is only the culmination of a very long and arduous process of individual and class struggle.

As we saw in the previous chapter, Marx believed there was a period of relatively free agency, "a golden age for labour", with the demise of the feudal and guild-systems. However, this period soon ended as the bourgeoisie developed and made effective their demands for large tracts of agricultural land and amounts of wage labour. These changes in objective circumstances were accompanied by important changes in producers' subjective experiences.

Initial attempts to have them do wage labour were often strongly, if usually individualistically, resisted. Marx suggested former producers even preferred – and pursued – robbery, beggary, and vagabondage rather than work for others under these conditions.[48] However, as both these and the more socially-legitimate alternative means of subsistence (independent farming and craftwork) became closed off to them this resistance was largely broken.

The experience of the latter, more independent forms of employment receded to the background of their collective and individual consciousness. But then, as impersonal and "dully compulsive" processes of competition for employment for the most part replaced those of direct, political, and legally-sanctioned coercion, so did the recognition that their labour is in fact still forced.[49] Similarly, the exploitative nature of capitalist relations became hidden behind their surface characteristics: the merging of subsistence and surplus labour in the same space and time,[50] the separation of the process of circulation from that of production, and the apparent freedom and equality of all buyers and sellers,[51] and so on. Largely because of these processes – the receding of awareness of, and aspirations for, independent labour, and the masking of the true, coercive and exploitative nature of the capitalist system – the latter began to appear natural, even legitimate.[52] It is at this point that Marx felt justified in referring to bourgeois claims of freedom and equality as totally illusory. Workers are not free agents, but at best highly paid slaves[53] who may *believe* that they are relatively free agents, that it is natural to not be free, or both.

Nevertheless, this absence of the subjective as well as objective prerequisites for transforming social relations did not make Marx pessimistic for the long-run, since such "vicious cycles" of atomization and systematization were already being broken during his own lifetime. Although the completion of the break would have to occur through the class conscious agency of workers themselves, the initial cracks would instead be unintentionally started by the bourgeoisie.

For one thing, the largely unintended consequences of the actions of the bourgeoisie both modify the capitalist system and expose its true nature. Out of competition comes not freedom and equality of opportunity, but a huge concentration and centralization of capital. This greatly simplifies the class structure and makes the parasitic nature of the capitalist class that much more obvious. As workers organize as a class and the state intervenes on the side of the bourgeoisie, the extent of the bourgeoisie's domination of society as a whole is also laid bare.[54]

For another, as indicated in the last sentence, workers do not remain alone for long. As noted earlier, the bourgeoisie itself brings them together in ever larger numbers, makes them interdependent, and helps break down traditional barriers among them. It also provokes them to organize *independently* of the bourgeoisie: it lowers wages, lengthens the working day, and forces workers to place a class interest in maintaining solidarity above such individual and sectoral interests as maintaining wages as such.[55] With collective praxes come successful resistance, and perhaps even small offensive victories, and hence both knowledge of the capitalist system and confidence in their collective capacity to modify it.[56]

Finally, workers' natures as individuals become modified in respects other than an increase in knowledge and confidence. Whereas the first provocation for them to organize themselves is usually a threat to their very physical subsistence – the deprivation of their biological needs – the expansion of capitalism vastly increases the number and variety of needs they experience and demand gratification for. These demands arise not only from advertising and the mere availability of new commodities, but also from workers organizing and then comparing their lot with that of the bourgeoisie. This clearly occurs with material goods. For example, items such as liquor and tobacco which were once only luxuries for the working class become "second nature" and make workers less tolerant of crises.[57] However, other "needs" and aspirations develop which are still less capable of being accommodated within the system.

Thus workers themselves begin to develop more, and demand even more, inter*personal* relationships with each other at work as well as in their "free time".[58] But through study groups and the like they also encourage each other to develop themselves as individuals,[59] and such concerns with self-development are reflected not only in demands for more free time,[60] but also for more control over the process of production itself, and social recognition for the indispensability of their contribution to it. The latter demands are especially likely to arise among those sectors of workers who have been educated in science to operate highly automated machinery.[61]

This brief account of how workers emerge as historic agents hardly does justice to the richness of Marx's own. Although I have purposefully stressed the role of individual and psychic conditions in social change, one has to keep in mind that Marx himself emphasized that as workers organize, the exigencies of the class struggle both take precedence over more individualistic concerns and greatly modify these individual concerns to begin with. The latter problem of how individuals' psyches are transformed in intergroup contexts is developed below in Chapter 7.

Nevertheless, in closing I would like to reiterate an argument from Chapter 1 – that workers do not cease being psychic beings simply because they are organized as, and function as, a class. Thus in Marx's own analyses of attempts at proletarian revolution during his lifetime, such psychological considerations are as prominent as those with regard to either the objective prerequisites for communism or the suitability of various strategies adopted by workers for the struggles at hand. Why, for example, were the revolutionary struggles of French workers in the late 1840s unsuccessful? According to Marx, the single most important explanation was that whereas the major provocation for worker unrest in the first place had been a severe economic depression, this circumstance had reversed itself by the time workers might otherwise have completed their revolt by seizing and keeping state power.[62]

NOTES

1.   *Manuscripts*, pp. 275–7, 302–4.
2.   *Manuscripts*, pp. 273–80, 332–3; *German Ideology*, pp. 31–2, 36, 41–3

(the reference to the production of new needs as "the first historical act" is on p. 42), 82, 87–8; *Poverty of Philosophy*, pp. 165–73; *Eighteenth Brumaire*, pp. 103–4; *Grundrisse*, pp. 87–94, 160–2, 226, 334, 527–8, 831–2.

3. *Manuscripts*, p. 298.
4. Ibid., p. 529; *Capital 1*, pp. 316–17.
5. For example, in the Asiatic mode individuals "relate naively to it [the earth] as the property of the community, of the community producing and reproducing itself in living labour" (p. 472). However, "Property, insofar as it is only the conscious relation . . . is only realized by production itself. The real appropriation takes place not in the mental but in the real, active relation to these conditions – in their real positing as the conditions of his subjective activity" (p. 493).
6. *Manuscripts*, pp. 278–9; *German Ideology*, p. 44; *Capital 1*, pp. 77–81.
7. *German Ideology*, pp. 54, 87–8.
8. Ibid. See also pp. 48–52, 289, 432, 438. Earlier, in *The Holy Family (Collected Works*, vol. 4, p. 36), Marx had suggested that capitalists as well as workers are "alienated" and therefore have an objective, long-term interest in changing the social relations, but the benefits of their class position relative to workers "buy them off" and prevent them from recognizing this interest. For the importance of individuals' motives and consciousness in Marx's late writings, see, for example, the *Grundrisse*, pp. 410, 457, 463, 542, and 597. Much of this material is presented in this chapter.
9. G. F. Hegel, *The Phenomenology of Mind* (New York: Harper and Row (Torchbook), 1967) pp. 228–40 (Chapter IV, part A). For Marx's use of the model, see the *Grundrisse*, pp. 243–4, 454, 457–8, 463, 516–17, 541–2.
10. *Manifesto*, pp. 492–8; *Grundrisse*, p. 597.
11. *German Ideology*, p.44.
12. Ibid. See especially 47–8, 87–8.
13. Dawe (op. cit.), for example, interprets Marx as having neglected the subjective side of agency (pp. 390–1) and offers his own alternative (e.g., pp. 376–8), which, however, may be much less in opposition to Marx's than Dawe claims.
14. *Preface*, p.183.
15. E.g., *Grundrisse*, pp. 486, 499. See below.
16. *Ideology*, p. 379.
17. *Manuscripts*, p. 313; *Holy Family*, p. 52.
18. *Grundrisse*, p. 486.
19. Ibid.
20. Pp. 472–3. As Bologh notes (op. cit., pp. 107–8). Durkheim's totemic theory of religion overlaps considerably with Marx's account at this point. For an application of the same logic to the fetishism of money, see the *Grundrisse*, p. 160.
21. Ibid., pp. 475–6.
22. Ibid., p. 475.
23. Ibid., p.476.
24. Ibid., pp. 487–8.
25. Ibid., p. 479.

26. *Manifesto*, p. 483; *Grundrisse*, p. 463.
27. See Notes 22–5, Chapter 2.
28. *Capital 1*, p. 82.
29. *German Ideology*, pp. 65–6.
30. "Since the instrument itself is already the product of labour, thus the element which constitutes property already exists as posited by labour, the community can no longer appear here in a naturally arisen, spontaneous form as in the first case – the community on which this form of property founded – but rather as itself, already produced, made, derived and secondary community, produced by the worker himself." *Grundrisse*, p. 499.
31. *German Ideology*, pp. 65–6.
32. *Grundrisse*, p. 506.
33. Ibid., p. 419.
34. Interestingly, in the few cases where slave revolts were successful the newly-freed producers demanded little more than what they already had. See Chapter 8.
35. *Capital 1*, p. 196.
36. *German Ideology*, pp. 65–6.
37. Ibid.
38. *Grundrisse*, p. 510.
39. See Notes 68 and 69, Chapter 2.
40. *Grundrisse*, p. 482; *Capital 1*, pp. 20–1; *Capital 2*, pp. 121, 478; *Capital 3*, pp. 289–90, 819. In fact, the accumulation of capital often leads capitalists to forego their own pleasure. See *Capital 1*, p. 557.
41. *Grundrisse*, p. 420; *Capital 3*, p. 484.
42. *Manifesto*, pp.491–3.
43. *Capital 1*, p. 313.
44. Ibid., pp. 264–81.
45. At one point Marx is reputed to have noted with satisfaction the decision of one group of workers to take more free time rather than an increase in wages. Referred to (but not cited) by Heller, op. cit., p. 91.
46. *German Ideology*, p. 80; *Grundrisse*, pp. 410, 749–50.
47. On Marx's conception of the proletariat as a "universal class", see especially Avineri, op. cit., Chapter 2.
48. *Grundrisse*, pp. 507, 736, 769–70.
49. See *Capital 1*, pp. 538, 669, 689.
50. *Grundrisse*, p. 590; *Capital 3*, pp. 791–2.
51. *Grundrisse*, p. 197; *Capital 1*, p. 172; *Capital 2*, pp. 120, 318.
52. For example, see note 49 above.
53. *Wage Labour and Capital*, p. 220.
54. *German Ideology*, p. 80.
55. For struggles over the length of the working day, see Note 44 above. For the provocative effects of absolute immiseration, see the *German Ideology*, p. 87; *Wage Labour and Capital*, pp. 225–6; and *Capital 1*, pp. 403–6, 596–9. The emergence of class solidarity as a paramount goal is referred to in *The Poverty of Philosophy*, pp. 210–11.
56. See Chapters 6 and 7 below.
57. See Chapter 4.

58.   *Manuscripts*, p. 313.
59.   *Grundrisse*, p. 287.
60.   See Note 45, p. 74.
61.   *Grundrisse*, p. 705.
62.   *Class Struggles in France*, p.137.

Part III
"Human Nature in General"

Introduction

We have already seen not only that it is legitimate to look for psychic processes common to all human individuals in Marx's theorizing, but that it is probably *necessary* to do so if one wants to fully understand his theorizing. For example, it has been shown that Marx regarded the relative independence of capitalist relations of production from the conscious control of individuals to itself depend upon these individuals' indifference toward each other and their own labour. This indifference must be explained *psycho*-logically – at least in good part – and presumably such an explanation must in turn rely heavily upon assumptions about human nature in general.

It is to the latter assumptions Marx appears to have employed that we now turn. I say "appears", because it is by no means always obvious what Marx regarded as the psychic processes common to human individuals in different historical epochs, classes, and so on.

It was not uncommon for Marx himself to label some as "natural", "animal", "peculiarly human", or whatever, but neither was it a rule of his that he do so. Nor did he always make his underlying psychological assumptions explicit in the first place. As Ollman has suggested, Marx may have been much less aware of his own assumptions about human nature than he was of those of the political economists, Hegelians, and others whom he set out to criticize.[1]

Other problems arise from the peculiarities of Marx's method of abstraction.

In the first place, as we saw in Chapters 1 and 2, for Marx individuals cannot always be neatly divided from each other; with the conditions which most affect their internal psychic states and overt activities being thought of as somehow "in" them as separate individuals, rather than in their interaction and the social context as a whole. Furthermore, as suggested in the previous chapter and to be elaborated upon in Chapter 7, the psychic characteristics of separate individuals may well be transformed when these individuals think and act collectively rather than individually.

Secondly, what we see in each historical epoch, according to Marx, is not human individuals neatly divided into two halves – into what is unique and what is common – but a complex interaction of the two. Thus we never find a "pure" need for food "uncontaminated" by historically- and class-specific "needs" for certain foods prepared in certain ways.[2]

How, therefore, are we to know whether a particular psychic process or characteristic described or implied by Marx is one he regarded to be part of human nature in general rather than simply specific individuals, perhaps functioning only individually, under highly specific circumstances?

The short and honest answer to this question is that unless Marx himself labelled a process or characteristic as general, we cannot in fact know for sure. On the other hand, we can apply Marx's method of abstraction to his own writings, and this is what I have attempted to do here. Specifically, I have tried to avoid presenting a process as general unless Marx employed it in his descriptions of individuals in more than one social formation, and, albeit less often, individuals functioning both relatively highly individually and relatively highly collectively.

Of course, the latter procedure does not *ensure* that the process in question is in fact universal, but it is at least better than the all-too-common practice of generalizing from descriptions of individuals in only one social formation or set of specific social circumstances.

Yet we have still to exhaust the problems to be solved before we can proceed to Marx's theory(ies) of human nature in general. To wit, how do we decide which among all the psychic processes Marx described most deserve our attention, and how do we then organize them so as to best indicate their importance?

For example, mention was made earlier of various of Marx's models which appear to constitute only a very general "shell" of human nature. The general model of agency employed in Chapter 3 is one example: it postulates that all human individuals are agents in the sense that much of their seemingly "natural" as well as human-made environment is produced by themselves, but the specific degree to which they can be considered agents varies a great deal, and the psychic and other conditions which permit one to explain these differences in degree are often not specified and related through cause-and-effect statements.

Certainly, such models have to be taken up in any account of human nature in general. Thus part of the model of agency employed in Chapter 3 will reappear in our treatment of responses to gratification and deprivation (Chapter 5), and the acquisition and modification of knowledge (Chapter 6). However, I complained earlier that all too many existing treatments of Marx on human nature are *too* general to be very useful in understanding Marx's specific explanations and predictions.

In keeping with this concern, I have generally left epistemological and other such questions for philosophers and concentrated upon the more substantive and cause-and-effect of Marx's analyses. I have also emphasized the more psycho-dynamic over the definitional, enumerative, and classificatory. In this respect what we have here should be considered only a first approximation.

Marx's theory of needs is the first component of his psychological anthropology we shall examine here. "Consciousness" is not taken up separately, although "knowledge" is, for reasons which will emerge eventually.[3]

NOTES

1. Ollman, op. cit., p. ix.
2. *Grundrisse*, p. 93.
3. I hope I will be forgiven, as Ollman apparently has, for relying so little on others' interpretations of Marx on human nature in general. Certainly, I think I could defend such a practice (and did more so in an earlier, and much longer, draft). I have already expressed many reservations about Ollman's rendering. In some ways I find John McMurtry's (op. cit.) more satisfying, but he does not organize his various observations in a manner which allows us to see and use the psychodynamic aspects of Marx's psychologic. To my mind, Lucien Sève's massive volume (*Man in Marxist Theory and the Psychology of Personality* (Sussex/New Jersey: Harvester/Humanities Press, 1978)) is at least as misleading as it is helpful, because he never really breaks with the Althusserians he sets out to critique, and in the process misrepresents Marx as having dispensed with the concepts of need and alienation, and as having derogated consciousness much more than was the case. Notwithstanding these fundamental differences, Monsieur Sève was a most gracious host when I visited him.

4 Needs and Wants

Presumably, any account of needs should first carefully distinguish between what human individuals "need", in the strict sense of *require* in terms of some (potentially) objective criterion such as their "normal" biological and psychological functioning and development, and what they "want", which may arise merely from a superficial desire or passing fancy. However, Marx can easily be interpreted to have first and foremost intended "need" in the broadest sense of *anything* which individuals *want* and therefore motivates them to think and act with regard to it.

Thus, according to Marx, there are sociological and psychological processes we shall come to shortly which lead individuals to treat as "needs", subjectively, what are only subjective "wants" objectively. That is, individuals *require* these objects, activities, or relationships in order to *feel* normal and healthy. For example, as Marx himself put it at one point, "Our desires and pleasures . . . are of a *relative* nature",[1] and at another, "what previously appeared as a luxury [for instance, spacious housing or liquor and tobacco to the working class] is now necessary".[2] "Necessary" here refers to the fact that workers are as likely to be motivated by a drive to acquire these "extras" as to acquire true necessities; that the "needs" for these former luxuries have now "become second nature".[3] This is reflected, Marx claimed, in the fact that workers insist that they have wages sufficient to purchase them and that even if they have experienced an absolute increase in their standard of living, they will remain dissatisfied and eventually rebel if this standard is less than what they feel is possible and socially justified and desirable.[4]

As I see it, this interpretation is correct. The inclusive meaning of need is not simply there, as we have just seen, but is the most frequent meaning, which suggests that it may indeed have been first and foremost in Marx's thinking. However, one would be in error to conclude that Marx therefore believed "need" in the literal sense of the term, and the distinction between it and "want", to be unimportant. Marx not only made many references to needs in the strict sense, but also to his own awareness of their importance in their own right.

The most obvious strict or "true" needs Marx referred to are biological – those for food, drink, protection from the potentially destructive forces of nature (clothing and shelter), and sex (at least in the form of sexual tension release). When he stated that "life involves before everything else eating . . .", etc., he was presumably referring to requirements for the "normal" functioning and development as well as the very subsistence of human individuals. Certainly, the former criterion is very much in evidence in Marx's later "economic" critiques of capitalism.[5] Yet there is no shortage of references to needs of a seemingly less biological nature.

Thus human individuals are said to have "social" needs not only for affiliation, which Marx claimed has biological roots in human individuals' natures as "herd animals", but for "social *inter*course",[6] which he did not elaborate upon but which presumably has to do with obtaining recognition and social support from others, and exercising and developing one's social skills, through communication, and so on. Marx may not have regarded gratification of these "social" needs to be as immediately necessary for individuals' normal functioning and development as is the case for needs having to do with their biological functioning, narrowly conceived, as could be concluded from his having labelled the social needs which put constraints on the length of the working day "moral" as opposed to "purely physical limitations". Nevertheless, when he wrote that "But both these limiting conditions are of a very elastic nature, and allow the greatest latitude"[7] (presumably for capitalists to maintain a long working day rather than for workers to be normal and healthy), he appears to have been assigning "social" needs a status as "true" needs, parallel to that of biological subsistence needs.

In addition to these needs which are "social" in the sense that others are the immediate objects of the need, and that the need in question can only be gratified through activities undertaken collectively, Marx described several needs whose objects are more immediately "individual" or "personal", and which can also be gratified through activities which are relatively solitary. One such object is *activity* itself: "It seems quite far from Smith's mind that the individual, 'in his normal state of health, strength, activity, skill, facility', also needs a *normal* portion of work, and of the suspension of tranquillity".[8] Another is a *variety* of activities: "Constant labour of one uniform kind disturbs the intensity and flow of a man's *animal* spirits, whch find recreation and delight in mere change of activity."[9]

Needs for affiliation and social intercourse, activity and variety are the true needs beyond those having to do with mere biological subsistence that we can be sure Marx was concerned with. Nevertheless, I think one can make a case that even the wants Marx regarded to be ideal ethically but neither objectively required by, nor even very subjectively effective in, the individuals of his own time – that is, the desire to help others gratify their needs, with no other return to oneself than the vicarious experience of pleasure,[10] and the desire to express and develop oneself as an individual with no external reinforcement other than perhaps others' recognition of, and pleasure from, one's own individuality[11] – are still rooted in these individuals' biological makeup, in this case especially their peculiarly human makeup.

The capacities in question are those which allow individuals to (a) distance themselves from their *own* needs and activities, and (b) vicariously experience *others'* pleasure and pain. They in turn make it possible for individuals to (a) direct their own activities toward *others'* gratification rather than their own, while still being able to obtain gratification for themselves indirectly, and (b) pursue activities which are *creative* – that is, unique rather than simply instinctual – and still gratify themselves, both directly through their own responses to their activities and finished products, and indirectly through their direct or vicarious experience of *others'* responses.

I admit to having done some extrapolating and filling in of holes here, but I do not think I have strayed very far from what is already in Marx's own writings. Thus the capacity of human individuals to distance themselves from their needs and activities, and its centrality for understanding both their normal and "alienated" functioning, was explicitly noted by Marx himself.[12] The capacity to empathize with, or "take the role of", another individual and respond to one's own action as he or she does and/or would is not treated as explicitly, but it is unquestionably there.[13]

Marx has often been accused of having been very lax on the problem of the precise mechanisms whereby individuals "fail" to exercise their uniquely human capacities, but if one examines his work closely I think one can find a great deal more there than he has usually been given credit for. I refer particularly to his having dealt with "the system of needs and system of labours" to the extent of having postulated (a) how individuals' needs are organized in their psyches, and (b) how individuals are likely to handle, psychically as well as practically, the deprivation of their needs, singly and plurally.

A key idea for Marx here is the *hierarchical structuring* of needs.

From what I can gather, Marx referred to this ideal explicitly only once. There he simply noted that an individual's rank-ordering of consumer "goods" in terms of value (presumably *use*-value) will "correspond" "to the hierarchy of his needs".[14] Nothing is said of the content of the latter, and one gets the impression that here Marx was referring less to *needs* in the true sense than to consciously-experienced *wants*. Nevertheless, the conception of true needs as hierarchically structured can be found throughout Marx's middle and late writings.

Specifically, when Marx noted in the *Ideology* that life involves before everything else satisfying those needs relating to one's very biological subsistence, he undoubtedly meant that these needs are the most urgent; and hence also the practical problem of highest priority for individuals thinking and acting collectively as well as individually.[15] As long as individuals think and act under conditions of extreme scarcity, affiliation and social intercourse, activity and variety (*for their own sake*), and certainly altruism and self-"actualization", will be "luxuries" that few of them can afford. This is presumably what Marx meant when he wrote that "in general, people cannot be liberated as long as they are unable to obtain food and drink, housing and clothing in adequate quality and quantity",[16] and that in lieu of "a great increase in productive power" which would correspondingly greatly decrease scarcity, socialism would be impossible, "because without it privation, *want* is merely made general, and with *want* the struggle for necessities would begin again, and all the old filthy business would necessarily be restored".[17]

Conversely, once individuals and collectivities have solved the problem of satisfying their own and others' biological/subsistence needs they can move on to concern themselves with "higher order" needs. Marx gave relatively few concrete examples of this process, but he did give a few, and it makes sense to interpret several others of his comments about real-life occurrences along these lines.

Indeed, the hierarchical structuring of needs provides a reasonable interpretation of his statement that "the satisfaction of the first need [for food, drink, housing and clothing], the action of satisfying and the instrument which has been acquired, leads to new needs".[18] However, the "new needs" he was referring to may well have been individuals' desires for (a) less taxing and more efficient means of production and (b) new consumer goods and services rather than higher order, true needs.

Marx once observed that "When communist *artisans* associate with one another, theory, propaganda, etc., is their first end. But at the same time, as a result of this association, they acquire a new need – the need for society – and what appears as a means becomes an end. . . . Such things as smoking, drinking, eating, etc., are no longer means of contact or means that bring them together. Association, society, and conversation, which again has association as its end, are enough for them; the brotherhood of man is no mere phrase with them, but a fact of life, and the nobility of man shines upon us from their work-hardened bodies."[19] He may have meant that as a function of their status as relatively highly paid skilled workers, to begin with, or because they have organized themselves collectively, they have been able to satisfy their biological/subsistence needs more satisfactorily than other workers have. As a consequence they have also been freer to develop intrinsic, truly inter*personal* attachments, which in turn have been stimulated by the particularly gratifying nature, as well as mere presence, of these particular others.

Nevertheless, the fact remains that Marx himself did not explicitly link this account of the development of new wants among artisans to the hierarchical structuring of their needs. In fact, the only concrete, empirical example of individuals actually proceeding up the hierarchy of their needs is this one: "The great mass of workers, whatever part they belong to, have at last understood that their material situation must become better. But once the workers' material situation has become better, he can consecrate himself to the education of his children; his wife and children do not need to go to the factory, he himself can cultivate his mind more, look after his body better, and he becomes socialist without noticing it."[20]

Thus far we have considered only the *practical* implications of the need hierarchy. These make up one of several seemingly rational elements in Marx's conception of human nature. In this instance Marx claimed that since everything else rests upon individuals subsisting biologically, they must and do attempt to gratify these needs before all others. On the other hand, we should recognize that Marx's conception of needy individuals was by no means wholly rationalistic. To wit, if the means for adequately satisfying their biological/subsistence – and sexual – needs are not available, objectively and/or subjectively (for example, through ignorance), such that they experience severe and long-lasting deprivation, individuals are likely to become "fixated" upon these needs. This means they will be prone to obsessive ruminations and stereotypic and ineffective actions; that they will find it difficult to concentrate upon other matters, including gratifying their other, higher order needs; and that the latter, lacking exercise, so to speak, are likely to atrophy.

Marx argued to this effect in the *Ideology*, where he attributed Max Stirner's egoistic obsessions with food and sex to his personal circumstances as a poorly-paid and solitary school teacher.[21] When Marx wrote in these same passages that "The communists have no intention of abolishing the fixedness of their desires and needs . . . [but] only strive to achieve an organization of production and intercourse which will make possible the normal satisfaction of all needs, i.e., a satisfaction which is limited only by the needs themselves",[22] he probably meant that individuals will always be forced to gratify some needs at the immediate expense of others; both practically because of the persistence of some degree of scarcity and socially necessary labour, and psycho-dynamically because of such inherent biological and psychological limitations as the inability to do several different activities at once or sustain interest in any one activity for a great length of time.[23] However, reconstructing the social relations of production, and the quality as well as quantity of socially necessary labour, will make it easier for individuals to gratify all of their needs, and especially the biological/subsistence, such that they will then be freer to establish priorities of needs and wants which are relatively unique; that is, truly personal.[24]

Since we have covered much terrain so far in this chapter, perhaps we should stop for a moment and summarize Marx's views on human needs; on which are most important and how they are organized psychically. I have attempted to do this in the table which follows.

	Object of Need	
Nature and Place in Hierarchy	Other, Species	Individual, Self
Highest, peculiarly human	*Others'* needs	"*Self*-activity" (Creativity, self-expression, recognition)
	Social *Inter*course	Variety
	Affiliation	Activity
		Sexual tension release
Lowest, least peculiarly human	Cooperative instrumental interaction	Shelter and clothing
		Hunger and Thirst

FIGURE 1   *Major needs and their hierarchical organization*

Now that we have done so, some readers will no doubt experience a glaring omission. Where, after all, are the nasty human passions of aggressiveness, avarice, and egoism? Did Marx believe them to be *un*natural?

Three answers to this question can be gleaned from the literature: (a) Marx considered such propensities to be totally historically specific, and in this sense "unnatural", even "artificial"; (b) they are partly natural and partly historically specific: they are developed forms of human needs in the true sense, but not *necessary* forms; (c) they are *also* totally natural, and can at best be suppressed or diverted in a communist society, through socialization which emphasizes duty to the community over self, or circumstances which permit individuals to gratify their more vulgar needs without harming others.

The first, largely Rousseauian, possibility has been by far the most popular interpretation of Marx on this problem. Heller, for example, sees Marx as having regarded egoism as an historically-specific adaptation individuals have made to scarcity, which over time has become somewhat functionally autonomous: what she refers to as a "quasi-instinct".[25] However, the third, largely Hobbesian, solution can also be found among Marxists.[26] On the other hand, Soper in particular has recently opted for the remaining interpretation of Marx. According to her, Marx may well have regarded some types and degrees of possessiveness and acquisitiveness to be natural. Thus working on land or with tools may naturally give individuals a sense of possessing them; just as individuals' aesthetic sensibilities, or even an inclination to be enamoured by "glitter", may lead to a "mania for possessions". However, proprietorial attitudes involving the exclusion of other members of one's own community and the accumulation of money for its own sake, independent of the use-value of the goods it can buy, are neither necessary nor inevitable forms of these natural inclinations.[27]

Unfortunately, one must agree with Soper that Marx's own accounts of the nasty passions are "fairly ravelled";[28] and for this reason there is no obvious basis for choosing one over another of the three possibilities, although one suspects that Marx leaned much more toward the first and second than the third. At a minimum, he probably attached more importance to anti-social tendencies than his critics have recognized; but, to anticipate Chapter 9 below, probably not enough.

We are therefore forced back to another problem we had earlier bracketed: the more general distinction between "needs" and "wants". We have gone about as far as we can to zero in on what Marx appears to have regarded as needs in the strict sense of the term; but what about *wants?* What did he see as the most important of these forms of human motivation; where did he see them as originating; and did he in fact regard them as *equally* as important as needs?

Wants are the myriad of things individuals through the ages have desired – but not necessarily "needed" in the stricter sense of the term. Needs and biological and psychological limitations probably constrain individuals in what they are likely to want, especially under conditions of naturally and/or socially produced scarcity; but the number and variety of wants is likely to be large to the point where they are very difficult to delineate. Perhaps for this reason, Marx did not attempt to do so.

Nevertheless, one gets the impression that he did not consider it impossible to identify the *major* wants of individuals in particular historical epochs. For example, as we saw in Chapters 2 and 3, in the early communal social formations the "prime" want is supposed to have been the perpetuation of the traditional community; in the capitalist formation either the accumulation of private property or simply self-preservation; and in the communist altruism and "self-activity". To the extent that this was indeed the case, it may have been because Marx believed that the social and psychological processes whereby individuals acquire wants are relatively few and common. Either way, since Marx put considerably more effort into identifying the latter than specific wants as such, it makes sense to start with the processes whereby individuals acquire wants.

One set of processes appears to be based on a relatively simple principle: individuals are likely to want what they have *learned* to want, and especially what they have learned to *expect* – what they are accustomed to. In keeping with some recent work in psychology, I shall refer to what individuals have learned to want and expect as the *"adaptation level"*.[29] Marx himself distinguished between two different components of the adaptation level: that which individuals acquire through the *customs and traditions* of communities and classes – a social, and often "moral" component, and that which they may acquire relatively solitarily through mere *familiarity and habit*.[30] In practice, of course, the two processes will usually work together. For example, particular workers will want liquor and tobacco both because they are customary wants of the working class and because they have provided these particular workers with pleasure in the past, and hence have become part of their individual repertoires of habits.

A second set of processes seems to be based upon another, perhaps less simple, principle: individuals are likely to want whatever is *available* for them to want. What is available is partly a question of custom and tradition ("culture") on the one hand, and familiarity and habit ("personality") on the other; but only partly. There may be a great deal of innovation, and individuals may well desire what is neither customary nor familiar.

Marx suggested that the use of money as a universal equivalent tends to create a "need" for it.[31] The same is true for the production of new consumer goods and services, and even art: "The need which consumption feels for the object is created by the perception of it. The object of art – like every other product – creates a public which is sensitive to art and enjoys beauty. Production thus not only creates an object for the subject, but also a subject for the object."[32]

But the innovations in question may be as much social and cultural as technical and material. For example, the community may have become divided into highly unequal classes, and/or the classes themselves may be stratified internally, with different kinds and amounts of consumption being among the major features which distinguish them. If social inequality has traditionally and habitually been regarded as natural – as unavoidable and legitimate – individuals in the lower social classes may not desire what is now available only to those in higher classes. However, perhaps especially after bourgeois revolutions, this condition may be met less and less; such that producers come to include in their "comparison level of alternatives" a "*social comparison level*"[33] which includes the levels of material and cultural consumption attained by other classes: "A noticeable increase in wages presupposes a rapid growth of productive capital. The rapid growth of productive capital brings about an equally rapid growth of wealth, luxury, social wants, social enjoyments. Thus, although the enjoyments of the worker have risen, the social satisfaction that they give has fallen in comparison with the increased enjoyments of the capitalist, in comparison with the state of development of society in general."[34]

Note that this passage is pregnant with not just one hypothesis – that workers will compare their lot with that of the capitalist and experience "relative deprivation" – but several.

Let us return for a moment to the adaptation level phenomenon. One can find other passages where Marx indicated his awareness that workers' adaptation levels may *decrease* rather than increase. For example, he noted that workers may come to expect nothing more than to barely subsist;[35] Irish workers may come to expect to live not simply on potatoes, but *scabby* potatoes.[36] Nevertheless, in the passage we have just quoted above Marx appears to have suggested that a situation of "rising expectations" is much more typical. There the direct object of desire is higher wages, but elsewhere he makes the same argument for "free" time: the more workers acquire, the more they will desire and expect.[37]

My reason for going back to the adaptation level is not simply to point to the hypothesis of rising expectations, but to note the relatively greater importance Marx appears to have assigned to the comparison level of alternatives, and especially the *social* comparison level, than to the adaptation level. Thus the psychologic behind the concept of the adaptation level would presumably lead us to predict that an increase in wages or free time which greatly exceeds the level workers have learned to want and expect should produce extreme satiation rather than deprivation – at least in the short run – before these levels become customary and habitual and expectations are therefore adjusted further upward. However, in the passage we have been examining Marx clearly argues that any such placating effects are completely counteracted by the experience of deprivation relative to workers' social comparison level: no matter how much the outcome of the class struggle may have favourably exceeded workers' expectations, they will remain dissatisfied as long as capitalists continue to benefit from the struggle even more.

Before proceeding it may be useful to note that both of the psychic phenomena we have just discussed – the adaptation level and the comparison level – are highly related to another phenomenon commonly referred to in the literature of modern social psychology: the *"level of aspiration"*.[38] Workers may aspire to no more than what they are accustomed to and what is currently available to them, or they may also aspire to what they see as now available only to others. Either way, what they are accustomed to is likely to constitute the *minimum* to which they aspire, and as we shall see shortly, Marx appears to have regarded workers' aspiration levels as crucial aspects of their psyches which both condition how workers react to social changes and partly determine – indeed, *define* – psychic alienation.

But here my own aspiration to move on to other aspects of Marx's psychological anthropology has pushed me beyond the immediate task at hand, which was to have been merely to complete the discussion of needs and wants. I shall do this as quickly as possible by making (a) a brief admission about identifying wants, and (b) some suggestions regarding the aforementioned problem of weighing the relative importance of needs and wants.

The admission is that I have never really intended to, nor shall, attempt to identify all of what Marx considered to be the major wants of individuals. I think he saw them as limited by individuals' needs, singly and through the hierarchy. For example, most of the demands workers make or are expected to make – for higher wages, more free time, cultural activities, etc. – appear to relate, psychologically, to their needs, whether they be "physical, social or intellectual". Nevertheless, as Soper has stressed,[39] the *specific* wants of individuals are likely to be *so* highly specific – geographically, culturally, and historically – that they have at best a dubious place in an account of human nature *in general* such as the one presented in this chapter. I am not opposed to identifying the typical wants of particular historical epochs and classes, and have already attempted to provide many of those Marx himself stressed (see above), but I shall not pursue the matter further here. However, in the final chapters we shall again confront the issue when we attempt to answer this question: have workers in fact demanded all that Marx predicted they would; and if not, why not?

As to the relative importance of needs and wants, I think Soper is correct that Marx regarded historically specific wants as *equally* as capable and likely as needs in the strict sense to motivate individuals,[40] at least in the absence of extreme scarcity, for reasons to be given in a moment. After all, we have just observed Marx arguing that the "relative" component of workers' wants will prevent them from being satisfied even though they may have what they absolutely "require". However, as noted earlier, I do not think it follows, as Soper sometimes implies, that Marx therefore *always* treated the two as equally important, and therefore for all intents and purposes *abandoned* the distinction.

In most of his later writings, of course, Marx's major purpose was to critique and offer an alternative for bourgeois political economy. When his more specific purpose was only to explain the exchange value and price of commodities, including labour power, the relevant "needs" were what Marx referred to at one point as "effective social wants";[41] that is, those desires, such as those for higher wages and more free time, which have received *organized* expression in the form of demands by unions and political interest groups and parties. Although true needs undoubtedly figure in these effective social wants, (a) many of them – for example, for social intercourse and expressing one's individuality *while working* – are not likely to figure very prominently, or at least very effectively (since at least in the short run, employers are unlikely to give in to them and workers are likely to adapt themselves accordingly), and (b) those true needs that do make their way into effective social wants may in fact be no more important in determining the value and price of material commodities or labour power than mere wants. (For example, workers may hold out for a wage increase not because they need one to continue to eat well, but because they want to buy a new automobile.)

However, this is only part of the story.

In the first place, true needs *may* be more important than mere wants, even in the determination of effective social wants. For example, when Marx wrote that French workers in 1848 had to either take action or *starve*,[42] he was in effect arguing that needs in the strict sense were so important that they were practically *synonymous* with effective social want. The very notion of the hierarchy of needs means that under such conditions of extreme scarcity true needs of highest priority come to the forefront and mere wants recede to the background.

Secondly, Marx obviously had many purposes besides explaining the value and price of labour power and other commodities, and predicting revolt. Psychic alienation and other states of non-well-being of individuals were among the many other phenomena he wanted to explain, and, as we shall see in the next chapter, the deprivation of true needs figures much more prominently than the deprivation of mere wants in Marx's explanations for *these* particular phenomena.

Let us now proceed to discuss the problem of how individuals respond to gratification and deprivation in general, and with specific reference to alienation and rebellion.

NOTES

1. *Wage Labour and Capital*, p. 216. My emphasis.
2. *Grundrisse*, p. 527. The example of housing is in *Wage Labour and Capital*, p. 216; that of liquor and tobacco in *Capital 2*, p. 407.
3. *Capital 3*, p. 859.
4. *Wage Labour and Capital*, op. cit.; *Wages, Price and Profits* in *Selected Works*, p. 220.
5. *Capital 1*, pp. 252–3; *Capital 3*, p. 795.
6. *Grundrisse*, pp. 84, 496; *Notes on Wagner*, excerpted in David McLellan (ed.), *Karl Marx: Selected Writings* (Oxford University Press, 1977), p. 581. The full text can be found in Terrell Carver (ed.), *Texts on Method* (Oxford: Blackwell, 1975).
7. *Capital 1*, p. 223.

8. *Grundrisse*, p. 611. My emphasis.
9. *Capital 1*, p. 322. My emphasis.
10. *Manuscripts*, p. 296.
11. "Comments on James Mill", pp. 220, 228 (*Collected Works, 3*); *Manuscripts*, pp. 274, 304; *Grundrisse*, p. 611.
12. *Manuscripts*, p. 276; *Capital 1*, p. 174.
13. Comments . . .", pp. 227–8. The emphasis on "human" is mine.
14. *Notes on Wagner*, in Carver, op. cit., p. 195.
15. *Ideology*, pp. 41–2.
16. Ibid., p. 38.
17. Ibid., pp. 48–9.
18. Ibid., p. 42.
19. *Manuscripts*, p. 313.
20. See McLellan, op. cit., p. 538. The passage excerpted there was written in 1869.
21. Pp. 255–6. He later suggested that a hungry man would have difficulty appreciating beauty.
22. *Ideology*, p. 256.
23. This interpretation differs from those of Ollman (op. cit., p. 232) and Soper (op. cit., p. 147), who see Marx as having naively assumed that there are few internal, psychic barriers to the full gratification of all needs.
24. This may be implied, for example, in *The Gotha Programme*, p. 324 (*Selected Works*), where communism is supposed to allow labour (free, and concrete?) to become "life's prime *want*" (my emphasis).
25. Heller, op. cit., p. 61.
26. Ibid., p. 106.
27. Soper, op. cit., pp. 111, 117, 126–7, 132, 150–1. The relevant passages from the *Grundrisse* are on pp. 222–4, 231.
28. Op. cit., p. 111.
29. Harry Helson, *Adaptation-Level Theory* (New York: Harper and Row, 1964).
30. *Wages, Price and Profit*, p. 225; *Capital 1*, pp. 168, 223; *Capital 2*, p. 407.
31. For example, see the passage Soper quotes on p. 117.
32. *Grundrisse*, p. 92. Marx himself may well have intended "want" rather than "need" here. The German word "bedurfnis" can be translated as either. Nicolaus, the translator of the *Grundrisse*, has opted for need.
33. The term "comparison level of alternatives" is John Thibaut and Harold Kelley's. See their *The Social Psychology of Groups* (New York: Wiley, 1959) pp. 21–4. Leon Festinger is best-known for the concept of social comparison level. See his "A theory of social comparison processes", *Human Relations*, vol. 7 (1954), pp. 117–40.
34. *Wage Labour and Capital*, p. 216. See also the *Manuscripts* (p. 314), the *Ideology* (p. 48), the *Grundrisse* (p. 597), and *Wages, Price and Profit* (p. 225).
35. E.g., *Grundrisse*, p. 285; *Wages, Price and Profit*, p. 225.
36. *Manuscripts*, p. 308.
37. See Note 45, Chapter 3. Also *Capital 1*, p. 225.
38. As with the other concepts introduced with regard to wants, this one

comes out of the "field theory" tradition inspired by Kurt Lewin, who may himself have been mildly inspired by Austro-Marxism. For a summary account of theory and research on the level of aspiration, see Morton Deutsch and Robert Krauss, *Theories in Social Psychology* (New York: Basic Books, 1965).

39. Op. cit., pp. 14–15, 46.
40. Ibid., pp. 5, 15–16.
41. *Capital 3*, p. 192.
42. *Class Struggles in France*, p. 67.

5 Responses to Gratification and Deprivation

To begin, let us suppose that in his thinking about how individuals respond to gratification and deprivation Marx had common principles of "reinforcement" in mind.

The most general of these principles is probably the so-called "Law of Effect": "Pleasure stamps in; pain stamps out."[1] This idea, that individuals pursue those activities which are gratifying and avoid those which are not, and especially those that are actually depriving, runs throughout Marx's writings. Marx's most obvious application of this is to alienation.

First, when labour is "forced" and "abstract" – compulsory, paced, relatively unskilled, and routine, and therefore lacking in creativity and other artistic qualities, individuals lack "organic links" with it[2] – they cannot express, "realize" or "affirm" themselves[3] by exercising their individual or "particular bodily and mental powers" and "skills".[4] It is not "self-activity".[5] (It goes without saying that they also cannot perform a variety of activities, or perhaps even be very active at all. Indeed, their labour may not even allow them to gratify their more narrowly biological needs very well.)

Secondly, because individuals are not able to gratify their needs – especially for creativity, self-expression and recognition, but perhaps also for variety and activity – through their labour, they experience their labour as depriving rather than gratifying. "Enjoyment" is "*separate*" from labour,[6] and labour is therefore experienced as "pain" and "suffering",[7] as a "sacrifice" and "denial" of self,[8] as "hated toil".[9]

Finally, because individuals experience deprivation while they labour, they (a) are not "attracted" to their labour – they are "repulsed" by it[10] and pursue as little of it as possible. They "shun" it "like the plague as soon as no physical or other compulsion exists", and engage in it only "irregularly".[11] Because the labours and products from which they choose are more or less *equally* depriving, individuals are (b) "indifferent" as to, or "disinterested" in, which they perform or produce.[12]

Marx appears to have made analogous arguments for the alienated nature of social relationships in the capitalist mode of production, but they presumably also apply to those in other modes where the social relations of production have similar characteristics.

Thus private ownership of the means of production and a division between mental and manual labour make for conflicts of interest and very different styles of life. The former makes interaction between individuals of different classes potentially depriving, and therefore threatening;[13] the latter gives individuals in different classes little in common which would make such interaction gratifying. Individuals of different classes therefore avoid each other; and where they cannot, they limit interaction to the barest amount necessary to fulfill their class roles. Capitalists write "No Admittance Except on Business" over their office doors. All they expect and demand of their workers is their raw labour power; all workers expect and demand of their employers is a job.[14] Because most interaction is in-role rather than interpersonal, because the personalities of individuals do not make much of a difference to how much gratification or deprivation one experiences, individuals are indifferent as to which members of the other class they interact with.[15]

The same principles apply to workers' relationships with each other. To the extent that they compete for employment and/or wages, they are threatened by, and avoid, *each other*.[16] Although workers are objectively interdependent and generally benefit from their interaction, this social nature of production and distribution is hidden behind private ownership of the means of production and individualized employment contracts.[17] Hence the depriving effects of competition may be more salient than the gratifying effects of cooperation. To the extent that the proletarianization of labour has made individuals as well as activities and products relatively indistinct, different individuals are likely to be regarded as *equally* gratifying or depriving, and, therefore, also with indifference.[18]

Among the other principles of reinforcement Marx employed is that of "*secondary* reinforcement" or "classical conditioning". Thus just as reinforcement theorists argue that stimuli which initially are only indirectly associated with pleasure or pain will eventually elicit the same responses as stimuli that are more directly associated, so Marx claimed that workers in the capitalist mode are not likely to even recognize the product as their own; and/or likely to regard it as hateful and tormenting, because the *activity* by which they have produced it has been externally directed, tedious, and therefore also painful. As he himself put it, "How could the worker come to face the product of his activity as a stranger, were it not that in the very act of production he was estranging himself from himself? The product is after all but the summary of the activity, of production".[19] Similarly, if the worker comes to regard his entire *life* as a sacrifice,[20] if he has "a sense of misery rather than well-being" *in general*, [21] it is because his major activity involves "suffering", "for what is life but activity?"[22]

We also find "instrumental learning" or "operant conditioning", not simply in the form of unconscious "habits", but of complex and conscious conceptualizations of reality. Thus in Marx's critique of Wagner, he noted that "the property that . . . things have of 'satisfying their needs' is impressed on their brains" when individuals repeatedly behave "actively, gaining possession of certain things in the external world by their actions".[23] But the same applies to working class consciousness: it is only after organizing as a class and concertedly pursuing their own interests as a class separate from the bourgeoisie that workers come to recognize both the class complicity of the state and their own power to seize and control it.[24]

These principles of reinforcement are clearly fundamental to Marx's thinking, not simply about human nature, but to his theorizing more generally. On the other hand, of course, we would be remiss if this were the *only* model of responses to gratification and deprivation we were to apply to Marx's theorizing about human nature, since, as we have already noted, Marx claimed that human individuals have capacities peculiar to their species which make both their needs and the nature of their experiences of gratification and deprivation very different from those of other animals.

For one thing, the capacity to distance themselves from their impulses and activities leads individuals both to reward themselves for their own individuality, and to react to barriers to gratification in a peculiarly human way. Specifically, whereas the more typically animal response is to *avoid* such barriers, at least the most *distinctively* human response is to seek out and remove or overcome them. Presumably, human individuals do this because (a) their ability to distance themselves gives them more flexibility, and therefore creativity and "rationality", which allows them to overcome barriers more easily, and (b) their capacity to vicariously experience others' experiences of themselves and reward themselves accordingly leads them to experience feelings of competence and pride in overcoming barriers. This seems to be the thrust of this statement of Marx's: "Certainly, labour obtains its measure from the outside, through the aim to be attained and the obstacles to be overcome in attaining it. But Smith has no inkling whatever that this overcoming of obstacles is in itself a liberating activity – and that, further, the external aims become stripped of the semblance of merely external natural urgencies, and become posited as aims which the individual himself posits – hence as self-realization, objectification of the subject, hence real freedom, whose action is, precisely, labour."[25]

For another, and this follows from the principles of reinforcement discussed above, when Marx claimed that "this overcoming of obstacles is in itself a liberating activity" he presumably meant that in overcoming obstacles individuals develop not only better cognitive and technical abilities and skills for overcoming other, more difficult obstacles in the future, but the *motivation* to seek out and overcome such obstacles.[26]

While these propositions also figure importantly in Marx's conception of human nature, they are highly conditional, and much more than in the global way that Ollman and McMurtry suggest; that is, that the circumstances individuals face in all pre-communist societies all but preclude the exercise of these capacities.[27] For example, even if we assume individuals are more or less conscious of what they need rather than simply feeling deprived in a diffuse way, these individuals may not recognize the barriers most responsible for their deprivation. If this were the case they would be unlikely to successfully overcome these barriers, and therefore also to develop the means and motivation to take on other such barriers in the future. Alternatively, they may clearly recognize the source of deprivation, but objective circumstances may prevent them from overcoming it anyway. One would presumably expect *these* individuals to avoid such barriers and/or situations where they feel deprived. Should they be unable to avoid either the barrier or deprivation, one might well expect them to react in either or both of two ways: to take steps to lessen the psychic pain of deprivation, and especially if this is not very successful, to "take out" their frustration in various ways, some of which may be more expressive, even "irrational", than instrumental and effective in removing the barrier.

These considerations suggest that an adequate theory of human nature should go far beyond simply postulating individuals to be either rational or irrational and provide a model of problem solving which elaborates upon individuals' responses, whether rational or irrational, to various specific circumstances. Although I cannot demonstrate that Marx used each and every component of such a model explicitly, I shall try to show how he repeatedly employed not just the imagery, but most of the propositions, of a model of "frustration and aggression".[28]

These propositions are as follows.

(1) Provided barriers are recognizable and individuals feel capable and powerful enough to remove or surmount them, individuals will initially respond to deprivation by *seeking out* and *dispensing with* such barriers.

(2) Should these individuals be unable to discover the actual barrier(s) to gratification, or should they discover that they are incapable or powerless to overcome them, their next response will be to *circumvent* them. In practice this usually entails withdrawing from the activity or relationship in question and pursuing alternatives.

Proposition 2 should apply to a primitive people's use of infanticide to cope with a severely limited supply of food as well as to the attempts of slaves, serfs, journeymen, and wage-labourers to escape the respective relations of production within which they find themselves. However, the latter barriers appear to have concerned Marx most.

Marx himself did not actually discuss this response on the part of slaves, but he did for the case of serfs. Many, Marx claimed, were ready to buy their independence where possible, and many who could not escaped to towns and cities.[29] Later, many of the tenant farmers and other free peasants, who had been cleared from the land to make way for large-scale capitalist enterprises, avoided wage-labour through vagabondage, beggary and robbery, and had to be coerced to do otherwise.[30] On the other hand, even those who voluntarily took on wage labour often left themselves escape routes, sending their wives and children "in" first and/or maintaining a family farm to retreat to.[31]

As the capitalist mode of production became more and more dominant, fewer and fewer wage labourers would have experienced more independent forms of labour, and hence have had high aspirations for them. Similarly, as capital became more and more concentrated, their objective chances of obtaining relatively independent employment woud have greatly diminished.[32] Nevertheless, Marx noted, wherever they could, wage labourers were prone to switch jobs and employers at an amazing rate.[33]

(3) Should individuals be unable to discover, dispense with, *or* avoid barriers to gratification they are highly likely to experience *frustration*.

Interestingly, given the much-toted thesis of a break in Marx's thinking about human nature, frustration as a consequence of prolonged need deprivation is only alluded to in his earliest, pre-historically-materialist writings. Labour and products, for example, are described as "hostile" and "tormenting",[34] and workers as feeling "unhappy" rather than "content",[35] and "restless"; presumably because they are not just poverty-stricken and "de-humanized", but because they are "conscious" and "painfully aware" of their own poverty and de-humanization.[36] However, with the *Ideology* one begins to find more direct references to both feelings of frustration as such *and* to their sources being not just in the deprivation of needs, but in the incapacity of individuals who are deprived to avoid depriving circumstances and find alternative means of gratification.

"For as soon as the division of labour comes into being," Marx wrote, "each man has a particular, exclusive sphere of activity, which is forced upon him and from which he cannot escape." "This fixation of social activity" is then characterized as "growing out of our control, *thwarting* our expectations, *bringing to naught* our calculations".[37] In the process, proletarians in particular are "completely shut-off from all self-activity":[38] "The contradiction between the individuality of each separate proletarian and labour, the condition of life forced upon him, becomes evident to him, for he is sacrificed from youth onwards and, within his own class, has no chance of arriving at the conditions which would place him in the other class."[39]

The proletarian's circumstances are unlike those faced earlier by serfs, who are said to have actually had more opportunities for social mobility. To wit, even if they could not escape to the towns and become petty bourgeois, as many did, they had various gradations of subordination and status they could move up into. Furthermore, because even the latter form of social mobility depended upon the serf's having accumulated property, he was not as likely as the worker to regard his continued subordination as reflecting upon him as an individual, and hence as personally degrading.[40] Marx considered this theme important enough to repeat it in the *Manifesto*.[41]

(4) Individuals have a relatively low tolerance for frustration. At the very least, there is a (specifiable) *limit* to how much they will tolerate.

Possible references to a threshold for frustration among producers in pre-capitalist formations include one to the slave as acquiescing to slave relations of production *only until* his "awareness that he cannot be the property of another", "his consciousness of himself as a person".[42] Others can be gleaned from the account of *The Class Struggles in France* from 1845 on. There economic hardship brought on by the potato blight and crop failures was said to have "increased the general ferment among the people", and an international industrial and commercial crisis which led to many bankruptcies among the French petty bourgeoisie to have "made the autocracy of the finance aristocracy still more *unbearable*" (p. 52, my emphasis).

Later, the peasantry and urban petty bourgeoisie are described as tolerating, even supporting, the ruling class because they wrongly regarded the proletariat as the source of their own hardships. However, once the bourgeoisie had provoked and defeated the latter in June 1848, the "bourgeois dictatorship" became "recognized officially" and "the middle strata of bourgeois society, the petty bourgeoisie and the peasant class, *had* to adhere more and more closely to the proletariat as their position became more *unbearable* . . ." (p. 69, my emphases).

Elsewhere in his account Marx suggested that French peasants in fact often put up with French governments in spite of serious *economic* hardship, but only until certain traditional *political* limits had been exceeded. The most important of these was a re-imposition of the wine tax, which tended to discriminate highly against peasants. According to Marx, this was *the* most important event leading to "the gradual revolutionising of the peasants" (pp. 120–2).

The same imagery is applied to wage-labourers, who are also portrayed as finding either or both of capitalist relations of production and wage-labour itself "unbearable". The idea that they too have limits beyond which they will act to relieve frustration is also frequently alluded to in Marx's accounts of class struggles.

Probably the most explicit statement of the proposition is Marx's claim that capitalist relations of production will only become "a power against which men make a revolution" after it has "become an 'unendurable' power", which in turn will only have occurred (soon?) after it has "rendered the great mass of humanity 'propertyless', and moreover in contradiction to an existing world of wealth and culture".[43] Otherwise one can again appeal to the accounts of *The Class Struggles in France*.

When Marx wrote that "The workers were left no choice; they had to starve or take action." (p. 67), he could well have been making the assumption we have been examining. But it is clearer in his and Engels' expectation that French workers would not accept certain political moves on the part of the government, especially the abolition of universal suffrage, which workers had already come to accept as one of their "natural" freedoms. Engels, at least, indicated this belief in his letters from Paris.[44]

(5) *Aggression* – especially against the source(s) of deprivation, but also against various other targets, depending upon the circumstances – is a highly likely response to frustration.

In the early writings we find statements such as these: "Eventually wages, which have already been reduced to a minimum, must be reduced yet further, to meet the new competition. This then *necessarily* leads to revolution."[45] The proletariat is not just abased but *"indignant"* "at that abasement"; "through urgent, no longer removable, no longer disguisable, absolutely imperative need – the practical expression of necessity – [it] *is driven directly to revolt against this inhumanity"*.[46] This famous passage, which begins with the claim that "The propertied class and the class of the proletariat present the same human self-estrangement", was recalled and reworked by Marx for what was to have been the final chapter of the first volume of *Capital*, and, when it is denuded of its abstract Hegelian imagery, the frustration–aggression hypothesis shines through even more clearly.[47]

If it needs noting, in between these writings Marx reiterated the frustration–aggression proposition time and again. Workers are eventually to *"make a revolution" "against"* "an unendurable power",[48] and in the meantime to "rebel" "against the prevailing relations brought about by the existing productive forces, and against the way of satisfying needs that corresponds to these relations", to engage in actions which "this stage of production daily engenders afresh".[49] It is the basis for both the sweeping generalizations about class struggles in the *Manifesto*,[50] as well as many of the more concrete analyses of those in France, where, for example, with regard to peasants and the petty bourgeoisie reference is made to their position becoming "more unbearable *and* their antagonism to the bourgeoisie more acute",[51] to "the innumerable bankruptcies among this section of the Paris bourgeoisie [the small epiciers and boutiquiers en masse], *and hence* their revolutionary action in February".[52]

In stressing the importance of frustration–aggression for Marx's theorizing I do not mean to imply that he regarded aggression and, certainly, *revolution*, as a *necessary* result of frustration. Clearly, he only expected revolution to occur when a number of other conditions are met; the major one being that workers are already highly organized as a class, and hence objectively capable of making one, as well as subjectively aware of the ultimate source of their frustration. Marx himself made this clear in most of the passages we have just cited.[53]

Nor am I suggesting, as has often been the case with those who have used the frustration–aggression hypothesis, that responding to frustration with aggression is necessarily an irrational act; an ill-considered "lashing out" which is neither effective nor intended to be. Rather, Marx was aware that aggression by workers is often a deliberate and highly practical response to frustration – a response which, at least in the forms of rebellion and revolt, arises as much from their *awareness* of the *source* of their deprivation as from the mere existence of the deprivation.[54]

(6). If the others who are barriers to gratification are not recognized as such and/or are too powerful for one to successfully aggress against, individuals are likely to *displace* aggression – upon (a) the means of production, (b) the product, (c) others less powerful than the source, and especially than themselves, and/or (d) themselves.

Thus, Marx wrote, precisely because the slave is treated only as an implement or animal which happens to be able to speak, "he himself takes care to let both beast and implement feel that he is none of them, but is a man. He convinces himself with immense satisfaction, that he is a different being, by treating the one unmercifully and damaging the other con amore. Hence the principle, universally applied in this method of production, only to employ the rudest and heaviest implements and such as are difficult to damage owing to their sheer clumsiness."[55]

French peasants often mistakenly attributed their destitution to the old landed aristocracy rather than the new grand bourgeoisie, which is why they also tended to support the Bonapartes more than the urban proletariat.[56] Similarly, for some time most peasants believed that the *proletariat* was the source of their own problems and therefore initially opposed the post-revolutionary government of 1848.[57] The Provisional Government also managed to protect itself from the proletariat, the petty bourgeoisie, and the more liberal members of the bourgeoisie by rewarding some proletarians while at the same time turning them into scapegoats for itself.[58]

As to the workers themselves, Marx made many references to *their* having displaced their *own* frustration and aggression against objects other than the bourgeoisie.

With the birth of the proletariat, workers "direct their attacks not against the bourgeois conditions of production, but against the instruments of production themselves; they destroy imported wares that compete with their labour, they smash to pieces machinery, they set factories ablaze, they seek to restore by force the vanquished status of the workman of the Middle Ages."[59] But even when workers have not taken out most of their frustration and aggression against the *means* of production they have not necessarily redirected it against the *bourgeoisie* or the relations of production. Rather, they not only compete with, but direct their hostility toward, each other. Direct competitors are especially likely to be scapegoats for aggression, as Marx noted has been the case with English against Irish, and southern white against black American workers. Indeed, at one point Marx claimed that the former displacement of aggression was the single most important explanation for the lack of revolutionary ferment among English workers.[60] But according to Marx, male workers also take out their frustration upon their own families.[61]

Marx does not appear to have attributed much importance to workers displacing aggression against *themselves*. Nevertheless, in discussing Stirner's suggestion that workers' dissatisfaction with themselves is a major source of rebellion Marx did agree that such dissatisfaction can, and sometimes does, occur. However, contrary to Stirner, he believed that mere dissatisfaction with oneself would hinder rather than promote revolution.[62]

(7) If individuals have no choice but to continue a depriving and frustrating activity or relationship, they will attempt to lessen the pain they experience. Typically, they will do so in either or both of two ways: (a) by *withdrawing* from the activity or relationship *emotionally*, usually by lowering their aspirations for gratification from it, and/or (b) by *seeking compensatory gratification* in alternative activities or relationships, usually by increasing their aspirations for, and involvement in, these alternatives.

The first "strategy", if we can call it that (this response need not be deliberate to the point of being consciously planned), is one of the most important components of psychic alienation.

If one is "indifferent" towards one's labours and relationships, one is often also emotionally neutral toward them; if such indifference is not a "natural" orientation, it is presumably an adaptation one has made (perhaps collectively rather than simply individually) to "unnatural" (historically-specific, "man"-made) conditions. This also appears to have been Marx's reasoning behind individuals' narrow, utilitarian ("instrumental" or "extrinsic") orientation toward others and labours. Specifically, such an orientation presupposes a lowering of initial aspirations for greater gratification of more needs, and that this lowering entailed, or at least was accompanied by, emotional withdrawal – not only from others and one's activities, but from one's own, and especially one's higher-order, needs.

In lowering one's aspirations in order to minimize pain, from whatever source, one comes to concentrate upon, and seek gratification for, one's lower-order needs: sexual tension release, material, and perhaps also social, security, and so on. Being neither acted upon nor reinforced, one's higher-order needs recede from one's consciousness, and perhaps atrophy more generally, as Sève has suggested.[63] The combined result of these psychic adaptations is that relationships and activities become mainly means toward narrow ends, rather than objects which fulfill a variety of needs, including those which require intrinsic involvement for their gratification.

References by Marx to labour having become only a means – for wages, consumption, and one's very physical subsistence – are legion and need not be quoted here.[64] However, that human relations also lose some of their distinguishing characteristics and are thereby reduced toward those of other animal species is a lesser-known claim of Marx's which may warrant illustration at this time. Thus in an early writing male–female relations are implied to have been largely reduced to male lust and female prostitution – from naturally *human* to simply "natural" (animal)[65] – and in a later writing this is given a fairly explicit psychological explanation: "Leaving aside the nonsense that the entire working class cannot possibly take the decision not to make any children, their condition, on the contrary, makes the sexual instinct their chief pleasure and develops it one-sidedly."[66]

One should note that the need hierarchy concept Marx employed here has a bi- rather than uni-directional psychologic. True, under *certain* circumstances one would expect workers to reduce their demands to those having to do with the gratification of lower-order needs. However, to the extent that they then *succeed* in forcing employers and others to provide the means for gratifying such needs, there should be a kind of "diminishing marginal utility" effect, and, as with the relatively highly paid skilled workers Marx was so optimistic about,[67] they should then move up the hierarchy to expect and demand that their *higher*-order needs be met. Nevertheless, Marx appears to have assumed that the more typical circumstance for most workers is that rises in real wages simply replace those wages lost during earlier economic crises.[68]

Much the same psychologic applies to the seeking of *compensation* through alternative activities and relationships: since it is difficult, if not impossible, for most individuals to gratify their higher-order needs through labour and the relations of production, they tend to pursue and/or involve themselves in "leisure" activities and "social" relationships where such gratification is, or at least is believed to be, less difficult. Thus the worker pursues food and drink, sexual intercourse and dressing-up, where he has more opportunity to "affirm himself" than he does at work, and his emotional involvement and self-identity vary accordingly. "The worker therefore only feels himself outside his work, and in his work feels outside himself. He feels at home when he is not working, and when he is working he does not feel at home."[69] He may also try to restore the dignity he has lost in submitting "willy-nilly" to the dictates of his employer by dictating to his own wife and children.[70]

In spite of Marx's own belief in the inevitability of proletarian revolution, it is important to recognize that the possibility that various forms of individualistic "withdrawal from reality" will lessen the likelihood of, if not preclude altogether, such a revolution is *already* built into Marx's own psychologic.

Thus even if the frustration–aggression–compensation model we have just examined were the only basis for Marx's having predicted proletarian revolution (which it is not), there are many opportunities within the model itself to predict the derailing of class conscious rebellion. Thus individuals may not in fact recognize the true barriers to gratification (Proposition 1), and even if they do, they may in fact be able to circumvent them (2). Even if they cannot, their threshold for tolerating frustration may not be exceeded (4), and even if it is, the frustration which ensues may be displaced (6), and/or the deprivation which would otherwise lead to frustration and aggression may be compensated for (7).

I do not mean to suggest that each and every one of the assumptions in the model is correct, nor that they never contradict each other. As we shall see in later chapters, several are of questionable validity, and Marx himself did not make his full psychologic explicit enough, and push it far enough, to appreciate its full implications. For example, if most individual workers were in fact to compensate by greatly lowering their aspirations, we might well expect them to feel much less frustration the next time around. That is, their tolerance for frustration in general would presumably rise. But again, for all such problems, Marx was still much more sophisticated psychologically than most of his critics have given him credit for.

However, having written this, I can imagine this retort: if Marx really was so sophisticated, and proletarian revolution is not in fact a necessary implication of his theory of human nature in general, then why on earth did Marx consider it to be inevitable? It may have been a case of wish-fulfillment on his part, but there are several other possibilities to consider.

One is that his specific predictions, as with *any* theorist's predictions, depend not only upon assumptions about human nature in general, but upon the existence of a host of specific social conditions – conditions which in this case were not fully in existence during Marx's own time, but only forecast by him for the future. Some of these trends and how they were, or presumably were, to affect individuals' deprivation, frustration, and responses to them, are as follows.

There should have been an increasing proletarianization of the labour force and frequency of economic crises, which in turn are supposed to have (a) made the ultimate barriers to gratification easier to recognize, and (b) harder to avoid. Of course, they should also have (c) increased deprivation and frustration, and (d) decreased the likelihood that workers will displace aggression upon each other (that is, with proletarianization, others who would previously have been different from oneself in skill and status will now be much more similar). They will have (e) made it more difficult to find compensatory gratification (relative and absolute deprivation and frustration will be higher, and means of gratification will be fewer), and (f) violated individual workers' aspirations, no matter how low workers will have adapted them.

I shall later argue that these specific expectations are much more questionable than Marx's theory of human nature in general. However, for the moment there is another answer to the question under consideration: there is still more to Marx's theory of human nature in general, and these elements are important for understanding Marx's expectation that workers would "make the revolution" – act class consciously and collectively rather than individually, with a "bourgeois consciousness". One of these elements is a general theory of knowledge, which led Marx to expect workers to view the trends he predicted in some rather than other ways; another is a general, but less explicitly general, theory of how and why individuals think and act differently when they identify with, and act as, groups rather than separate individuals. Let us take up these remaining components.

NOTES

1. E. L. Thorndike, "Animal intelligence: an experimental study of the associative processes in animals", *Psychological Monographs*, 1898, 2 (No. 4 – whole No. 8).
2. *Grundrisse*, p. 104.
3. "Comments on James Mill", pp. 218–20, 227–8; *Manuscripts*, pp. 272, 274; *Ideology*, p. 66; *Grundrisse*, pp. 297, 611.
4. *Capital 1*, pp. 174, 398.

5. *Ideology*, p. 87.
6. Ibid., p. 418.
7. *Manuscripts*, p. 302.
8. Ibid., p. 274.
9. *Manifesto*, pp. 490–1; *Capital 1*, p. 604.
10. *Ideology*, p. 481; *Grundrisse*, p. 611.
11. *Manuscripts*, p. 274; *Grundrisse*, p. 462; *Capital 1*, p. 449.
12. *Ideology*, p. 66; *Grundrisse*, pp. 104, 297.
13. For an elaboration of this psychologic in Marx, see my "Face-to-face: The alienating effects of class, status and power divisions", *American Sociological Review*, vol. 41 (October 1976), pp. 819–37.
14. *Capital 1*, p. 195.
15. "Comments . . .", pp. 219–21; *Grundrisse*, pp. 241–3.
16. *Ideology*, p. 75; *Manifesto*, p. 492.
17. E.g., *Grundrisse*, pp. 585–90. See also Chapter 6, below.
18. *Manuscripts*, pp. 278, 324–6; *Grundrisse*, pp. 156–7, 241–2.
19. *Manuscripts*, p. 274.
20. Ibid., p. 281.
21. Ibid.
22. Ibid., p. 275.
23. McLellan, op. cit., p. 581.
24. For example, see *The Class Struggles in France*, and Chapter 7 below.
25. *Grundrisse*, p. 611.
26. *Capital 1*, p. 481.
27. Ollman, op. cit., p. 135; McMurtry, op. cit., p. 43. See also Avineri, op. cit., p. 69.
28. The classic work here is John Dollard, L. W. Doob, N. E. Miller, D. H. Mowser, and R. R. Sears, *Frustration and Aggression* (New Haven: Yale University Press, 1939). For a review and critique of subsequent work see Billig, op. cit., Chapter 5.
29. *Ideology*, pp. 64–5; *Capital 3*, p. 795.
30. See Note 48, Chapter 3.
31. *Grundrisse*, p. 586.
32. *Manifesto*, pp. 491–2.
33. *Capital 1*, p. 458.
34. "Comments . . .", p. 228; *Manuscripts*, pp. 278–9.
35. *Manuscripts*, p. 274.
36. *Holy Family*, p. 36.
37. *Ideology*, p. 47.
38. Ibid., p. 87.
39. Ibid., p. 79.
40. Ibid.
41. Ibid., pp. 485, 495.
42. *Grundrisse*, p. 463.
43. *Ideology*, p. 48.
44. *Collected Works, 10*.
45. *Manuscripts*, p. 270.
46. *Holy Family*, pp. 36–7. All emphases are mine.
47. *Results of the Immediate Process of Production*, op. cit., p. 509.

48. *Ideology*, p. 48.
49. Ibid., p. 432.
50. E.g., p. 492.
51. *Class Struggles in France*, pp. 69–70. My emphasis.
52. Ibid., p. 52.
53. E.g., *Ideology*, pp. 49, 87–8.
54. For the latter, practical motivation for aggression, see the *Class Struggles in France*, p. 67, or *Ideology*, p. 80.
55. *Capital 1*, p. 191 (footnote).
56. *Eighteenth Brumaire*, pp. 186–90.
57. *Class Struggles*, p. 61.
58. Ibid., pp. 62–4.
59. *Manifesto*, p. 492. See also *Capital 1*, pp. 403–4.
60. (with Engels) *Ireland and the Irish Question* (Moscow: Progress, 1971) p. 294.
61. "Peuchet: On Suicide", in *Collected Works, 4*, p. 605.
62. *Ideology*, pp. 398–9. The last emphases are mine.
63. Sève, op. cit., p. 325.
64. E.g., "Comments . . .", p. 228; *Manuscripts*, p. 274; *Wage Labour and Capital*, pp. 202–3; *Grundrisse*, pp. 196, 289.
65. *Manuscripts*, pp. 295–6.
66. *Wages*, in *Collected Works, 6*, p. 433. Thanks to Roy Broadbent for calling my attention to this passage.
67. See Notes 19 and 20, Chapter 4, and *Capital 1*, p.458.
68. *Wages, Price and Profit*, pp. 220, 223.
69. *Manuscripts*, p. 274.
70. See Note 61, above.

6 Knowledge

There may well be as much controversy surrounding Marx's theory of knowledge and related phenomena such as ideology as there is about his views on human nature more generally. Did Marx reject "the classical definition of truth" and replace it with a conception of truth about reality, indeed, of reality itself, as constructed and proven in the process of modifying nature through praxis? Are individuals' observation and experience of reality direct or immediate, as philosophical "empiricists" have usually claimed, or only mediated through collective and individual praxes? If the latter is the case, what are these praxes and precisely how do they relate to individuals' knowledge?

The first two questions are both interesting in their own right and "barriers" between us and Marx's social psychology of knowledge. However, severe limitations of space have precluded me from giving them the attention they deserve here. Nevertheless, I shall state my own position on these problems before proceeding further. In brief, it is that (a) *no*, Marx did *not* reject "the classical definition of truth", at least to the point of being uninterested in what is "out there", "objectively", but (b) *yes*, he did maintain that all of humans' *experiences* of that reality are not direct, but necessarily *mediated* by social and psychic processes, (c) many of which are *common* to all known societies *and individuals*. Furthermore, (d) if one examines some of the most-often-cited "constructivist" interpretations of Marx's theory of knowledge, one will find them agreeing not just with argument (b), but (a) and (c) as well.[1]

Having said this, I shall begin my presentation of Marx's anthropology/psychology of knowledge at what some will find a most unusual and problematic starting point: the seemingly "objective" nature of reality "external" to individuals. Yet we shall arrive at the "internal" nature of individuals' psyches almost before we know it.

THE OPACITY OR TRANSPARENCY OF SOCIAL REALITY

A very basic assumption of Marx's theory of knowledge appears to be this one: particular social processes can be more or less opaque or transparent; that is, observable, recognizable, comprehensible, and therefore also informative. The less opaque, and more transparent, they are, the more likely individuals are to accurately and fully – "truly" – know them. In effect, most of the propositions we shall take up in this section exemplify Marx's use of this assumption.

(1) The more, and more *different*, social processes in reality, the less likely individuals are to know any one well, let alone which are most central, which have most effect upon others.

Marx may have had some such assumption in mind when he suggested that French peasants, while actually much more heavily exploited by the grand bourgeoisie, mistakenly believed their ultimate exploiters to be the old landed aristocracy,[2] in that he may have meant to suggest that where several modes of production co-exist, or at least where the classes which made up previous relations of production have not yet died away, it is relatively easy for the members of some classes to fail to recognize who their true, or more serious, class enemies are.

Another aspect of Marx's theorizing which is consistent with such an assumption is his claim that the demise of the petty bourgeoisie more generally will have revolutionary consequences for the working class. Thus he implied that this increasingly marked tendency would not simply close off one of the few escape routes previously open to workers, but simplify the reality of capitalism for both former members of the petty bourgeoisie and longer-time wage-labourers to the point where they could hardly help but recognize its true nature.[3]

(2) The more *overlap* among different social processes in reality, the more difficult it is for individuals to know any one well.

There is a wealth of separate hypotheses of Marx's which appear to have been based upon such an assumption.

One is Marx's comparison of the relatively enlightened serf and the relatively ignorant worker on the matter of surplus labour. This is supposed to be no mystery for the former, who, for example, may be forced to divide his working time between his own plot of land and that of the lord. However, it may well be for the latter, since the labour for his own subsistence and that for the exploiter occur in the same space and time.[4]

Several other hypotheses concern the peculiar nature of commodity exchange relations – the fact that they tend to embody many different processes within the same general process.

Thus while commodities have both use and exchange value, the confluence of these two very different qualities in the same good or service lessens the likelihood that either quality will be fully understood. For example, although its *exchange*-value is the quality which most determines how a capitalist seller relates to a commodity, its *use*-value may be the quality which most moves a working-class consumer, who may therefore assume that the value of goods and services in his or her own society is inherent and fixed. Alternatively, the economist who is most interested in explaining how capitalists think and act, and in helping them do so more effectively, may erroneously assume that goods and services have no inherent value whatsoever.[5]

On the other hand, Marx noted, workers' capacity to labour, their *labour-power*, is a commodity which, as a "service" rather than a finite, material "good", is still more mystifying. If one sells a good one loses a tangible object, and nothing more, and usually, at least, immediately receives a good or promise of a good in return. Workers tend to believe that the same is the case with their labour: they contract with their employer to labour enough to acquire the means to gratify their needs and wants, and expect to receive in wages what they believe to be *the* value of that labour.[6]

Marx suggested that the very fact that they are not paid until long after they have laboured, that they have in effect advanced the capitalist a long line of credit, is itself peculiar and mystifying.[7] However, of more concern to us here is the fact that because of the very nature of the exchange of *labour* for a wage, the worker cannot help but lay at the disposal of the capitalist the relatively limitless use of his or her entire labour-*power* rather than simply the much more limited amounts of labour s/he intended to offer. As a consequence, s/he may not recognize the distinction between necessary and surplus labour, between that portion of his or her labour necessary to gratify his or her own needs and wants and that portion which serves as a means for "capital" to gratify "its" needs.[8] In other words, exploitation is hidden beneath the overlapping of the exchange of labour-power and specific quantities of labour. A related hypothesis is that workers do not recognize the highly socialized nature of the labour process because their labour contracts with their employers are individual.[9]

Some of Marx's claims regarding conflict *within* the working class may fit in here. Specifically, if deprivation and frustration arising from domination and exploitation by their employers coincide with those arising from competition with fellow workers, as is likely, workers may well mistakenly blame each other rather than their employers. Similarly, if their working class competitors also happen to be black or Irish, they may be still more likely to be taken for the root cause of workers' own deprivations.

Finally, the aforementioned tendency for workers to blame machinery *per se*, an *apparently non-human* process, for either or both their own lack of employment or the extremely intense nature of their actual labour may lie, in part, with the superimposition of mechanization upon the other, older means of dominating workers and extracting surplus value. In this case the *means* for more efficient domination and extraction is mistaken for the *source*, perhaps even the motivated agent, of social change.

(3) The more *separate* in time, space and institutionalized sphere of society (certain) social processes are from each other, the more difficult it is for individuals to know the true *relationships among them*.

This proposition may seem to contradict the previous one, but note that it refers to individuals' knowledge of the relationships *among* several different processes rather than any one singly. Furthermore, the processes covered by this proposition often appear to be somewhat different from those covered by the former.

For example, to the theoretically sophisticated observer, the exploitation of workers' labour power clearly presupposes their prior domination: they have no choice but to sell their labour-power, and while all they desire and intend to sell is a definite amount of their labour, they nevertheless have no choice but to hand over a relatively unlimited amount of labour-power to their employers. However, in contrast to slaves and serfs, neither the worker's person nor labour is legally owned and politically controlled by the employers who exploit labour-power. These relationships are contractual, at least formally.[10] This separation of domination and exploitation presumably makes it difficult for workers to see the connection between the two.

Similarly, domination itself is in fact partly political and legal as well as "economic", in that it occurs indirectly through private property rights to the means of production, and through legal enforcement of these rights by the state. Indeed, the latter has sometimes amounted to *politically enforced* labour, as with government enforcement of anti-loafing laws and injunctions against striking. However, the more typical disjuncture in space, time, and institutionalized sphere of political–juridical domination "hides" the true relationship between these two sets of processes.

The same might be said for the separation of each of domination and exploitation from both (a) the physical *person* of the exploiter, and (b) the use of "brute", *physical* force.

Thus whereas there could be little doubt in the slave or serf's mind that he was dominated and exploited, and as to precisely who was doing the dominating and exploiting, there can be much for the wage-labourer. With the advent of the joint-stock company s/he may have many, and for the most part unseen, employers, and even if this is not the case, those who control the immediate process of production and with whom s/he is most likely to interact are likely to be intermediaries, and perhaps even non-humans (machines), rather than the employers themselves. In other words, invisible employers make for "invisible threads".[11]

Similarly, "Direct, political, and especially *physical* force, outside economic conditions, is of course still used, *but only exceptionally.*"[12] Furthermore, when it *is* used the agent exercising it is much more likely to be the state than the employer.

(4) The more repetitive, stable, and longer-term social processes are (for example, through institutionalization), the more likely they are to be regarded as "natural" and inevitable.

Thus social relations are likely to appear socially "stable" and "independent from mere chance and arbitrariness", which then increases the likelihood that they will become entrenched "as custom and tradition", after first, the "mere repetition" of their reproduction, and subsequently, the "regulation" and "orderly form" of this reproduction "in the course of time". Presumably, the *institutionalized* regulation, especially through legalization, of these same social relations then further increases their repetitiveness, stability, and appearance of being natural.[13]

In the passage we have just quoted Marx was attempting to explain how "labour rent" could emerge and become legitimate within the very womb of feudal relations of production. However, we have also already seen him apply the same principles to how capitalist relations come to appear natural. Workers come to look upon "the conditions of that mode of production as self-evident laws of nature" because first, the initial resistance of producers to this mode of production has been broken by political–legal force and then workers' dependence upon capital, and second, with such resistance now being much less frequent and effective, capitalist relations of production are reproduced more smoothly and less problematically. There is still "compulsion" involved in their reproduction, but this compulsion is now indirect and "dull" rather than "direct" and acrimonious.[14]

The corollary of the general assumption guiding this section, which presumably kept Marx from despairing that "the" revolution would ever occur, is that *should reality change, its nature should also become much more apparent.*

If the bourgeois society of his own time contained a number of different modes of production and plethora of classes and strata, its appearance would eventually become greatly simplified as large capital "gobbled up" small capital, the petty bourgeoisie all but disappeared, and other aspects of proletarianization greatly homogenized the working class. (This is the converse of Proposition 1.)

Whereas the most important features of capitalist relations of production were then overladen with a variety of superficial features, the former would come to be superimposed upon the latter (Proposition 2). Thus once labour has become very highly socialized, automated, and productive, so little labour time will be necessary that the workers cannot help but recognize that the bulk of their labour is surplus labour expropriated by their employers for their own purposes. By then workers' contracts with their employers are likely to be wholly collective rather than individual, and the value their employers place on both their own labour-power and the material goods they produce almost wholly exchange- rather than use-value.

If in Marx's own time the analytically separate spheres of bourgeois society were also relatively separate empirically, all this was supposed to change (Proposition 3). With economic crises and spiralling conflict between capital and labour, the state would be forced to intervene more on the side of capital. With capital breaking up the working class family by employing wives and children, and then replacing all workers by machinery, as well as failing to prevent economic crises, workers would have to organize as a class on a national and "political", rather than simply local and "economic", level. These changes should all lead workers to draw important connections between both the different aspects of their own activities and relationships (the economic, political, and social; the public and the private) and the different aspects of capitalist relations of production (capital's control over the state and private life, the state's class-bias, and so forth).

As we noted with regard to Proposition 4, Marx considered the capitalist system to have attained a certain stability and legitimacy by his own time. Its relations of production had been reproduced on a relatively long-term basis, and with a minimum of "breaks". Economic crises occurred only every ten years or so, and political force to achieve the economic compliance of labour had largely receded into the background. However, as we have just seen, all of these conditions were to change, and with them the legitimacy of capitalist relations of production and bourgeois political rule. A system which cannot provide enough employment and goods and services at affordable prices cannot be regarded as legitimate; nor can a ruling class whose rule cannot ensure even stability, let alone impartiality.

If we now reflect upon the assumptions and propositions discussed up to this point we could well arrive at a conclusion which would both startle Marx's various neo-Hegelian interpreters and lead many to accuse us of gross inconsistency (even indecency). After all, aren't these proposals both purely "structural" or "sociological" and vulgarly materialist or "reflectionist"? Is the point not that the reality of social relations is simply "reflected" in the "mirror" of individuals' minds, that the latter's knowledge of reality is completely determined from without and impervious to change until external reality has somehow changed *itself*?

Both the long and short answers to these questions are decided nos. The short answer – the one we shall take up immediately – is that if through no other means, all of individuals' knowledge of reality is mediated by perceptual and reasoning as well as motivational processes; by processes which are general as well as specific to individuals in different social formations. The long answer – to be taken up later – is that as we saw in Chapter 1, for all Marx's appeal to organic imagery, he did not in fact believe that social institutions and systems bring about social changes by themselves, and the same is true for knowledge: it is acquired and changed through "praxis", through individuals' conscious attempts to gratify their own needs and wants. Let us expand upon the first of these answers.

What must Marx have assumed about the human psyche in order to have made the proposals discussed above? I say "must" because he himself has told us very little about these still-more underlying assumptions. However, the following would seem to be "good bets" for each of the propositions, respectively.

(1) There are limits to how much information individuals can, or at least are likely to, process well; to how well they can reorganize and simplify information about reality. The more and complex the information, the less organized and accurate will be their knowledge of it.

(2) The more difficult it is for individuals to distinguish among social processes *empirically* – the more confounded they are in reality as it is "immediately" perceived – the more difficult it is for them to distinguish among them *analytically* – to know their true nature and relationships with each other.

(3) The less *proximate* social events and processes are in time and

space, the more difficult it is for individuals to draw accurate inferences about *cause-and-effect* from them.

That Marx may have had some such assumption in mind is consistent with a number of his own suggestions. For example, the aforementioned tendency for French peasants to blame workers rather than the grand bourgeoisie for their own dire straits may have been heavily dependent upon the fact that government aid to workers was the most *recent* source of frustration they had encountered, and upon their false assumption that because workers were closely associated with the government's actions, they must somehow be the ultimate *cause* of them. Similarly, the more typical belief that the state in bourgeois society is neutral vis-à-vis the class struggle in the "economic" sphere of society may rest in part on the fact that (a) the persons who make up the government may not themselves be capitalists, and (b) political decisions appear to be made far away in space and time from the workplace.

(4) *Changes* in social reality are more informative about cause-and-effect relationships than are stability and continuity.

Social events which continually re-occur, social processes which appear to have no beginning and no end, may not even be recognized as separate events and processes. Even if they are, they are likely to be regarded as "natural", as rooted in humans' biological–animal nature if not nonhuman and even supernatural to begin with, and as therefore also unchangeable and inevitable. Conversely, observable changes in social reality call into question such assumptions for the lay person and social scientist alike. If Marx had such an assumption in mind when he proposed Proposition 4, it may help explain his claim that the events which are by far the most instructive for workers are precisely revolutions, where the entire structure of bourgeois society is rapidly and fundamentally changing.[15]

IGNORANCE AND INTEREST: THE PARTICULAR VANTAGE POINT OF THE INDIVIDUAL

In his 1859 retrospective on the development of his own social scientific knowledge Marx wrote of three conditions which he regarded as seminal for his own progress: "The enormous material for the history of political economy which is accumulated in the British Museum, the favourable vantage point afforded by London for the observation of bourgeois society, and finally the new stage of development upon which the latter appeared to have entered with the discovery of gold in California and Australia . . ."[16]

An important implication of this comment would seem to be this: even if social reality is relatively transparent and the individuals who observe it have a great deal of interest in discovering the true nature of that reality, and capacity to do so, *these individuals will remain ignorant of important aspects of that reality if they observe it from a vantage point which is narrow or otherwise unfavourable.*

From Marx's various writings I gather that an individual's vantage point will be more favourable, (a) the more developed the dominant, or soon to be dominant, mode of production is in his or her own society; (b) the more s/he has "straddled" more than one mode of production in his or her own lifetime; and (c) when s/he has been a member of more than one class.

Marx's belief in the validity of the first proposal is attested to in many different writings. His explanation for the failure of Aristotle to discover the law of value was that commodity exchange relations were not developed enough in his own society at the time for him to have been able to do so.[17] The "German ideology" is an ideology in the sense of a system of beliefs about reality which is very partial, even "illusory", because the individuals who developed it did so in a society which was relatively primitive economically *and* politically – so much so that even the struggle between the aristocracy and the bourgeoisie had not progressed very far.[18] French analysts had the advantage of a polity which was far advanced of its economy, but a full appreciation of the capitalist mode of production required observing England, which was both economically and politically advanced over Germany and France, and Marx considered himself to have been fortunate to have been able to not only examine England, but to have compared it with the other societies he had occasion to observe, if often unwillingly.

Arriving at Proposition (b) has entailed more extrapolation on my part, but it nevertheless seems to be a reasonable conclusion to have drawn. Thus, for example, when Marx wrote that "Man's reflections on the forms of social life, and consequently, also, his scientific analysis of these forms, take a course directly opposite to that of their actual historical development. He begins, post festum, with the results of the process of development ready to hand before him",[19] he presumably meant that the advantage of being able to view a social process after it has developed can easily be offset if one simply comes in at the "tail end" of the process and does not even view existing reality *as* simply the *end* of a *process*. Being able to move from country to country and observe the process at several stages of development, as Marx himself did, is one palliative for the problem, but having experienced a change in the dominant mode of production within one's *own* society might well have the same effect. This appears to have been part of the point of Marx's reference to "The advance of capitalist production" having developed "a working class which . . . looks upon the conditions of that mode of production as self-evident laws of Nature"; that is, after a certain point in time there are few members of the working class who have experienced an alternative mode of production, and hence who could and would compare present conditions with those surrounding previous modes.

Proposition (c) is still more tentative as an interpretation of Marx himself, and to the extent that he did in fact propose it, it may only apply to "downward", and not "upward", social mobility. Here I am thinking especially of the enlightenment Marx expected the former member of the petty bourgeoisie to experience as s/he loses out in competition with the grand bourgeoisie and "sinks" into the proletariat.[20] Again, however, such a proposition is at least consistent with his general reasoning about how the narrowness of one's own vantage point can restrict one's knowledge of social reality.

But the narrowness of one's own experience – whether one views reality through a regular or "wide-angled" lens, if I may extend the imagery Marx himself used in the *Ideology* – is far from the only "personal" limitation upon the acquisition of knowledge. Rather, *one's perception of reality and processing and retention of information about it is likely to be selective, and to be more or less so, depending upon the nature of one's own needs, wants and interests.* As I see it, Marx appears to have had two more specific propositions relating to this assumption in mind.

One we have already touched on in the chapter on needs and wants. This proposition holds that when individuals' lower-order needs are seriously deprived for a considerable length of time, these individuals are likely to become fixated upon objects related to these needs, and therefore also less interested in, and attuned to, the deprivation of higher-order needs and the sources of that deprivation. Hence, for example, individuals who are starving would not be expected to be very concerned that their relationships with others or their own labour are not intrinsically gratifying, or in discovering the true sources of such deprivations.

Another relevant proposition is that the more any one order, or all orders, of an individual's needs are met within an existing reality, the less likely s/he is to be interested in, and knowledgeable about, the nature of this reality. At least, the less interested s/he is likely to be in acquiring knowledge which would help and lead one to change this reality. Clearly, this is the thrust of Marx's well-known claims that workers are likely to have more insight into the true nature of capitalist relations than are capitalists.[21]

Before proceeding to the next section I would like to leave the reader with two observations about the latter two propositions.

One such observation is that Marx appears to have had not one but two different psychic processes in mind for each proposition. Thus the selectivity of individuals' knowledge is assumed to occur not only because they are uninterested in acquiring knowledge which is impractical, but because they actively avoid, and perhaps even "repress", aspects of reality they may still perceive or know to be true. Here we might recall Marx's references to the capitalist as someone who is not only "blinded by competition", but someone who has an interest in *"drawing the veil over"* various aspects of the reality he encounters.[22]

The other observation is that Marx's own superior powers of observation did not prevent him from contradicting himself (again). Thus whereas the first proposition about interest leads us to predict that those who are severely deprived will not be especially insightful into the social relations within which they exist, the second leads us to predict that it is precisely these individuals, who have the least stake in the status quo, who will be most driven to discover its true nature. However, the co-existence of these two seemingly contradictory propositions may not lie simply with Marx's failure to bring his psychologizing together in the same space and time. Instead, the problem may simply be that Marx assumed fixation would occur when individuals are "individualized", and insight when they are thinking and acting collectively. We shall return to this possibility in the next chapter.

MEDIATION BY PRAXIS

If one were to ask Marx's interpreters how he thought individuals acquire knowledge, most would quickly answer that for Marx knowledge of reality comes *not* from *contemplating* it passively, but through doing, through *acting*. Individuals learn about external reality and themselves in the process of consciously and actively *adapting* themselves to, and actually *changing*, reality. Put otherwise, knowledge is mediated by individuals' *praxis*.[23]

However, we should recognize that Marx never believed that *all* praxes are *necessarily* enlightening. Rather, in the middle stages of capitalism individuals' everyday practices tend to put into practice and reproduce "ideological beliefs" about the capitalist mode of production and bourgeois society. Hence, for example, having claimed that "In capital–profit, or still better capital–interest, land–rent, labour–wages, in this economic trinity represented as the connection between the component parts of value and wealth in general and its sources, we have the complete mystification of the capitalist mode of production, the conversion of social relations into things . . .", Marx went on to explain such mystification, at least in part, as a consequence of the particular praxis of the "agents of production". Thus, "it is just as natural" for them as for bourgeois economists "to feel completely at home in these estranged and irrational forms of capital–interest, land–rent, labour–wages, since these are precisely the forms of illusion in which they move about and find their daily occupation".[24]

Unfortunately, however, this is one of many places where Marx alluded to psychic processes without spelling them out, and we cannot be sure of which ones he was thinking. Perhaps the most parsimonious is that of limited experience: ideological beliefs themselves provide only a partial view of reality (by definition), and practices based solely upon them are likely to simply reinforce rather than modify individuals' initial beliefs. On the other hand, presumably such beliefs must, and must continue to, "work". Such an argument is consistent with a number of his claims; for example, that even something as basic as the dependence of their own existence as capitalists upon the extraction of surplus value is not likely to be very much appreciated by capitalists, until, that is, their own workers have withdrawn their labour-power by striking.[25] The same psychologic presumably applies to Mepham's point about the wage form "working" for workers; that is, only when it *ceases* to work for workers would one expect them to seriously question this configuration of ideological beliefs about capitalist relations of production.[26]

Relatively stable and unproblematic everyday practices therefore appear to have been among the circumstances Marx believed would lead to and reproduce "the reification of the consciousness of the proletariat".[27] Another such circumstance is the degree to which individuals are, and believe themselves to be, "free agents". Indeed, one suspects that Marx was well aware that instability is far from a sufficient condition for the development of a revolutionary praxis; that the latter presupposes proletarians who *already* recognize the dependence of their social relations upon their own activity and feel confident in their collective capacity to transform them, at least to a considerable extent.

Marx himself suggested at least two conditions (and a third we shall take up shortly) which hinder individuals from recognizing themselves as agents, as the makers, or at least *potential* makers, of their own history. One is where individuals do not now *consciously plan* their own activities and relationships, whether or not in the latter they are dominated by a class of exploiters. (The structure and content of their activities and relationships may simply have been handed down to them by previous generations and accepted through "tradition, education and habit".) The other is where individuals' everyday activities, and perhaps their "private" social relationships, may be consciously planned, but not in a very *collective* manner.[28] After all, social *relations* are structured relationships among many different individuals in at least several distinct "roles". For this reason, as Berger and Luckmann have suggested, *unilateral* attempts to transform one's social relationships may lead to feelings of impotency rather than agency.[29]

Related to the latter is a second suggestion of Berger and Luckmann as well as Marx: social relations which have been established and institutionalized by others besides those with whom we ourselves directly relate – whether these others are those in previous generations who have unwittingly and unfairly passed on their own relations to us as "dead weight",[30] or simply others of our own generations who, in structuring *their* relationships in certain ways make it next to impossible for us to do anything very different with our *own* immediate relationships[31] – are likely to be relatively impervious to our attempts to change and gain new information about them, and hence to make us fatalistic about the prospects for fundamental social change. (As we shall see in the next chapter, Marx expected organization as a *class* to change all this.)

A third, albeit perhaps less important, potential source of belief in one's own agency (given its greater historical specificity) is individuation. As we saw in Chapters 1 and 2 above, Marx claimed that most individuals in most social formations do not even clearly *distinguish* themselves from the community as a whole; particular others in the community, even if these others oppress and exploit them; and/or from the means of production, their own labour, and the product. To the extent that individuals do not in fact distinguish themselves from the things they have produced, one would not expect them to (a) see themselves as agents, (b) attempt to change their products and themselves, and thereby also (c) *increase* their sense of themselves as agents.

On the other hand, again as we have already seen, Marx saw conditions especially characteristic of the capitalist social formation as promoting certain *false optimisms* about agency at the same time that they prevent certain *true* facts from being recognized. Thus the less their own actions are *directly* controlled by others, and the greater the *number* of courses of action open to them, even if the consequences of these actions and the actions themselves are almost identical, the more individuals are likely to believe that they are free and possess individuality, that they have choices which they make solely on the basis of their own, internally-generated, needs and wants.

Hence, for example, as compared to those which bind the slave to his or her master, the "threads" which bind the wage-labourer to his owner are "invisible" because "The appearance of independence is kept up by means of a constant change of employers, and by the fictio juris of a contract."[32] Similarly, because producers are no longer *legally* restricted from purchasing most consumer goods and services, they wrongly assume that they are actually free in this and many other respects; that this is "proof" that "freedom" is synonymous with bourgeois society.[33] To the extent that individual members of such a society experience themselves as being compelled rather than free, they assume that this compulsion comes only from the most proximate source of their own thoughts and action: their own needs and wants.[34]

To recapitulate, there are a host of conditions surrounding individuals' praxes which Marx believed (probably correctly, as we shall eventually see) would often promote not a subjective sense of agency, but of impotency or alienation. Alternatively, he suggested, certain other conditions especially characteristic of individuals' praxes in bourgeois society would foster an equally false belief in their own efficacy and freedom.

This said, there are at least two further problems to be dealt with in this section of the present chapter. One is to correct any impression the reader may have derived from my own presentation of Marx on praxis that individuals' praxes are necessarily, or even ever at all wholly, *individualistic* enterprises; the other is to explain how, if so many conditions surrounding individuals' everyday praxes promote false beliefs about freedom and agency, Marx could still expect workers to acquire true (accurate and complete) knowledge of the reality of bourgeois society.

In fact, of course, Marx considered others to mediate our conceptions of reality in a myriad of ways.

Many of the processes whereby this social influence is effected are initiated by others *intentionally*. They may deliberately *instruct* us about the nature of reality, and in this manner "socialize" us in the family, in the school, or on the job. They may also do this less personally, as when members of the ruling class promote racist and sexist beliefs through "the press, the pulpit, the comic papers, in short, by all the means at the disposal of the ruling classes".[35] Alternatively, or in addition, they may *selectively control our access to independent information*, as when the bourgeoisie monopolizes the means of production of information and exercises its own censorship, and is therefore able to have its own ideology become the "ruling ideas".[36] Given that so much of what we learn about reality derives from our own attempts to adapt to, and modify it, others can control our knowledge still more indirectly by *controlling us and/or our immediate environment*. By thus preventing us from experimenting with our environment and ourselves, or at least from doing so successfully, others can prevent us from developing true knowledge of that environment and our own actual or potential agency.

On the other hand, I would agree with Mepham and others that Marx was more likely to emphasize social influence processes which are less dependent upon the deliberate intentions of ruling classes.

One such process is that of *"taking the role of"*, and often subsequently *"identifying with"*, *others*. Thus even when an individual artist or other creative person produces something relatively individually, what s/he learns about external reality and him/herself hardly depends simply upon experiences unique to him or herself. Nor, although it is obviously extremely important, is the sharing of experiences with others simply a matter of sharing the same *language* and other aspects of the same culture. Rather, how a given individual interprets his or her own activities and products depends upon vicariously experiencing *others'* experiences of his or her own activities and products.

We have already quoted Marx to this effect earlier in this part, and hence need not do so here.[37] However, note that there is no great leap between individuals being pleased about their own products and creative capacities because they know *others* are pleased with them and these same individuals being ashamed of themselves because they have violated a social (e.g., bourgeois) norm.[38]

Another social influence process is simply that of the *reinforcing effect reciprocal interaction has upon individuals' beliefs* in external reality and themselves. Thus reciprocity not only helps create a stable and non-problematic reality for the individuals concerned, but provides social and, seemingly, also "physical" and "factual" support for, and therefore reinforces, each individual's initial conception of reality and him or herself.[39] Although he did not put it in quite this way, Marx himself appears to have had some such process in mind.[40]

What light, then, can we throw on the remaining problem of this section: the process whereby individuals de-mystify themselves through their own praxes?

One popular interpretation of Marx on this question is that human individuals are conceived as inveterate experimenters and their relationships as inherently unstable and problematic, such that changing "projects" and "definitions of the situation" are equally inevitable.[41] It is not difficult to comprehend the appeal of such an answer over that of structuralists, which has tended to be that everyday "material" practices and the ideology which is embedded in them have a "life of their own", and only change through externally-generated contradictions. After all, the former is a more flattering view of "human nature" and promotes faith and optimism. However, I find the suggestion that "things are always changing" little more helpful than that "things are always the same".

As I see it, Marx's expectation that workers would "see the light" was based upon a number of highly contingent propositions about the course of development of *capitalism* rather than an "iron law" deriving from a few assumptions about the inherent features of all human individuals or all human relationships. To be sure, workers' experimentations with reality *if and when* it becomes problematic – and Marx *did* expect it to become problematic – are among the confluent events which lead workers to enlighten themselves, but for Marx, and unlike various phenomenologists, reality is far from *always* problematic enough to provoke a great deal of experimentation. Although for Marx the reality of capitalism remains problematic as long as individuals begin with inadequate knowledge of it and act relatively unreflectively and atomistically rather than truly collectively, such that their everyday practices have consequences which they cannot foresee and control, it may nevertheless become stable enough for individuals' adaptations to it to become routine and appear natural. Under such circumstances the initial provocation for change is indeed likely to come from "without", in the sense that what makes reality problematic enough to initiate a search for new knowledge is not an invariant quest for truth in each individual worker, but the unintended consequences of their own and others' beliefs and actions. If this interpretation is correct, all we can do here is point to various social trends which Marx thought would change the circumstances workers face, and hence also their own praxes.

The concentration and centralization of capital and economic and political crises, which themselves are the largely unintended consequences of *capitalists'* adaptations to the circumstances *they* face, are cases in point. They not only provoke workers to organize on an evermore class-wide level, which itself is supposed to aid them in acquiring true knowledge (see the next chapter), but to subvert the previous praxes of individual workers which had hitherto given them the illusions of freedom and equality. Thus during crises a great many workers are no longer able to find *any* employment, let alone change employers at will; they have so little "purchasing power" that the equality of opportunity and freedom proclaimed in bourgeois ideology come to be seen as mere formalities; and so forth.

NOTES

1. For example, consider Leszek Kolakowski's "Karl Marx and the classical definition of truth" (pp. 58–86 in *Marxism and Beyond* (London: Pall Mall Press, 1968). After having forcefully argued the constructivist position, Kolakowski then in effect admits there is a reality *somewhat* independent of individuals' experiences of it, an "external world" of "objects" which helps "create" our "cognitive being" (p. 87). How else are we to interpret his denial of an *"absolutely* independent" reality (p. 67; my emphasis), and his recognition of the dependence of scientific analysis upon consensual rules of evidence (p. 82)? Similarly, having disputed the possibility of an *"entirely* universal and nonhistorical theory of knowledge", he concedes that there may exist "immutable human needs and relations" which are a *"constant"*, "the *primary* material of our cognition" (pp. 78–9; my emphases). The latter claim is clearly more extreme in the direction away from his initial position than are the claims I have made in this work.
2. *Eighteenth Brumaire*, pp. 190–1.
3. *Ideology*, pp. 48, 79, 87; *Manifesto*, pp. 491–2.
4. *Capital 3*, pp. 791–2.
5. *Wages, Price and Profit*, pp. 213–14; *Capital 1*, Chapter 1.
6. *Wage Labour and Capital*, p. 201; *Wages, Price and Profit*, pp. 209–10.
7. *Wages, Price and Profit*, p. 213; *Capital 1*, p. 170.

8. See Note 6.
9. *Grundrisse*, p. 585.
10. *Capital 3*, pp. 791–2.
11. This is an extension of Marx's suggestion that "The Roman slave was held by fetters; the wage-labourer is bound to his owner by invisible threads" (*Capital 1*, p. 538).
12. *Capital 1*, p. 689.
13. *Capital 3*, p. 793.
14. *Capital 1*, p. 689.
15. This seems to be implied in the *Preface*, p. 183.
16. Ibid., p. 184.
17. *Capital 1*, p. 65.
18. *Ideology*, pp. 39, 55–7; *Manifesto*, Part III.
19. *Capital 1*, p. 80.
20. *Manifesto*, pp. 491–2.
21. *Holy Family*, p. 36; *Results* . . . , p. 508.
22. *Capital 3*, pp. 43, 168. As with the "withdrawal from reality" discussed in the previous chapter, the parallel with the thinking of Freud is apparent. Unfortunately, these many parallels, which, as suggested earlier, are ironic given the criticisms neo-Freudians have often levelled against Marx, cannot be pursued further here. However, I have taken matters somewhat further in a separate paper, "Marx and Freud: Aliens or bedfellows?", presented to the World Congress of Sociology in New Delhi, in August of 1986.
23. For example, see Theses 1 and 5; *Ideology*, pp. 30, 36–7, 39–41.
24. *Capital 3*, p. 830.
25. *Capital 1*, p. 200.
26. Op. cit. (see Note 104, Chapter 1).
27. Lukács, op. cit., p. 83.
28. *Ideology*, pp. 47–8, 83; *Grundrisse*, pp. 585, 590; *Capital 1*, p. 82.
29. Peter Berger and Thomas Luckmann, *The Social Construction of Reality* (Garden City, N.Y.: Doubleday (Anchor), 1967) pp. 58–9.
30. *Ideology*, p. 54; *Eighteenth Brumaire*, p. 103.
31. This may have been what Marx meant by his statement that "It is not a question of what this or that proletarian . . . at the moment regards as its aim" (*Holy Family*, p. 37). Certainly, he made many references to capitalists having little choice as to how to treat their workers because of competition (e.g., *Capital 1*, p. 257).
32. *Capital 1*, p. 538.
33. *Grundrisse*, p. 283.
34. Ibid., p. 245.
35. *Ireland and the Irish Question*, op. cit., pp. 293–4.
36. *Ideology*, p. 59.
37. See Chapter 4, Note 13.
38. Berger and Luckmann, op. cit., pp. 131–5, 155.
39. Ibid., pp. 149, 152–3.
40. E.g., see the passage quoted above and referenced by Note 24.
41. The existentialist and phenomenological/"symbolic interactionist" roots, respectively, for the latter interpretations can be found in, for

example, Jean-Paul Sartre's *Being and Nothingness* (New York: Simon and Schuster (Pocket Books, Washington Square Press, 1966), and Herbert Blumer's *Symbolic Interactionism* (Englewood Cliffs, N.J.: Prentice-Hall, 1969).

7 A General Psychology of Intergroup Relations

For the sake of continuity with the immediately preceding chapters I shall assume, as did Marx himself at many points in his writing, the existence of a mode of production, such as capitalism, which has been in existence long enough that traditional groupings from previous social formations have been largely broken down, but not long enough that the majority of producers have organized themselves as a group/ "class-for-itself". However, conceiving of individuals as chickens and groups as eggs is only an analytical device. Groups are *also* chickens. Indeed, as we saw in Chapter 1, for Marx the most primeval chickens – and those most important for historic change – are groups rather than individuals, and on numerous occasions we shall have to acknowledge this fact.

(A) SOME GENERAL PSYCHOLOGICAL PRINCIPLES OF GROUP FORMATION

To suggest that Marx employed *general*, let alone also *psycho*logical, principles of "group" formation will no doubt seem heretical to many. After all, he never even provided a complete theory of *class*, to say nothing of social groups in general. Nevertheless, this is precisely what I intend to suggest.

In taking this stance I by no means deny that Marx regarded class as a highly peculiar species of group. Although he did not get around to spelling out the distinctive features of classes, we do know that classes are *defined* by their members' ownership or non-ownership, and control or lack of control over, the means of production. As a consequence, in societies dominated by one or another class, a large proportion of the population may be denied the means for their own subsistence. What makes classes especially important, therefore, is the fact that membership in them determines whether, and how much, one's most basic needs are gratified.[1] Classes also tend to be pivots around which both smaller and larger groups organize: they usually form as alliances among families, but also tend to be the basis for nation states and international relations.[2]

But there is every reason to believe that Marx still treated classes as species of groups. Thus, as we shall see shortly, he offered very similar explanations for the formation of groups as diverse as families, occupations, guilds, classes, and nations. Indeed, Marx often used other groupings, including the family, as models for – in fact, evolutionary prototypes of – classes. "The division of labour in which all these contradictions [in this case, those of capitalism] are implicit," he and Engels wrote, "[is in turn] based on the natural division of labour in the family and the separation of society into individual families opposed to one another . . . ."[3] Certainly, Marx's "class-for-itself"[4] – or, as he put it at one point, "compact group"[5] – would meet social psychologists' criteria for a "group". Here individuals identify themselves, and "associate" with, others (and, as we shall see, vice versa) over more than one or two collective actions.[6] They have traditional interpretations of the circumstances they are likely to face, such as a reimposition of the wine tax, and these as well as their common "conditions of life" are likely to perpetuate "customs".[7] There is likely to be a minimum amount of solidarity in, and loyalty to, the group, as with workers who forgo wages in order to maintain the existence of their union. And, of course, processes of leadership are likely to be very much in evidence.

An important additional feature of groups stressed by Marx is their *ideology* – their distinctive interpretation of reality which is not only likely to be highly partial, but also highly apologetic for the existence, interests, and/or activities of the group.[8] Among other things, this ideology is likely to portray the group's own, partial interpretation as nearly universal and impartial, as, for example, with the suggestion of the economically and politically powerless "German ideologists" of Marx's own time that religion is the root of all evil.[9]

We could not hope to take up all of these characteristics of groups in detail here, even if Marx himself had. What we shall do instead is only take up those aspects of each of the features of groups as they apply to the specific psychological propositions considered here.

The first such proposition may seem overly simply, a truism, but it is nevertheless central:

(1) Individuals attempt to group or regroup when they share gratifications in common to protect, or barriers to remove and deprivations to ameliorate.

The barriers individuals share in common may simply be natural. On the other hand, other groups whose members' interests are opposed to one's own are among the most important barriers Marx took up.

As noted in Chapter 3, Marx explained the emergence of the city-state in ancient Greece and Rome as in part the coming together of separate landed proprietors to protect themselves from both each other and invasion from without. In medieval Europe individuals organized themselves into towns for similar reasons, although in these cases the threat was as much from the landed proprietors of their own society as from outsiders. Within the towns themselves craftsmen organized themselves into guilds in large part because of "the necessity for associating against the association of the robber-nobility" and "the growing competition of the escaped serfs swarming into the rising towns."[10]

It was the persistent and increasing threat from the feudal nobility which subsequently led certain sectors of the town populations to organize themselves *across* towns as a (national) class – the bourgeoisie. The latter was the specific reference point for a statement of Marx's, hereafter referred to as the SIS statement, to which we shall return several times in this chapter: "The separate individuals form a class only insofar as they have to carry on a common battle against another class; in other respects they are on hostile terms with each other as competitors."[11] However, the proposition clearly applies equally to the proletariat, who in turn initially organize only in order to protect themselves from the bourgeoisie's pursuit of *its* own interests.[12]

The word "initially" in the last sentence is meant to signify an important qualification about Marx's account of grouping. Although Marx implied that it occurs because it is, *and is perceived by individuals to be,* a more effective, and perhaps necessary, means of protection or amelioration than is individual action, he in no way suggested that individuals conceive and plan full groups-for-themselves before the process of grouping begins. As have contemporary social psychologists, so too Marx thought of group/class formation as following a number of stages; the first of which may involve a series of relatively disjointed collective acts, such as food riots or machine smashings, whose inspiration is as much expressive as instrumental. The "compacting" of collective action into longer-term groups, social movements, and classes-for-themselves is much more an "emergent" process than one pre-planned by individual participants, although, obviously, there may be varying degrees of pre-planning.[13]

(2) Any given objective interest in organizing (for example, a class interest) may not in fact be recognized and acted upon if there are other, competing interests.

In our discussion of typical responses to gratification and deprivation in Chapter 5 we noted Marx's claim that "social mobility" (that is, the movement of *individuals* and/or families between social classes) – and even individuals' aspirations for, and expectation of, it – hindered, and perhaps prevented, serfs and journeymen from organizing as classes-for-themselves. The independent artisans, notaries, and so on who eventually formed the bourgeoisie were also in this position initially. What with, according to Marx, "social mobility" becoming completely blocked for them, wage labourers are in a considerably different position. Nevertheless, in other respects Proposition 2 very much applies to them as well as to previous "classes" of individuals.

First, in the early stages of capitalism, and often much later as well, most workers think of themselves as individual proprietors of their own labour who individually contract with their employers to sell that labour. Other employees are regarded as competitors, for employment itself, and for varying slices of the wealth produced by their labour. This individualistic and competitive orientation leads individual workers to either avoid and be indifferent to, or/and be hostile toward, each other, rather than to combine into groups.[14]

Second, the first groupings of workers are not by class but by order of entry to the labour market and protection of these relatively privileged positions. The crafts retain certain aspects of their traditional organization and modify them as they need to. Skilled labourers more generally subsequently do the same. Adult males attempt to exclude or "ghettoize" women and children, the dominant racial, ethnic and national groups the subordinant.[15]

Third, competition along these various lines continues to disorganize the proletariat long after it has already organized itself well beyond the level of local occupations, and participated as a class-for-itself in the official political arena of bourgeois society. It is even more beset with disorganizing competition than the bourgeoisie was during the period of its own ascendancy.[16] For example, that between English and Irish, and even French and German workers, was at various times described as the single most important "secret" of the impotence of the English proletariat, the most numerous and organized of Marx's own time.[17]

Of course, as we saw earlier, Marx assumed that in time these various competing interests among workers would greatly decrease with (a) the general deskilling or "proletarianization" of labour, and (b) trade and commerce and other forms of "intercourse" among occupations, localities, and nations. *On the other hand,*

(3) Competing interests need not disappear in order for general, objective (for example, class) interests to be recognized and acted upon. Rather, collective action by groups of individuals with opposing interests, and especially occasional collective responses to such actions, may make general interests salient and superordinant to those which have previously divided individuals or groups from one another.

We have already seen several applications of this proposition with regard to Proposition 1; that is, the formation of city-states, towns, guilds, and classes by private proprietors faced by a common, collective enemy. This reasoning is well-captured in his previously-quoted SIS statement. Were it necessary, many independent pieces of evidence for this, Proposition 3, could be mustered. For example, there is said to be a division within the bourgeoisie between "mental and material labour" (between its practitioners and, for example, its academic theorists), a division which "can even develop into a certain opposition and hostility between the two parts". However, "whenever a practical collision occurs in which the class itself is endangered they automatically vanish".[18] As we have had several occasions to note, the same was claimed to be true for workers, who, when they find their association is attacked by their employers, act together in spite of their individual interest in maintaining a continuous income.

What perhaps most needs stressing here is Marx's belief that among the several different classes to be found in bourgeois society, wage-labourers are those for whom the principle of superordinant goals is most likely to apply. Their "natural" class enemy has had considerably earlier access to societal wealth and power, and is smaller and initially much better organized and prone to move against other classes. Furthermore, unlike the landed aristocracy, the peasantry, and the urban petty bourgeoisie, wage-labourers have no means of subsistence of their own to retreat to in the face of action against them by the bourgeoisie and its representative agent, the state.[19] Finally, whereas in their own revolutions the urban bourgeoisies and peasantry were able to, and did, divide privately-owned property among themselves, and thus ensure competition amongst themselves in the future, the proletariat will take over means of production which are too large, complex, and integrated to be divided amongst themselves. This provides them with the highly unique superordinant goals of public ownership of the means of production and the abolition of *all* classes, including their own.[20]

While the latter arguments are exceedingly interesting and, taken at face-value, fairly plausible, they are far from unproblematic. For one thing, it is questionable that workers will necessarily be *forced* to develop superordinant goals, since this presupposes that their class enemy, the bourgeoisie, either cannot, or is unwilling to, share enough of collective wealth to prevent them from doing so.[21] For another, whereas the bourgeoisie has its own state and a long-standing body of "ruling ideas" to help it develop superordinant goals, the proletariat has no such ready-made machinery – except, perhaps, loose populist traditions – and must begin more-or-less from scratch.[22] And, of course, with our own benefit of hindsight, we now know that extremely large-scale industry does not in fact necessarily require full public ownership and the abolition of classes. Rather, private "joint-stock companies" can be much larger than Marx envisioned, and even where they have been dismantled by proletarian revolutions, they may be ruled by bureaucratic elites in a manner not all that different from their capitalist predecessors.[23]

Another potential problem with Marx's argument regarding the special applicability of the principle of superordinant goals to proletarians is one actually recognized by Marx himself, but then either forgotten or underestimated. Specifically, if superordinant goals can develop *within* classes, why cannot they also develop *between* classes? Marx acknowledged the existence of "aristocracies of labour" – for example, within the British working class and vis-à-vis it and the working classes of Ireland and the Continent – but he saw such tacit alliances with capital as inevitably short-lived.[24] Although the principle of superordination might just as well lead one to expect that international competition would bring capital and labour together as push them apart, Marx was much more willing to consider the latter than the former.[25]

(4) Group/class formation and organization are greatly hindered by such objective circumstances as geographical dispersion, limited means of transportation and communication, and large numbers. However, where there is a particularly strong will to organize, individuals will frequently find a way to do so. Alternatively, even where there is *not* a particularly strong will initially, particularly favourable objective circumstances for organizing make it especially likely.

The first part of this proposition may strike one as an overly voluntaristic reading of Marx, but there is some evidence that Marx indeed thought along these lines. At least, this seems to be implied in the following passage: "It is evident that large-scale industry does not reach the same level of development in all districts of a country. This does *not*, however, retard the class movement of the proletariat, because the proletarians created by large-scale industry assume leadership of this movement and carry the whole mass along with them, *and because the workers excluded from large-scale industry are placed by it in a still worse situation* than the workers in large-scale industry itself."[26]

Here Marx appears to have assumed that the "worse" situation of workers in small-scale industries makes them especially eager to organize, so much so that, although they do not have good means for doing so directly at their disposal, they go out of their way to seize upon the example and existing organization of workers in large-scale, urban industries. Indeed, he was later to claim that "[economic] crises first produce revolutions on the Continent [.] Violent outbreaks must naturally occur [first] . . . in the extremities of the bourgeois body [rather] than in its heart, since the possibility of adjustment is greater here [in the latter] than there [in the former]".[27]

We probably should not interpret Marx as suggesting that workers are likely to overcome *any* barriers to organization, no matter how numerous or large. One is reminded, for example, of his admonition to Utopian socialists not to moralize against workers for competing amongst themselves. "To demand the opposite", Marx cautioned, "would be tantamount to demanding . . . that individuals should banish from their minds conditions over which in their isolation they have no control."[28]

The objective "conditions" Marx was referring to here are "the big industrial cities and cheap and quick communications," which are "the *necessary* means" for a union of workers, "if it is not to be merely local". There seems little question that he himself stressed the second rather than the first component of Proposition 4. This is suggested by his claim, taken up above in Chapters 2 and 3, that the first stimulus for organization often comes not from workers, but from the bourgeoisie, who – unintentionally, of course – put workers in close contact with each other by congregating them in large industries in the cities. It is more directly evident in the claim that whereas it took the bourgeoisie centuries to organize themselves as a (national) class, because of huge advances in transportation and communication proletarians will be able to do the same in mere decades.[29]

Nevertheless, it is important to recognize that both components of this proposition are in Marx, that the latter is paradigmatic of several others we shall take up in this chapter, and that all of them are problematic.

The problem is this: Marx continually offered explanations for social phenomena which specify several different conditions, *all* of which are at one time or another labelled "necessary". In this case, the ways or "means" for organizing are characterized as necessary, but as we also saw earlier, Marx was equally adamant that the will or "motive" to organize is necessary. (The example taken up earlier was that of the highly numerous and organized British working class which nevertheless lacked the will to make the revolution.[30]) However, Marx then proceeded to predict that high degrees of class organization were on the immediate horizon even when one or another of the two sets of necessary conditions was, by his own admission, insufficiently developed!

Now, one can attempt to rationalize away this problem by crediting Marx with having implicitly employed sophisticated explanatory models which are "interactive" or "multiplicative" rather than simply "linear" and "additive", as is perhaps suggested, for example, by Hegelian and/or more generally systemic notions of "totality" such as one finds in the early work of Lukács.[31] The idea here would go something like this: as long as both the variables will and way, motive and means, are above zero, one does not require both to be extremely high. Rather, even if only *one* is, it will make up for deficiencies on the other because it combines with the other *multiplicatively* rather than additively.

This is an appealing argument, but I suspect that it is wrong, and that in his more sober and old-fashioned moments, Marx himself knew this all too well. Although it makes excellent sense to posit that conditions interact rather than simply combine in a mechanistic manner, wills and ways are too important in their own right to make up for serious deficiencies in one or the other. The above-mentioned observations of the British proletariat by Marx himself seem to bear this out.

(B) HOW INTERGROUP RELATIONS TRANSFORM THE PSYCHES OF INDIVIDUALS

Here we switch from observing Marx theorizing about relatively unattached individuals in the process of organizing themselves into groups, to how relatively developed groups affect their individual members. For the most part, the propositions and the order in which they are taken up pertain to those discussed in Chapters 4 through 6.

(1) Intra-, and especially inter-, group interaction both makes individuals more aware of *existing* needs, wants, and deprivations and creates *new* ones. Among other things, group interaction changes the reference point for relative deprivation from *individuals'* own past history and present alternatives to inequalities between *groups*.

Let us begin with *intra*-group experiences.

One of the consequences of association among communist artisans is that "they acquire a new need" for "association, society and conversation," a need which goes well beyond their original purposes in associating, which were to organize themselves as a class through "theory" and "propaganda".[32] Since, as we have seen, Marx regarded affiliation as a basic need in-and-of-itself, "acquiring a new need" presumably means either or both becoming aware of this existing need and/or developing aspirations and wants for things which are already needed. This interpretation is supported by a later statement that "English and French workers have formed associations in which they exchange opinions not only on their immediate needs as *workers*, but on their needs as *human beings*."[33]

How, then, does this increased awareness come about?

In the first passage quoted above Marx could be construed to imply simply that individual workers become aware of their needs for affiliation and social intercourse simultaneously and independently once they have begun to associate. However, in the second he explicitly refers to a process which is not only emergent, but dependent for its emergence upon prior *social interaction*; in this case upon discussion in which there is an "exchange" of "opinions", and, perhaps, also social influence. Furthermore, we have had several occasions to note the importance Marx attributed to group culture and the socialization of new members into it through tradition, and this presumably applies to the awareness of needs and development of new aspirations and wants.

However, it bears noting that discussion and various forms of inter-individual and group influence *need not* lead to individual members becoming more aware of their needs and/or developing new wants. The group may instead promote ignorance. It may also mislead individuals as to the true sources of their own activities, and perhaps even create "false needs". Marx himself was aware of this possibility,[34] but he seldom used the term "ideological" to decribe the ideas which constitute the weapons of the proletariat presumably because he thought that proletarians, being more numerous and having less of a stake in the status quo, are in a much more favourable position than capitalists to develop an ideology which also contains a scientific analysis of capitalism.[35]

I have few qualms about the logic of the latter claim, but I do have some. First, as Plamenatz suggested, it is by no means obvious that having to adapt to others who oppress and exploit one (often relatively passively) *necessarily* requires one to have more insight into theirs and one's own motives than does having to oppress and exploit them oneself (often relatively actively).[36] Secondly, the expectation that the proletariat as a whole will develop a sound basis for a scientific analysis of capitalism presupposes a proletariat which is not itself internally stratified and wracked by substantial conflicts of interest.[37] However, as we have just seen in the first part of this chapter, Marx himself noted that the latter condition is often not met.

Having thus slipped into using examples of *intergroup struggle* rather than simply intragroup interaction anyway, let us deal with the latter explicitly.

Perhaps most importantly, as suggested by the corollary to Proposition B1, in the process of struggling against their employers, workers in particular begin to compare their own situation *as a group* with that of their employers *as a group*. As Marx himself put it, workers then begin to measure their wages *in proportion to* their employers' profits. The size of this proportion then becomes "a real moment of economic life itself", a "decisively important" moment, in that (a) they now begin to demand a larger share of the surplus value they have created, and (b) when they do not receive it they become much more aware both of surplus value as the source of profit and that their own group's relationship to their employer's is not one of an equitable exchange.[38]

Nor, as noted in Chapters 3 and 4, are these changes in the quantity and quality of social comparison and relative deprivation restricted to aspirations with regard to lower-order, subsistence needs and consumer wants more generally. Thus the ratio of "free" to "working" time also enters their calculations as workers discover (a) their own needs for social intercourse and self-development, and (b) that their employers control an unnecessarily large share of their time as well as the material wealth produced during their working time. Along the way, furthermore, wants with regard to the *status* of their own *group*, as well as their esteem as individuals, will have been deprived by the collective actions of employers against it. Industrialization and mechanization will have threatened, if not altogether reduced, the status of traditional occupational groups within the category of producers; state representatives of employers will have insulted peasants and workers alike by attacking and removing traditional group symbols or imposing unwanted ones;[39] and so on.

Yet Marx's formulations contain a number of presuppositions, not all of which are explicit, and unproblematic.

First, Marx's expectation that workers' comparisons will become collective rather than individualistic was based on the prior assumptions that (a) individual social mobility is almost totally blocked, and that in large part because of this (b) workers have in fact organized themselves as a class. Obviously, however, there may be gradations of status instead of simply two classes in conflict, and individuals may function *as individuals* who, having been fortunate or unfortunate enough, depending upon one's point of view, to have someone "below" them "on the ladder", feel relatively *privileged* rather than deprived.

We noted before that Marx was well-aware of such conditions among serfs. He also noted their existence for the bourgeoisie in the early stages of the transformation of feudalism.[40] However, he appears to have resisted the conclusion that they might also continue to apply to workers, and this despite various of his observations which might have led him to think otherwise: the feelings of superiority among craft workers, of men versus women and children, of the English versus the Irish.[41]

Second, Marx assumed that social comparison and the subsequent recognition of inter*group* inequality *necessarily* leads to feelings of relative deprivation. Surely, however, the latter need not follow the former, even when individuals are highly organized as groups rather than functioning individually. The old caste system of India is the classic counter-example, but others, such as the estate system in the middle stages of feudalism, might also apply. The expectation of relative deprivation presupposes still other conditions; to wit, that the groups doing the comparing have beliefs about morality and justice which make inequality illegitimate. Yet on this problem Marx was cryptic, seemingly sloppy, and certainly confusing.

On the one hand, for example, Marx himself emphasized that principles of morality and justice are highly specific historically. For instance, those related to individualism as opposed to authority, and, one presumes, equality versus hierarchy, are supposed to have come into their own only in the 18th century.[42] But on the other,

Marx's own accounts of serfs' recognition of, and rebellion against or avoidance of, exploitation could be construed to depend upon their adherence to such principles. The same could be said for some of his descriptions of slaves, who on one occasion are portrayed as about to recognize themselves as "persons", and, having done so, to revolt against the system of servitude.[43]

This being the case, how are we supposed to proceed? Should we presume that Marx occasionally fell back into a practice for which he vehemently criticized Hegel, Proudhon, and others; that is, of presupposing a system of "*natural* rights"? This is in fact a common practice among contemporary analysts which has even been explicitly recognized by some users themselves.[44] One doubts that this is what Marx had in mind, yet it is by no means obvious precisely when and why principles of equality arise, and, most importantly for our understanding of contemporary bourgeois society, why one would expect workers to see capitalism as an entire system as unjust, even if they *have* come to believe in principles of equality.

After all, by Marx's own admission the dominant system of morality and justice for most of the life of bourgeois society is likely to be the *bourgeoisie's*, and the beliefs embodied in that system stress the fairness of the exchange of equivalents, of commodities at their value. It is debatable that even Marx himself regarded workers' exchange of their labour-power for a wage as unjust, since on average this wage is likely to tend toward the true value of labour-power.[45] Either way, it is doubtful that even *organized* workers will *necessarily* see inequality between classes as immoral and unjust.

Recall first that what is stressed in bourgeois justice is not equality in the *distribution* of *communal* wealth, but only equality in *opportunity* for initial access to *ownership* of, and control over, *means of production*. That such principles can foster a misguided psycho-logic of justice is a fact of which Marx himself was well aware. Specifically, rather than recognizing that capitalists are leaders of industry because they inherited or otherwise unfairly came to own it, workers often believe that capitalists became capitalists because they are natural leaders.[46]

Recall also Marx's own claim that what is usually conceived as *workers'* contribution to industry, by workers themselves as well as capitalists, is not even the actual commodity they contribute – that is, their own labour-*power* – but only certain fixed quantities of *labour*. To the extent that workers do indeed have this conception of what they contribute, they may well not see the profits and living standards of their employers as having resulted from exploitation. Even when they are dissatisfied with their wages, their feeling that justice does not obtain may lie only with a claim that some nebulously-defined "pie" has not been fairly divided, and not with the much stronger one that they have a *right* to most of it because it arises only from their own labour-power.

Surely the latter claim presupposes an *alternative* system of justice; a system which need not be *totally* unique, or even completely different from the bourgeoisie's, but nevertheless very distinctive. Its own system of morality and justice served the bourgeoisie well in its battle against the aristocracy, but conditions were then considerably different from those faced by the proletariat, even in Marx's own time. Whereas the artistocracy had been very much smaller than the bourgeoisie, the ratio of at least small capital owners to propertyless manual labourers in Marx's own day was much larger, and although it is far from a very accurate conception of the present state of affairs, it is still a common one among today's workers. The bourgeoisie could easily point out that whereas they worked, and often productively, the aristocracy did not and were only able to exist through taxing those who did. In other words, exploitation was simple, blatant, and easily labelled unjust. Workers may or may not believe that what their employers do is very productive, but many, and perhaps most, are not very familiar with their employers anyway, and believe that most of their managers and supervisors *do* at least "*work*".[47]

That this dilemma did not cause Marx himself to despair can probably be explained by two expectations of his. One is that the reality of bourgeois society would drastically change for the worse. With the concentration and centralization of capital it becomes very difficult for the bourgeoisie to argue that there is in fact equality of opportunity. More importantly, absolute immiseration undermines the claim that capitalism is even a rational, let alone moral and just, system.[48] The other expectation is that in the meantime various groups of workers will have been at work fashioning their own system of justice. The materials out of which this new system emerges are the principles of liberty and equality proclaimed earlier by the bourgeoisie and the new circumstances faced by workers: their lack of opportunity to have their needs and abilities as individuals determine even their employment, let alone upward mobility; to have their *individual* contributions to production measured in the face of a highly *socialized* division of labour; etc.

(2) Intergroup action/struggle makes individual group members

more aware of, and knowledgeable about, *barriers* to gratification, even those, such as the social relations of production, which are not only most general and important, but least immediately visible.

The passage cited earlier with reference to collective bargaining and "fraternal" comparison appears to contain this proposition as well. Specifically, this process is alleged to make workers aware that capitalist relations of production and distribution do not in fact entail free and equal exchange. Rather, the "semblance" of the latter is replaced with the recognition of the real nature of the social relations as the greatest barrier to gratification.

We could garner many other passages to support this interpretation. In a large proportion of such passages Marx argued that class struggles usually begin with only very low levels of class consciousness on the part of workers, but that the latter then develops greatly with the former. For example, at one point Marx suggested that "As the bourgeoisie develops, there develops in its bosom a new proletariat, a modern proletariat; there develops a struggle between the proletarian class and the bourgeois class, a struggle which, before being felt, perceived, appreciated, understood, avowed and proclaimed aloud by both sides, expresses itself, to start with, merely in partial and momentary conflicts, in subversive acts."[49]

This being the case, let us proceed to the more interesting problem of *how* workers and other group members are supposed to learn more by acting collectively, and *why* Marx believed that this knowledge would be more accurate than that gained individually.

From what I can gather, Marx implicitly provided three solutions to these problems.

First, groups are alleged to provide individuals with unique perspectives and other resources for interpreting existing social phenomena which are already collective. For one thing, their cultural traditions often contain perspectives which keep their individual members on the lookout for certain barriers, as French peasants did by instructing their children to beware of governments which deliberate about wine taxes. For another, when individuals confront further aspects of their environment for the first time, they find that doing so collectively has certain advantages. As with many contemporary social psychologists,[50] here Marx appears to have assumed that groups tend to be better problem solvers than individuals. As suggested earlier in the passage about communist artisans discovering their most human needs after associating, individuals in groups are able to both pool the knowledge they have gained from their past, individual experiences, and come up with unique, new knowledge by "brainstorming" and other such processes.

A second set of solutions concerns collective phenomena, or, at least, certain aspects or degrees of them, which really only *emerge* after individuals have grouped, and, often, thereby provoked reactions from groups of individuals with opposing interests. Indeed, if one recalls Marx's SIS statement, then one realizes that *class* itself (class-*for*-itself, that is) is among such emergent phenomena.

Marx offered many different scenarios for how individuals expand their knowledge of the barrier, the capitalist relations of production, through class struggle.

In one, employers congregate workers in a central location, only to discover that they have combined. These employers then drastically alter working conditions to counter this threat to their interests: they employ such "fore" people as foremen, supervisors, and the like, but then also replace workers with machinery, indicating that their interests are partial and incompatible with those of their employees.

In another scenario French workers organized themselves politically and forced the bourgeoisie to introduce universal suffrage. However, after exercising their new-found rights by electing representatives from their own classes, workers and peasants soon discovered the truth about bourgeois rule: if the bourgeoisie cannot rule with the support of parliament it will rule without it.[51]

In a third solution collectivization is seen as increasing the "scientific", experimental features of individual members' relationships with their environment that were described in Chapter 6. To wit, in part because, as we shall see with the next proposition, individuals become more confident in their capacity to modify their environment, collectivization increases the likelihood that they will deliberately *attempt* to modify it. Either way, "strength in numbers" increases the likelihood that they will in fact modify it. These modifications then tend to be more informative than those which occur through individual action or which occur while groups merely contemplate them passively. For example, because individuals can now see that changes have resulted from their own group's actions, they learn more about cause–effect relationships.

These latter arguments seem eminently reasonable, but there is reason to believe that Marx was overly enamoured with the likelihood and size of the modifications which come with group action compared to their quality and content. Most curiously, he often claimed that group *defeats* – for instance, in the case of the French producing classes in 1850 – are more informative than group successes.[52] In this particular case Marx may well have been correct, but to generalize from these circumstances to defeats in general is to take too narrow a view of their effects.

Perhaps most importantly, whereas from successes individuals and groups at least learn that they have done something correctly in their attempts to modify their environment – and perhaps also what that something is – from failures they are likely to obtain information which is much less specific and useful. Thus they know that they have done something wrong, but by no means what they must do in the future to "get it right". This reasoning flows from the same principles of reinforcement that we saw Marx to have drawn upon in other respects of his theorizing (see Chapters 5 and 6), and there is no reason to believe that they should apply less to individuals thinking and acting collectively than to those doing so individually.

Over and above this problem, defeat can have other, and still more serious, consequences. Specifically, it can greatly decrease individuals' and groups' *confidence* in their capacity to modify their environment. This brings us to our next proposition.

(3) Group and intergroup action and struggle gives individuals a greater feeling of *power to remove* barriers to gratification.

According to Marx, workers' education in the "school of labour" is "not in vain" because it is not simply "stern", but "steeling". "In their associations," for example, English and French workers "show a very thorough and comprehensive consciousness of the 'enormous' and 'immeasurable' power which arises from their co-operation."[53]

That Marx believed both workers' actual strength and their subjective beliefs in it derive in good part from their numbers, when "concentrated" and "combined", is clear. "[T]he 'power of the individual'," he wrote, "very much depends on whether others combine their power with his; with the development of industry the proletariat not only increases in number; it becomes concentrated in greater masses, its strength grows, *and it feels that strength more*."[54] Much less clear are the nature and sources of the psychic experiences which provide these feelings of strength.

The statements I have just quoted imply that the mere perception of large numbers of others organized into the same group makes workers feel more powerful to take on barriers. Perhaps they feel that they now face their employers not individually, but with many others than their employers have with them. However, given the centrality of praxis in Marx's explanations for the acquisition of knowledge in general, one would expect Marx to argue that collective praxes are more likely than individual ones to provide such feelings, and recognition, of power.

If we do assume a primitive sense of power in mere numbers and organization, then we might expect organized workers to be more likely than individualized ones to experiment with, and attempt to change, their environment. The latter could also result from a feeling that other group members will support one and share in any responsibility for the consequences of such attempts.[55] This is a major thrust of the next proposition. Whereas the *absence* of attempts to change often leads to "avoidance conditioning" (since individuals do not know that they could safely act in a particular way, they do not, and consequently do not learn the truth),[56] the *presence* of such attempts when they are collectivized, and therefore much more powerful, now provides them with *evidence* of this power, and this should make them much more conscious of it.

This scenario is a relatively straightforward incidence of the learning processes mentioned earlier. Yet it is problematic as an interpretation of Marx's own reasoning. Why? Because in numerous places he stressed that the outcome of even workers' *collective* attempts to alter their working conditions and other aspects of their environment is much more likely to be *defeat* than victory. "*Now and then* the workers are victorious," he claimed, "*but only for a time.* The real fruit of their battles lies, not in the immediate result, but in the ever-expanding union of the workers."[57]

This appears to be a major problem with Marx's analysis. If they typically experience failure rather than success, workers will presumably come to feel more power*less* than power*ful*. The more they attempt to change their environment without actually changing it for the better, the more powerless they should feel. And attempting to do so collectively may well *increase* this sense of powerlessness. Thus they may well reason that "If we cannot even change things with these highly organized numbers, then reality must *really* be impenetrable."[58] There is some reason to believe that Marx was at least aware of the problem. For example, in 1864, in " 'a sort of a review of the fortunes of the working classes' since 1845", Marx noted how a series of defeats had in fact resulted in severe demoralization and apathy among British workers. "[I]n point of fact," he claimed, "never before seemed the English working class so thoroughly reconciled to a state of pol..ical nullity."[59]

(4) Especially because intergroup action/struggle increases both individuals' knowledge of, and confidence to remove, barriers to gratification (Propositions 2 and 3), it also changes the manner in which they respond to deprivation and frustration. Specifically, whereas individuals functioning *as individuals* are most likely to respond by either circumventing difficult barriers, or, if this is not possible, displacing aggression and/or withdrawing and compensating, individuals functioning *as groups* are more likely to aggress directly against, and remove, such barriers to gratification.

For future reference I shall label this proposition the "Contingency Hypothesis". This is not to suggest that whether or not, and the degree to which, individuals function collectively rather than individually is the only contingency Marx considered important in explaining and predicting the various forms which responses to deprivation and frustration can take. Rather, how individuals respond clearly depends upon which options are objectively open to them. Thus, according to Marx, the more sporadic and less successful revolts of serfs and journeymen as compared to wage-labourers had a great deal to do with the fact that social mobility was much more open to the former than the latter.[60] Similarly, he implied that vagabondage, begging, and even robbery were the preferred responses of formerly independent producers who had been involuntarily cleared from the land because such responses were more available to them then than later – after Henry the Eighth and other authorities had passed anti-loafing laws and cracked down on crime – and certainly than to modern wage-labourers.[61]

This alternative "contingency" hypothesis is also an important one of Marx's. If individuals can circumvent barriers and thereby avoid having to expend a great deal of effort "banging their heads against walls" which, assuming they are recognized to begin with, are correctly perceived as close to impenetrable, then they will do so. Furthermore, having been able to circumvent barriers and obtain compensatory gratification *individually*, such individuals will be much less prone than less successful individuals to *organize* to *remove* the original barriers. Nevertheless, cross-cutting all these historically specific accounts of how various categories of producers respond to deprivation and frustration is the contingency contained in Proposition B4.

That serfs so seldom attempted to eradicate feudalism itself, at least on their own, was a result not simply of the fact that they, as individuals, had escape routes, but that they were relatively isolated from others in the same situation. The same was true for journeymen.[62] That formerly independent producers solved their problem of subsistence by pursuing largely individualistic as well as (officially) illegitimate occupations occurred not only because the latter means were more available to them than to modern wage-labourers, but because they too were relatively individualized to begin with.

This interpretation is borne out in Marx's various accounts of bourgeois society during his own time.

Crime was still explained, indeed, sometimes *defined*, as "the struggle of the *isolated individual* against the predominant relations".[63] The initial responses to wage-labour take the form of individual acts of sabotage rather than direct revolt, not because revolt is in principle unavailable to individuals (although *successful* revolt clearly is), but because, being so unorganized initially, individual workers are unlikely to either see capitalist relations of production themselves as the major barrier, or to believe they are powerful enough to take on and remove them. The latter come with workers' organization, especially as a class, and it is at that point that Marx described workers' responses as changing from individualistic acts of aggression or withdrawal to collective revolt.[64]

This should not be taken to mean that Marx believed there is some magic point at which workers suddenly organize and remain organized, such that their typical responses to deprivation and frustration subsequently become collective revolt instead of individualistic aggression and withdrawal. To the contrary, workers often function relatively individually, either because they or those who have preceded them at a particular workplace have never organized themselves very independently of their employers, or because their organization has been broken down by competition.[65]

As we saw in Chapter 1, it is this very fragmentation or, as Marx himself often labelled it, "atomization", which explains the fact that their social relations of production and state are objectively beyond the control of the majority of members of bourgeois society. As we have just observed in this chapter, this same atomization is most responsible for both individuals' ignorance of the nature and role of their social relations and their belief that they and their society as a whole are beyond their control.

Here the pivotal role of Proposition B4, the "Contingency Hypothesis", becomes evident. The logic behind Marx's optimism about proletarian revolution is very heavily a logic of inter-*group* rather than inter-individual relations. To the extent that workers do in fact organize themselves well as a class, there are socio- and psycho-logical processes –

most, but not quite all, of which we have already examined – which propel them to successfully revolt. *However*, to the extent that workers are not well-organized to begin with, *by Marx's own psychologic* they are more likely to respond to the privations and provocations which would otherwise propel them toward revolution individually rather than collectively. As others have also noted, very large amounts of "alienation" probably *hinder* revolution more than they facilitate it.[66]

(C) HOW INTERGROUP RELATIONS IN PART OBVIATE THE EFFECTS OF THE INTERESTS, IGNORANCE AND INTENTIONS OF INDIVIDUALS

As may be recalled from Chapter 1, in the present work I have assumed that adequate explanations for almost all phenomena, whether individual or collective, must include conditions from *both* levels of analysis. The stress here upon analyses at the level of individuals is in no way intended to imply that those at the collective are unimportant, or even less important than the former. Rather, in emphasizing the individual level of analysis I have attempted to redress the imbalance in other interpretations of Marx's theorizing. In the rest of this chapter I shall qualify the earlier material still further by suggesting that Marx often assumed anything but a one-to-one relationship between the psyches of individual members and the interests and activities of groups. Instead, he appears to have argued that the greater the extent to which individuals have organized themselves as a "group-for-itself", the less the subsequent nature of their group and intergroup relations will depend upon the nature of their own interests, beliefs, and intentions, whether taken singly or aggregatively.[67]

As I see it, Marx employed at least three sets of socio-/psycho-logical processes to explain discrepancies between the actions of groups and the interests, knowledge, and intentions of their individual members. The most obvious one has to do with leadership, but there are several others. Thus in the process of struggling against their employers workers are supposed to develop highly "cohesive" groups where long-term solidarity takes precedence over their individual, short-term interests. Furthermore, beyond pressures to maintain the integrity of the group/class as such, concerted action is greatly aided by the development of political programs (and, presumably, unique ideologies) which, among other things, allow members to adjudicate conflicts of interest within the group and live with compromises which often satisfy no one completely.

Let us take up each of these explanations in some detail. As usual, I begin by formulating them as propositions in which I attempt to make their more psychological aspects explicit.

(1) *Inter*group struggle increases identification with, and loyalty to, one's "ingroup"; and consciousness of, "negative identification" with, and hostility toward, the "outgroup". It therefore also indirectly enhances *intra*group cohesion and organization.

Most of the evidence that Marx had some such proposition in mind is indirect, in that it relates inter- and intra-group organization without specifying that increasing ingroup and decreasing outgroup identification and loyalty are among the important processes linking them. Some of this evidence is contained in material touched upon in the discussion of previous aspects of Marx's conception of intergroup relations. One thinks especially of such claims as that "Now and then the workers are victorious, but only for a time. The *real* fruit of their battles lies, not in the immediate result, but in the ever-expanding union of the workers."[68]

The best indications of Marx's employment of increasing identification and loyalty can be found in two passages in *The Poverty of Philosophy*.

In one, quoted earlier in this chapter with regard to a different proposition, Marx wrote that "As the bourgeoisie develops, there develops in its bosom a proletariat, a modern proletariat; there develops a struggle between the proletarian class and the bourgeois class, a struggle which, before being felt, perceived, appreciated, understood, avowed and proclaimed aloud by both sides, expresses itself, to start with, merely in partial and momentary conflicts, in subversive acts" (p. 175). I take this to mean that sharp "cognitive differentiation" between, and positive and negative identification with, the in- and out-group, respectively, are among the important consequences of class struggle which further its development.

In another part of the same passage Marx described this phenomenon, already referred to above (Chapter 3): "If the first aim of resistance was merely the maintenance of wages, combinations, at first isolated, constitute themselves in groups as the capitalists in their turn unite for the purpose of repression, and in the face of always united capital, *the maintenance of the association becomes more necessary to them than that of wages.* This is so true that English economists are amazed to see the workers sacrifice a good part of their wages in favour of associations, which, in the eyes of these economists, are established solely in favour of wages" (p. 211; my emphasis). I take this to mean that after struggling together workers come to identify themselves with each other to such an extent that they put the long-term interests of their group or class ahead of their short-term, narrower interests as individuals.

Just how important Marx regarded these phenomena of increasing identification and loyalty can be seen in the following sentences in this passage: "In this struggle – a veritable civil war – all the elements necessary for a coming battle unite and develop. Once it has reached this point [presumably, where workers put the interests of their class over their short-term interests as individuals], association takes on a political character". Exactly why the latter, political aspects of organization are so important is the subject of the next proposition.

(2) The development of political programs and parties greatly increases the cohesiveness of groups, and in fact is *necessary* for the concerted, and, in the long-run, successful, action of *classes*.

In the passage in the *Poverty* from which we have been quoting Marx referred to the bourgeoisie as having developed in two stages, "that in which it constituted itself as a class under the regime of feudalism and absolute monarchy, and that in which, already constituted as a class, it overthrew feudalism and monarchy to make society into a bourgeois society".

The former stage "began by partial combinations against the feudal lords". Marx did not say whether these particular combinations were explicitly political, but when he proceeded to discuss the second stage the existence, and necessity, of such combinations is clear. Specifically, the only way the bourgeoisie could abolish feudalism was to coalesce with other estates, and the only way they could do *that* was develop a political program calling for the abolition of *all* estates (pp. 211–12). Even after they had largely broken the rule of the aristocracy, the bourgeoisie or at least a large and influential portion of them – discovered that the further development of their organization of production was hampered by competing interests within the class. Perhaps most importantly, certain sectors of the bourgeoisie were against specifically industrial development. The bourgeoisie as a whole also found itself in struggles against the bourgeoisies of other nations.[69]

These problems led to two further developments, both of which were political.

First, the bourgeoisie reconstituted the "executive of the Modern state" as "a committee for managing the common affairs of the whole bourgeoisie".[70] Although Marx and Engels themselves did not explicitly say so here, one presumes that they were referring more to the "relatively autonomous" than narrowly "instrumental" functions of the state. Thus rather than simply bend to the pressure of one or another sector of the class, state officials adjudicate interests – within the bourgeoisie itself as well as between it and other classes – in the long-term interests of the class as a whole, and plan for the future in terms of infrastructure for industry and legitimating bourgeois rule.[71]

Second, it reconstituted its own political parties in such a way as to make them more appealing to the other new classes which emerged with them and with which they still required alliances, in some cases against remnants of the aristocracy, or even certain conservative sectors of the bourgeoisie itself, but especially for its struggles against the bourgeoisies of other nations.[72]

When they wrote that "Each step in the development of the bourgeoisie was accompanied by a corresponding political advance of that class.", this is presumably what Marx and Engels were referring to; that is, at every stage of its development as a *class* (for-itself) the bourgeoisie was plagued by conflicts of interest, both internally and between other classes with which it had to coalesce; conflicts of interest which could only be overcome *politically*. Furthermore, since each of these conflicts of interest tended to be different, they required somewhat different political solutions.

Marx's use of the development of the bourgeoisie as a model for the development of the proletariat was explicit. The very *emergence* of the proletariat as a *class* as opposed to merely small, local and/or sectoral groups is described co-terminously with its specifically *political* organization: "Economic conditions had first transformed the mass of the people of the country into workers. The domination of capital has created for this mass a common situation, common interests. This mass is thus already a class as against capital, *but not yet for itself*. In the struggle, of which we have pointed out only a few phases, this mass becomes united, and constitutes itself as a class for itself. The interests it defends *become* class interests. But the struggle of class against class *is a political* struggle."[73] Marx not only reiterated many of these very words in a later writing, but, in an earlier one, provided the interpretation stressed here. "[F]or proletarians – " he wrote, "*owing to the frequent opposition of interests among them* arising out of the division of labour – no other 'agreement' is possible than a political one directed against the whole present system."[74]

Just as dealing with competing interests is a major function of the state and the bourgeoisie's political parties, so it is of the proletariat's communist parties. The latter are portrayed as having "no interests separate and apart from those of the proletariat *as a whole*", no "sectarian principles of their own". "[T]hey always and everywhere represent the interests of the movement as a whole."[75]

The above discussion of political parties leads us rather naturally to the question of leadership, since the aforementioned political processes may presuppose it. One can imagine political parties and programs coming about through the initiative of a "rank-and-file" who come to recognize their importance in limiting competition among themselves. However, if there is a *great* amount of competition it is difficult to see how common, *class* action could occur without *someone(s)* initiating steps in this direction, and this is surely one of the defining features of leadership.

On the other hand, there are many types and degrees of "leadership". When, as we saw earlier, Marx suggested that urban workers in large factories tend to "lead" more ruralized workers in small industries into the class struggle, he used the term more in the sense of providing an example than actually exhorting them to do so. Indeed, note how he went on to suggest that the "led" may well do the leading when it comes to actually revolting. Leading in the sense of a vanguard party or other elite planning and carrying out its own program through propaganda and agitation is quite another matter, qualitatively and quantitatively.

Did Marx himself see such elites as playing an important role, and if so, how important did he perceive this role to be relative to the initiative of the rank-and-file? I have not been able to find an answer to this question with which I am completely satisfied. This being the case, I have chosen to begin by playing "devil's advocate" for the affirmative position that Marx believed leadership to be very important indeed. On the other hand, after doing so I then want to heavily qualify such an interpretation.

(3) Rank-and-file members of a group can be, and often are, led (and *mis*-led) far (and "deep") in some directions in spite of interests, beliefs, and intentions of their own which would otherwise have taken them in quite another direction.

Much of what Marx preached and practised about leadership leads us toward this proposition.

The *Manifesto* portrays "The Communists" as "on the one hand, practically, the most advanced and resolute section of the working-class parties of every country, *that section which pushes forward all others*; on the other hand, theoretically, they have over the great mass of the proletariat the advantage of clearly understanding the line of march, the conditions, and the ultimate general results of the prole-tarian movement" (p. 49; my emphasis). Furthermore, it is well-known that Marx and Engels were worried enough about the effects of Bakunin and his followers taking over the First International that they actually moved its headquarters to New York City![76]

Marx's analyses of specific movements with which he was not so directly associated do not consistently give leadership anywhere near as much attention as his own programs and practices would suggest, as we shall see in a moment. Nevertheless, there is no question but that *some* do. The *Brumaire* is an obvious case in point.[77] My problem with ending the matter here is that Marx's account of these struggles while they were still in progress, *The Class Struggles in France*, gives no such great weight to leadership. True, the masses of workers who under-took various collective actions had leaders, and many of the latter (Blanqui, Raspail, Deflotte, etc.) were drawn from the revolutionary communist party and its sympathizers. Yet these leaders are described as individually "heading up" large masses of workers as, for example, they marched on the Hotel de Ville, rather than leading the entire struggle *as a party* (pp. 54, 88).

At this point in Marx's analyses the doctrinaire Utopians are portrayed as having vigorously attempted to lead and divert the working class from its revolutionary path, but as having had very little success, individually or as entire parties. They had more effect upon peasants (p. 97), but the latter too are said to have been inspired much more by their own immediate, collective experiences of voting to have their interests represented in the Provisional Government but then failing, and of repression, and the *example* of the proletariat as a whole (pp. 122–5).

One hesitates to make much of this first analysis of the class struggles in France, since it is easy to think of plausible reasons for the de-emphasis upon leadership besides Marx's belief in its unimportance relative to other processes. One might argue, for example, that Marx simply did not have as much information about these events while they were in progress as when they had ended. One also wonders whether strategic considerations might not have made Marx reticent about acknowledging the role of leaders while the working class seemed to be on the verge of success.

On the other hand, if these alternative interpretations were true one might well expect Marx to have "gotten his act together" and given leadership its due in his account of the Paris Commune in *The Civil War in France*. After all, as with the *Brumaire*, this account was *ex post facto*: Marx had information about the ending as well as the course of the struggles, and he did not have to worry about his identifying leaders and assessing their leadership compromising their position. Yet here we find Marx not only referring infrequently to the necessary role of leaders, but positively emphasizing the initiative of the masses, in controlling and dispensing with poor leaders as well as in acting collectively against their class enemies.[78]

Leadership definitely figured into Marx's analysis. For instance, had the ruling class under Thiers not cut off communication between Paris and the countryside, the Parisian Communards would allegedly have become the "intellectual leaders" of the peasantry (p. 297). Furthermore, the Communards themselves thought enough of Blanqui as a leader to offer the Archbishop of Paris and any number of priests in exchange for his release, and Thiers is said to have refused the offer because "He knew that with Blanqui he would give to the Commune a head . . ." (p. 308). Nevertheless, one is left with an impression that these leaders reflected the highest development of the class as a whole more than that they actually directed it. For instance, "armed working men" and the Central Committee are written of as if they were interchangeable (p. 285). Either way, the former are characterized as exercising at least as much control over their leaders as vice versa, including deposing them when they were inept or opportunist (p. 299).

These latter considerations lead me to think that Marx might have qualified Proposition 3 in the following manner:

(4) When rank-and-file members have organized and developed themselves well as a group-for-itself, they can struggle successfully against an opposing group without requiring very much in the way of leadership from elite individuals or parties. Alternatively, even when rank-and-file members are not especially prepared and knowledgeable, great gains can be made through the influence of effective leaders.

Were one to presume this to in fact have been Marx's own position, one might again question this form of "multiplicative" logic.

A successful revolution surely requires *both* a highly developed rank-and-file *and* good leadership. Neither can in fact substitute for the near absence of the other. One might also regard Marx's analyses as rather unfair to revolutionary leaders. To wit, in those where the working class appeared to be making great gains, almost all the credit was given to the rank-and-file, whereas in those where the movement as a whole failed to result in revolution, leaders were usually shouldered with most of the blame![79]

At a minimum, I think it fair to conclude that Marx did not pay enough attention to problems of leadership, not only to the organizational dimensions later taken up by Lenin, Gramsci and others, but to the socio-/psycho-logical problems of how and which leaders emerge, how they exercise influence, and how and why they are retained, or dispensed with, by the rank-and-file. On the other hand, of course, in light of the crude state of social psychological knowledge during Marx's time, this may not be so fair a judgment after all.

NOTES

1. This is also why Marx believed the proletarian has no choice but to make the revolution. See the *German Ideology*, pp. 46–9, 55, 86–7.
2. Ibid., pp. 45–6, 64.
3. Ibid., p. 44.
4. *Poverty of Philosophy*, p. 211.
5. *Manifesto*, pp. 492–3.
6. *Ideology*, pp. 76–7.
7. Ibid. See also the *Class Struggles in France*, pp. 118–19.
8. E.g., see the *Ideology*, p. 61. The interpretation of Marx on ideology employed here is closer to Bhikha Parekh's (*Marx's Theory of Ideology* (London: Croom Helm, 1982)) and Joe McCarney's (*The Real World of Ideology* (Sussex/N.J.: Harvester/Humanities Press, 1980)) than to Althusser's ("Ideology . . . ," op. cit.). On one hand, in using both the criteria of partiality and apology – of ideology as an evaluative weapon for the promotion of group/class interests – it is much more specific than Althusser's. On the other, unlike Althusser, I restrict ideology to the structure and content of beliefs and ideas rather than all "material" practices. While it is true that Marx himself sometimes claimed that the former closely reflect the latter (e.g., *Preface*), if one simply collapses material practices and ideas it is difficult to formulate and test hypotheses about what is partial and/or apologetic and what is not.
9. See Note 18, Chapter 6.
10. *Ideology*, p. 34.

160   *Marx and the Missing Link: "Human Nature"*

11. Ibid., p. 77.
12. *Poverty of Philosophy*, pp. 210–11; *Manifesto*, pp. 492–3.
13. See especially the latter passage.
14. *Ideology*, pp. 75, 77, 83, 86; *Poverty*, pp. 195, 210–11; *Wages*, pp. 423–4; *Manifesto*, pp. 490–6; *Wage Labour and Capital*, pp. 225–6; *Grundrisse*, pp. 157, 161, 239–50; *Capital 1*, pp. 96, 519–20.
15. *Manifesto*, pp. 487, 491; *Wage Labour and Capital*, p. 226; *Capital 1*, pp. 330–1; *On the Irish Question*, pp. 293–4. Marx claimed there was even competition between mothers and their own children (*Capital 1*, p. 375).
16. *Ideology*, p. 75; *Manifesto*, p. 493.
17. *On the Irish Question*, pp. 293–4; *Inaugural Address to the First International*, in McLellan, op. cit., pp. 534–7.
18. *Ideology*, p. 60.
19. Ibid., pp. 49, 52; *Manifesto*, p. 494; *Grundrisse*, p. 510.
20. *Ideology*, pp.52, 78–9, 87–8; *Poverty*, p. 212; *Manifesto*, p.495.
21. Thus several of Marx's critics have argued, and claimed to have demonstrated, that technology and the increasing productivity of labour allow for workers' real income to rise, whether the rate of surplus value or exploitation remains constant or also rises. See George Lichtheim, *Marxism: An historical and critical study* (London: Routledge and Kegan Paul, 1961) pp. 187–90, and Geoffrey Kay, *The Economic Theory of The Working Class* (London: Macmillan, 1979) pp. 44–53, 72–8. Indeed, Lichtheim argues that if the rate of surplus value remains constant, as Marx himself often assumed, real wages *must* rise.
22. Indeed, Marx himself often made derogatory references to these traditions, even when they are revolutionary ones. For example, see the *Brumaire*, pp. 103–6, and *The Civil War*, p. 299.
23. However, whether the Soviet Union and other such socialist societies can be accurately and fruitfully regarded as "state capitalist" is another matter. For one critique of this conception, see Hillel Ticktin's "The contradictions of Soviet society and Professor Bettleheim" *Critique*, 1976, No. 6 (Spring), pp. 17–44.
24. Letters to Engels, 6 April, 1863; Kugelmann, 29 November, 1869; Meyer and Vogt, 9 April, 1870. In McLellan, pp. 585, 590–2.
25. *Ideology*, pp. 74–5.
26. Ibid.
27. *Class Struggles in France*, p. 134.
28. *Ideology*, p. 75.
29. *Manifesto*, p. 493.
30. *Ideology*, p. 78.
31. Lukács, op. cit., p. 13.
32. *Manuscripts*, p. 313.
33. *Holy Family*, p. 52.
34. *Brumaire*, p. 128.
35. On this point, see McCarney, op. cit., pp. 111–26, 138–9.
36. Plamenatz, op. cit., p. 178. On the other hand, there is some evidence that individuals who have coercive power over others (for example, fathers in families) have less insight into those they rule than the latter have into the ruler (for example, see Darwin Thomas, David Franks and

Janet Colonico, "Role-taking and power in social psychology" *American Sociological Review*, vol. 37 (October 1972), pp. 605–14.
37. *Grundrisse*, p. 597.
38. *Manifesto*, pp. 485, 487, 491–2; *Class Struggles*, pp. 122–3, 127–8; *Civil War*, p. 295.
39. *Ideology*, p. 79.
40. Indeed, one wonders whether Marx's own references to the "lumpenproletariat" as "scum" and the like might not have had something to do with his own impoverished, but not quite so impoverished, living conditions. See, for example, the *Manifesto*, p. 494; *Class Struggles*, p. 62.
41. *Poverty*, p. 170.
42. *Ideology*, p. 79; *Grundrisse*, p. 463.
43. Barrington Moore is a case in point. See his *Injustice: The Social Bases of Obedience and Revolt* (White Plains, N.Y.: Sharpe, 1978).
44. Allen Wood argues this point forcefully in his "The Marxian critique of justice" pp. 3–41 in Marshall Cohen, Thomas Nagel and Thomas Scanlon (eds), *Marx, Justice and History* (Princeton University Press, 1980) pp. 21–2.
45. *Capital 1*, pp. 314–15.
46. See Chapter 9, below.
47. *Manifesto*, pp. 495–6.
48. *Poverty*, p. 175.
49. James H. Davis has reviewed this literature in *Group Performance* (Reading, Mass.: Addison-Wesley, 1969) Chapter 3.
50. *Class Struggles*, p.131.
51. Ibid., pp. 47, 54–9, 66–7.
52. *Holy Family*, pp. 37, 52–3.
53. *Ideology*, p. 362; *Manifesto*, p. 492.
54. On the effects of anonymity and "diffusion of responsibility" see, for example, Leon Festinger, A. Pepitone and T. M. Newcomb, "Some consequences of deindividuation in a group" (*Journal of Abnormal and Social Psychology*, vol. 47 (1952) pp. 382–9.), and Bibb Latané and John Darley, *The Unresponsive Bystander: Why Doesn't He Help?* (New York: Appleton-Century-Crofts, 1970).
55. O. H. Mowrer, *Learning Theory and Behavior* (New York: Wiley, 1960). Although Martin Seligman does not use the term, parts of his analysis of *Helplessness* (San Francisco: W. H. Freeman, 1975. E.g., pp. 37–40.) appear to rely upon this process.
56. *Manifesto*, p. 493.
57. See Chapter 9, below.
58. *Inaugural Address*, in McLellan, op. cit., p. 535. The first part of this quote is McLellan quoting Marx.
59. *Ideology*, pp. 65–6, 79.
60. Ibid., pp. 68–9.
61. Ibid., pp. 65–6.
62. Ibid., p. 330; my emphasis.
63. *Manifesto*, p. 492.
64. *Ideology*, p. 77; *Manifesto*, p. 493. The later statement reads "This organization of the proletarians into a class, and consequently into

a political party, is *continually* being upset again by the competition between the workers themselves" (my emphasis).

65. Psychic alienation, that is. On this point see the references to C. Wright Mills and Melvin Seeman in my "Psychic alienation in Marx . . . ," op. cit.

66. However, having said this, I want to dissociate the present interpretation from most others, such as Lukács', which have tended to be unduly holist and anti-psychological. Interestingly enough, Lukács himself later discounted some such aspects of his early work as a naive attempt to "out-Hegel Hegel" (op. cit., p. xxiii).

67. *Manifesto*, p. 493; my emphasis.

68. Ibid.

69. Ibid., p. 486.

70. See David Gold, Clarence Lo and Erik Olin Wright, "Recent developments in Marxist theories of the capitalist state" *Monthly Review*, vol. 27 (October, November 1975) pp. 29–43; 36–51. For reviews of later developments in these debates see Robert Jessop's *The Capitalist State: Marxist Theories and Methods* (Oxford: Martin Robertson, 1982) and Martin Carnoy's *The State and Political Theory* (Princeton: Princeton University Press, 1984).

71. *Manifesto*, p. 493.

72. *Poverty*, p. 211; *Manifesto*, pp. 490, 495.

73. *Poverty*, p. 211; my emphasis.

74. *Ideology*, pp. 371–2; my emphases.

75. *Manifesto*, p. 497; emphases mine.

76. E.g., see Marx's Letter to Bolte, 23 November 1871 (in McLellan, op. cit. pp. 587–9). For a secondary account, see Henry Collins and Chimen Abramsky, *Karl Marx and the British Labour Movement* (London: Macmillan, 1965) Chapter 13, and pp. 298–300.

77. Op. cit., pp. 110–11, 130–4, 146, 184–8.

78. Op. cit., pp. 291–2, 306–10.

79. According to some "worker intellectual" friends of mine, Marx was only accurately reflecting long-standing working class traditions; that is, the norm is for working leaders themselves not to take credit for successful campaigns they have led, but only blame for the unsuccessful ones. However, other such friends take a much more critical view of union leaders and argue that the reverse is the case. I am not in a position to pronounce one or the other as more correct. On the other hand, one need only read newspapers and watch television to observe many cases of the latter, self-serving practice. To my mind, our own "working class hero", Bob White, the head of the Canadian Autoworkers Union, partially illustrates the point, in that a documentary of an historic struggle between the union, General Motors, and the previously international United Autoworkers Union, and White's recently published autobiography, give the impression that much more of the credit for the CAW's many successes should go to Bob White personally than to the militancy of rank-and-file autoworkers. Indeed, if we are to believe White, it has mainly been his firm control over the latter which has permitted these victories.

Part IV

Evaluating Marx's Theories of Human Nature "Empirically"

Introduction

There are many ways to evaluate a theory. One can look for ambiguous or incomplete explanations, and those which are inconsistent or contradictory, and/or one can examine underlying assumptions and specific explanations and predictions and try to establish whether or not they are supported by evidence oneself and others can "see", or, perhaps, at least agree *seems* to be "there". I have already attempted to do the former while presenting Marx's various theories of human nature. Here we take up the latter.

Presumably, reasonably complete "tests" and positive "proofs" of Marx's theories of human nature should include the following:

(1) proof that the *modes of production* Marx postulated have both existed and centred around the characteristics he claimed to be most important;
(2) that they have "*dominated*" entire societies and historical epochs;
(3) that "*individuals*" in particular modes of production, societies, and historical epochs have been characterized by the lack or presence of individuation and free and historic agency;
(4) that the characteristics of individuals specified in (3) covary with those of the modes of production in (1);
(5) that such characteristics of individuals can be better explained by the features of modes of production than by other aspects of a society's environment or culture; and
(6) that the psychic processes Marx assumed are common to *all* individuals in *all* modes of production, societies, and historical epochs are *in fact* that common.

However, it is a tall order for one individual to uncover and present all such information, even from secondary sources, since it requires that s/he be an anthropologist and ancient and modern historian as well as an economist, sociologist, and psychologist. For these reasons I have had to lower my aspirations considerably and concentrate upon some criteria more than others. Specifically, I have asked whether, *given* the existence of certain modes of production with certain forces and relations of production, one can use Marx's theories to explain the relative absence or presence of individuality and autonomy, and free and historic agency; and whether, comparing individuals *across all* modes of production, the psychic processes Marx assumed are common turn out to be so. Nevertheless, we must still consider whether we can in fact take Marx's modes of production as "given" and "dominant". Parenthetically, although Marx was a "dialectician" and not simply a "logical positivist", he would have regarded it legitimate to perform such "tests". Indeed, the methodology we have seen Marx prescribe for constructing theories of human nature seems to *demand* some such procedure.[1]

THE VALIDITY AND DOMINANCE OF MODES OF PRODUCTION

According to many critics, Marxist and otherwise, there has never *been* an "Asiatic mode of production", and certainly not one (a) with all of the characteristics Marx assigned to it – that is, large-scale irrigation, with it and land communally owned and administered, and production carried out primarily by peasants who are neither slaves nor serfs and who pay tribute to representatives of the community as a whole, in good part in exchange for these representatives' public works – and (b) which applies, or ever applied, to all "Asian" or "oriental" and none, or only a few, non-Asian societies.[2] Logically, these critics argue, Marx of all people should not have postulated the existence of societies with centralized states, but no classes, based upon private ownership of land and other means of production, and self-sufficient villagers who were nevertheless heavily dependent upon centralized state authorities. Empirically, furthermore, it can be shown that Asian societies, the original civilizations included, have not lacked rainfall and good soil, private ownership of land and technology, and local initiative for irrigation and a host of other industrial and commercial pursuits by such private owners. They have had slave and feudal, in addition to, if not always instead of, tributary or "pre-bendal" relations of production.[3]

These criticisms are all well-taken, as are others which suggest that Marx was unable or unwilling to rise above the racism and European chauvinism of those upon whom he primarily relied for his theorizing about Asian societies; that is, such representatives of English imperialism as Maine, and German nationalism as Hegel. Calls for rejecting the "Asiatic" mode of production altogether are therefore far from frivolous. I do not believe that we can or should let Marx "off the hook" for these various prejudices, but neither am I alone in being reticent about doing so. Instead I shall assume that for all his faults, Marx was "onto something" important with his "Asiatic" mode of production. My reasoning is as follows.

First, while Asian peoples and others whom Marx recognized as having established the first civilizations – that is, the Egyptians and other peoples of the Middle East, and the Aztecs and Incas of the Americas – were in dire need of neither water nor local, private enterprise, they both had available to them, and made good use of through irrigation, good sources of water. As we would expect from Marx's own theorizing more generally, it was probably precisely these favourable environments and technological advances which permitted the production of the surpluses, wealthy non-productive classes, centralized states, and marvellous arts and sciences which we associate with these early civilizations.

Second, while there was no lack of private property classes in these early civilizations, it is nevertheless true that the *largest* and most *politically powerful* "owners" – or legally, more likely administrators – tended to be first monarchs and then the high priests of temples (in size, that is – historically priests usually came first). Given that this was the case, and that large owners who were legally private had usually been courtiers or military officers who had initially received their land as grants from monarchs, such private owners tended to either be heavily dependent upon state officials and/or unable to successfully compete with, and expand their own enterprises relative to, state enterprises.[4] Therefore, whereas Marx was logically inconsistent and empirically naive not to have recognized the existence of private property classes in the early Asian civilizations, and full-fledged feudalism in India from at least the Mughal period, he was far from completely off-base in arguing for the importance of legally communal property and centralized state administration.

In fact, Marx's account of early "Asian" societies in the *Grundrisse* may provide the basis for a reasonable explanation for this apparent exception to his general theory of the state; that is, the existence of state ownership and control which dwarfs, initiates, and controls private enterprise. Interestingly enough, Marx's account of how "oriental despots" may have emerged and become seen as the legitimate representatives of the community as a whole (or better, how single individuals rather than the entire community or a single clan became identified as such representatives and then became despots) is not unlike those of such contemporary archaeologists as Gordon Childe (a self-proclaimed Marxist) and Robert McC. Adams (who does not so identify himself).[5]

Thirdly and finally, with regard to the AMP, while it may seem contradictory for Marx to have maintained that early Asian villages were both self-sufficient and heavily dependent upon state authorities for the initiation and administration of public works, the facts are far from totally inconsistent with the modified characterization suggested here. Thus on one hand villagers manufactured goods for urban and "international" markets far more than Marx claimed, but because they usually had to obtain their raw materials, transportation, and traders through state enterprises they were indeed highly dependent upon state officials. On the other, although those who were peasants were more self-sufficient, they too were often highly controlled by state officials bent upon maintaining high quantities and qualities of tribute. Thus peasants were often required to obtain their seeds from the royal granary, not to leave their villages during planting and harvest, and to pay tribute in amounts as high as 20 or 30 per cent of their products.[6] Yet precisely to lessen the likelihood of rebellion, this control was often exercised through village rather than city officials. For the same reason, conquerors routinely left Asian communities with their own religions.[7]

Marx regarded the forms of property which allegedly predominated in classical antiquity and the Germanic tribes of that time to have evolved out of the Asiatic form,[8] but again the facts do not warrant such a simple conclusion. One might make a case for classical antiquity, in that (a) before they were apparently destroyed by barbarian invaders, the Cretan and Mycenaean civilizations seem to have been on a course little different from those of the Indus Valley and elsewhere in Asia, and (b) there is evidence for cultural diffusion from the latter to the former.[9] However, this was clearly *not* the case for Germanic peoples. That their traditional, "barbarian" ways of life were modified after they were first colonized by the Romans and then themselves invaded and conquered Rome is beyond doubt,[10] but to argue, as Marx did, that before these developments they had more private ownership is pure fantasy. To the best of our knowledge, before colonization the separate family units about which Marx wrote possessed their own flocks and herds, but there was *no* private, individual ownership of arable land and pasture; rather, arable land was usually "owned" by the local clan as a whole and reallocated to different families every year, and there were at most only slight differences in wealth among the latter.[11]

Marx was probably correct in assigning less *communal* property to the early Germanic than Asian and Mediterranean peoples, but he was clearly wrong to imply that more of it had been whittled away by private owners. The actual sources of the difference presumably lie elsewhere: in the fact that the Germanic tribes were much more primitive, and not more developed, than the Asians and Mediterraneans; and that as such, because property of *any* kind was probably less developed there,[12] and therefore also *both* classes based upon *private* property *and* centralized *states*.

As to why Marx was so off-base with his "Germanic" "mode of production" (note that he said very little about production in his accounts; and still less suggesting either distinct technologies or relations of production) we can only speculate. Interestingly enough, the sources most used by contemporary scholars – the observations of Tacitus and Caesar – were also available to Marx. Given that this is the case, one suspects that Marx violated his own professed methods of systematic, comparative historical research, and instead relied too heavily upon *Hegel's* account of individuation and agency in *The Philosophy of History*, where Asians are unfairly derogated and Germans are chauvinistically seen as a people chosen by history to make history.

Few scholars have questioned Marx's assumption that early classical antiquity was characterized by relatively self-sufficient, landowning, farming families. However, the nature and dominance of the subsequent modes of production of which Marx wrote are matters of considerable contention. According to some researchers, slavery was less a separate mode of production which characterized particular societies and historical epochs than a cultural practice which has existed in most areas of the world in most historical epochs; has resulted mostly from conquest, and whose motivating force has been to confer status upon slave-owners rather than to procure labour-power. Nor, so the argument goes, has slavery *ever* amounted to a "dominant mode of production", since there has never been a society in which even a majority of producers have been slaves.[13] Parallel arguments have been made with regard to feudalism: if slaves are at least politically and legally tied to particular owners, serfs have seldom if ever been tied to the land rather than the latter, nor have *they* ever constituted a majority of producers.[14]

However, in these cases Marx has been defended by prominent non-Marxists as well as Marxists. Thus Moses Finley has argued that slavery should be regarded as having been dominant in all of ancient Greece and Rome, the Caribbean, Brazil, and the antebellum southern United States, not because the majority of producers were slaves, but because there were ruling classes in those societies who ruled because they exploited slave labour, and because most of the rest of those societies were "coloured" by the existence of the slave mode of production.[15] In effect, Marc Bloch took a similar position with regard to feudalism in medieval Europe. Marx was probably erroneous in taking the Roman coloni, who *were* legally tied to the land, as his model for serfs more generally, but in countries such as France, whose feudalism was among the purest and most dominant in Europe, serfs did eventually become bound to the soil rather than the lord *per se*.[16]

Although Marx does not appear to have regarded the guild-system as ever having been dominant in the original, statistical sense mentioned above, he has encountered no less opposition from subsequent scholars. Thus far from having been restricted to medieval Europe, guilds were frequent and strong in the Far East, even in ancient times.[17] Contrary to Marx's characterization of them as self-governing bodies of craftsmen, guilds both came to prominence primarily as associations among merchants and dissipated as, true, associations among craftsmen as well as merchants, but usually those heavily dependent upon, and controlled by, the latter.[18] This is not to say that there were not societies and periods where guildsmen were relatively self-governing, but even where these conditions were met, the internal workings of the guilds were seldom as egalitarian and meritocratic as Marx insinuated, since it is doubtful that many individual guildsmen got to make their own tools or achieve master status simply by producing a "master" or "proof" piece.[19]

On the surface, there may seem to be more agreement on the validity of Marx's rendition of the capitalist mode, but here too it is far from complete.

As for its early stages, it does not appear, as Marx contended, that manufacturing was a necessary step between the "putting out" and factory systems. Rather, putting out or "cottaging" often entailed a division of labour even before the appearance of middlemen; and manufacturing first developed, and often remained, as an adjunct to putting out. In fact, the factory system often developed more or less directly from the latter.[20] Parallel problems attend Marx's accounts of mechanization, in that, for example, even by the time of the revolutions of 1848, most participants were still skilled artisans who were at most employed in small factories which were only partially, if at all, mechanized.[21] Indeed, heavy industry was little evident in most industries, even in England, until well into the 20th century, and the initial effect of mechanization was sometimes the creation of as many or more new occupations and skills as it destroyed.[22]

If there is little question that most of the conditions Marx wrote of eventually came to dominate bourgeois society, they have remained far from unitary and unchanging. Perhaps most obviously, a large sector of the economy still consists of small, and often relatively technologically-primitive, private enterprises, and the severe market conditions he expected have often applied only to them and not to the other major enterprises which have developed since his own day; that is, both large private oligopolies and public monopolies.[23] Automation has become extremely important, as Marx brilliantly foresaw, but not universally so, and since its introduction there have been still further complications.

The emergence of other kinds of production besides that of heavy industry employing "blue collar", "manual" labour has led to a relative percentage drop in the latter, but I do not see how we can take seriously claims for "*post*-industrialization", or even "*de*-industrialization"[24], since what appears to be occurring most is not a net loss of industry from the point of view of capitalism as a global system, but a relocating of industry ("*re*-industrialization"?) from high to low wage areas of the world, or even single nations. However, there is a contradictory, if still subsidiary, trend toward "re-cottagization"; that is, the "contracting out", by large public as well as private enterprises, of work formerly done by their own employees to small, competitive industries, or, in the case of both clerical and accounting work (performed on personal computers) and handwork (such as sewing), even to single individuals.[25]

If capitalism no longer looks quite the same as it did to Marx, "communism" might well be unrecognizable. Of course for him legally communal ownership of industry was only a first step, or rather, a *second* step. To wit, it would occur only after workers themselves had taken it and the state over, and run them collectively. "State communism" is surely a contradiction in terms, but given the absence, or non-dominance, of the market in most professedly socialist countries, so, presumably, is "state capitalism".[26] In fairness to those who have sincerely attempted to establish Marx's vision of communism, the conditions under which such attempts have hitherto been made have almost never been those Marx claimed are necessary; that is, (a) in highly developed capitalist economies, where (b) industrial workers have constituted the vast majority of the population, and (c) made their revolutions more or less by and for themselves in many countries more or less simultaneously, so that the proletariats of single nations would not be forced into "war communism".

These circumstances place those who would evaluate Marx's theories of human nature in a quandary. On the one hand, it seems unfair to Marx to test his predictions about individuation and agency and the reformation of human nature more generally under conditions which he himself thought would subvert such developments. On the other, *not* to examine human nature in "actually existing socialism" is to lay the analyst open to the charge that s/he is not prepared to consider the possibility that Marx's theories are Utopian to begin with, and/or criticize "communist" regimes which have deliberately limited individuation and agency. I have chosen the first option here, but I hope that given my efforts to be critical of Marx's theories as they apply to other modes of production, I will not be judged too harshly on the second count. I admire those Marxists who have been brave and honest enough to pursue the second option,[27] and I would like to have had the time, space, and expertise to have contributed to that task here.

MISSING MODES, ACTIVITIES AND RELATIONS, AND INDIVIDUALS

We have just seen how some of Marx's "modes of production" (for example, the Germanic) are of dubious status, both as distinct modes of *production* and as "dominant" at particular stages of evolutionary development (thus if it existed, the Germanic mode surely preceded rather than succeeded the Asiatic). Here we must face a more serious problem: Marx's total omission of the hunting and gathering or "foraging" mode of production; a mode which, as Richard Lee has noted, "was not only the original mode of production, but . . . a way of life that characterized the first 80 or 95 per cent of the total life of the human species".[28]

This omission can probably be attributed to three sources. The first was Marx's less-than-critical-enough use of *Hegel's* models of individuation and agency. In this case, Hegel had explicitly excluded African peoples, many of whom were foragers at the time, for racist reasons; that is, according to him they not only had not civilized themselves, which was untrue, but *could* and *would* not.[29] The second is related to the first: Hegel's neat conceptual model portrayed individuals as going from a complete lack of individuation and historic agency to the complete development of both, and for some reason Marx appears to have wanted to retain this neatness. Perhaps for the latter reason, Marx simply collapsed foraging peoples into the same, individual-less and agentless category as Asiatics.[30] But there is a third potential source which is less damaging to Marx's self-concept as a rigorous and unbiased scientist: as with most others of this time, Marx was very ignorant of "tribal" peoples when he wrote the *Ideology* and the *Grundrisse*, which contain his theories of individuation and agency; his interest and knowledge having been increased only in the 1870s, after he had read Morgan and other anthropologists.[31] Whatever the reason, we shall see that this omission is serious indeed, since when one examines foraging peoples closely one discovers that one cannot in fact simply extend Marx's model "back" to them. Rather, one must revise the model fairly drastically.

There are at least two other important criticisms of this nature. One is that Marx made a fetish of labour and the production of material goods to the detriment of other activities and relations – such as sex and kinship, communication and language, power and political domination, ethics and religion – which may be equally, or even more, general to human nature and its historical modification.[32] The other is that he ignored the *specific* role of *women*, both in material production and in social relations outside it. At best, these critics argue, he treated women simply as if they were not "there" in material production – or no different from men – and "women's" activities and relationships outside it as unimportant for the development of individuation and agency. At worst, Marx is supposed to have regarded the latter as *natural* and women as "second-class", in effect, *animal* members of the human species.[33]

My own inclination is to recognize these as valid criticisms of Marx's methodology, but to give him the benefit of the doubt theoretically and treat the competing claims as empirical questions which could well be, but have not yet decisively been, answered in favour of Marx's critics.

Such a stance seems particularly valid for the first set of criticisms, on at least two grounds. One, it is not clear that these particular critics have interpreted Marx correctly in the first place. Specifically, whereas there is no question that he assumed material production heavily dominates *bourgeois* society, his point seems to have been that in all previous societies, including the next one back (the feudal), religious and/or political considerations usually held the economic in check.[34] Furthermore, in his thinking the economy is no longer to play anywhere near so important a role in communist society as it has in bourgeois society.[35] We shall eventually see that Marx tended to forget these, his very own, arguments, and to underestimate the importance of religion and politics *per se* in societies with pre-capitalist modes of production. We shall also see that the lives of many primitive peoples have been far less dominated by material production than Marx and other Victorians assumed. Nevertheless, and this is my second argument, it does not follow that material production has therefore been any *less* important for understanding human nature and human society than sex, communication, or religion. This is a matter for empirical research rather than *a priori* pronouncements on either side.

I would make a parallel, but weaker, provisional defence of Marx against feminist criticisms. Clearly, he did ignore women or assimilate them to his own, male-biased categories, but it is far from obvious that his conceptions of human nature will *necessarily* turn out to be irretrievably patriarchal. True, through "their own activities" as well as those "of men", women have probably played a much greater role in history than Marx assumed, but his assumption that, through their domination of material production, men are much more likely to have been free and historic agents may have been *true* until recently.[36] Furthermore, while certain of his models of human nature in general, such as that of frustration and aggression, might not apply to women, this too is far from obvious. (Were one to attack their children, one would probably learn otherwise.) Similarly, while nurturing and other propensities which have usually been associated much more with the female of the species are admittedly less in evidence than others in Marx's theory of needs and wants, the *need* to gratify *others'* needs is not only *there*, but at the top of the need hierarchy and the pinnacle of hu-"manity" (see Chapter 4).

What I am suggesting is not that we defend Marx's productivism and sexism, but that we follow his prescribed methods for inferring what is and is not common to human nature, and that to follow such a procedure means not privileging Marx's critics' presumptions any more than his own. In keeping with this proposal, I have made an attempt to check his claims against evidence about activities and relationships other than those of material production, and of those of women as well as men. Unfortunately, however, evidence for the latter is often either missing or unknown to me. This is an important challenge for future research.

IDENTIFYING INDIVIDUATION, AGENCY AND HUMAN NATURE IN GENERAL

Limitations of time, space, and knowledge – and my own impatient character – have precluded my establishing rigorous indicators of these features of individuals and undertaking primary research to see whether or not they can be "seen" first-hand. Instead, I have usually left definitions and indicators to my own and the reader's intuition and freely reinterpreted the work of others. However, in the long run more rigour and original reasearch is probably necessary.

The most obvious problem for any such research is that there is precious little direct information about the nature of individuals in previous societies and epochs, although, ironically, given the work of contemporary anthropologists we actually know much more about "tribal" peoples than we do about those of ancient Asia and the Mediterranean, and even Medieval Europe. Both the paucity of first-hand accounts of the character of individuals in various societies and epochs and Marx's own characterization of religion and philosophy as ideology have led me to concentrate more upon the objective circumstances individuals are likely to have faced and to extrapolate from such circumstances what individuals were *probably* like. Nevertheless, there is undoubtedly much more information available, "objective" as well as "subjective", secondary as well as primary, than that I have used here.

For instance, on the more or less objective side, it would be interesting to examine the languages of ancient societies. For example, that in Medieval English the word "individual" was apparently only an adjective referring to entire communities rather than biologically separate "individuals" presumably indicates that there was not much individuation in such communities,[37] and one wonders what one would find in Egyptian hieroglyphics or Sanskrit.[38] Similarly, particularly since I shall argue shortly that Marx appears to have underestimated the importance of religion and philosophy, I probably should have examined the different systems of them much more thoroughly than I have here. Finally, although we have no autobiographies of peasants or slaves in ancient or medieval times, we do have some for slaves in the antebellum South and wage labourers in Victorian England,[39] and it would be worth examining them for indications of subjectively experienced individuation, agency, and various, allegedly universal, human propensities.

As for identifying the latter, I have also employed rather liberal criteria. In most cases, for past societies I have taken as evidence for the occurrence of certain psychic processes observations from secondary accounts which would seem to follow *if* one were to *assume* the existence of such processes. In a few I have merely taken respected historians' use of such concepts as relative deprivation, frustration, or a tolerance limit for the latter as an indication of the apparent usefulness of such concepts. By itself, of course, the second criterion is extremely dangerous. Usually, however, even where I have not been able to combine it with the first, more independent procedure, I have eventually been able to compare such claims with the more direct, and often experimental, tests of such general processes by contemporary social psychologists.

NOTES

1. For a defence of this position, see my "Using Marx's theory of alienation empirically" (op. cit.), and Chapter 1 above (especially the material with regard to Notes 32 and 33).
2. For Marx's versions of the AMP which stress the centrality of irrigation, see particularly "The British in India" *New York Daily Tribune*, June 25th, 1853, pp. 83–9 in Shlomo Avineri (ed.), *Karl Marx on Colonialism and Modernization* (Garden City, N.Y.: Doubleday, 1968) pp. 85–6. However, in the version I have relied most upon here – that in the *Grundrisse* – he did not emphasize it as much. There he claimed only that "aqueducts" are "very important among the Asiatic peoples," and by the first volume of *Capital* "the regulation of the water supply" was only "[o]ne of the material bases of the power of the state over the small disconnected producing organisms in India" (pp. 481–2, fn.; emphasis mine). Similarly, while Marx probably did believe his AMP was common to almost all early Asian societies, he also believed it characterized some ancient slavic peoples and the Aztecs and Incas of the Americas, although in the case of the latter two he claimed that their AMP was imposed through external conquest rather than internal evolution (*Grundrisse*, p. 490). The latter qualification is apparently wrong. Here see Robert McC. Adams' *The Evolution of Urban Society: Early Mesopotamia and Prehispanic Mexico* (Chicago: Aldine/Atherton, 1966) p. 21.
3. For these various criticisms of Marx's AMP, see Daniel Thorner, "Marx on India and the Asiatic mode of production" (*Contributions to Indian Sociology*, vol. 9 (December 1966), pp. 33–66); S. Naqvi, "Marx on pre-British Indian society and economy" (*Indian Economic and Social History Review*, vol. 9 (March 1972) pp. 380–412); Perry Anderson, *Lineages of the Absolutist State* (London: New Left Books (Verso), 1979); Bryan Turner, *Marx and the End of Orientalism* (London: Allen and Unwin, 1978); and Kate Currie, "The Asiatic mode of production: Problems of conceptualizing state and economy" (*Dialectical Anthropology*, vol. 8 (April 1984), pp. 251–68). Thanks to Bhula Bhadra for pointing me towards most of this literature. For a comprehensive critique of Marx's treatment of the AMP vis-à-vis India, see her PhD

dissertation at McMaster University. For some primary research indicating local, private initiative for irrigation, see Robert McC. Adams' *Land Behind Baghdad* (Chicago: University of Chicago Press, 1965) and Nirmal Sengupta's "The indigenous irrigation organization in South Bihar" (*Indian Economic and Social History Review*, vol. 17 (April–June 1980), pp. 157–89); for the presence of multiple modes of production in ancient Asian societies, see M. Rostovtzeff's *The Social and Economic History of the Hellenistic World* (Oxford: Clarendon, 1967. vol. 1) and Kwangchih Chang's *The Archaeology of Ancient China* (New Haven: Yale University Press, 1974).

4. Rostovtzeff, op. cit.; Adams, 1966, op. cit., pp. 48–51, 125–6.
5. V. Gordon Childe, *What Happened in History* (Harmondsworth: Penguin, 1982) pp. 100–10, 135–7, 169–70; *Social Evolution* (New York: Meridian, 1963) pp. 140–5, 160); Adams, 1966, op. cit., pp. 45, 63–76, 90–4.
6. Rostovtzeff, op. cit., pp. 276–98, 308.
7. Ibid., pp. 291, 300, 329, 435–7, 443; D. D. Kosambi, *Ancient India* (New York: Pantheon, 1965) pp. 50–1; Lawrence Krader (*The Asiatic Mode of Production* (Assen: Van Gorcum, 1972) p. 172 claims that Marx himself was ambivalent on the whole question of interference.
8. *Grundrisse*, p. 497; *Capital 1*, p. 82 (fn.).
9. See Childe, 1982, op. cit., pp. 172–9; 1963, op. cit., pp. 126, 160–7; Moses Finley, *Early Greece* (New York: Norton, 1970) pp. 38–43, 54–6; *Economy and Society in Ancient Greece* (Harmondsworth: Penguin, 1983) p. 211.
10. E. A. Thompson, *The Early Germans* (Oxford: Clarendon, 1965) pp. 60–3, 71–2, 92.
11. Ibid., pp. 3–9.
12. The form of property does not appear to go from nearly complete communal to nearly complete private, as Marx implied, but from not much property at all, besides weak individual ownership of tools, weapons, clothing and shelter, to communal ownership of land and other natural resources, to more private. There is a passage in the *Grundrisse* (pp. 490–1) where Marx could be construed to have conceded this, in that he referred to both hunting and pastoral peoples as relating to their hunting and grazing lands "as their property, *although they never stabilize this property*" (my emphasis). However, even here, Marx claimed, these peoples regard their proprietorship to be stable enough to make war on intruders. In fairness to Marx, this issue is still disputed by contemporary anthropologists. For example, see Eleanor Leacock and Richard Lee (eds), *Politics and History in Band Societies* (Cambridge: Cambridge University Press, 1982), pp. 8–9, 85–108, 466, and 475–6 versus pp. 180, 191.
13. See especially Orlando Patterson, "Slavery", *Annual Review of Sociology*, vol. 3, 1977, pp. 407–49; *Slavery and Social Death: A comparative study* (Cambridge: Harvard University Press, 1982).
14. Marc Bloch, *French Rural Society* (Berkeley: U. of California Press, 1966) pp. 66–7, 90; *Feudal Society* (Chicago: U. of Chicago Press, 1961) pp. 176–80.

15. *The Ancient Economy* (London: Chatto and Windus, 1973) pp. 71–3, 79; *Ancient Slavery and Modern Ideology* (Harmondsworth: Penguin, 1980) p. 9.
16. Bloch, 1966, op. cit., pp. 86, 104–5; 1961, op. cit., pp. 257–64, 279.
17. Rostovtzeff, op. cit. Jeannine Auboyer, *Daily Life in Ancient India* (London: Weidenfeld and Nicolson, 1965) pp. 102–6. George Unwin, *The Gilds and Companies of London* (London: Cass, 1963). Anthony Black, *Guilds and Civil Society in European Political Thought from the Twelfth Century to the Present* (London: Methuen, 1984) pp. 3–7.
18. Henri Pirenne, *Early Democracies in the Low Countries* (New York; Harper and Row, 1963) pp. 128–9; *Economic and Social History of Medieval Europe* (London: Routledge and Kegan Paul, 1936) pp. 184–5, 200–4. George Unwin, *Industrial Organization in the Sixteenth and Seventeenth Centuries* (London: Cass, 1957) pp. 15–19.
19. Pirenne, 1963, op. cit., pp. 88, 165, 210–11; Unwin, 1957, op. cit., pp. 47–8; 1963, op. cit., pp. 91–2.
20. Paul Mantoux, *The Industrial Revolution in the Eighteenth Century* (New York: Harper and Row, 1961) pp. 89–90, 250, 365–7, 476. Maurice Dobb, *Studies in the Development of Capitalism* (New York: International Publishers, 1963) pp. 143–4. Fernand Braudel, *The Wheels of Commerce*, vol. 2 of *Civilization and Capitalism, 15th-18th Century* (New York: Harper and Row, 1982) pp. 298–303, 372–3, 404. Raphael Samuel, "Workshop of the world: steam power and hand technology in mid-Victorian England", *History Workshop Journal*, vol. 3 (Spring 1977), pp. 6–72.
21. Harold Perkin, *The Origins of Modern English Society, 1780–1980* (London: Routledge and Kegan Paul, 1969) p. 179. William H. Sewell, *Work and Revolution in France* (Cambridge: Cambridge University Press, 1980) pp. 143, 266.
22. Samuel, op. cit.
23. The classic statement on these changes by Marxists is Paul Baran and Paul Sweezy's *Monopoly Capitalism* (New York: Monthly Review Press, 1968).
24. For the former characterization, see Alain Touraine's *The Post-Industrial Society* (New York: Random House, 1971) and Daniel Bell's *The Coming of Post-Industrial Society* (New York: Basic Books, 1973); for the latter, Robert Laxer (ed.), *[Canada] Ltd* (Toronto: McClelland and Stewart, 1973) and Barry Bluestone and Bennett Harrison, *The Deindustrialization of America* (New York: Basic Books, 1982).
25. Laura C. Johnson, *The Seam Allowance: Industrial home sewing in Canada* (Toronto: Women's Press, 1982). Heather Menzies, *Women and the Chip* (Montreal: Institute for Research on Public Policy, 1984).
26. Hillel Ticktin, "Socialism, the market and the state", *Critique*, vol. 3 (Autumn 1974), pp. 65–72.
27. E.g., Michael Burawoy, *The Politics of Production* (London: New Left Books (Verso), 1985).
28. *The !Kung San: Men, women and work in a foraging society* (Cambridge: Cambridge University Press, 1979) p. 437.
29. *The Philosophy of History* (New York: Colonial Press, 1899) pp. 91–9.

30. *Grundrisse*, p. 84.
31. Here, see especially Lawrence Krader (ed.), *The Ethnographical Note-books of Karl Marx* (Assen: Van Gorcum, 1972).
32. Some of the better-known critiques of Marx's "productivism" are Jurgen Habermas's *Knowledge and Human Interests* (Boston: Beacon, 1971. Chapters 2 and 3), Jean Baudrillard's *The Mirror of Production* (St. Louis: Telos Press, 1975), and Marshall Sahlins' *Culture and Practical Reason* (Chicago: University of Chicago Press, 1979).
33. See the excellent review in Allison M. Jaggar's *Feminist Politics and Human Nature* (Sussex/Totowa, N.J.: Harvester/Rowan and Allanheid, 1983).
34. E.g., see the material in Chapter 2 referenced by Note 8, and the *Grundrisse*, p. 485.
35. E.g., see the material in Chapter 2 referenced by Note 61.
36. Jaggar herself notes this possibility (op. cit., p. 134).
37. The observation is Raymond Williams'. It is cited in Dawe, op. cit., p. 376.
38. And speaking of languages, I read French and German, but for reasons of convenience I have rarely used sources in them here. Clearly, this is not defensible as a collective and long-term research strategy.
39. Some of the research I draw upon does use the former. For the latter, see David Vincent's *Bread, Knowledge and Freedom* (London: Methuen, 1981).

8 Individuation and Agency Revisited

EXCURSUS ON "TRIBAL" SOCIETIES: THE MISSING STARTING POINT

Although few if any of Marx's theories were constructed on the basis of systematic observation of "tribal" societies,[1] I am impressed by how well they fit many of the facts about them. In particular, the more sophisticated a people's technology, and, presumably, therefore also the greater the surplus available to them, the more and more differentiated their "culture", material and otherwise, and the more likely they are to have private ownership of land and other means of production; *both* commodity exchange *and* slavery, feudalism, or other coercive forms of labour; centralized political and legal decision-making dominated by a small minority of the community, such as male elders and/or property owners; repressive laws and punishments for transgressing them; and centralized, institutionalized religions with full-time priests.[2]

These facts have important implications for individuation and agency, in that, presumably, the more developed their technology and surplus (a) the more division of labour, craftsmanship, and "culture" the individual members of a community have available to them to develop themselves, both *within* subsistence labour itself, and in their capacity to *avoid* strenuous and time-consuming manual subsistence labour in the first place. However, the more technology and surplus (b) the greater will be the proportion of individuals who are *denied much access* to the potential advantages outlined in (a), and to the other spheres of activity, such as more and more complex political, legal, and religious decision-making; where those who do participate in them supposedly do get opportunities and develop themselves, and to act as agents for the community, themselves, and/or their rank or class. In fact, because of (b), (c) *constraints against* individuation and agency should be greater for the majority of producers, the more technology and surplus are available to the community as a whole.

Now, how much individuation and agency one would expect to find among foragers, people with the most primitive of technologies, will depend upon just how few and low the facilitating circumstances they face are, and how many and high the constraining. Since he assumed foragers to be little more than "herd animals", to have levels of individuation and agency very near those of the majority in the early Asian civilizations (that is, near zero), Marx must have presumed they were favoured with very few and low facilitating circumstances, and encumbered with many and severe constraining circumstances. Certainly, his earlier-quoted proposition that "The less social power the medium of exchange possesses . . . the greater must be the power of the community which binds the community together" (see Chapter 2) implies that he believed the latter to be the case. Furthermore, when combined with his propositions about the role of technology and surplus, it points to a decidedly productivist thrust in his thinking. To wit, while a complex division of labour and exchange are far from the only important bases for social cohesion, they are more or less automatic consequences of technological innovation and surplus production, and once all four processes have emerged they necessarily come to undermine, and greatly overshadow, if not altogether replace, earlier forms of cohesion based on religion, politics, and, although Marx himself did not say so, perhaps also informal "public opinion". However, Marx has now been taken to task for both his presumptions and his productivist premises.

Thus for the most part, the subsistence technologies of foragers are not only well-adapted to particular environments – after all, as noted earlier, they have permitted such peoples to survive for tens of thousands of years – but also permit a great deal more leisure than Marx would ever have thought possible. Time studies indicate that the "work week" for many, and perhaps a majority, of foragers is as short as twelve hours. Such peoples do not appear to be especially anxious about obtaining enough nourishment, and spend most of the rest of their time doing such things as socializing, or simply sleeping.

To be fair to Marx, this alleged revolution in our knowledge about primitive peoples – the so-called "original affluent society" hypothesis[3] – has probably gone too far, in that there are large differences among foraging peoples in the length and onerousness of their subsistence activities, depending, as we have already seen Marx himself suggests, upon the natural abundance or scarcity of their respective environments. Proponents of the OAS hypothesis themselves concede that there are exceptions in the other direction, and a close perusal of the ethnographic data indicates that these exceptions are in fact many, and that they extend well beyond the Eskimo of the Arctic to not only many of the Indian tribes of the sub-Arctic, but to those in the

American southwest and South America.[4] Furthermore, the very distinction between "work" and "leisure" appears to be fairly historically specific, if not necessarily bourgeois, and therefore rather questionable. Certainly, most hunters and gatherers do not even have words for "work" and "leisure" as we conceive them, and some considerable amount of the time the OASers classify as "leisure" is in fact spent consulting others – or spirits – on how best to hunt or gather, and/or in attempting to influence the outcome of a hunt or move by performing magic.[5]

On the other hand, there is no getting away from the fact that Marx exaggerated the length and onerousness of the subsistence labour of foragers. Furthermore, although he was anything but wrong in assuming that they had little surplus production at their disposal, he appears to have been incorrect in assuming that the explanation for this lies mainly in the primitive nature of their technology. Interestingly enough, one of the major alternative explanations for the lack of a surplus among foragers – a low level of wants and aspirations[6] – is one of which Marx himself was well aware and might have himself marshalled for this purpose. However, here he appears to have preferred the more narrowly technological over the social psychological. Similarly, his characterization of "tribal" societies as "primitively communist" *might* have led him to another alternative explanation for the absence of a surplus in foraging societies – the cultural requirement that most things be shared with others.[7] Again, however, it did not.

There are also problems in applying Marx's account of the effects of the division of labour and exchange upon individuation and agency to "tribal" societies.

Marx was correct that among most foragers, most labour is divided *within* the family rather than *between* families. As a consequence such families tend to be self-sufficient. However, it by no means follows that the individual members of such families have little opportunity to develop much individual skill and initiative. To the contrary, the often rigid division of subsistence labour between the sexes means that each is heavily dependent upon the specialized skills of the other, with the consequence that each family member must usually be highly skilled in his or her respective tasks. Certainly, ethnographers report substantial individual differences in knowledge and skill among hunters and gatherers,[8] and their child-training practices tend to stress self-reliance over obedience, while among peoples with somewhat more technologically advanced modes of production the emphasis is reversed.[9]

Another interesting and important observation about such societies is the presence of more, and more individualistic forms of exchange practices than Marx was aware of. As Marx would have predicted, the absence of much division of labour beyond the family does not lead to a great deal of individualized exchange, especially of a narrowly self-interested nature. Nevertheless, one often *does* find forms which, while also often ritualized, are still fairly individualized and inter-*personal*. The "song-cousin" relationship among Eskimos is a good case in point, and others can be found among hunters and gatherers on other continents.[10]

Alternatively, if we now consider *constraints against* individuation and agency, we find far fewer and weaker such constraints among foragers than Marx postulated for early Asian societies with irrigated agriculture. Thus as we have already noted, families, and sometimes even their individual members, tend to be relatively self-sufficient economically, and even when they are not, labour sharing tends to be cooperative and voluntary. "Political" as well as "economic" decision-making (in fact, neither is clearly demarcated, from the other or from other spheres of activity) tends to be highly democratic. Leaders of the hunt or fishing expedition achieve their position because of their skill and other personal qualities, and their status in one sphere seldom generalizes to others. "Political" decisions, such as to break camp, are usually made by all adult members of the nomadic band, including women. The "legal" systems of such societies also tend to be informal and interpersonal. One initially finds only 'self-redress" and "advisor" means of resolving differences. Elders' councils and adjudication by chiefs only predominate later, in "ranked" societies where there is a more developed technology and some surplus.[11]

Now, it would clearly be wrong to paint foragers as completely egalitarian and free.

In the first place, there is usually a fairly rigid division of subsistence labour by age, and especially sex. On the other hand, there tends to be equality within age and sex categories, and the work of women is both crucial and tends to be regarded as such, as indicated by the fact that most conflict among foragers tends to revolve around women and sexual relations. Just as women tend not to be excluded from decision-making in general, although there are exceptions,[12] so they are not prevented from becoming shamans. (In general, religion among foragers tends to be very informal and individualistic.[13]) Similarly, foragers tend to be permissive about pre-marital sex, individual choice of a marriage partner, and divorce, with economic transactions at marriage and severe restrictions upon pre- and extra-marital sex generally coming only with further technological and social evolution.[14]

Secondly, there seems little question that informal "public opinion" in small nomadic bands where everyone knows everyone else and there is little "privacy" can often stifle individuality and autonomy. On the other hand, since there are few formal means for enforcing cultural norms in these societies, including serious ones such as incest, they are seldom rigidly and successfully enforced.[15]

My point here is not to counter the "herd animal" conception of primitive peoples with that of the "noble savage". To go on from the relative egalitarianism and self-reliance of foragers to refer to them as "individualistic" peoples, as some cultural anthropologists are wont to do,[16] is to go much too far. Most hunters and gatherers not only appear to be more communal than individualistic in the "independent", "self-interested" and "selfish" senses of the term,[17] but to be so for many of the reasons claimed by Marx. Furthermore, to suggest that there tends to be much more individuation and a freer agency in "band" societies with foraging technologies than Marx's own account would lead us to expect is by no means to suggest that there is a great deal of individuation and agency relative to Marx's standards of perfection. Primitive peoples cannot legitimately be said to lack creativity in either their subsistence labour, their art, or their "culture" more generally. Nor do they lack individuality, either "objectively", or necessarily even in their knowledge of themselves as individuals.[18] On the other hand, given that he viewed the degree of individuation in Classical Antiquity to have been severely limited, as we saw earlier, Marx would probably have belittled the accomplishments of foragers still more, and were we to accept the particular standards he appears to have been using in that comparison – although it is by no means obvious that we should – it would be difficult to disagree with him.

This is particularly true for his criterion of *historic* agency. Marx took it as axiomatic that the members of a collectivity must consciously modify nature to some considerable extent before they can even begin to "make history", and this assumption is still popular among anthropologists, whether or not they have Marxist leanings.[19]

If one looks at such indirect evidence as the nature of a society's beliefs about nature and history one might well conclude in favour of Marx's claims. Thus the religious beliefs of hunters and gatherers tend to be not just fairly individualistic and personal, but animistic: the many spirits who govern the universe and must be appeased are regarded as various inorganic or organic parts of nature itself (the sun, the bear, etc.). Alternatively, belief in a Supreme Creator, especially in human form, tends to be much more frequent among agriculturalists. There are also interesting differences in the nature of the games played by the two categories of peoples. Specifically, whereas the vast majority of hunters and gatherers play games of *chance*, a large majority of even simple horticulturalists instead play games involving *strategy*.[20]

On the other hand, if we look at contemporary foraging-band societies it is not difficult to find examples of far-reaching social changes and equally consequential refusals to change, with many seemingly being both conscious and voluntary, and, incidentally, relatively non-productivist. For instance, the Mbuti "pigmies" Turnbull studied were well aware of their neighbours' agricultural technology, but appeared to have consciously rejected it because they observed that it required much more, and more onerous, labour. They opted instead for symbiotic trading relationships with these wealthier, but far less leisurely, neighbours.[21] An "historic" as well as "rational" decision, shouldn't one say?

If we can agree that the original condition of human nature was *not* in fact a complete *lack* of individuality and freedom, but some combination of community on the one hand and a not inconsiderable degree of individuality and freedom on the other, let us proceed to the *later* "communal" modes.

The next one to consider, of course, is *not* the Asiatic, with its irrigated agriculture, but the *Germanic*, since before Roman colonization the Germanic peoples were organized as tribes or clans and were not anywhere near so technologically developed. Many tribes did grow root crops, vegetables, and grains, and some used ploughs and fertilizers as well as crop rotation. However, there was only a very limited use of iron and a crude, home-made pottery, and most tribes were primarily pastoralists who still relied heavily upon hunting and gathering.[22] We noted earlier that there was no private, individual ownership of arable land and pasture, and presumably the division of labour and commodity exchange were similarly relatively undeveloped.

Leadership of subsistence and military activities was usually informal; that is, based only upon personal qualities. Different activities tended to be led by different individuals. There were no central chiefs, each tribe tending to have several, relatively equal, chiefs who were also *elected*. Reallocation of land and settlement of disputes were apparently conducted by the leading men of each tribe. They had little if any coercive power. With few exceptions, the central councils about which Marx wrote were called only in the case of war.[23] Even after Roman intervention had led to larger differences in wealth, leading men in peacetime as well as war, and permanent chiefs, local councils of warriors had more power than the councils of leading men, and chiefs could be overruled by the local councils of leading men. Indeed, they could be deposed, and even expelled or executed. The "rank-and-file" members of a village probably did not propose policy changes, but they too could apparently vote chiefs down, and most decisions were probably more or less unanimous. This "tribal" democracy extended even to the battlefield, in that battles were often led by several chiefs rather than a single commander, and even there their influence was much more through example and advice than coercion.[24] This relatively anarchistic form of military decision-making probably had much to do with the eventual colonization of these peoples.

Again, as with still more primitive "tribal" societies, community control of the individual was probably extensive. We know, for example, that there were "crimes against the community" which were punishable by death. These appear to have included treachery, cowardice, desertion, and even homosexuality. However, providing he stayed within these boundaries, "no free warrior could be bound, whipped or beaten by his fellows".[25] Women may well have been much more heavily constrained, but if so it would have been in keeping with other societies at analogous stages of socio-technical development.

If we extrapolate in this manner from the circumstances they typically faced, we might well conclude, with Marx, that the early Gemanic peoples were more individuated and freer agents than the early Asians. On the other hand, were we to do so we would have to disagree fundamentally with his reasoning. To wit, such fortune must have been a function of a much *lesser* degree of evolutionary development. But what *of* early "Asians"?

THE LATER "COMMUNAL" MODES: THE "ASIATIC" AND THE MEDITERRANEAN

Clearly, the existence of *multiple* modes of production in the early Asian civilizations – not just the AMP as described in the Introduction to Part IV, but both directly church- and state-administered and large-scale, private agricultural, manufacturing, and trading enterprises employing guild or wage labour in addition to, or instead of, slave, serf, or tenant labour – has profound implications for Marx's claims regarding individuation and agency, in that true "slaves of the community", whether real or only figurative, must have been relatively few. The enabling conditions for the individuation and agency of many small, quasi-independent producers as well as large-scale private owners must have been considerably greater than Marx maintained, while the constraints against them were probably also fewer. We do know that the economic and other activities of large private owners were much less closely controlled and taxed than were those of others; whether these others were directly supervised by church or state authorities or nominally independent and forced to pay tribute.

Given these very different circumstances from those posited by Marx, we should expect much more individuation and agency, certainly in absolute terms, although, for the reasons discussed above, perhaps less than in the early Germanic people. Is this the case? Obviously, more direct evidence for individuation and agency among early Asian producers is extremely difficult to come by. If we start further up the social scale we do find a successive emergence of paramount rulers as "tenant-farmers of the god", "kings", and divine individuals with highly inflated egos,[26] and this progression (?) does seem to indicate individuation and a change from representative to free agency. Furthermore, large private owners often appear to have been fairly enterprising. In fact, although there are no extensive records about class conflict for ancient times, those we have indicate that even small producers aspired to be more independent and grated under the expropriation of tribute. Thus they often petitioned authorities in great numbers, and even left their traditional plots of land and villages *en masse*.[27]

One can also make a case that most Western observers of the Orient, and especially those upon whom Marx relied, have misunderstood Eastern religions and other ideological aspects of the social structure. For example, the major Hindu values include hard work, the accumulation of private property, and individual pleasure, as well as duty to the gods and their earthly representatives.[28] If the same cannot be said of Buddhism, its prescriptions at least freed its adherents from responsibilities to gods and ancestors and fostered *self*-contemplation and control.[29] Confucians retained their identity as individuals despite their unity with nature, and the initial conception of *human* nature as passive ("yin") eventually gave way to a conception of it as greedy, selfish, and capable of influencing non-human nature (in effect, "yang", at least in being active, if not always positively so).[30] In practice if not always in theory, the Zoroastrian and Muslim religions of the Near East have often been still more aggressively individualistic.[31]

Nevertheless, it is difficult to avoid concluding that individualism has in fact taken much more of a back seat to communalism in the Orient than in the West for most of history as we know it. Certainly, the familialistic and individualistic values of Hinduism have been subordinant to the communal and authoritarian; the only legitimate resolution of conflict between the two having been to renounce real-world activities altogether and pursue a course of passive contemplation.[32] While Buddhism and Confucianism have had more room for outright criticism of caste-systems and other aspects of the social structure, they too have idealized transcendence of active, worldly individuality through inner contemplation.[33] For all the fierce independence of nomadic peoples in Middle Eastern history, despotic centralized authorities have often been able to legitimate their rule by following Muslim religious principles to the letter.[34]

Many observers of contemporary India claim that individuals are *still* treated not *as such* but as inseparable elements of hierarchically-structured social relations. Thus an individual is not regarded as a "person" until he or she has married. If s/he dies before s/he has done so s/he is considered to have been incomplete as a person. (Even now, some women kill themselves upon the death of their husband.) The individual is said to seldom act autonomously; that is, without thinking of his or her familial and wider communal duties, and often others do not hold the individual *personally* responsible for his or her own actions.[35] (Conversely, if a woman "fails" to marry or becomes divorced, her sisters are also stigmatized.[36])

All this is not meant to suggest that the individual is *never* regarded as a unique being. Thus the soul or ego is still treated as somewhat separate from one's "person", which is in effect a social role.[37] Yet this "inner self" is often just that: something one is more likely to passively retreat to than overtly act upon in one's relationships with others.

If the latter claims are at all accurate Marx's treatment remains highly problematic, in that it does him little good to have been correct in his assessment of the relative degree of individuation and agency in (at least some) "Oriental" as compared to Western societies if the conditions he used to *explain* these differences had either never existed, existed only in a diluted form, or long since disappeared. A leading contender of Marx's own account, of course, would be explanations, such as Max Weber's, which rely heavily upon the peculiar religious and status institutions of Eastern societies such as India.[38] But as we have already seen him to have done with the "culture" of less developed peoples, Marx appears to have both misunderstood and underestimated the importance of India's caste and religious system.[39]

By the time *Mediterranean* peoples established their second round of civilizations, they may well have been more highly individuated and freer agents, as Marx claimed. After all, by then even the earlier "kinglets", as Childe called them, had been broken up, leaving only smaller, landowning farmers and warlords.[40] Of the Homeric legends, Moses Finley has written that "never before or since have gods been so much like men (apart, of course, from their inability to perish) . . . what a step it was, after all, to raise man so high that he could become the image of the gods. . . . What they [Homer and Hesiod] did, both in the action itself and in its substance, implies a human self-consciousness and self-confidence without precedent".[41]

But in *his* content analysis of the Homeric legends Joel Kovel claims to have found no "abstract terms referring to the person". "There is no generic term for *person, self, mind,* or even *body* in the *Iliad* and *Odyssey."* The word "psyche" *is* there, but at that point it refers only to "the force that keeps men alive and leaves upon death" rather than "an endogenous self" which is the seat of "motivation and action". According to Kovel, it was not until about the sixth century that "psyche" came to be used in the broader sense of a 'living self' and the lyric poets began to "write of themselves, their passions, longings and – most significantly – aloneness".[42] As Finley has noted, this is also the time at which religion became more personal and potters, painters, and sculptors first began to sign their works.[43]

Nevertheless, even then "the individuality of the archaic poets remains a relatively unalienated social product. The other is always included in the address."[44] Similarly, artistic creations generally remained within the confines of custom and fashion.[45] The concept of the more fully-developed individual with a psyche in the sense of *"the self,* or the seat of consciousness", having "the quality of activity" and "moral responsibility", had to wait for Plato.[46]

To recapitulate, although Homer's heroes may have been somewhat more individuated than their Asian counterparts (although this has yet to be substantiated), they were a long way from being fully individuated and free. Furthermore, the differences in individuation and agency between the Homeric and Platonic periods may well have been as great as those between Asian and Mediterranean civilizations in their earliest forms.

Now, these trends are perfectly consistent with Marx's own account. After all, the first difference was explicitly claimed by Marx on the basis that property ownership, the division of labour and commodity exchange were more developed in the former than the latter region, and we now know that this may well have been the case. Similarly, that there were large differences within early Mediterranean civilizations themselves would not have surprised Marx. Presumably, he would simply have claimed that such changes in individuation and agency were preceded by the further privatization of property, and so on.

On the other hand, the latter reasoning presumes a simple linear development of individuation and agency which does not appear to have occurred. At least, a good case can be, and has been, made that the Sophists and other pre-Socratic philosophers were much more "individualistic" – self-interested and cynical about and detached from, society – than Socrates and other thinkers of his generation. Thus for all his having used the aphorism "Know thy*self*" to describe his own philosophical system, Socrates urged the citizens of Athens to greatly increase their allegiance to the community.[47] Of course, whether this reflected a general trend in that direction is another matter. Conceivably, Socrates was attempting to stem a huge tide in the *opposite* direction. Whereas his philosophical forerunners' concern to protect their interests against those of society may have reflected the reticence of private landowners to abrogate their independence to the community, Socrates' own call for allegiance to the state may have reflected the fact that the latter increasingly came under attack from private interests from within as well as other states from without.[48]

The one matter which may seem glaringly missing in the present account is *historical* agency. Specifically, just as individuation and free agency appear to have been higher in the early Mediterranean than "Asian" civilizations, should one not say the same for "democracy", and with it, the possibility and actuality of historical change; that is, conscious change undertaken by and for community members at large? The answer is unquestionably yes, but here too one should be careful not to exaggerate the differences from early "Asian" societies. Thus neither the Spartans nor the Romans developed anywhere near the degree of democracy that the Athenians did; the degree of democracy in the latter was itself fairly limited;[49] and, as Marx himself pointed out, this modicum of democracy was eventually subverted by the development of slavery and large differences in property ownership.

Since we have already moved a considerable way from Marx's own accounts of individuation and agency in early societies it may make sense to pause for a moment and summarize the various qualifications which have been made. Figures 2 and 3 represent an attempt to do this.

Figure 2   *Marx's Ordering of Modes of Production, Historically, and by Individuation (In) and Agency (Ag)*

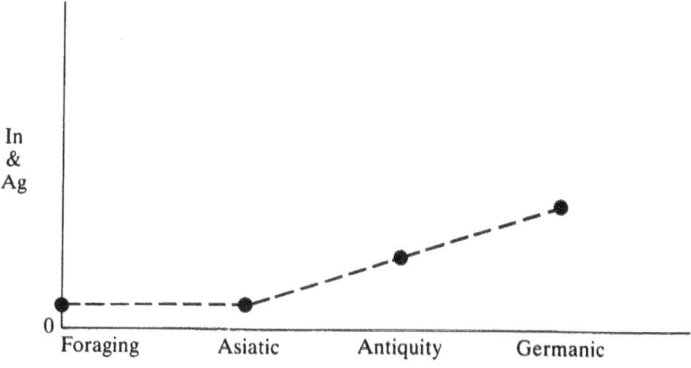

Figure 3   *Revised Ordering*

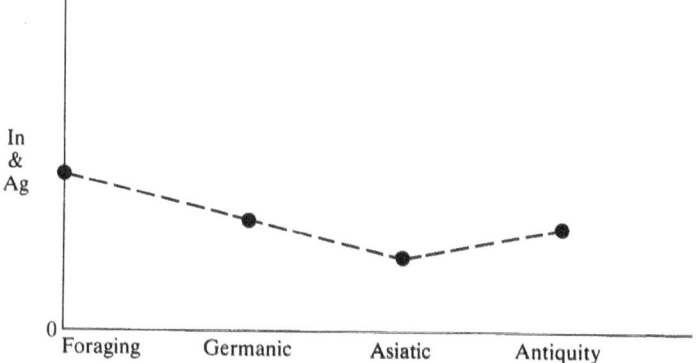

Marx's original claims are graphed in Figure 2. The qualifications graphed in Figure 3 can be summarized as follows. First, individuation and agency, far from being *less* in "tribal" than "Asiatic" societies, as Marx appears to have argued, are much *greater*. They progressively *decrease* as one proceeds from band societies with hunting and gathering or "foraging" modes of production to others with pastoral and agricultural modes. Individuation and agency probably *were* higher in early Germanic than "Asiatic" and Mediterranean societies, but only because they were at a much *earlier* stage of development. Marx should have placed them between societies with pastoral modes of production and those with settled agriculture, but neither classes nor states, rather than with "civilizations" with both.

"PERSONALIZED" AND NOT-SO-PERSONALIZED EXPLOITATION

(1) Slavery

In effect, we find many contemporary scholars implying that Marx probably also underestimated the objective individuation and agency of slaves.

Thus the vast majority of slaves in ancient Greece and Rome are said to have worked side-by-side with their small-scale, farmer-owners rather than in large work gangs with overseers, or in relatively small households.[50] In fact, many rose to positions of considerable responsibility, and even authority; slaves having not only been teachers and doctors, but policemen and magistrates.[51] Such arguments have even been made for the antebellum South, where in one, admittedly atypical, version of the thesis agricultural slaves were said to have had *contractual* relationships with their owners,[52] and in another, less extreme version, many other slaves were artisans who often did wage-labour for others besides their owners and got to keep a large proportion of their earnings for themselves.[53]

Some slaves in Classical Antiquity were actually permitted to own and alienate property, and even some of those in the antebellum South, the Caribbean, and Brazil were allowed to both have their own garden plots and sell the produce grown in them. Indeed, according to Orlando Patterson, most of the urban population of Jamaica were dependent upon the independent commodity production of slaves for fruit, vegetables, and poultry.[54] Other aspects of the legal status, *de jure* as well as *de facto*, of slave owners and their slaves are said to have moderated the de-individuating and oppressive effects of slavery. Thus legal as well as informal social constraints are alleged to have largely prevented owners from excessively dominating and exploiting their own slaves,[55] and while slaves had very few legal *rights*, they nevertheless had a number of *duties* in common with full-fledged citizens, and, like the latter, were held *personally* responsible for such crimes as theft and murder. Finally, much has been made of manumission – of slaves in the New as well as the Old World having been able to obtain their freedom legally, by actively working for others and paying off their owners rather than simply having to rely upon the benevolence of the latter.[56]

All of these circumstances having to do with property, the division of labour, commodity exchange, and political–legal control by the community, are implied to have mitigated the effects of the slave mode of production upon the person of the slave; that is, he or she was much less constrained from thinking and acting as an autonomous individual as one might imagine. However, in conceding the validity of many of these qualifications to Marx's account of slavery we must be careful not to go too far in the other direction. Nor is the danger here restricted to the extreme characterization of the master–slave relationship as contractual – a view which now appears to have been decisively refuted.[57]

Thus if the large, closely supervised work gang was not the *most* typical circumstance faced by slaves, neither was it so infrequent as to have affected an insignificant number of them.[58] Either way, there is a great deal of evidence that slaves in most circumstances, including those in one-to-one and relatively personal relationships with their owners, were usually heavily constrained.[59] Furthermore, the mobility of slaves in ancient times *within* the condition of slavery has been exaggerated, in that (a) relatively few obtained the above-mentioned occupations, (b) for the most part, they obtained them because freemen and women did not want them,[60] and (c), either way, being legally a slave usually mitigated any status one might otherwise have gained from such occupations.[61] As to the New World, only a small percentage of slaves – at most five – were artisans who could contract their labour out to non-owners,[62] and with the exception of Jamaica, those who could engage in other forms of quasi-independent commodity exchange were still fewer.

The same is true for legal rights. While Patterson may well be correct that "there has never existed a slaveholding society, ancient or modern, that did not recognize the slave as a person in law",[63] he would be wrong to make much of this fact. For one thing, the very legal status of slave owners as *property* owners greatly compromised most of the potential control of the community over them: to interfere when another slave owner mistreated his slaves was to risk having oneself interfered with and/or to give slaves in general the idea that they had rights which might legitimate revolt.[64] For another, there was clearly a double standard in both the laws and the way in which they were applied to owners and slaves.[65]

The claims for manumission must be taken more seriously. Whereas Marx would have us believe that there were few positive incentives for the slave to work hard and otherwise conform to the wishes of his or her owner, there were in fact a number of them, including, in some cases, the desire to please someone with whom one shared a relatively intimate, if paternalistic, relationship,[66] and at least in ancient times the prospect of manumission was probably very important in this regard.[67] Indeed, manumission appears to have been consciously used by the Greeks for this purpose.[68] On the other hand, it is doubtful that the majority of slaves in ancient Greece had the opportunity to become free, or even believed themselves to have had it. Nor, for that matter, did manumission usually entail attaining all the rights of citizenship.[69] Furthermore, in the New World, where supplies of new slaves were cut off at a relatively early period, manumission was less frequent and more haphazard.[70]

A second major problem – whether slaves *experienced* themselves as separate individuals and at least aspired to be free and historic agents – is more difficult to investigate.

One thing we do know about the slave societies of ancient Greece and Rome, the sometime tendency for Russian scholars to take Marx and Engels' statements in the *Manifesto* as empirically-established fact notwithstanding[71]: they were not riven by more-or-less open class conflict, let alone consciously transformed by their slaves. Although there were several large-scale rebellions, they were neither frequent nor anywhere near class-wide.[72] Nor, for that matter, do the myriad acts of sabotage reported for the antebellum South appear to have been as frequent in the earlier period.[73] On the other hand, the absence of much overt resistance and revolt is hardly good *prima facie* evidence that the slaves of antiquity did not experience themselves as separate individuals and aspire to freedom.

Among the suggestive evidence for the opposite conclusion are these additional facts. First, the Greek and Roman ruling classes not only feared their slaves, but had good reason to; that is, there were enough cases of slaves killing their masters to make such a fear realistic.[74] To the extent that ancient slaves did appear to have "slavish" *personalities*, the latter can probably be attributed more to the necessity of adapting themselves to the oppressive circumstances they encountered than to either the standpoint from which they began their careers as slaves or a developed "second nature". At a minimum, some of the sayings of ancient slaves, such as "If you don't like being a slave, you will be miserable; but you won't stop being a slave," are remarkably similar to those indicating the "coming-to-terms" process among modern wage labourers.[75]

Many of the debates about the subjectivity of slaves in the antebellum South, Caribbean, and Brazil parallel those for antiquity. Thus in opposition to the claims of such racist scholars as U. B. Phillips – who maintained that North American slavery was benign, both because owners were benevolent and slaves in effect were helpless children who needed direction – Russian-inspired social scientists like Herbert Aptdecker stressed the importance of rebellion and revolt by American slaves.[76] Then, as has been the case with ancient slavery, other scholars such as Kenneth Stampp stepped into the fray to suggest that while open class conflict and revolt were infrequent, slaves *both* accommodated themselves to slavery *and* resisted and rebelled in a great many ways when they could get away with it. Although the latter actions did not allow them to consciously transform the whole system of slavery, it did force most owners to adapt to their own slaves much more than if these acts of resistance and rebellion had not occurred.[77] What is distinctive and interesting about the latter debate is its subsequent recycling, with the original position that slaves actually had slavish *personalities* now being restated in more psychologically sophisticated, and non-racist, terms by Stanley Elkins.[78] Thus the "sambo" personality is said to indeed have been prevalent in the American South; not because of any peculiar racial characteristics of black people, but because the conditions under which slaves in the United States were obtained and controlled were unusually harsh and brutal.

Most of Elkins' many critics would agree that many, and perhaps most, slaves in the American South often felt humiliated and degraded, and that they may well have accepted their masters' views of them at various points in time. Yet few see the "sambo" syndrome as having been as common as Elkins claims it was, and even fewer would regard it as a question of enduring personality – that is, of a "second nature".[79]

Most of these criticisms are readily available in a number of compendia,[80] such that we need not detail them here. But what of *Marx's* meagre account of the subjectivity of the slave? Is there anything here which might help us determine whether or not, as Marx implied, slaves typically began by accepting their masters' view of them as passive instruments but then came to reject such a view in favour of one of themselves as active agents? If anything, the evidence indicates that the sequence was probably as much in the reverse direction. Indeed, rejection may have been greatest at the *earliest* point of the relationship between a particular master and his slave; when, for example, the newly-arrived African had recently experienced freedom and his or her aspirations for it were therefore highest. At any rate, it was these slaves who tended to be the most proud and rebellious.[81]

But perhaps we are being too hasty here, for Marx appears to have postulated that particular sequence on the assumption that slaves were relatively "individualized" to begin with, but that they eventually organized themselves collectively, if not often on a class-wide basis. However, we should probably also reject this qualifying assumption, at least in its present form, in that most slaves were probably *always* associated with a slave community with some considerable degree of solidarity.[82] Nevertheless, we do know that both the composition and solidarity of American slave communities were precarious, what with some of their members being sold or killed and others competing for the favour of the master and his family. Just as Marx was well-prepared to see the class organization of wage labourers as dissipating rather than simply increasing, so we might expect him to concede the same for slaves, had he had better information about them.

Given the latter consideration, perhaps our problem can be re-phrased as follows: did the likelihood of rebellion increase under conditions which would be likely to have fostered prior collective organization? In his comparative study of slavery, Patterson claims to have discovered that rebellion has been most likely to occur under the following circumstances: a very high ratio of slaves to owners, and of absentee to resident owners.[83] Presumably, in these circumstances there would have been both more opportunity for slaves to organize themselves and a greater objective chance of overpowering the class of owners. Furthermore, as Patterson himself suggests, the smaller the non-slave portion of a society, the less likely slaves would be to depreciate themselves to begin with; that is, one's own slavery would be explained as a calamity of the community as a whole, brought on by conquest from without, rather than an event reflecting upon one's own worth as a person.[84] This reasoning might well help explain why there were many more, and more successful, slave revolts among the helots than other slaves in ancient Greece, and in the Caribbean than in the antebellum South.[85]

(2) Feudalism

Some of the major qualifications we should make to Marx's conception have already been alluded to in the Introduction. For one thing, serfs were tied to the land rather than the person of the lord only in some societies at certain periods within the Middle Ages. This circumstance was not a very general one. For another, the majority of producers were usually "free" tenants rather than serfs. In fact, *wage-labour* existed from the beginning, and it increased considerably even in the early Middle Ages.[86] Yet it is not clear that these particular provisos require us to greatly modify Marx's account of individuation and agency during this epoch.

This is so because, even though serfs were often not legally tied to the land of the lord, not only themselves but also legally-free tenants of the lord ("villeins") – indeed, even wage labourers in the vicinity – were almost always under his legal jurisdiction. This had far-reaching consequences for villeins and wage labourers alike, in that the former, at least, were subject to almost all the same demands of the lord for labour services and tallage as were serfs. While they did not have to ask his permission to marry, and while they could marry whomever they (or their families) chose (serfs were usually required to marry other serfs), they still had to use the lord's premises and officials, and as such were "fined" for doing so, just as they were for using his grain and woollen mills.[87] Lacking land to possess or rent, wage labourers were not much better off.

Given the latter considerations, more major problems with Marx's account lie elsewhere. At least four sets of important qualifications require discussion: (a) large regional variations in the degree to which political–legal relations were actually feudalized, (b) in the allocation and use of arable land and pasture, and (c) in the degree to which serfs and other producers were naturally organized to resist the lord's control, and (d) large differences over time *within* the overall period of the Middle Ages.

Of the first set of circumstances, we should keep in mind that serfdom *per se* does not constitute *feudalism*. The latter occurs only when there is a hierarchy of power and jurisdiction.[88] In some countries and regions the typical lord had few other lords above him, and consequently had more or less free rein in how he governed his own estate; but in others the reverse was the case.[89] One might expect that having a monarch at the top of the pyramid would buttress and fortify an otherwise weak landlord, but it appears that more often strong monarchs greatly limited his jurisdiction. The latter occurred in Germany, where monarchs not only held court in competition with local lords, but themselves appointed judges to the *lord's* court. Most of the French aristocracy, on the other hand, did not have to contend with monarchical control for most of the feudal epoch. In England the latter began with a smaller proportion of serfs, and with it relatively weak lords *and* monarchs. However, having conquered the country from without, the Normans were apparently able to replace and/or strengthen both.[90]

On the economic front, in regular "open-field" systems plots were left unfenced so that the combined flocks and herds of the community could graze on the stubble. In other open-field systems peasants were at least permitted to have highly irregularly shaped plots and use more discretion in the methods by which they worked them. But the larger contrast is between all open-field and "enclosed-field" systems. In the latter plots *were* fenced off from each other and communal flocks and herds were *not* permitted to graze on them. Marc Bloch went so far as to characterize the latter system as having had a "climate of individualism", and its participants *"independent* habits' (my emphasis), which included "respect for the principle of keeping oneself to oneself".[91]

On the class struggle/political front, as Marx himself had suggested, peasants appealed to 'custom' as a means for resisting or encroaching upon the lord's domination and exploitation. However, such customs and habits *also* varied a great deal by region and country, and with them, presumably, peasants' individuality and autonomy. One such variation was whether or not peasant communities had strong and long-standing traditions of popular assembly. They were especially characteristic of the Anglo-Saxons, but also of some of the tribes of Germany itself, and of Scandinavia. Again, most French peasants lost out on this score as well as the others discussed above, although we should not exaggerate the participation and power of "rank-and-file" peasants in such assemblies during that period to begin with.[92]

With regard to time, marked changes away from collectivism and political conservatism were under way long before the emergence and ascendency of the bourgeoisie as a class.

In the very early Middle Ages several families often worked a portion of the lord's estate in common, rather than as single families. This portion, known as the "manse", appears to have begun as a unit of assessment devised by lords to insure collective responsibility for services, rents, and fines.[93] But the family, more narrowly conceived, was also important. Its members usually insisted that work be shared and marriages arranged, and often successfully maintained possession or ownership of the same plots for generations, and even forestalled the emergence of primogeniture.[94] Individuals were identified with their kin to such an extent that "The honour or dishonour of one of the members of the little group reflected upon them all", such that feuds and vendettas were extremely common, and this often led to the suppression of individuality and autonomy. As Bloch put it, "in the most normal circumstances, a strong sense of community was quite compatible with a pretty callous attitude towards individuals. As was natural perhaps in a society in which kinship was above all regarded as a basis of mutual help, the group counted for much more than its members taken individually."[95]

However, by the mid-Middle Ages the manse had effectively disappeared; for example, by the end of the 12th Century in France, the most feudalized of European societies. Not only had the *de facto* inheritance of plots by individual *families* often become *de jure*;[96] rather, there had also been (a) a considerable amount of geographical movement away from the kinship group and its holding by English peasants, and presumably no small amount of intra-familial strife,[97] and (b) a marked tendency for *individual peasants* to have bought not only the plots upon which they had traditionally worked, but portions of the lord's own demesne, and even their own freedom. These developments apparently resulted from a "cash crisis" – and, in good part because of the plagues, also a labour shortage – for lords, and the fact that serfs were often able to buy their plots and freedom with *cash* indicates another development which Marx greatly underestimated: their production for, and participation in, urban as well as local markets.[98]

Parallel changes can be seen in class struggle and historic agency.

As we have already noted, in the beginning peasants appear to have appealed to custom in their struggles with their lords, but this was mainly for the purpose of maintaining the status quo, of keeping their lords from increasing services, rents, and fines, and decreasing the size of communal pasture and woodland.[99] Their consciousness at the time has also been labelled a *"negative class consciousness"*; that is, much more of a sense of who they were *against* than who they *themselves* were (a class with common interests).[100] Along with this, they tended to view the world in religious terms. This meant not only imputing much more agency to supernatural entities than their lords and themselves, but employing religious rather than secular ideologies in their class struggles.[101]

On the other hand, by the mid-Middle ages peasants had both helped precipitate the aforementioned crisis by leaving estates in large numbers,[102] and learned to take collective advantage of it. The latter meant not just whittling away at the lord's jurisdiction and power by forcing him to sign 'charters', but sometimes obtaining their complete freedom from him *en masse*.[103] Others may be correct in assuming, as had Marx, that in most regions peasants would not have been able to "finish off" feudalism on their own, without the aid of their respective bourgeoisie. However, even they indicate that in most cases peasants themselves had *already* transformed feudal relations of production beyond anything resembling what they had started out as.[104] Clearly, any claim that the *bourgeoisie* of these times were much better organized and class conscious is probably unfair to the peasantry, as Marx often was. For example, some researchers claim that the most active participants in the English revolutions of the 1640s were not especially likely to be members of the bourgeoisie.[105] Either way, there is no denying that most were *Puritans*, such that religion was still a major – perhaps *the* major – ideological weapon in the struggle. Interestingly enough, the most egalitarian ideals and purposes of the time were not those of Cromwell *et al*, but of those closer still to the peasants; that is, the "diggers" and "levellers".[106]

(3) The Guild System

Marx himself considered this mode to have had many contradictory characteristics. Thus craftsmen produced their own tools and had a modicum of artistic licence, yet they had to do so within the confines of traditional, local markets and methods; they could achieve master status merely by demonstrating their own skill, yet they also had to struggle against their own masters' attempts to dominate and exploit their labour.[107] Having seen the guilds as economically conservative to the point of losing out in competition with emerging capitalist organizations, Marx presumably gave them little credit for helping with the final political fight against feudalism either. The same contradictory quality can be seen in subsequent research, but in the latter the scales more often tip in the direction of collectivism for conservative class interests than that for individual development and recognition and progressive social change.

Apparently, most craftsmen began their careers in guilds as employees of merchants and/or municipal authorities (often one and the same). As such they were very heavily controlled indeed, and from *without* to boot. Thus in the "low countries" Henri Pirenne studied most closely (Holland, Flanders, the north of France, and Italy), the craftsman had to practise his trade at an open window so that both the general public and city inspector could see him at work. Not only was he forbidden to hire non-guild members, advertise or undercut the prices of his fellow guildsmen; rather, "he was . . . forbidden . . . to work longer than between the bell which proclaimed from the belfry the beginning and the end of the day's work". Furthermore, "*It was penal for a craftsman to use or invent new tools. . . .*" "It would be impossible to restrict the individual's economic liberty more severely," Pirenne concluded. Why, therefore, did these craftsmen apparently accept such conditions? Because municipal authorities helped them achieve full protection from competition; from without, by restricting guild membership to long-term, legally-free residents of the towns, and from within, by requiring strict equality among masters, and perhaps, although Pirenne did not say, social mobility within the guild for apprentices and journeymen.[108] Pirenne implied, furthermore, that the guilds' emphasis upon the quality of the product was at least as much in exchange for this protection as an end in itself.

Eventually, however, competition from the countryside and abroad and inequalities within the guilds, especially between merchants bent upon supplying external markets and craftsmen concerned almost exclusively with the local market, led the craft members of most guilds to struggle for their independence. Nevertheless, this process did not occur universally, nor was it always successful. For example, George Unwin claimed that journeymen as well as craftmasters were much better organized in Germany than they were in France or England; yet Pirenne maintained that the fight for independence was actually much *less* successful in the former than the latter.[109] In many cases, it appears, these struggles for independence coincided with, and greatly aided, revolutionary movements for municipal freedom and reform.[110] But more important for our present purposes are these questions. First, did independence bring a lessening of restrictions upon individual craftsmen or, at least, did they become more oriented toward the quality of the product and the artistic development of the craftsman? Second, did the attainment of master status become easier or, at a minimum, more meritocratic; that is, based upon the demonstration of skill, and perhaps individual creativity?

Pirenne's answer is unequivocally *no*. "The new control," he wrote, "was, at the same time, much more active and much more minute than the old one . . . The later we come down, the greater the number of restrictive measures." Furthermore, its purpose was still further away from controlling quality in the interest of consumers and toward protecting members from competition. Thus the latter came to consider "the craft guild as a family property, passing naturally from father to son. It reduced the time of apprenticeship in favour of the sons of 'masters', while making it still longer and still more expensive for newcomers. Similarly it raised difficulties in the way of the 'brother' who came from outside to gain an entrance." There was much attention to the physical, social, and moral welfare of members, including those who were old and no longer working, but this concern for "brotherhood and equality . . . was limited" to "the narrow circle of the calling". "[T]he crafts, as organized in the 14th century, had reached a state of perfect equilibrium. Henceforth they were not to develop further, *either in numbers or in craftsmanship.*"[111]

George Unwin was a bit kinder. The professional honour of guildsmen was not just a question of selfish motives; for example, when the doctors of London incorporated they treated even those patients who could not afford to pay them. Similarly there were indeed periods where apprentices and journeymen could reasonably expect to become masters.[112] Nevertheless, he admitted, the religious and charitable motives of the guilds had "*never*" been primary, and the "*most distinctive*" feature of the London guild was its *court* where "unruly apprentices were whipped, journeymen on strike were imprisoned, and masters offending against regulations were fined".[113] As for mobility within the guild, this did not last for very long, since, as Pirenne was also to later argue, with the halt in the growth of the population of the towns and the guilds' traditional production only for the local market there was no longer enough production to go around. What occurred then was *both* the loss of status for many *existing* masters *and* new qualifications for attaining mastership in the first place which were so severe, and deliberately so, that usually only the sons of masters could meet them.

Entrance fees were raised. Apprentices who had completed their terms were often in debt to their masters, and new rules were sometimes made that they not work for anyone else until that debt was paid; or, even where they were paid, that there be a minimum of, say, three years before the completion of apprenticeship and the attainment of mastership, or that the would-be master be at least 24 years of age. The latter often had to bear "the cost of a dinner or 'drinking' ", and "the production of an elaborate masterpiece, which embodied in some cases the work of several months, and involved the use of expensive material. It should be added that the sons of masters were generally exempted from most or all of these conditions." Unwin emphasized that some of these requirements were relatively late developments; for example, in the case of the London guilds the masterpiece did not appear until the 16th century. Nonetheless, it had been in existence on the Continent much earlier, and many of the other requirements occurred in England as early as 1350![114]

If we are to believe these two classic accounts – and Unwin's, at least, is well-documented with quotes from guild court records – there was little individuality or autonomy in the guild system, even for masters, let alone apprentices and journeymen. It is *very* doubtful that *either* got to make their own tools, as Marx claimed, and, therefore, to also have experienced themselves as free, let alone historic, agents. Craftsmen were among those who struggled for the initial immunity of towns from feudal obligations, and their subsequent fight for independence from merchants and municipal authorities would have put them on the side of those who made municipal revolutions in, for example, Ghent and Florence in the 14th century.[115] There are also indications that guild rules notwithstanding, some masters attempted to stockpile products for distribution in markets beyond the local. On the other hand, the merchants who again came to dominate the guilds as well as fellow craftsmen were usually able to squelch such attempts.[116] Furthermore, at the time of various crucial movements to finish off feudalism – for example, the peasants' revolts in England in the 1380s and 90s and the revolutions of the 1640s – the masters of the major guilds were usually abstaining, or even on the opposing side.[117]

Not surprisingly, there *were* those who were in, or who *had* been in, the guilds who did not fit the above mould, but they tended to be those who had never been fully admitted, or who had been thrown out, rather than those who experienced themselves as historic agents because they made their own tools. Thus journeymen, many with no hope whatsoever of ever becoming masters, not only went on strike, but organized on a far wider basis than Marx maintained. Indeed, these organizations were often close to *class*-wide. That they were unsuccessful seems to have had little to do with the reasons Marx advanced; that is, paternalistic relationships between masters and journeymen and the latters' expectation of becoming masters themselves. Instead, these circumstances had long since passed, and the outcome can be attributed to the effective efforts of masters to either smash such competing organizations, or to co-opt them within the guild itself.[118] The others who did not fit the mould were the small masters who were demoted within, and subsequently left, the guild, or had never gained admittance in the first place. They often hawked their wares in the street and formed organizations of *their* own. If guild masters were seldom among the participants of the political revolutions of the time, journeymen and small, independent masters *often* were.[119]

To be sure, subsequent accounts have not always been so unflattering, and some may require us to qualify the above as well as Marx's. For example, not all guilds were so economically conservative, and many survived well into the 19th century; presumably in part because of this greater economic adaptability,[120] and in part precisely because their *political* conservatism put them on the side of those who usually won the class battles of the day. Nevertheless, some recent renderings idealize the guilds as much as, or more than, Marx had. For instance, with one hand Fritz Rörig wrote that "an internal political mood existed which guaranteed the worker living conditions such that he was relieved of the trouble of struggling for existence and, provided he was personally able, could do some extraordinary things. This was the explanation of the urban art which was so eminent in the medieval town and which we admire today", and with the other that "Certainly the creative artist felt only too strongly the narrowness of the world dominated by the guilds". (Here Albrecht Dürer is quoted to this effect.)[121] Similarly, Anthony Black has made two, rather dubious claims. One is that "individuation and association went hand in hand . . . [T]he evidence does not tell us that medieval communes and guilds had a particularly holistic or collectivist mentality." The other is that the latter provided both the model, and often the means, for the bourgeois revolutions.[122] Finally, other research tends to corroborate rather than contradict that of Unwin and Pirenne.[123]

CAPITALISM

(1) A Golden Age for labour, or a "Cultural Renaissance"?

It would be difficult to pinpoint a time in the 14th or 15th centuries when there was an especially golden time for agricultural labour. We do know that feudalism underwent a crisis at about that time, and that a shortage of labour was very much a part of it. On the other hand, its major sources appear to have been either internal (increasing fiscal pressure upon lords from those higher in the hierarchy and responses by peasants, such as fleeing the land or simply buying their freedom, which left lords with too little labour), or external to capitalism as well (principally, decimation of the labouring population through the plagues). True, some lords dealt with the crisis by becoming employers of agricultural wage-labour, and the relative cheapness of land and desire for gentry status led some members of the urban bourgeoisie to do the same, but apparently these did not occur frequently enough to vastly increase the demand for wage-labour.[124]

Marx would seem to have been on firmer ground for the case of urban labour, in that the rise of the mercantile bourgeoisie and incorporation of towns and cities do seem to have increased the demand for labour in the form of construction and manufactured goods. For example, of Florence in the 1400s, Agnes Heller notes instances of employers granting concessions to workers and explains them by the supposed shortage of labour. Similarly, Jacques Le Goff notes that during the same period, French textile workers began their struggle over the length of the working day by attempting to have it *extended* rather than shortened, in order to increase their income.[125] Certainly, the urban-based aristocracy and rising bourgeoisie, who wanted to distinguish themselves from others and enhance their status in the community by owning unusual houses and other luxury goods, including visual, musical, and literary portraits of themselves, provided artists, musicians, writers, and other craftsmen with new opportunities for employment.[126]

The "cultural" concomitants of these trends were many. Even by the end of the 13th century, attitudes toward labour and various trades and professions had already undergone drastic revision. Whereas before all labour, and especially manual labour, had been denigrated, it now in effect became a standard of value to which almost any trade or profession, religious or secular, intellectual or manual, commercial or productive, could appeal for legitimacy.[127] And, of course, the next two centuries was also the period of "the" "Renaissance", and the evidence for a dramatic increase in individuation and agency during that time is striking.

Portraits captured the mannerisms as well as physical features of individuals as never before, and the *self*-portrait came into existence. Literature saw not only the revival of a much more self-conscious lyric poetry, but plays which indicated awareness of a private self distinguishable from one's public performance, a performance which involved self-control not just for the purpose of appeasing authorities and "public opinion", but, through "tact" and other forms of manipulated self-presentation, for influencing others. Full-fledged autobiographies came into existence, and these indicated not only individuals' awareness of their own individuality, but, in the form of choice and responsibility, shame and guilt, free agency as well. Along with these changes came a new awareness of the individuality and autonomy of *other* individuals besides onself, and of the possibility and desirability of friendship and love relationships involving personal choice and reciprocity.[128]

The changes in religious and secular thinking were every bit as marked. Although a focus upon internal contrition, even individual intention, rather than simply external sanction, had emerged in earlier religious renaissances,[129] one now saw glimmerings of the individual relationship with God which was to characterize the Protestant Reformation. But matters did not stop there: humans were seen to affect, rather than simply reflect, nature as well as God; society as well as history – indeed, sometimes human nature too – was seen as evolving instead of merely repeating the past; and humans, who could now sometimes even recognize several historical periods within their own lifetime, also developed some awareness that they "make" history. Finally, the art of personally influencing both other individuals and historical events became the discipline of politics, one of the first "social sciences" besides history, and some scholars went so far as to design "communist" "utopias" in order to rectify the social injustices and personal excesses of the time; utopias where individuals were, if not *completely* free, at least enough to choose their employment and govern themselves.[130]

The latter developments may seem to clinch Marx's case. Admittedly, it is difficult to imagine a convincing explanation for them which would not have both the rise of the bourgeoisie in general and the consequent demand for craft and manual labour at its core. Nevertheless, a number of qualifications should probably be made.

For one thing, many of the above trends appeared considerably earlier than the 14th and 15th centuries. For another, these centuries were probably less golden for labour than Marx claimed. For example, the aforementioned French textile workers very quickly changed to fighting for a *shorter* working day as their employers took advantage of them, and rather than make concessions, in these cases employers used "draconian measures" to quell their revolts. Furthermore, despite the general re-evaluation of labour by the end of the 13th century, the gap between intellectual and manual labour not only remained, but subsequently increased. Perhaps most of the new demand for labour still came from the aristocracy, and most of the benefits in terms of choice of employment and variety in work went to elite art craftsmen.[131]

Attempts to invoke a golden age for labour as an explanation – and, certainly, as *the, sole* explanation – for the cultural Renaissance are still more questionable. While it is true that the humanism of the time was often more limited, conservative, cynical, and self-serving than has usually been recognized, even some of those Marxists who have leaned toward the other extreme of writing it off as bourgeois ideology have had to concede that it was far more than that.[132] Marx and Engels themselves did not *explicitly* take the latter position, yet as Anderson has noted, their neglect of the Renaissance is both unwarranted and cause for suspicion.[133] Certainly, if they regarded it as superficially as they did the Protestant Reformation,[134] we should be more than simply suspicious.

(2) The ascendancy of the bourgeoisie, the capitalist mode of production, and the "industrial revolution"

Many of the things I have to say here have already been said, in the Introduction to Part IV, and in the previous sections of this chapter. They can be summarized as follows. First, the putting out or cottage system was the dominant form of capitalist production for centuries longer than Marx thought. Second, along with this, *merchant* capital continued to be extremely important, with a division of labour in manufacturing having begun within the cottage system, and having subsequently received its greatest impetus from merchant capitalists rather than either master craftsmen, acting individually or in association, or other industrial capitalists. Third, the factory system itself, and especially the mechanization of labour, also occurred much later; and its development was much slower and more uneven than Marx believed. Yet we must now add a few more: (a) The "industrial revolution" often occurred in *agriculture* long before it did in secondary, urban industry, as Marx usually implied. (b) The initiative for this came as much from large, landowning members of the aristocracy and merchants, as from members of the urban, industrial bourgeoisie who were extending their holdings into agriculture. (c) The latter, purely industrial bourgeoisie often appeared only *after*, and not before, the industrial revolution. (d) The political revolutions often attributed primarily to the urban, and eventually industrial, bourgeoisie – for example, in the case of England, those of the 1640s and the 1830s – should probably be credited more to the initiative of agricultural producers, both small and independent and large and aristocratic, and of merchants.[135] Put otherwise, the 'most revolutionary role' Marx imputed to the industrial bourgeoisie was much less and much later.

The latter interpretation of history (primarily English) flies in the face not only of Marx's, but that of such popular contemporary historians as Maurice Dobb and Christopher Hill. According to the latter, the English bourgeosie had already gained ascendancy with the political revolutions of the 1640s. While there had been some large-scale capitalist industry even in the 16th century, the political revolutions of the 17th had a more or less direct effect upon their appearance and growth. Thus the industrial bourgeoisie is said to have used its newly-acquired political power to first deny producers access to their own land, and then introduce machinery so as to take away their skills and make them more tractable, as well as to save labour.[136] However, these latter claims are difficult to sustain in light of the aforementioned facts, and of many others.

We have already noted that the urban bourgeoisie of *any* stripe were not prominent in the revolutionary events of the 1640s. Harold Perkin and R. S. Neale, the major proponents of the alternative interpretation mentioned above, also point out that there *was* no large-scale, industrial bourgeoisie-for-itself (or perhaps even in-itself) in the *18th* century.[137] There was considerable resistance to technological innovation among merchant–capitalist employers as well as among their employees and guildsmen. Nor did those who were successful in inventing and/or employing industrial machinery by any means necessarily foresee the various uses to which it was eventually put. For example, the idea of using machinery to *replace* labour was usually only apparent *after* its employment had produced resistance among workers.[138] Either way, "the landowning aristocracy retained a virtual monopoly of political power throughout most of the *nineteenth* century in England".[139]

Why, therefore, did the industrial bourgeoisie take so long to emerge, organize itself, and gain ascendancy? Was there something unique about the class/political culture of England that allowed the bourgeoisie to achieve their aspirations for individuality and autonomy with relatively little resistance from the aristocracy and the producers they wanted to employ as wage-labourers? For example, had the aristocracy been weakened by earlier movements for democracy, and producers by enclosures and the absence of alternatives? Perhaps, although some of the abovementioned facts suggest otherwise. Alternatively, had the former perhaps been *strengthened* by links to mercantilism and the latter by the *persistence* of alternative means of subsistence? (The latter appears to have been the case in Germany.)

Of course, there are still other possibilities. The bourgeoisie may never have developed very high aspirations for individuality and autonomy in the first place, or Marx's theory of agency may itself be faulty. These issues are obviously important for evaluating the latter, but at this point we are not in a position to resolve them.

(3) The "making" of the working class

Given that the industrial *bourgeoisie* took so much longer to emerge and become politically dominant than Marx thought, we should not be surprised that the same was the case with the urban proletariat. But this is far from the only qualification we must make to Marx's analysis.

A second one is that, for the most part, the producers who initially fought industrialization and mechanization were not those whose individuality and freedom were most immediately and directly affected – that is, wage-labourers in factories – but spinners, weavers, and other craftsmen in the putting-out system. To be sure, their fear that they would not be able to compete with mechanized factory labour was not the only motive behind their rebellion. Rather, they appear to have been equally concerned that they would themselves have to become factory labourers, and that in the process they would lose whatever individuality and freedom they already had.[140] Nevertheless, this does not change the fact that Marx misrepresented these early rebellions as specifically proletarian. Indeed, the fact that the cottage craftsmen were as, and perhaps more, likely to find allies among small and medium-sized employers of farm and factory labour as/than the latter labourers themselves has led some analysts to suggest that these movements were "populist" rather than working class.[141]

Thirdly, although Marx was wrong to have represented the initial response to industrialization and mechanization as proletarian, he was also incorrect to portray it as simply a primitive, "pre-political" response to frustration; a "blind lashing-out" where producers mistakenly attributed the ultimate source of the problem to machines rather than men in capitalist relations of production. At least the English "Luddites" were nowhere near that naive. Furthermore, in most areas they were well-organized on the local level and their acts of sabotage were usually explicitly designed to force employers and state officials to take their interests into acount. That their methods were crude was more a matter of the state of repression at the time than their own lack of "class" consciousness (the Combination Acts prevented them from either peacefully withdrawing their labour or petitioning Parliament), and these methods, while understandably not achieving all that they were intended to, were anything but totally ineffectual.[142]

Fourthly, few would dispute that factory workers *per se* eventually became better organized and more class conscious. In addition to the studies by E. P. Thompson and others, one might note the statistical trend away from jurisdictional and other disputes between rival groups of artisans or neighbourhoods – which predominated in France, Germany, and Italy until the early 19th century but then largely disappeared – toward attempts by some, presumably working class, groups to defend longstanding positions against the attempts by other, usually ruling class, groups to erode them by the mid- to late 19th-century. However, the same researchers who discovered this trend, the Tillys, also found that *offensive* attempts by the former to *better* their own position did not become prominent until the *20th* century.[143] The latter is especially interesting given recent re-analysis of mid-19th century England and France.

According to earlier accounts such as Thompson's, by the time of the constitutional crisis surrounding the Reform Bill of 1831 the English working class had "made" itself to the point where it was on the brink of revolt. Although the latter was averted, working class consciousness then took a large leap and laid the basis for the Chartist movement; one of the first nearly class-wide attempts by workers to act on their own behalf, independently of the bourgeoisie.[144] However, while the failure of workers to obtain suffrage through the Chartist movement did lead to wider class organization along syndicalist lines and several general strikes, the movement itself does not appear to have been working class and conscious enough to have advocated overthrowing the state and expropriating the employers of wage-labour, or even much milder socialist measures. Instead, given that they demanded only the end to their exclusion from the official political arena, and, through this means, some limitation of employers' dictatorial control over conditions of employment, workers in the Chartist movement may not have moved much beyond the program of the bourgeois radicals with whom they had coalesced.[145]

Parallel reinterpretations have been offered for France. Marx himself had claimed that the majority of Parisian workers were both proletarianized and organized and class conscious enough to act as a class-for-itself in the revolution of 1848. This meant that they acted more or less as a block on the side of the revolution and had a distinctly working class program. Yet we now know that (a) the majority of the producers who participated were still skilled artisans who were at most employed in small factories which were only partly, if at all, mechanized; (b) contrary to Marx's casting of participants as solidly proletarian and recruits to the Mobile Guard as "lumpen", both groups were drawn from the same pool, the majority of whom were un- or under-employed artisans; and (c) while the demands of Parisian workers were sometimes more socialist than those of English Chartists, the most central and persistent was that the "right to labour" be enshrined in the constitution. Furthermore, as in England, workers' anger was directed more against the state and more long-standing class enemies than the employers of industrial labour.[146]

Now, as we saw with regard to the rise of the bourgeoisie, that Marx was so off-base in his characterization of the timing and nature of the early development of Europe's working classes need not totally invalidate his general theories of individuation and agency, nor even all of his historical applications. Perhaps most importantly, there is evidence that the above periods coincided with increases in individuation and autonomy for many workers, in that workers' clubs stressing mutual support and self-improvement had emerged, as well as a proliferation of autobiographies by *workers* rather than just members of the "middle" classes.[147] Furthermore, working class organization and rebellion do seem to have coincided with, and presumably in part resulted from, deprivation; both absolute (unemployment, and sometimes destitution) and relative (to previous standards of wages and independence, and to increasing *inequality* between strata and classes).[148] Finally, some of the preferred explanations for the failure of these movements, while not exactly like Marx's, are nonetheless consistent with his theories of human nature in general.[149]

It is the more specific nature and importance of workers' experiences which are more in dispute. For example, were real wages and standards of living decreasing or increasing in the early 19th century, in general, and for factory labourers in particular? Alternatively, how much and how fast were alternatives to factory labour receding? Did producers voluntarily go into factories to increase their standard of living, or were they much more likely to have been forced in by the destruction of independent means of subsistence? These issues have not been resolved,[150] but *if* cottage labour was *both* more poorly paid *and* more available to factory labourers than Marx believed, as appears to have been the case, then it may explain why the latter may have been proportionally less represented than cottagers and other artisans in the working class movements of the time.

Other controversies concern alternative aftermaths of different working class movements. For instance, why did the English movement remain more reformist after the demise of Chartism than the French after the defeats of the late 1840s? One possibility has been suggested by Perkin: because the English ruling class did not give in on either the demand for the vote or that to regulate working conditions, but did give in on certain, more minor issues, workers "learned by failure and success", respectively, to chart a course in a still more pragmatic direction.[151] French workers actually had much success in the short run, since the more liberal and democratic governments in

France at the time wanted to obtain workers' support against the aristocracy. However, once their expectations and aspirations had been raised, governments more reactionary than the British came to power and took away all previous gains.

(4) "Advanced" or "Late Capitalism"

It is tempting to extend the latter analysis to later times. Such an account might be outlined as follows.

Many capitalists have now been *forced* to bargain with their employees, because working classes have by now organized more extensively than earlier; and because the latter have forced the state – the political representative of the bourgeoisie, but now much more "relatively autonomous", because the bourgeoisie have been unable to prevent economic and political crises on their own – to minimally protect workers' organization as a means of legitimating the capitalist system as a whole. Many more capitalists have also become *willing* not only to bargain with their employees, but to pay them considerably more, at least in absolute terms, as a means to buy peace. Among other things, whereas Marx usually presumed that increased wages mean decreased profits, oligopolistic capitalist and monopolistic public employers have often been able to increase the pie to be distributed between capital or management and labour by increasing the productivity of labour, and/or to pass on wage and benefit increases to consumers and taxpayers.[152] The "pot" has also been "sweetened" with other "goodies", not only considerable job security, benefits, and sometimes mobility within the company, but occasionally even a bit (but only a bit) of "sharing" in profits and "participation" in decision-making with regard to workers' own working conditions.[153]

The above scenario is at least consistent with the fact that workers have been more likely to strike a relatively good deal in those countries whose capitalist economies and liberal–democratic polities are most developed, and to rebel against the system as a whole in those which are less developed. Although differences in national as well as class culture are clearly important, as Marx himself was aware, it is interesting that among developed Western nations themselves, workers have in turn bargained better deals where they have vastly outnumbered and out-organized their employers (e.g., in Sweden), and rebelled where their employers have been more numerous, more aristocratic, and least willing to bargain away wages and working conditions (e.g. in Italy and France).

However, needless to say, such an analysis is far too crude to explain all that we wish to. For one thing, of course, it underplays the role of coercion on the part of the capitalist class and the state. Neither has been willing to bargain about "management's rights" to own and control the means of production, the work process, and the product, and as Michael Mann has suggested, it is probably precisely because of this that unions, concerned with *their* survival and prosperity, have been so economistic and unwilling to fight battles about ownership and control.[154] As a direct consequence of the latter, the working conditions of even most unionized "blue", and many "white, collar" workers, while less military-like and oppressive than Marx expected them to be, nevertheless do not permit much individuality and autonomy, with the result that most workers remain psychically alienated from their labour. For example, as Marx himself forecast, those who become independently wealthy through winning a lottery subsequently avoid labour "like the plague".[155] Nor have most workers been able to compensate for the lack of opportunities for individuality and autonomy at work in their time *outside* of work, what with long work weeks, shift-work, the considerable time required to get to and from work, and the "spill-over" effects of the nature of the work itself.[156] Given their responsibiltiy for reproducing *others'* labour-power as well as their own, *women* workers have had still less, and less autonomous and individualized, leisure than have men.[157]

For another, those workers who have been fortunate enough to have struck the above-mentioned bargain (but usually at the cost of their own individuality and autonomy) have seldom constituted even a *majority* of the working classes of developed liberal-democracies. Rather, the above model applies only to unionized workers in the oligopolistic private and monopolistic public sectors, and not to those, often non-unionized, in the small "sweatshops" in the competitive sector, or to the many others who are "chronically" (sic) un- or under-employed. Single women, native people, other racial and ethnic minorities, and immigrants figure prominently in the latter two sectors, and a substantial proportion of workers in them are both poverty-stricken in absolute terms and forced to work under the very military-like conditions which Marx mistakenly generalized to all workers. Their lack of options has often meant lower aspirations regarding wages and benefits, yet because they usually enter the labour force through "segmented" markets and remain in "job ghettos", they have competed directly with dominant male workers far less than Marx expected.[158]

The latter circumstances point to a number of others which surely are crucial for understanding the working classes of the 20th century; that is, the highly uneven development of both capitalist economies and their working classes. Many workers have yet to experience the full mechanization of their labour, let alone its automation. Others are privileged to work under the highly automated conditions about which Marx prophesied. They have not gotten to study and control production itself to anywhere near the extent he anticipated, nor have they necessarily, or even usually, developed high aspirations for such control.[159] On the other hand, they *have* gotten relief from many of the oppressive conditions other workers have experienced, in that they often work in small groups which range over a wide area of the plant, "reading dials and pushing buttons", with relatively loose and informal supervision and lots of time to socialize.[160]

But the fact that many workers have had relatively high wages and less than highly oppressive working conditions, and therefore also a sizeable stake in the capitalist system, is only part of the point I want to make here. Another is that the "de-skilling" and other processes which Marx believed would homogenize wages and working conditions and give workers coincident interests in organizing as a *class* have in fact been uneven to the point that there continue to be many, indeed, may have been a vast increase in, *competing* interest groups *within* the working class "in-itself". In fact, some "mass production" workers still retain much of the traditional control that the crafts had over the process of production itself.[161] It is also worth noting that this same unevenness applies to workers' *communities*.

Marx maintained that workers would be naturally organized in the latter as well as at work, since they would inevitably be concentrated in the immediate vicinity of their workplace. However, most traditional working class communities have been radically transformed since his time. This is true not only of North America, but of England and other European societies, where it is far from uncommon to find mixed-class "bedroom communities" far away from members' workplaces and without much of a sense of either community or class.[162] At a minimum, some researchers suggest, we must distinguish among "traditional" working class communities, usually but not always restricted to single industry towns, which are in turn often isolated from other communities; "deferential" communities, where workers' working and living conditions are likely to be so mixed by class that they are not likely to have developed an independent working class perspective in the first place and "privatized" bedroom communities where workers seldom see and socialize with their workmates and often appear to have lost a sense of working class community and consciousness. While this rendering is far from unproblematic, there does seem to be a decided trend away from the first, and toward the last, type of "working class" community.[163]

Although the evidence does not indicate that "embourgeoisement" is a necessary, or even common, consequence of "privatization",[164] it does suggest that most workers have lost many of previous generations' opportunities to mobilize their local communities in support of their industrial struggles, and to act independently as a class in the arena of politics more generally. Along with this loss of community has been an increase in feelings of powerlessness with regard to both work and politics.[165] Have workers nevertheless "gained" more of a sense of themselves as "autonomous *individuals*"? This is an interesting but highly controversial issue. Indeed, to phrase it in this manner is to prejudge the matter by insinuating that working class communities have traditionally stifled individuality in the first place.

The facts of the matter are highly mixed. Marx himself, of course, sometimes suggested that workers would have to "lose themselves in the proletariat" in order to achieve circumstances favourable for their own individuation *collectively*, and historians such as Thompson have noted demands for uniformity as well as self-improvement in the initial formation of the working class.[166] The evidence for the 20th century is similarly mixed, in that traditional working class patterns of interaction have sometimes been described as both highly personalized and de-manding of group loyalty.[167] When blue collar workers are studied as "individuals" they are more likely than their upper status white collar counterparts to socialize their children to be "other-directed"; that is, to stress conformity to others in the interest of avoiding punishment rather than voluntarily following the dictates of one's own conscience. On the other hand, this is only a relatively weak statistical tendency. The same is true for decision-making within the family: while blue collar women have sometimes been found to have less power in the home, the differences are seldom large, and they vary considerably by a number of specific circumstances, as do class differences in child-rearing.[168] Those who have gone as far as to coin the term "working class authoritarianism" have pointed to the intolerance workers have often had for communists and other "deviants", but where such a tendency has existed, it has not been general to all workers or all issues. Perhaps most importantly, it has been especially characteristic of workers in the United States, whose rulers have been excessively anti-communist; and even there, blue collar workers have been more likely than others to favour welfare legislation and other means of redistributing wealth.[169]

Either way, whereas the break up of working class communities does seem to have disrupted traditional interaction patterns, and especially those associated with the extended family, it is by no means clear that this new freedom "from" past working class loyalties has necessarily left individual workers free "to" develop themselves as individuals. Aside from the persistence of the aforementioned constraints upon work and leisure, many workers appear to have sacrificed themselves to the individuation and social mobility of their *children*. The loss of a community and extended family which both accepted them as individuals merely because they were members and justified their work and life as part of the working *class's* unique contribution to society appears to have led to a loss of security and self-esteem, which have *also* hindered workers from developing themselves as individuals.[170]

Thus far we have more or less followed Marx's own general models for individuation and agency, but often plugged in very different, specific, "initial" conditions: much less deprivation, and consequently a much greater stake in the capitalist system, for many workers, but also much less class organization and a sense of their own power to change the system even if they wanted to; much deprivation for other workers and the "reserve army of labour", but too little organization for them to change the system in spite of their greater objective interest in doing so.[171] But there is a further set of conditions which should also be considered; that is, a decrease in the coherence and visibility of a class enemy for the working class. We have already noted how the state has become relatively autonomous, and therefore less obviously class-biased, but the same must be said for the capitalist class itself. While Marx was dead-on in his scenario of the increasing concentration and centralization of capital, he did not anticipate, or at least attribute enough importance to, both the so-called "managerial revolution" and the vast proliferation of other occupations which he considered to be "unproductive". If in his own day the latter amounted to a few "overseers", clerks, and engineers, we now have a host of other white collar occupations, including "professions", associated with marketing, employee and public relations, accounting, and so forth. The latter developments are important not only because they have made the capitalist nature of our system more opaque, but because they have often changed the reference groups with which workers have compared themselves from those of their capitalist employers to those much closer in wages and working conditions to themselves. As a consequence, *relative* as well as absolute deprivation has probably decreased for most workers.[172]

But before we despair and say "Farewell to the Working Class" as an historic agent,[173] there are some further, potentially revolutionary, qualifications to the above analysis. To wit, in the past decade or so the implicit deal between employers, both private and public, and relatively privileged workers has been coming undone, and with it the seemingly non-partisan stance of the state. The replacement of workers by automated machinery, and, because of *this particular* trend, the swelling of the ranks of the reserve army by those who can in fact expect never to work again, has indeed occurred; yet as suggested earlier, its importance has been overrated. In the immediate future the more fundamental problems appear to be (a) the internationalization of the market, and capital; (b) competition from "foreign" capital (often not so foreign), and falling rates of profit; (c) the *relocation* of *mass*, *labour-intensive* production to low wage areas, leaving considerable unemployment in its wake; and, consequently, (d) the need for national and municipal states to increase social welfare far beyond their traditional sources of revenue; that is, the taxing of the personal income and consumption of the working and middle classes.[174]

The immediate consequences of these trends have been disastrous for many workers, including those who have been relatively privileged until recently. Workers have had to not just say "Hi Tech, Goodbye Jobs", but to listen to their employers say "Accept all these concessions or we will contract work out to small, more competitive firms (You can still work – for *them* – but at half or two-thirds of your present wages, and few benefits), or move our operations to areas where workers' demands are more reasonable. (For example, southern American workers will work for minimum wage, and *Mexican* workers for 69 cents an hour!)"[175] In many cases, of course, employers have not even waited for workers' answers. When workers have called on "their" governments to do something about these events, they have often found them to be more avowedly conservative, less sympathetic, and even less likely to help than previously. Indeed, in many cases the employer doing the contracting out or relocating *is* "their" government![176]

As Marx suggested was the case in the early 19th century (perhaps exaggeratedly – remember the Luddites), "organized labour" appears to have initially been "stunned" by these developments. Fear for their very jobs has often meant workers accepting not only the wage and benefit concessions their employers have demanded, but various forms of class-collaboration at and beyond the workplace, such as "productivity deals"; drastic technological changes in exchange for promises of more job security and workers' participation for those who are left; joint lobbying for protective tariffs against foreign competition; and participation in planning the economy with employers' federations and state officials (to a token degree, certainly).[177]

Because the occurrence and effects of the crisis have been uneven, these trends have sometimes exacerbated old divisions within the working class or created new ones between, for example, those lucky enough to retain any job at all and those who have not been so lucky. Those who have been strong enough to resist concessions, or even continue to extract concessions from their employers, such as auto and postal workers in Canada, have sometimes fallen victim to envy and scapegoating by other, less fortunate workers. In some of these cases (woodworking and auto) the Canadian sections of "international" (North American-wide) unions have felt that the only way to avoid being dragged down by their U.S. brothers and sisters is to leave these unions.[178] In other cases, traditionally strong unions such as those of the British miners have misjudged their own strength and that of their employers and lost even after mounting a concerted defence against concessions.

When one couples this lessening of the numbers and clout of organized labour, and indeed, its seeming *dis*organization, with direct attacks on union rights and the dismantling of many welfare programs, one sees movement as much *back* to the *pre*-industrial times of the 19th century as forward to a post-industrial society. However, just as the conditions of those times led many to oppose industrialization, so current conditions have forced many sectors of organized labour to oppose "de-industrialization", so-called, and this opposition may well spread and deepen to the point where fundamental changes to the very nature of capitalism are the most likely solution.

In the first place, even retrenchment has had its advantages, as, for example, unions which have seen their membershp shrink drastically have sought amalgamations with others outside as well as inside their own industries. The prospects for wider organization of the class have therefore increased at the same time that layoffs have decreased them.

Secondly, the same fears have forced some of the larger and still relatively powerful unions and union federations to attempt to organize the previously unorganized much more seriously than earlier. Because this has meant concentrating upon white collar and/or women workers in, for example, sales and banking, it may well help break down these traditional divisions.

Thirdly, the weakening of its economic bargaining power and political clout has forced organized labour to seek coalitions with other groups in the community traditionally still more removed from itself; not just the unemployed, welfare recipients, the elderly and others threatened with cutbacks in state welfare, but white collar professionals and churches concerned with education and other community services. Such coalitions have been relatively few, and they have often dissolved along sectoral lines. However, that they have occurred at all is reason for hope.

Now these turns by organized labour are admittedly defensive. They are attempts to prevent the further erosion of its earlier, sometimes relatively privileged, position, rather than to make a socialist revolution. However, the last decade has also seen a fourth trend: the emergence of new, or long-out-of-use, strategies by labour which more directly challenge capital's ownership and control of the means of production and production itself.

A (very) few unions have managed to get collective agreements giving them some control over the introduction and effects of technological change, and others have attempted to exercise such control through their community; by, for example, having municipal governments receive assurance that employers will be responsible for the effects of "tech change" upon their employees in exchange for community services.[179] To date these attempts have not been very successful, but they have made workers more aware of the need for *them* to take control and more angry when they have not been able to do so.

When companies have announced that they are relocating and laying off their employees, the latter have sometimes taken over their plants. Their demands have more often been better severance pay than worker or community control of the plant as such, but the latter has sometimes occurred as well, with workers on occasion trying to buy the plant and equipment themselves and at other times demanding that the state do so.[180] Again, such strategies have seldom resulted in successful workers' ownership and control, let alone wider revolution, but they have entailed workers taking matters into their own hands and forcing public debate about the disadvantages of capitalism.

These latter developments bear some considerable similarity to those of the previous century. Specifically, political–economic changes are undermining the modicum of job security and control producers have come to expect, and they are fighting to retain or regain them in ways that challenge those who are currently much more in control. The outcome of this class struggle may also be a replica of that of the earlier period, but it need not be.

NOTES

1. I say "so-called", because a relatively small proportion of primitive societies actually deserve the label tribal; that is, they are seldom organized on the level of tribes, whether objectively or subjectively. See especially Morton H. Fried, *The Evolution of Political Society* (New York: Random House, 1967), pp. 154–74.
2. In addition to the studies by Hobhouse et al., Udy, Mandel and myself and my colleagues described in my *Social Psychology* . . . (op. cit., Chapter 7), see Fried, op. cit., Gerard Lenski and Jean Lenski (*Human Societies* (New York: McGraw-Hill, 1974)), and Katherine S. Newman (*Law and Social Organization: A comparative study of pre-industrial societies* (Cambridge: Cambridge University Press, 1983)).
3. Marshall Sahlins, "The original affluent society", pp. 1–39 in *Stone Age Economics* (New York: Aldine, 1974). See also Lee, op. cit., pp. 431–41.
4. E.g., Sahlins, "Notes on the Original Affluent Society", pp. 85–9 in Richard Lee and Irven DeVore (eds), *Man the Hunter* (Chicago: Aldine, 1968). Lee, op. cit., p. 441. June Helm (ed.), *Handbook of North American Indians*, vol. 6, *The Subarctic* (Washington: Smithsonian Institution, 1981) pp. 130, 144, 190, 201, 339. Julian Steward, *Basin-Plateau Aboriginal Sociopolitical Groups* (Washington: Smithsonian Institution, Bureau of American Ethnology) Bulletin 120, 1938, pp. 1, 9, 20, 33, 46, 64, 73, 75, 134, 142, 152, 231. Julian Steward (ed.), *Handbook of South American Indians* (Washington: Smithsonian Institution, Bureau of American Ethnology) Bulletin 143, vol. 1, 1946, pp. 48, 55, 246, 261. Vol. 3, 1948, pp. 461, 463. Some ethnologies even lead one to question whether the OAS hypothesis applies uniformly to foragers in Africa and Australia. E.g., see Lee and DeVore, op. cit., pp. 89–92, 203–4, 325.
5. Maurice Bloch, *Marxism and Anthropology* (Oxford: Oxford University Press, 1984) p. 91. Although he cites no specific data, the latter can be found in, for instance, Jane Christian and Peter Gardiner's *The Individual in Northern Dene Thought and Communication* (Canadian Ethnology Service Paper No. 35. Ottawa: National Museums of Canada, 1977), p. 59; and Annette Hamilton's "Descended from father, belonging to country: Rights to land in the Australian Western desert" (pp. 85–108 in Eleanor Leacock and Richard Lee (eds), *Politics and History in Band Societies* (Cambridge: Cambridge University Press, 1982)), p. 92. Incredibly, Lee (op. cit., pp. 210, 250–2) acknowledges these facts

but then removes any work-related activities which are *pleasurable* from the category of subsistence labour! It would be difficult to find a more "alienated" way of thinking about labour.

6. Sahlins, op. cit., pp. 37–9.
7. Sahlins, "On the sociology of primitive exchange" pp. 185–275 in *Stone Age Economics*, op. cit., pp. 187–90, 212–15. Lee, op. cit., pp. 118, 437, 460.
8. Ibid., pp. xx, 244.
9. Herbert Barry, I. L. Child and M. K. Bacon, "Relation of child training to subsistence economy", *American Anthropologist*, vol. 61 (February 1959), pp. 51–63. Interestingly, these researchers attribute the reversal not to the emergence of a surplus *per se*, but to the appearance of private property in herds, etc., which children are trained to look after well. The tendency for foragers to stress the importance of self-sufficiency and *self*-control in general is noted in ethnologies too countless to cite here. Let me just say that they exist for all of the major areas of the world, including those, such as the Arctic, where the environment is most harsh and potential surpluses the lowest.
10. David Damas (ed).), *Handbook of North American Indians*, vol. 5, The Arctic (Washington: Smithsonian Institute, 1984) pp. 287, 331–41, 354, 403–4, 436. D. P. Sinha, "The Birhors" pp. 371–403 in M. G. Bicchieri (ed.), *Hunters and Gatherers Today* (New York: Holt, Rinehart and Winston, 1972). Lee, op. cit., p. 365. Leacock and Lee, op. cit., pp. 66–7, 198–9.
11. See Note 2, above.
12. Newman, op. cit., pp. 144–53. The position of women appears to have been lower among Eskimos and Australian aborigines. For example, see Lee, op. cit., p. 454. For the fact that the position of women is generally better among foragers than pastoralists and agriculturalists, see Kathleen Gough, "The origin of the family", *Journal of Marriage and the Family*, vol. 33 (November 1971), pp. 760–71.
13. Damas, op. cit., pp. 221, 244, 334, 343, 407, 497. Helm, op. cit., p. 184. Steward, "Ethnology of the Owens Valley Paiute", *University of California Publications in American Archaeology and Ethnology*, 1932–4, vol. 33, pp. 233–350, pp. 308–11; 1946, op. cit., pp. 343, 440–1, 463. Bicchieri, op. cit., p. 211.
14. Damas, op. cit., pp. 176–9, 192, 286, 493. Helm, op. cit., pp. 192, 261, 301, 319, 344. Steward, 1938, op. cit., pp. 242–3; 1946, op. cit., pp. 76, 324–7, 442; 1948, op. cit., pp. 367, 460–1. Bicchieri, op. cit., pp. 419–21. Leacock and Lee, op. cit., p. 180. Lee, op. cit., pp. 450–4. Lee and DeVore, op. cit., p. 107. For the last comparison, see Lenski and Lenski, op. cit., p. 200.
15. Lee, op. cit., pp. 24, 244, 345, 397, 457–61. Colin Turnbull, *The Forest People* (New York: Simon and Schuster (Touchstone), 1962) pp. 111–14.
16. For example, Christian and Gardiner, op. cit., p. 12.
17. For accounts stressing that the respect foragers have for individuality and autonomy usually occurs within a cooperative, communal context, see Helm, op. cit., pp. 191, 720–6, 737–8; Leacock and Lee, op. cit., pp. 7–9, 12–13, 30–3, 113–15, 148, 180.

18. E.g., Bicchieri, op. cit., pp. 41, 416–17, 438–9; Christian and Gardiner, op. cit., p. 97; Steward, 1932–4, op. cit., pp. 423, 357; Damas, op. cit., pp. 341, 440, 494; Helm, op. cit., pp. 183, 191, 720; Leacock and Lee, op. cit., pp. 12–13, 113. However, there is by no means consensus on this and the preceding claim. As one instance, see p. 33 of the last reference.
19. *German Ideology*, p. 44; *Grundrisse*, pp. 107, 472, 499. V. Gordon Childe, *Man Makes Himself* (New York; New American Library (Mentor), 1951). Lenski and Lenski, op. cit., pp. 156–7. Lee, op. cit., p. 117. Leacock and Lee, op. cit., p. 294.
20. Lenski and Lenski, op. cit., pp. 106, 157–8.
21. See especially Leacock and Lee, op. cit., pp. 213–22, 357–62, 384–8. The most common argument is that many foragers have so much self-conscious control over their social relations that they are often able to incorporate and control, not just trading relations with outsiders, but sometimes even the consequences of wage-labour. Lee (op. cit., pp. 446–7) even claims that their very continued subsistence requires a considerable amount of fairly conscious planning on the part of the bushmen he studied, and that their tendency to aggregate in larger numbers at certain periods requires still more agency. One could mount an analogous argument for the population control exercised by Eskimo bands. The same might be said for some contemporary North American Indian bands (Leacock and Lee, op. cit., pp. 355–68, 380–5).
22. E. A. Thompson, op. cit., pp. 3–9.
23. Ibid., pp. 10–13.
24. Ibid., pp. 35–45.
25. Ibid., pp. 46–8.

The Later "Communal Modes"

26. For the first two stages, see Childe, 1982, op. cit., pp. 108–10; for the latter, Joseph Campbell, *Oriental Mythology; The masks of God* (Harmondsworth: Penguin, 1976) p. 101.
27. Rostovtzeff, op. cit., pp. 320–1; Kosambi, op. cit., p. 52. Certainly, there was a great deal of rebellion by Mughal times. For example, see Irfan Habib, *The Agrarian System of Mughal India (1556–1707)* (London: Asia Publishing House, 1963) pp. 305, 329–30, and Bipan Chandra, "Karl Marx, his theories of Asian societies, and colonial rule" (*Review*, vol. 1 (Summer 1981), pp. 13–91) p. 61.
28. P. T. Raju, "The concept of man in Indian thought", pp. 220–319 in S. Radhakrishnan and P. T. Raju (eds), *The Concept of Man: A Study in comparative philosophy* (Lincoln, Nebraska: Johnson, 1966) 2nd Edition, p. 228.
29. Ibid., pp. 268–9, 278.
30. Wing-Tsit Chan, "The concept of man in Chinese thought", pp. 172–219 in Radhakrishnan and Raju, op. cit., pp. 187–8, 204–5, 211–12.
31. Mary Boyce, *A History of Zoroastrianism* (Leiden/Koln: E. J. Brill, 1975).
32. Raju, op. cit., pp. 228, 232–4, 249. Madelaine Biardeau, "Ahamkara: The ego principle in the Upanisad", *Contributions to Indian Sociology*,

No. 7 (October 1965), pp. 62–84, 82–3. Louis Dumont, "The functional equivalents of the individual in caste society", ibid., pp. 85–99, 91–2. *Homo Hierarchicus* (London: Paladin, 1972) pp. 230–3, 283–4. Ronald B. Inden and Ralph W. Nicolas, *Kinship in Bengali Culture* (Chicago: University of Chicago Press, 1977) p. 84. Richard Lannoy, *The Speaking Tree: A study of Indian culture and society* (Oxford: Oxford University Press, 1974).

33. Raju, op. cit., pp. 280–1; 278.
34. Anderson, *Lineages* . . . , op. cit., pp. 498, 511, 515, 518.
35. Dumont, 1965, op. cit.; 1972, op. cit., pp. 279–82. Inden and Nicolas, op. cit., p. 84. Akos Ostor, Lina Fruzzetti and Steve Barnett (eds), *Concepts of Person: Kinship, caste and marriage in India* (Cambridge, Mass.: Harvard University Press, 1982) pp. 4–5. Anthony T. Carter, "Hierarchy and the concept of person in Western India", pp. 118–42 in Oster et al.
36. I read about such cases in recent newspapers. On the problem of ritual impurity between castes, see Dumont, 1972, op.cit., p. 225, and Ostor et al., op. cit., pp. 13–14.
37. Carter, op. cit., p. 126.
38. *The Sociology of Religion* (Boston: Beacon, 1963) pp. 15–16, 41–3. For contemporary critiques of Marx and Marxists along these. lines, see Dumont, 1965, op. cit., p. 98; 1972, op. cit.; and Steve Barnett, Lina Fruzzetti and Akos Ostor, "Hierarchy purified: Notes on Dumont and his critics", *Journal of Asian Studies*, vol. 35 (August 1976), pp. 627–46.
39. For an example of Marx's ridiculing of the importance of Oriental religions, see his letter to Engels, June 2, 1853, in *Selected Correspondence*, op. cit., pp. 80–1. For a contemporary Marxist dismissing caste, see especially Dipankar Gupta, "Caste, infrastructure and superstructure", *Economic and Political Weekly*, 1981, vol. 16 (No. 51, December 19th), pp. 2093–2104. However, not all Marxists have taken this position. For example, see Kosambi, op. cit., pp. 15–16, 34.
40. Childe, 1963, op.cit., pp. 124, 161.
41. M. I. Finley, *The Ancient Greeks* (New York: Viking, 1964) pp. 12–13.
42. "Mind and state in ancient Greece", *Dialectical Anthropology*, vol. 5 (May 1980), pp. 305–16, pp. 305–6.
43. Finley, 1964, op. cit., p. 154. *Early Greece* (New York: Norton, 1970) pp. 143–5.
44. Kovel, op. cit., p. 306.
45. Finley, 1970, op. cit., pp. 143–5.
46. Kovel, op. cit., pp. 306–7.
47. John Wild, "The concept of man in Greek thought" pp. 56–121 in Radhakrishnan and Raju, op. cit., pp. 60–5, 69–71. See also Finley, 1964, op. cit., who refers to "the 'new' individualism" (p. 139) and concomitant changes in the nature of poetry (pp. 77–8) and pottery, painting and sculpture (pp. 142–3).
48. E.g., see Finley (*The Ancient Economy* (London: Chatto and Windus, 1973) pp. 34–5), who argues that Socrates was exceptional in *not* seeing personal wealth as both necessary and good.
49. Finley, 1970, op. cit., p. 110.

Slavery

50. Finley, 1980, op. cit., Chapter 4. Thomas Wiedemann, *Greek and Roman Slavery* (London: Croom Helm, 1981) p. 133.
51. Ibid., pp. 155–8. Patterson, 1982, op. cit., pp. 88–9. M. I. Finley, *Economy and Society in Ancient Greece* (Harmondsworth: Penguin, 1983) p. 127.
52. Robert W. Fogel and Stanley L. Engerman, *Time on the Cross: The economics of American negro slavery* (Boston: Little, Brown, 1974).
53. Eugene D. Genovese, *Roll, Jordon, Roll: The world the slaves made* (New York: Random House (Vintage), 1976), pp. 388–93.
54. Orlando Patterson, *The Sociology of Slavery: An analysis of the origins, development and structure of negro slave society in Jamaica* (London/Cranbury, N.J.: Associated Universities Presses, 1967/9) p. 182.
55. See Genovese, op. cit., pp. 40–3.
56. Patterson, 1982, op. cit., pp. 22–3, 132–3, 196, 200. See also Wiedemann, op. cit., p. 51.
57. Herbert G. Gutman, *Slavery and the Numbers Game* (Urbana: University of Illinois Press, 1975); Paul A. David, Herbert G. Gutman, Richard Sutch, Peter Temin and Gavin Wright, *Reckoning with Slavery* (New York: Oxford University Press, 1976). This is not to suggest, on the other hand, that all of the issues surrounding this debate are clear and clearly resolved. See Patterson, 1977, op. cit., pp. 413–14.
58. See especially G.E.M. de Ste Croix, *The Class Struggle in the Ancient Greek World* (London: Duckworth, 1981) pp. 114, 120, 133, 144.
59. E.g., see Genovese, op. cit., p. 341.
60. For example, policemen had long hours and low pay, and being a magistrate hindered one from engaging in political intrigue and other means for pursuing one's self-interest (Wiedemann, op. cit., p. 155).
61. Ibid., and p. 4; Patterson, 1982, op. cit., pp. 79–89, 305. The latter even claims that the more powerful and wealthy a slave was, the *more* s/he was held in contempt!
62. Genovese, op. cit., p. 390. See also Gutman, op. cit., pp. 47–8.
63. Patterson, 1982, op. cit., p. 22.
64. E.g., see Genovese, op. cit., pp. 45–6. However, he stresses the interest owners had in *not* allowing their fellow owners to be brutal, since this tended to discredit slavery in general (see p. 41).
65. Ibid., pp. 37–41, 599–621. See also his *The Political Economy of Slavery* (New York: Pantheon, 1965) pp. 54–5, 74. In brief, whereas owners had many more rights than duties vis-à-vis their own slaves, the latter had many more duties than rights. Owners could usually get away even with killing their own slaves, let alone selling them and thereby breaking up families, whereas slaves seldom got away with any crimes, except, perhaps, that of breaking implements or stealing chickens.
66. Genovese, 1976, op. cit., pp. 5, 115, 125, 304–5, 341, 590–1, 597.
67. Finley, 1983, op. cit., p. 110; Patterson, 1982, op. cit., pp. 100–1, 132–3, 261.
68. This statement by Aristotle (see Wiedemann, op. cit., p. 186) is precisely to the point: 'It is essential that each slave should have a clearly defined

goal (*telos*). It is both just and advantageous to offer freedom as a prize – when the prize, and the period of time in which it can be attained, are clearly defined, this will make them work willingly.'

69. Finley, 1983, op. cit., pp. 122–3; de Ste Croix, op. cit., pp. 174–9. Patterson himself (1982, op. cit., p. 260) almost appears to concede this.
70. Genovese, 1976, op. cit., p. 57.
71. See Patterson, 1977, op. cit., p. 411, for a brief review of these claims.
72. Finley, 1983, op. cit., pp. 107–10; 1980, op.cit., pp. 114–15; de Ste Croix, op. cit.; Genovese, op. cit., pp. 587–660. See also the latter's *In Red and Black: Marxian explorations in Southern and Afro-American History* (New York: Pantheon, 1971) pp. 125–7, and the editor's introduction to Bracey Meier Rudwick (ed.), *American Slavery: The question of resistance* (Belmont, Calif.: Wadsworth, 1977).
73. Perry Anderson, *Passages from Antiquity to Feudalism* (London: New Left Books (Verso), 1978) p.79.
74. Indeed, in Rome there was a law specifying that when a slave killed his or her master, *all* slaves in that household must be executed (Wiedemann, op. cit., p. 188).
75. Ibid., pp. 77, 195. See also Finley, 1980, op. cit., pp. 114–15. For similar sayings by wage labourers, see my *Social Psychology* . . . op. cit., p. 125.
76. U. B. Phillips, *Life and Labor in the Old South* (Boston: Little, Brown, 1929). Herbert Aptheker, *American Negro Slave Revolts* (New York: Columbia University Press, 1943). For reviews, see Patterson, 1977, op. cit., pp. 425–6, and Rudwick, op. cit.
77. *The Peculiar Institution: Slavery in the Ante-Bellum South* (New York: Knopf, 1969 (1956)). See especially Chapter 3. Also Genovese, 1976, op. cit., pp. 303, 656.
78. Stanley Elkins, *Slavery* (Chicago: University of Chicago Press, 1959).
79. E.g., see Genovese, 1976, op. cit., pp. 124–32, 597–8, 617. See also Finley, 1980, op. cit., p. 116; Patterson, 1967, op. cit., pp. 178, 260. This is the position taken by most of Elkins' critics in Ann J. Lane (ed.), *The Debate Over Slavery: Stanley Elkins and his critics* (Urbana: University of Illinois Press, 1971), including Roy Simon Bryce-Laporte (pp. 269–92) and George M. Fredrickson and Christopher Lasch (pp. 223–44).
80. Lane, op. cit.; Rudwick, op. cit.
81. Patterson, 1967, op.cit., pp. 261, 275; Genovese, 1976, op. cit., p. 592.
82. E.g., ibid., pp. 317, 450, 622–5, 635, 654.
83. Patterson, 1967, op. cit., pp. 274–8; 1982, op. cit., p. 181.
84. Ibid., pp. 99–101.
85. That there *were* more revolts in the former than the latter is well-documented. For example, see Patterson, 1967, op. cit., pp. 273–83; 1977, op. cit., p. 427; 1982, op. cit., p. 259; and Genovese, 1976, op. cit., pp. 111, 587–660. However, I do not mean to suggest that how the slaves viewed themselves was the only, or even *major*, factor in determining whether or not they rebelled. On this point, see especially Patterson, 1977, op. cit., pp. 415–16, who, nevertheless, goes much farther in discounting such conditions than I would.

Feudalism

86. Marc Bloch, 1966, op. cit., pp. 66–7, 90; 1961, op. cit., pp. 176–80. Rodney Hilton, *The English Peasantry in the Later Middle Ages* (Oxford: Oxford University Press (Clarendon), 1975) pp. 125–6.
87. Bloch, 1966, op. cit., pp. 76–85; 1961, op. cit., pp. 171, 250–2, 272. Hilton, 1966, op. cit., pp. 128–35, 219. *Bondmen Made Free: Medieval peasant movements and the English rising of 1381* (London: Methuen, 1977) pp. 15, 59–61.
88. Bloch, 1961, op. cit., p. 279; de Ste. Croix, op. cit., p. 136.
89. Bloch, 1966, op. cit., p. 103; 1961, op. cit., p. 212. Hilton, 1966, op. cit., pp. 127, 227.
90. Bloch, 1961, op. cit., pp. 188–9, 218, 247–8, 271–4. Hilton, 1966, op. cit., pp. 127, 240–3; 1975, op. cit., pp. 116–21; 1977, op. cit., pp. 43, 140–5. However, on p. 150 of the latter work Hilton cautions us not to exaggerate the degree of centralization the Normans were able to achieve.
91. Bloch, 1966, op.cit., pp. 41–58.
92. Ibid., pp. 78, 178; 1961, op. cit., pp. 372, 431. Hilton, 1966, op. cit., pp. 152–4; 1975, op. cit., p. 54.
93. Bloch, 1966, op. cit., pp. 150–2; 1961, op. cit., p. 131.
94. Bloch, 1966, op. cit., p. 166; 1961, op. cit., pp. 132, 137, 141–2, 185. Hilton, 1966, op. cit., p. 89; 1975, p. 13.
95. Bloch, 1961, op. cit., pp. 123–5, 135, 226–7. Hilton, 1966, op. cit., pp. 150–1; 1975, op. cit., pp. 56–8.
96. Bloch, 1966, op. cit., pp. 91, 160–6; 1961, op. cit., pp. 133, 190–1, 205–10. Hilton, 1977, op. cit., p. 38.
97. Alan Macfarlane, *The Origins of English Individualism* (Oxford: Blackwell, 1978). See also Bloch, 1961, op. cit., p. 134; Hilton, 1966, op. cit., p. 166; 1975, op. cit., Chapter 3.
98. Bloch, 1966, op. cit., pp. 102, 106–7, 111, 115–16, 126–8, 140–5, 172, 198, 254, 276–8. Hilton, 1966, op.cit., pp. 85, 123, 136–8, 167, 219; 1975, op. cit., pp. 64–9; 1977, op. cit., pp. 15–17, 68–9, 74–5, 80–3, 90–2, 106; Chapter 3.
99. Bloch, 1966, op. cit., pp. 223–33; 1961, op. cit., p. 242.
100. Hilton, 1977, op. cit., pp. 130, 220.
101. Bloch, 1961, op. cit., pp. 81–6, 148. Hilton, 1977, op. cit., pp. 18, 21, 97, 103, 207–12, 221.
102. Dobb, op. cit.
103. See Note 98.
104. However, the degree to which the impetus for these changes came from within feudalism itself is a matter of some dispute. For a useful compendium of some of this material, see Rodney Hilton's edited volume, entitled *The Transition from Feudalism to Capitalism* (London: New Left Books (Verso), 1978).
105. For example, see Lawrence Stone's "The bourgeois revolution of Seventeenth-Century England revisited", *Past and Present*, No. 109 (November 1985), pp. 44–54.
106. Christopher Hill, *The World Turned Upside Down: Radical ideas during*

the *English Revolution* (Harmondsworth: Penguin (Peregrine), 1984).

The Guild System

107. Black, op. cit., p. 10.
108. Pirenne, 1963, op. cit., pp. 88–9; 1936, op. cit., p. 186.
109. Unwin, 1957, op. cit., pp. 48–52; 1963; op. cit., p. 350. Pirenne, 1936, pp. 184–5, 200–4. However, several English researchers maintain that many, and perhaps most, guilds there were not very independent either. For example, see Unwin, 1963, op. cit., p. 241, and D. M. Palliser, "The trade gilds of Tudor York", pp. 86–116 in Peter Clark and Paul Slack (eds), *Crisis and Order in English Towns, 1500–1700* (Toronto: University of Toronto Press, 1972) pp. 94, 106.
110. Unwin, 1957, op. cit., p. 18; 1963, op. cit., pp. 47–9, 61–6, 155–60. Pirenne, 1963, p. 128.
111. Pirenne, 1963, op. cit., pp. 163–6, 210–11; 1936, pp. 187, 207–8.
112. Unwin, 1963, op. cit., pp. 172–3, 221–31.
113. Ibid., pp. 28, 201.
114. Unwin, 1963, op. cit., pp. 91–2, 264–5, 347; 1957, op. cit., p. 48.
115. Ibid.
116. Unwin, 1963, op. cit., pp. 225–31, 350–1.
117. Unwin, 1957, op. cit., pp. 207–10. Clark and Slack, op. cit., p. 25. Hilton, 1977, op. cit., pp. 190–1.
118. See Note 116.
119. See Notes 115 and 117.
120. Unwin, 1963, op. cit., pp. 1–2, 346–9. Palliser, op. cit., p. 86.
121. Fritz Rörig, *The Medieval Town* (Berkeley/Los Angeles: University of California Press, 1969).
122. Black, op. cit., pp. 65, 58.
123. E.g., see Palliser, op. cit., and Lauro Martines, *Power and Imagination: City-States in Renaissance Italy* (New York: Knopf, 1979).

A Golden Age/Renaissance

124. Bloch, 1966, op. cit., pp. 143–4.
125. Agnes Heller, *Renaissance Man* (New York: Schocken, 1981) pp. 51–2. Jacques Le Goff, *Time, Work and Culture in the Middle Ages* (Chicago: University of Chicago Press, 1980) pp. 45–7. However, he interprets this demand as a response to increasing prices for goods and services and decreasing wages rather than simply a result of increasing opportunities.
126. E.g., Martines, op. cit., pp. 246–9.
127. Le Goff, op. cit., pp. 63–7.
128. Heller, op. cit., pp. 130, 157, 205–9, 231–17, 241, 244, 262–3, 294–5. See also Stephen Greenblatt's *Renaissance Self-Fashioning* (Chicago: University of Chicago Press, 1980) pp. 2, 11–7, 30, 36, 46–53, 157, 232, 235–6.
129. See especially Colin Morris, *The Discovery of the Individual, 1050–1200* (London: SPCK, 1972). Also Le Goff, op. cit., pp. xii, 39–41, 62–3, 112–13.
130. Heller, op. cit., pp. 179, 184, 189, 194, 330–8, 365, 391, 436–7, 440, 444–5.

Greenblatt, op. cit., pp. 33–43, 85–8, 99, 115, 129, 163, 212.
131. Le Goff, op. cit., pp. 46–7, 69–70, 121. Martines, op. cit., pp. 246–9. On the other hand, the latter notes that even though these art craftsmen were versatile, they had to "scurry around" to obtain commissions.
132. Martines, op. cit., pp. 191–210. See also Le Goff, op. cit., pp. 62–3, whose inspiration from Marxism appears considerably weaker.
133. Anderson, *Lineages* . . . , op. cit., pp. 148–9 (fn).
134. Karl Marx and Friedrich Engels, *On Religion* (New York: Schocken, 1964) pp. 97–109, 152–3, 189, 269–71, 299–300. One should perhaps note that all of these particular references are to Engels alone.

The Ascendancy of the Bourgeoisie

135. Perkin, op.cit., pp. 213–14. R. S. Neale, "Introduction" and " 'The bourgeoisie, historically, has played a most revolutionary part' ". Pp. 2–27 and 84–102 in Eugene Kamenka and R. S. Neale (eds), *Feudalism, Capitalism and Beyond* (London: Edward Arnold, 1975).
136. Dobb, op. cit., pp. 18–22, 97, 106, 122, 209. Hill, *From Reformation to Industrial Revolution* (Harmondsworth: Penguin, 1969), pp. 17, 127.
137. Op. cit. See Note 135.
138. Mantoux, op. cit., pp. 213, 218. Dobb, op. cit., p. 289. That mechanical innovations often did not even save labour in the first place, has been well-documented by Samuel, op. cit., pp. 47–8. He argues that given the large supply of labour in England, as compared, for example, to North America, this was seldom necessary.
139. Neale, op. cit., pp. 90–1.

The "Making" of the Working Class

140. Mantoux, op. cit., pp. 408–9. E. P. Thompson, *The Making of the English Working Class* (New York: Random House (Vintage), 1963), Chapters 8 and 9. George Rudé, *The Crowd in History* (London: Lawrence and Wishart, 1982), p. 180. Perkin, op. cit., pp. 131, 145–6.
141. Craig Calhoun, *The Question of Class Struggle: Social foundations of popular radicalism during the Industrial Revolution* (Chicago: University of Chicago Press, 1982).
142. Thompson, *Making* . . . , op. cit., pp. 62, 303–9, 541–75. Rudé, op. cit., pp. 84–9.
143. Charles Tilly, Louise Tilly and Richard Tilly, *The Rebellious Century, 1830–1930* (London: Dent, 1975) pp. 233–4, 279, 281.
144. Thompson, *Making* . . . , op. cit., pp. 826–30.
145. Perkin, op. cit., pp. 209–12. Gareth Stedman Jones, *Languages of Class: Studies in English working class history, 1832–1982* (Cambridge: Cambridge University Press, 1983) pp. 53, 60, 91, 106–11, 157, 168.
146. William H. Sewell, *Work and Revolution in France* (Cambridge: Cambridge University Press, 1980) pp. 143, 154–5, 266, 283. Mark Traugott, *Armies of the Poor: Determinants of working-class participation in the Parisian insurrection of June 1848* (Princeton: Princeton University Press, 1985) pp. 7–10, 171–4.

147. Thompson, *Making . . .* , op. cit., pp. 672–3, 743. Vincent, op. cit. Dennis Smith, *Conflict and Compromise: Class formation in English society, 1830–1914* (London: Routledge and Kegan Paul, 1982) p. 137.
148. Mantoux, op. cit., Chapter 3. Dobb, op. cit., Chapter 7. Thompson, *Making of . . .* , op. cit., Chapter 10. Perkin, op. cit., pp. 125–49.
149. E.g., Perkin's. See Note 151.
150. See Note 148. The main issues have been the importance of the enclosure system for forcing producers into the factories versus the ready availability of factory labour through population increases and a rise in the real wages and standards of living for factory labourers.
151. Perkin, op. cit., p. 381.

"Advanced" or "Late" Capitalism

152. For example, see George Lichtheim, *Marxism* (New York: Praeger, 1965) pp. 188–90, and Geoffrey Kay, *The Economic Theory of the Working Class* (London: Macmillan, 1979), Chapter 4 and pp. 72–8. Ernest Mandel (*Late Capitalism* (London: New Left Books (Verso), 1978) p. 178) claims that Marx was in fact not only aware that increases in productivity can allow the rate of surplus value and real wages to rise at the same time, but that this may be the rule rather than the exception; however, I am not at all convinced that this is an accurate interpretation.
153. On the first matter, see especially Michael Burawoy's *Manufacturing Consent* (Chicago: University of Chicago Press, 1980). On the second, for Britain, see Stephen Wood, *Industrial Relations and Management Strategy* (Cambridge: Cambridge University Press, 1983); for the U.S., Derek Jones and Jan Svejmar (eds), *Participatory and Self-Managed Firms* (Lexington, Mass.: Lexington Books, 1982); the U.S. and Canada, Donald V. Nightingale, *Workplace Democracy* (Toronto: University of Toronto Press, 1982). Such schemes actually pre-date Marx, and he was aware of them and ridiculed their effects. See Harvie Ramsey, "Cycles of control", *Sociology*, vol. 11 (September 1977), pp. 481–505 (p. 483). However, he clearly underestimated the subjective effects they would have upon workers. Here see especially Nightingale. For critiques of these schemes and their alleged effects, see Ramsey, op. cit.; Woods, op. cit. James Rinehart, "Appropriating workers' knowledge: Quality control circles at a General Motors plant", *Studies in Political Economy*, No. 13 (Spring 1984), pp. 75–97. Don Wells, *Soft Sell: "Quality of working life" programs and the productivity race* (Ottawa: Canadian Centre for Policy Alternatives, 1986).
154. *Consciousness and Action among the Western Working Class* (London: Macmillan, 1973) p. 21.
155. *Manuscripts*, p. 274; *Grundrisse*, p. 462. E.g., H. Roy Kaplan, *Lottery Winners* (New York: Harper and Row, 1978). His results for the case of Canada were much the same as these for the U.S. See Julianne Labreche, "Land of the small-time spenders", *MacLean's*, December 11, 1978, pp. 21–2.
156. E.g., see the studies reviewed in Archibald, *Social Psychology . . .* , op. cit., pp. 162–4.

157. Martin Meissner, Elizabeth W. Humphreys, Scott Meis, and William J. Scheu, "No exit for wives: sexual division of labour", *Canadian Review of Sociology and Anthropology*, vol. 12 (November 1975), pp. 424–39. Martin Meissner, "Sexual division of labour and inequality: Labour and leisure", pp. 160–79 in Marylee Stephenson (ed.), *Women in Canada*, 2nd edition (Toronto: New Press, 1977). See also Jaggar, op. cit., p. 80.

158. Pat and Hugh Armstrong, *The Double Ghetto: Canadian women and their segregated work* (Toronto: McClelland and Stewart, 1978). Michele Barrett, *Women's Oppression Today* (London: New Left Books, 1980). David Gordon, Richard Edwards and Michael Reich, *Segmented Work, Divided Workers* (Cambridge: Cambridge University Press, 1982).

159. As claimed, for example, by such proponents of the "new working class" thesis as Serge Mallet (*The New Working Class* (Nottingham: Spokesman Books, 1975). *Essays on the New Working Class* (St. Louis: Telos Press, 1975). Here, see particularly Duncan Gallie's *In Search of the New Working Class* (Cambridge: Cambridge University Press, 1978).

160. E.g., Robert Blauner, *Alienation and Freedom* (Chicago: University of Chicago Press, 1964). However, as many researchers have noted, not all workers in automated plants get to work with the automated machinery. For example, see H. Kern and Michael Schumann (*Industriearbeit und Arbeiterbewußtsein* (Frankfurt am Main: Europaische Verlagsanstalt, 1970)) and Theo Nichols, Peter Armstrong, and Huw Beynon (*Workers Divided* (London: Fontana, 1976). *Living with Capitalism* (London: Routledge and Kegan Paul, 1977)).

161. The classic restatement of the de-skilling hypothesis is Harry Braverman's *Labor and Monopoly Capital* (New York: Monthly Review Press, 1974). For some empirical critiques, see Andrew Friedman, *Industry and Labour: Class struggle and monopoly capitalism* (London: Macmillan, 1977); Ken Kusterer, *Know How on the Job: The important working knowledge of "unskilled workers"* (Boulder: Greenwood Press, 1978); Richard Edwards, *Contested Terrain* (New York: Basic Books, 1979); Stephen Wood (ed.), *The Degradation of Work?: Skill, deskilling and the labour process* (London: Hutchinson, 1982).

162. E.g., Peter Wilmott and Michael Young, *Family and Class in a London Suburb* (Harmondsworth: Penguin, 1968). John H. Goldthorpe, David Lockwood, Frank Bechhofer, and Jennifer Platt, *The Affluent Worker in the Class Structure* (Cambridge: Cambridge University Press, 1969).

163. The classification scheme is David Lockwood's. See his "Sources of variation in working class images of society", pp. 98–114 in Joseph A. Kahl (ed.), *Comparative Perspectives in Stratification* (Boston: Little, Brown,, 1968). For critiques, see K. Roberts, F. G. Cook, S. C. Clark, and Elizabeth Semeonoff, *The Fragmentary Class Structure* (London: Heinemann, 1977); M. Bulmer (ed.), *Working Class Images of Society* (London: Routledge and Kegan Paul, 1975); Eve Brook and Dan Finn, "Working class images of society and community studies" (pp. 125–43 in Centre for Contemporary Cultural Studies, *On Ideology*, op cit.); Howard H. Davis, *Beyond Class Images* (London: Croom Helm, 1979). For a relatively unsuccessful attempt to apply the conception to Canada,

232   *Marx and the Missing Link: "Human Nature"*

see Vincent Keddie, "Class identification and party preference among manual workers" (*Canadian Review of Sociology and Anthropology*, vol. 17 (February 1980), pp. 24–6).

164. Goldthorpe et al., op. cit.
165. E.g., a clear majority of blue collar workers in Canada feel that the federal government is influenced by the interests and wishes of "big business" and very little by those of labour. See my *Social Psychology* . . . , op. cit., pp. 146–7. For some general, non-specifically class, trend data indicating substantial increases in feelings of political powerlessness since the 1960s, see Robert S. Gilmour and Robert B. Lamb, *Political Alienation in Contemporary America* (New York: St. Martin's Press, 1975) pp. 16–21, 53–4, and Harold D. Clarke, and Jane Jenson, Lawrence LeDuc, and Jon H. Pammett, *Absent Mandate: The politics of discontent in Canada* (Toronto: Gage, 1984) pp. 39–40.
166. Thompson, *Making* . . . , op. cit., p. 623.
167. For a review of these claims by Richard Hoggart, Herbert Gans and others, see my *Social Psychology* . . . , op. cit., pp. 154–64.
168. Ibid., pp. 171–2, 189–93, 204. For a more recent study of machoism and other indications of sexism among groups of male blue collar workers, see Paul Willis's *Learning to Labour* (Westmead: Saxon House, 1977). However, there is no white collar comparison group in this study.
169. Again, see *Social Psychology* . . . , op. cit., pp. 193, 204.
170. Richard Sennett and Jonathan Cobb, *The Hidden Injuries of Class* (New York: Knopf, 1972). Nichols and Beynon, op. cit.
171. Mann, op. cit., p. 70.
172. E.g., see Walter Runciman, *Relative Deprivation and Social Justice* (Harmondsworth: Penguin, 1972); Nichols, Armstrong and Beynon, op. cit.
173. This is the title of a book by André Gorz (London: Pluto Press, 1982).
174. See Note 27 in the Introduction to Part IV, and James O'Connor's *The Fiscal Crisis of the State* (New York: St. Martin's Press, 1973).
175. For example, as I began writing this chapter, these items appeared in the Toronto *Globe and Mail*: "[British print] Unions at Canadian-owned papers to sign no-strike pact" (September 23, 1986, p. A15); "Railways hand labour unions severe concession demands [including a 5% wage rollback]" (October 2, 1986, p. A13).
176. In a recent Canadian case, the federal government contracted cleaning work out to a private firm. Many of the same workers were hired by the latter, but at $2.50 or so less an hour.
177. For the former, see, e.g., Martyn Nightingale, "UK productivity dealing in the 1960s" pp. 316–33 in Theo Nichols (ed.), *Capital and Labour* (London: Fontana, 1980). The latter is currently going on in the U.S. auto industry (*Globe and Mail*, October 10, 1986, p. B2).
178. Canadian autoworkers have already left and formed their own union, the Canadian Auto Workers Union. Representatives of Canadian woodworkers have yet to make the move, but they speak as if it is inevitable (Jennifer Hunter, *Globe and Mail*, September 16, 1986, p.B5).
179. For tech change clauses in collective bargaining agreements, the

Canadian Union of Postal Workers has one of the best. Control through municipalities has apparently been attempted in Norway, and has been discussed by organized labour in Canada. Here see David Noble, "Present tense technology", Part two, *Democracy*, vol. 3 (Summer 1983), pp. 70–82.

180. In one celebrated English case, workers threatened with layoff developed an elaborate plan to convert their plants from manufacturing arms to consumer goods. See Hilary Wainwright and Dave Elliott, *The Lucas Plan: A new trade unionism in the making?* (London: Allison and Busby, 1982).

9 How "General" is "Human Nature"?

DO WE NEED "NEEDS" AND "RELATIVE DEPRIVATION"?

Let us retrace our steps to the accounts of hunters and gatherers discussed in the previous chapter and reexamine them with regard to Marx's conception of needs and wants "in general".

On the corroborative side, we do find that general needs are sometimes referred to, especially in accounts of socialization practices. Furthermore, the needs discussed go beyond interdependence and self-preservation to belongingness and sharing, and often to at least some degree of self-sufficiency and "assertion".[1] Moreover, in at least some schools of anthropological thought something like a need hierarchy is presumed. For example, in the "cultural ecology" of Julian Steward and "cultural materialism" of Marvin Harris the relative absence of a highly developed culture and selfish individualism are attributed to poor environments, crude technologies, and the consequent deprivation of subsistence needs.[2] Finally, social comparison and many of its usual effects – arrogance and envy – have been reported for foragers, who themselves typically insist upon sharing and equality in order to avoid them.[3]

On the disconfirming side, one seldom sees needs referred to outside discussions of the socialization of children. Nor is it obvious that some of the practices referred to, such as sharing, in fact constitute prepotent needs, since they often have to be normatively regulated, even in the absence of scarcity. Furthermore, some of the needs stressed by Marx himself – for activity, for variety, and self-expression and development – are anything but prominent. Indeed, many analysts claim foragers operate on a "least effort" principle, such that they work only enough to subsist, and then spend most of their "leisure" doing non-effortful activities.[4] Moreover, self-sufficiency and assertion among foragers are said to have more to do with the survival of the group and its members than with the self-expression and development of the individual as such. Finally, the conceptions of how needs are psychically organized are as likely as not to be quite different from, even incompatible with, Marx's need hierarchy.

In one popular type of account, various needs or propensities are

235

organized as competing opposites, with equal rather than differential prepotencies. Thus foragers are said to struggle with tendencies to *both* share *and* accumulate wealth, to be both equal and individually distinctive, dependent and independent, nurturant and aggressive, and so on.[5] That one side of the respective antinomy wins out is more a function of practical and cultural reasoning than any natural hierarchical ordering. For example, since most foragers are nomadic, the accumulation of wealth is simply impractical, but since sharing is also more likely to be normative, acquisitiveness tends to be suppressed and repressed.[6]

Another is still less compatible with Marx's. On the one hand, here too it is assumed that humans have a multitude of capacities and needs, no one set of which, including that of bio-subsistence needs, is any more necessary than another for the existence of humanity. On the other, no human need transcends its own cultural context enough to allow one to predict the specific thoughts and actions of individuals in different societies, let alone a culture as a whole. In this case these criticisms have been explicitly applied to Marx as well as Steward and Harris. In fact, Sahlins, its chief proponent, attempts to stand them on their heads; that is, the absence of both much "economic" activity and a surplus of material wealth or culture is attributed to the absence of many wants and the cultural value placed upon sharing, rather than vice versa.[7]

Unfortunately, at this point we have no obvious means of choosing among these various conceptions. Marx may well have read into human nature his own values and inclinations toward hyperactivity and craftsmanship,[8] and to have underrated the importance, *in their own right*, of the nasty passions of aggressiveness and acquisitiveness. Nevertheless, his critics are themselves anything but free of bias, as was indicated in the previous chapter.[9] More importantly, a case can be made that his own position was not as different from theirs as it might seem, and that their criticisms of his empirical claims need not constitute a refutation of his underlying theory of needs.

In the first place, that most foragers have been relatively "affluent" does not invalidate the claim for a need hierarchy. If the initial condition of scarcity is not in fact met, the assumption that subsistence needs have priority is not tested. But where the initial condition *has* been met – that is, where the natural environment faced by foragers has been severe and their technologies primitive – the rest of their culture has also tended to be relatively limited.[10] Furthermore, Sahlins himself has noted that sharing often breaks down during famines.[11]

These facts, and especially the second, are clearly in line with the existence of a need hierarchy.

Secondly, there is no denying that the latter is in more trouble when subsistence needs *are* well-gratified and foragers still do not (a) develop wants for new material goods and/or (b) become more concerned with gratifying needs for variety and self-expression. However, even here one must be careful not to misconstrue Marx's own position, and, perhaps, that of foragers themselves. As we saw earlier, Marx's method was not to abstract needs from their specific cultural–historical contexts. Presumably, he would not have expected individuals to automatically desire new goods and services unless they were there to be desired, and the means for storing, carrying, and protecting them were available. The institution of private property is one such means whose existence Marx was careful to avoid presuming. Similarly, as noted in Chapter 8, just as most foragers have been less poor than Marx assumed, so they have been more active and creative than many of their would-be admirers have maintained. To assume otherwise one would have to use questionable criteria from our own alienated existence, such as the separation of "hobbies" from "work", and so on.[12]

If we now move on to *the communal modes of Asia and the Mediterranean*, we find somewhat parallel arguments for cultural relativity and against needs in common with people in other social formations. Thus precisely because individuals did not distinguish themselves from the Asian collectivity, as Marx claimed, they are not likely to have experienced themselves as free agents and "needed" variety or self-expression and development. If individuals *qua individuals* had few needs beyond subsistence, neither did they have high aspirations with regard to such material needs, since this would have required private ownership and social comparison which themselves necessitate circumstances which were lacking; that is, a culture which is individualistic and egalitarian rather than collectivist and hierarchical.[13]

I have already expressed qualified agreement with the latter position in the previous chapter, but I am not at all sure that (a) the higher-order needs on the individual side are in fact missing from the official religions and philosophies of Asiatic societies; (b) that their being less in evidence than higher-order needs with regard to other members of the community necessarily reflects the actual state of affairs at all accurately; or even (c), that social comparison was as infrequent, and individual aspirations as low, as such analysts claim.

Thus the four values of Hinduism have usually been seen as constituting a hierarchy, with "wealth" being more related to survival than accumulation as such. "Enjoyment", which seems to have aspects of "intrinsic motivation" (see below), is said to presuppose the obtaining of "wealth". Furthermore, both are necessary for, but less ethically good than, one's duties to others *and* one's own "self-realization", albeit the latter involves much more becoming one with nature and god than the expression and development of an individually unique and autonomous personality. If some degree of self-assertion is evident in this philosophy, it is still more so in Confucianism.[14]

Given that such philosophies counsel subordinating the individual and his or her self-expression and development to the community and its official representatives, their portraits of human needs and wants differ considerably from Marx's. Yet if one regards them as ideological attempts to control individuals rather than simply accurate descriptions (after all, most were written by Brahmins or official court philosophers), their counsels of constraint can often be seen as acknowledging the very aspects of human nature which seem to be missing or under-emphasized. Surely, for example, the call to denigrate and deny one's own needs and desires implies that one *has* them in the first place, and the reasoning offered is precisely that contained in Marx's; that is, if one does not lower one's adaptation level and level of aspiration, one is sure to be miserable, given, of course (conveniently), that scarcity and deprivation are inevitable.[15] Many argue that the original purpose of India's caste system was to legitimate inequality by preventing social comparison and mobility. For example, different rules of justice were to apply to different castes. However, here too the ideologues left nothing to chance and proclaimed that castes were still interdependent: even the lowest make important contributions to the community, and for this reason those of high caste must attend to the needs of those of low as well as vice versa. Yet authorities were not above deliberately encouraging social comparison, envy and strife among armed tribes they wanted to subdue.[16]

Certainly, there is lots of evidence that social comparison and relative deprivation occurred in Asian societies right from the beginning. Thus the wealthy families of the Indus cities made a point of not displaying their wealth, apparently because they lacked a militarized state to protect it. Many centuries later, after distributing agricultural production equally among members of the community, some Punjabi tribes actually *burned* the surplus so that it would not be bartered and wealth from it accumulated differentially! Finally, as noted earlier, there have been peasant revolts throughout most of India's history, and there is good reason to believe that social comparison and relative deprivation have figured prominently in their etiology.[17]

What the above analysis does not tell us, of course, is whether lower class/caste Indians have been motivated by higher as well as lower order needs. In this regard, I find the following additional observations suggestive. That their rulers seldom fully and directly enslaved them is often attributed to these rulers' knowledge that the absence of some degree of independence would lessen productivity and increase the likelihood of rebellion. The same rationale is usually suggested for the practice of having tribute collected by an official of one's own village rather than the court. Presumably, it was only after such attempts at manipulation failed that rulers resorted to terrorism. That this occurred relatively frequently implies that many did indeed grate at being controlled and exploited by others. The same is true for the occasional *en masse* desertion of villages. Finally, if we jump all the way to the present, we find some observers of India claiming that children's needs for relative autonomy and recognition as individuals are still being deprived, and that various maladies – insecurity, aggressiveness, etc. – have resulted from this deprivation.[18]

Needless to say, ancient Greece has been a more important source of ideas about human nature in the West. The ideal of both craftsmanship in particular and self-expression and development in general can be found here. Although there too the latter were primarily in the service of the community, they had more importance in their own right than they did in most Asian philosophies. The notion of a need hierarchy was also more explicit, in that both sharing and individual development were seen as motivated by needs beyond either material subsistence or religious salvation. Indeed, it was the ancient Greeks who first suggested that humans have not only a capacity for individual perfection, but an inherent drive to achieve it.[19]

Social comparison and other sources of relative deprivation were similarly recognized by the Greeks. Thus rather than trust matters to the need hierarchy, Aristotle and others proposed limiting extremes of wealth and poverty so as to ensure cooperation rather than competition. That the propensity for invidious comparison proved too strong to be eradicated by this means is suggested by its persistence, if often in seemingly strange forms. For example, individual members of the Greek ruling class often bragged about how much they paid in taxes, and hence how much they supported others and the state![20] Education was designed to promote sympathy and altruism instead of self-centredness and acquisitiveness. Stoicism appeared after there had been greater centralization of wealth and power, and one then found much the same call to deny one's own needs and lower one's aspirations as we have just noted for early Asian societies.[21]

On the other hand, some scholars have argued that the afore-mentioned ideals of craftmanship and self-development were neither fully valued nor accurate descriptions of the orientations of producers in classical antiquity. (Indeed, as we saw earlier, Marx himself was partly of this opinon.) According to this interpretation, the Greek ruling classes denigrated *any* manual labour, including craft labour, and craftsmen themselves were much more "extrinsically" than "intrinsically" motivated.[22]

Needless to say, we cannot hope to resolve these disputes here, but as usual the truth appears to be somewhere between the two extremes. Thus while the ruling classes did, at best, give only grudging respect to craftwork, this may have been because it quickly overlapped with slave labour, and/or because competition with the latter tended to keep remuneration low. It may have been precisely this relatively low status which made intrinsic involvement in the work itself difficult. Put otherwise, it may have been more a case of the deprivation of one need (recognition and esteem) preventing the gratification of another (self-expression and intrinsic involvement) than that the latter did not exist. In fact, there is some evidence for intrinsic involvement in manual labour in ancient Greece.[23]

What, therefore, of *slave labour* itself?

Most observers have assumed that specific reactions to slavery were the result of an interaction between common human needs and adaptation to specific social circumstances. While self-preservation and security seem to have been foremost amongst the concerns of slaves, retaining some degree of freedom and dignity also figured importantly. Understandably, this usually meant preserving some minimum room for the latter *within* accommodation. Often this entailed only being lazy and evasive, or taking pride in one's physical strength, musical or other artistic abilities, or even superior morality to that of one's master. However, sometimes aspirations for freedom and dignity were so strong that slaves were willing to sacrifice the gratification of lower, more basic needs. For example, they would accept manumission even though it meant leaving the rest of their family in slavery, or run away or rebel and run a high risk of not preserving one's very biological being.[24]

As with most explanations which rely upon needs, this one is difficult to evaluate. Nevertheless, in support of it I add the following observations.

First, as noted by all slave-owning classes, most slaves have to be coerced to labour for their masters. The explanations commonly offered for this fact are not unreasonable; that is, slaves are not internally motivated because their own needs, both biological (because they are poorly fed) and psychic (because they do not act independently and cannot express themselves, acquire respect as individuals, and so on) are deprived. Further facts in line with this reasoning are that (a) the same slaves who were lazy and "irresponsible" could be the exact opposite when they were hired out and permitted to keep a portion of the proceeds, or when they worked their own garden plots, and (b) slave owners themselves often preferred serfs or wage-labourers for this reason, and accordingly sometimes freed their own slaves.[25]

Second, whereas open rebellion and other forms of overt aggression by slaves have been rare, *flight* has not. Furthermore, unqualified submission has probably been as rare as overt rebellion.[26] Third, slaves have almost always had low status, and the explanation for this is obvious: independence has been nearly universally valued, and slaves have not had it. Fourthly and finally, slaves have almost always desired freedom, even when (a) they have seen no possibility of acquiring it, and (b) they have accepted the ideology of their masters that they are inferior and do not deserve it.

Of course, as many have observed, it is not very helpful to simply assume the existence of fully operative needs for freedom and dignity, since their absolute deprivation has seldom been in a one-to-one relationship with the above reactions. For example, the brutality of owners is a poor predictor of rebellion.[27] Instead, one must take social comparison, specific aspirations, and *relative* deprivation into account. Thus those slaves who were by far the most likely to rebel were those, such as the Spartan helots and newly-arrived, African-born slaves in the American South, who (a) had recently experienced freedom themselves and (b) were therefore most likely to compare themselves unfavourably with both their masters and other producers who were free. Furthermore, rebellion was most likely after expectations and aspirations had risen because of relatively *indulgent* masters, *prosperous* times, and increasing *inequality* among slaves as well as between them and their masters.[28]

There is little question that freedom was also highly valued in the *feudal* epoch.[29] However, can we legitimately treat this as indicative of a 'need'? It is tempting to do so. For one thing, researchers often argue that the more deprived of freedom peasants were, the more vociferously they demanded it and the more likely they were to flee or rebel.[30] For another, some treat freedom as a requirement of a higher order than subsistence and security. For example, the original pledge of allegiance to the lord is interpreted as a return for the lord's protection, which peasants found palatable only because the original emphasis was upon the latter rather than complete subordination. The latter was in fact fiercely resisted, and was accomplished only after the application of much force.[31] Also in line with a need hierarchy is the occasional suggestion of conflict between, on the one hand, peasants' desires for more material comfort and freedom for themselves, and, on the other, between each of these and the requirement of mutual help from each other.[32]

Either way, the vast bulk of claims about serfs and other peasants in Medieval Europe point to the more variable aspects of the desire for freedom and its relative deprivation. Thus it was lords' attempts to encroach upon established customs regarding the balance of control over separate plots, the commons, village assemblies, and so on, which seem to have provoked the *most* conflict. The expectations and aspirations of either side tended to rise after it had made some headway against nature and/or the other, and oppression was often experienced as worse after good than poor years for agricultural production. Allegedly, the freer serfs became, the more "irksome" their few remaining duties to work the demesne became, and the more the lord had to sweeten the load, by, for example, feeding them well while they worked. Social comparison is also implied to have been very important. Thus there was much differentiation, comparison, and competition among peasants themselves, with those whose fines were higher than others having felt more deprived. Similarly, the districts where serfs felt most deprived and extracted the most concessions from lords were those with the largest proportions of peasants who were *already* free.[33]

Interestingly, underlying the most prominent debate about the demise of feudalism is the same issue we discussed concerning slavery; specifically, whether serfs were motivated primarily by absolute or relative deprivation. Thus Dobbs' original argument was that in attempting to increase their revenues in the crisis of the 14th and 15th centuries, lords *over*exploited and dominated their serfs, such that the latter's very subsistence as well as desire for freedom was gravely threatened. They therefore fled more to avoid starvation than obtain freedom as such. It was the ensuing shortage of labour which permitted

those serfs who remained to extract concessions and eventually transform feudalism.[34] Sweezy, on the other hand, argued that the most
important motivator was not how much serfs were deprived of subsistence and freedom in absolute terms, but "the rise of the towns",
which "opened up to the servile population of the countryside the
prospect of a freer and better life".[35] However, eventually Dobb
conceded that relative deprivation was *also* important, and defended
his original explanation as having in fact included Sweezy's emphasis
on the mere existence of towns.[36]

As to the *guilds*, craft masters wanted autonomy from merchants,
other capitalists, and municipal officials; journeymen unquestionably
wanted to become masters, presumably through a combination of a
desire for a secure subsistence, relatively independent productive
activity, and recognition and status.[37] There are even more direct hints
of the need hierarchy in the literature. For example, guild controls
were more likely to be elaborated in prosperous than poor times.[38]
Similarly, it was presumably precisely the assurance that most guild
members' lower-order needs would be met that allowed for whatever
degree of intrinsic motivation in work itself there was.[39]

On the relative side, the structure of the guilds can be seen as a more or
less deliberate attempt to prevent competition and conflict by limiting
expectations and comparisons. With so many steps and years to become a
master, an apprentice or journeyman was likely to compare himself with
others beside the master and increase his expectations and aspirations
slowly; with methods, amounts, and the quality of production standard-
ized, all members were unlikely to make unfavourable comparisons and
feel deprived.[40] But rather than leave matters to this structure, masters
also directly exhorted their journeymen not to envy masters' working and
living conditions.[41] We have already seen that this was often unsuccessful
(see Chapter 8), but this too appears to have been a consequence of
relative deprivation, of the fact that masters not only dominated and
exploited those below them, but violated their expectations of becoming
masters.[42] Furthermore, the way guild members related to conflicts
between the aristocracy and the urban bourgeoisie on the one hand, and
the peasantry on the other, is said to have depended upon which of their
own needs were deprived, and by how much.[43]

There is a heavy emphasis upon adaptation and social comparison
levels in the literature on *industrialization and the early working class*.
However, in the better-known studies there is a concern with both
absolute and relative deprivation, and both lower and higher-order
needs. For example, of the food riots which occurred in the late 18th

and first half of the 19th century, E. P. Thompson writes that while low wages, the high cost of bread, and "famine or extreme scarcity" were obviously important, "even this violence shows a motive more complex than hunger . . ." "[The rioters] *expected* to buy their provisions in the open market, and even in times of shortage they *expected* prices to be regulated by *custom* also." In addition to exercising their own, direct control over the market, they wanted to punish retailers who were violating the customary morality of the community.[44]

The importance of the factory system was not so much that it drastically reduced the producers' standard of living. Indeed, factory labourers were often better off materially than others; but their *share* of communal wealth went down, so much so that they *felt* as if they had experienced an absolute decline. They also became less independent and self-determining in their labour, and therefore suffered a loss of status. The handloom weavers who opposed the factory system so strenuously were occasionally put out of employment and into "extreme distress" by the introduction of power looms; but more typically they were not, and either way, what they resented more was the indirect taxation which followed the power loom and/or the prospect of the discipline of factory labour, and especially having to *serve* those machines. Their greater opposition compared to other producers, therefore, was a function of their initially higher independence and status, of their higher *aspirations*. Similarly, the latter are alleged to have made them among the most despairing and pitiless of those who had to succumb to the factory system.[45]

Whether explicitly or implicitly, debates about workers' motivation have dominated much of *industrial and political sociology* in the 20th century. The primary concern has been the same issue which has arisen for all previous modes of production; that is, the relative weight to be given to general needs and specific wants. However, other issues have also been prominent. One is whether Marx's conception of general needs is itself adequate, or whether a very different one, such as that provided by Freudian or existentialist theory, is required. Another is whether existing accounts of both needs and wants might be seriously male-biased, and hence not applicable to over half the human species. I shall take up each of these issues in some detail, and then end with an examination of contemporary psychology.

(1) The relative weight of the general and the specific

The "Great Depression" of the 1930s has often been considered a test of Marxian theory which the latter has obviously failed. After all, one had drastic deprivation of subsistence needs but no revolutions. But quite aside from the questionable accuracy of both the premise and conclusion of this argument (the majority of workers neither came all that close to biological annihilation nor accepted their deprivation passively), commentators have pointed to a different interpretation which is also suggested by Marx's theory of needs. In particular, workers may have been too preoccupied with subsisting to be concerned with higher-order issues of workers' control, or even with lower-level forms of cooperation among themselves. More typically, researchers have stressed the limits to workers' social comparison and relative deprivation. Thus they felt that most people, and especially those with whom they were most likely to compare themselves, were "in the same boat", or even *"worse off"* than themselves.[46] Many workers saw the crisis as an abnormal situation which could not be blamed on anyone, and some workers, especially in the United States, largely blamed themselves for their plight.[47] Others simply saw no alternative and lowered their aspirations.

Changes in the occupational structure during and after this period, including the proliferation of "white collar" workers, led to a growing number of sociological studies whose authors in effect also took stands on the relative importance of general needs and specific aspirations. A notable example is C. Wright Mills. According to him, a concern with independence is a social value and individual habit which has not affected most workers in the present period – for example, they have not rebelled against being propertyless or supervised by others – because neither their workmates nor themselves have·ever experienced it. Work itself "has no intrinsic value", and the ideal of craftsmanship is just that: a social value which did not appear until the Renaissance, has long since been lost, and therefore no longer motivates workers.[48]

While this stance seems to indicate total opposition to the idea of general needs, Mills can in fact be shown to have been highly ambivalent and ambiguous on the issue, in that he himself claimed not only that "For most employees, work has a generally unpleasant quality", but that the *explanation* for this is that they have "few positive gratifications from their daily round". What would such positive gratifications be but those which pertain to general needs? Here too we need only turn to Mills himself to see what these presumably are: a "psychological" "tie between the product and the producer" which allows the latter both "consummatory satisfaction" and "positive satisfaction from encountering a resistance and conquering it", and so on.[49] Interestingly, one of the first systematic studies of alienation from work by a sociologist was undertaken by a student of Mills, and both the use of, and evidence for, such general needs is rampant and explicit.[50]

In his study of the effects of various technologies on workers' experience of work, published in the early 1960s, Robert Blauner assumed that in order to be involving, jobs must have variety and allow freedom of movement and self-expression. However, the extent to which deprivation is likely to be consciously felt and expressed through, for example, dissatisfaction, will depend greatly upon whether workers actually aspire to have control over, and initiative and meaning in, work. This, in turn, will be affected by whether workers are educated and/or otherwise exposed to alternatives to their present employment. For instance, Blauner claimed that these conditions were not met for the southern textile workers he studied, such that they did not feel very alienated from their labour even though it was objectively lacking in variety and responsibility.[51]

The criticisms Goldthorpe et al. were to make of Blauner were in good part an extension of his own argument about aspirations; that is, workers are so likely to have past experiences which have led them to lower their aspirations for personally fulfilling work – to the point where they treat labour as a mere commodity – that they are not greatly affected by how much technology and other specific working conditions do or do not allow variety and self-expression.[52] As others have noted, the problem with their own test of this reasoning is that their samples are small and suspiciously stacked against the counter-hypothesis.[53] This is not meant to detract from the argument that aspirations and relative deprivation are at least, and perhaps more, important than needs in general in affecting workers' responses to work. Certainly, other studies of the period attest to this.[54] Nevertheless, it hardly follows that one can legitimately deny the existence of needs common to, and providing the foundation for, such specific wants and aspirations.

In my own opinion, the better reviews of the research of this period make use of both absolute and relative deprivation. Michael Mann, for instance, explains relatively high levels of job satisfaction not by assuming that most workers either have few needs or that their working conditions gratify them, but by suggesting that they compare their jobs with what they realistically expect they could get rather than an abstract ideal, and then "steadily" lower their "aspirations" with each new work experience. Similarly, he (in effect) treats issues of control over production as higher-order, or emergent as compared to wages, job security, and other issues related to subsistence. Although workers do not often concern themselves with control, even when they are highly paid, this is presumably because management's steadfast refusal to bargain about it makes such a concern unrealistic.[55]

The 1970s saw a spate of empirical case studies by more overtly Marxist sociologists, primarily British, who took issue with many of the specific claims of both Blauner and Goldthorpe et al. For example, Huw Beynon, Theo Nichols, and Peter Armstrong questioned whether the lowering of aspirations to an "instrumental" orientation toward work is that widespread and complete, and whether it necessarily gives workers a stake in the system and limits the potential for revolt.[56] On the other hand, their own analyses of auto and chemical workers rely heavily upon the very same, realistically low, expectations and aspirations.[57] Furthermore, many of their other observations about contemporary workers – for example, that they neither know much about what their employers do or earn, nor, therefore, compare their own lot with them and feel especially deprived[58] – are very much in keeping with Marx's view of needs and wants.

The late 70s and early 80s also produced a number of first-hand (and first-rate) ethnographies of workers which contain strident criticisms of Marx for having allegedly overly emphasized coercion and greatly underestimated workers' active participation in the domination and exploitation of their own labour-power.[59] In the case of Michael Burawoy, he and his fellow machine operators eagerly treated exceeding production minimums as a game to be mastered; in that of Paul Willis, the working class youth he observed apparently looked forward to heavy, monotonous, manual labour as a confirmation of their own masculinity, relative to white collar men as well as women in general, and to working class youth who conform to the middle class standards of their teachers.[60]

These studies, and, incidentally, many others,[61] do provide an important antidote to Marx's more sombre portrayals of workers; who instead are often highly creative, individually as well as collectively, in *making* objectively alienating work more challenging and interesting. Again, however, these researchers' underlying models of human nature are not much different from those of Marx himself, in that both Burawoy and Willis assume (a) general needs for variety and self-expression, and that (b) the above-mentioned orientations of workers are creative attempts to achieve compensatory gratification of them.[62] Similarly, both researchers make extensive use of social comparison and adaptation level processes.[63]

(2) The nature of general needs

Beginning in the late 1920s, Marxists with an interest in Freudian theory began to question whether workers are motivated primarily by *either* the subsistence *or* higher-order needs suggested by Marx and subsequent Marxists. According to these critics, a concern with *sexual* pleasure is usually at the root of workers' thoughts and activities, with both healthy interpersonal relations more generally and intrinsic involvement in work being impossible in the absence of an unrepressed sexuality. Wilhelm Reich in particular claimed that having groups of working class women and youth discuss their sexual problems was more effective in radicalizing them than any amount of political analysis which appealed to workers' other needs.[64] Researchers continue to claim that those who are sexually liberated are also more likely to be liberated in other ways.[65]

One of the several problems I have with the latter claims is that the research upon which they are based provides an even less direct test of the importance of various needs than does the research immediately discussed above, in that explicit rebellion against capitalist relations of production is much further removed from needs and their deprivation than are experiences of work and rebellion against particular working relationships and conditions. Another is that either way, it hardly follows from the above findings that sexuality is as important as, let alone more important than, needs more directly related to particular individuals' subsistence. After all, religious celibates seem to subsist relatively well without gratifying their sexual needs, while severe hunger does not permit the same degree of adjustment.

Finally, although he placed much less emphasis upon sexual needs, Marx's own need hierarchy at least included them among those which are primary. When he wrote of workers moving up to concern themselves with others' needs and their own self-fulfillment, perhaps he too took it for granted that their sexual requirements would already have been at least minimally met. Marx did not see his higher-order needs as mere derivatives of the sexual; but then, even if we concede that some of the energy for higher-order activities might be sublimated libido, Freudians have yet to demonstrate that the former can be completely reduced to the latter anyway.

It was precisely the latter concerns which led to the second alternative taken up here: a combination of "ego" and "existential" psychology. According to these approaches, the "stumbling block" which makes it difficult for workers to concern themselves with others' needs and their own self-development is the deprivation of neither their subsistence nor their sexual needs, but a need for supportive/nurturant relationships with others and a well-defined, secure social identity. Eric Fromm was one of the first to offer such an approach, but its application to workers was more explicitly undertaken by Sartre and others in the 1950s.[66] In one influential American study, Robert Lane found the workers he interviewed to be greatly concerned with their low social status and attempts to avoid recognizing it or having it emotionally charge the rest of their lives. For example, they tended not to compare themselves with middle class people, and when they did they tended to deny that class differences are important.[67]

In their extension of this line of reasoning Richard Sennett and Jonathan Cobb reinterpret most claims about the motives of workers, or at least those in the United States. Thus workers' apparent authoritarianism is a consequence of neither a harsh and depriving childhood nor an attempt to compensate for such treatment at work, but a quest for respect as an individual in exchange for one's sacrifice for others. Consumerism is not the result of a desire to accumulate for its own sake or to obtain personal compensation for the deprivation of higher-order needs with regard to work. Rather, it is an attempt to provide for one's family and, through this, to prove to them and others that one is a worthwhile individual who deserves recognition and respect. Sennett and Cobb claim that unlike Lane's workers, theirs did not avoid comparing themselves with middle class people, nor did they go on to deny the importance of class; they instead battled each other for respect, precisely by making invidious comparisons with regard to how much each had sacrificed.[68]

This analysis is difficult to corroborate, particularly because, as Sennett himself notes, the United States is a country which makes workers' social identity and self-esteem especially problematic.[69] But even if we allow Sennett the benefit of the doubt, we can make a case that his analysis is not as different from Marx's as it might seem. Thus rather than being completely equal in priority to physical subsistence, workers' quest for freedom and dignity is said to have become more frequent and salient of late precisely because workers are now better-fed.[70] Similarly, while Sennett's workers compared themselves with middle class people, they did so *as individuals*. Given that this was the case, perhaps it is not surprising that they engaged in an "inner-class warfare" similar to, if much more convoluted than, the one Marx himself insisted would occur under these circumstances.

(3) Are Marx's needs and wants only those of the "malestream"?

In recognizing that needs for variety, self-expression, and development have been suppressed and repressed in women, do we really want to argue that they are male rather than fully human needs? Hardly.

The "reproductive" activities which are still relegated mainly to individual women have been motivated by a variety of needs and wants; from women's own biological subsistence, to that of their spouses and children, to love of the same, and so on. However, as Meg Luxton has ably documented, they have usually been much more than any of these,[71] and there seems little question that where the conditions surrounding "housework" have approximated those of factory and office work, women have typically experienced them in much the same way as men and women have usually experienced the latter. Similarly, while many women in contemporary capitalist societies continue to see their primary role as that of housewife and mother, a majority not only work outside the home, but are as likely as men to say that of all of their activities, they depend most upon their *paid* labour for personal satisfaction. Indeed, in some studies women have put *more* importance on how interesting their paid labour is, and been *more* dissatisfied when interest is lacking.[72]

As I see it, while studies of women workers indicate that women have indeed had different experiences from men on the shopfloor as well as at home, they do not require us to propose a different system of general needs or processes of relative deprivation for women than men. Thus as Anna Pollert herself has noted, the tobacco workers she observed and interviewed found their "unskilled", repetitive work boring and meaningless, and had lowered their aspirations and concentrated upon its economic aspects. As with Nichols and Armstrong and Willis, some even took pride in being tough and able to endure it, and were most insulted when management called them personally stupid because of the stupefying nature of their work.[73] As with Burawoy and Willis, their shopfloor culture appears to have been implicitly designed to both give them more control over their work and work relations, and to overcome boredom. Perhaps not surprisingly, however, it was also feminized.[74] Similar conclusions can be drawn from subsequent studies.[75]

The same can be said for experiences of relative deprivation. For example, although Pollert claims that most of her workers were young and felt highly deprived precisely because they were not prepared for factory labour, Ruth Cavendish suggests instead that hers had not expected their work to be satisfying and were "instrumentally oriented" even before they came to their current job. They also did not expect to stay in factory work.[76] Most of these researchers claim that women too compare their own jobs to others – to their own in the past, to others open to themselves now, and/or to those of friends and others in the present – *and*, incidentally, that for them as well the typical consequence was that they viewed their own relatively *favourably*. This was especially true if they were immigrants.[77]

Having said this, I do not mean to underplay the differences in *content* between the expectations, comparisons, and aspirations of male and female workers. Thus the reason that most women did not expect to stay on their jobs was not that they would get a better paying job, or perhaps start their own business, but that they were, or expected to become, full-time wives and mothers. Shockingly, they often thought of themselves as dependent upon men even if they were single or middle-aged with little objective hope of leaving their jobs! Put otherwise, for many their "career" was marriage and a family rather than paid labour.[78] The reason many viewed their own jobs relatively favourably was not only that they had compared them with other jobs *in general*, but with those typically performed by *women*. In this regard, many were thankful to have avoided the loneliness of the full-time housewife, and, given the competitiveness of their own industry and the competition among women to work in it, to have any paid labour at all.[79]

(4) Meanwhile, back at the ranch (psychology)

Among many criticisms of the concept of need are the following. Many activities and/or objects may gratify the same need, but if they become *very* many one might question whether it makes sense to use "need" in the first place. The claim that individuals have done something because they "needed" to is often too facile, even circular. Many circumstances are likely to intervene between a need and an activity, and these circumstances would presumably need to be part of an explanation for the latter. Alternatively, precisely because these circumstances are likely to be many, an individual may refrain from doing something *in spite of* "needing to". As a consequence of these various considerations, need arguments are open to the charge of being irrefutable.[80]

This list barely scratches the surface, since the claims by need theorists have often been outlandish. On the other hand, I find many of their critics to be equally excessive. For example, in one review Gerald Salancik and Jeffrey Pfeffer make statements such as these: "The repeated failures to find empirical support for theories of universal human needs (Turner and Lawrence, 1965; Hulin and Blood, 1968) led to an acceptance of the idea that different individuals had different needs, or at least different strengths of the same needs"; "It is difficult to maintain the position that needs, particularly higher-order needs, are instinctual in the face of little evidence for the generality of needs [the same two studies are cited here] and of the convincing social learning literature (Bandura, 1969) which argues that most behavioral dispositions are acquired through learning."[81] However, this is clearly a misuse of very little data.

Turner and Lawrence classified 47 jobs in 11 companies according to whether or not they permitted interaction with workmates, variety in the place and operation of the work itself, and knowledge, skills, and responsibility. This classification, which seems to fit the degree to which work permitted the gratification of higher-order needs rather well, in turn predicted absenteeism *very* well, and better than such unique characteristics of individuals as their education or seniority, even when the effects of the latter were partialled out statistically. In fact, the researchers' *own* conclusion here is diametrically opposed to Salancik and Pfeffer's: "Our evidence suggests that in general good attendance records were . . . to a large extent the consequence of greater interest in and involvement with the work itself."[82]

Our would-be critics of any theory of needs conveniently underplayed this set of findings and instead focused on another which did not support the researchers' findings so clearly. Specifically, there was no overall correlation between the above-mentioned "task attributes" and job satisfaction. Rather, it occurred for workers in towns, but not cities. In the latter satisfaction varied only with knowledge, skill, and responsibility. Salancik and Pfeffer take these findings as evidence for the extreme relativity of wants and reactions to work; however, here too the researchers themselves did not. Rather, they noted that in cities, "monotonous and unchallenging work" tended to be more highly paid, and wondered whether it was "the result of a conscious or unconscious effort to counteract an expected negative response". They also suggested that city workers, having been more used to such alienating work, might also have come to expect it more. This combination of lower expectations and higher compensation led our researchers to further suggest that "The favourable response of both Town workers to complex tasks and City workers to simple tasks can be interpreted as alternative expressions of the same underlying human tendency to value highly a sense of control and predictability in the environment."[83]

When we now turn to Hulin and Blood, we find that they too both rely extremely heavily on Turner and Lawrence, and also conveniently misinterpret them! All that their review appears to establish is that (a) there are often individual differences in how workers respond to the same job attributes, and (b) "job enlargement" experiments have not been uniformly successful in increasing job satisfaction and productivity, and lessening absenteeism and turnover. But here again our would-be critics would do well to return to Turner and Lawrence, who noted that in enlarging jobs, many experimenters have in addition actually *decreased* interaction, autonomy, and responsibility. They themselves recommended that wherever possible managers increase the latter as well as enlarge jobs.[84]

Such experiments in "participative management" and "job enrichment" have rightly been controversial, since they have (a) almost always been initiated by management rather than labour; (b) often been used for the purpose of keeping out, or undermining existing, unions; (c) been token in altering, if at all, the balance of power between management and labour, and (d) conveniently ended during economic downturns and/or after labour has gained more power through them than management was willing to give up.[85] On the other hand, there is another way to look at such experiments: given their typically token nature, they have been amazingly effective in altering workers' orientation toward their work. Thus in one review, published, incidentally, in the same year as Hulin and Blood's, Paul Blumberg concluded that "There is hardly a study in the literature which fails to demonstrate that satisfaction in work is enhanced or that generally beneficial consequences accrue from a genuine [sic] increase in workers' decision-making power."[86]

I suggest, therefore, that as with other disciplines, industrial psychology has established that workers indeed have many needs in common beyond those of mere subsistence. What has *not* been obtained is hard evidence for the existence of a need *hierarchy* such as that postulated by Marx. Most research has dealt with Abraham Maslow's formulation. However, there are problems with both it and purported tests of it. On the first count, Maslow's conception has been accused of greatly de-emphasizing social needs and indicating other biases in favour of competitive capitalism, including blaming its victims rather than itself.[87] On the second, most "tests" have tended to be either fairly casual observations or precise, quantitative analyses with questionable indicators of needs and deprivation.[88]

Nevertheless, the evidence for a need hierarchy is not quite as weak and inconclusive as the above implies. For one thing, one obtains better results even with the latter procedures if one simplifies Maslow's needs by distinguishing between "maintenance" needs for subsistence and security, "relatedness" needs for belonging and nurturance, and "growth" needs for self-expression, recognition, etc.[89] For another, there is a fairly consistent tendency for those workers whose lower-order needs are presumably most deprived – that is, blue collar workers – to place more importance on the related issues of job security, pay, and other "extrinsic" attributes of work than do white collar workers, and for the latter in turn to put greater stress on higher-order needs for autonomy, responsibility, and self-expression.[90] Furthermore, although most of these researchers have either neglected to study women or to consider whether their needs might differ from those of men, Ellen Betz's results support her argument that since full-time housewives are more dependent upon others for the gratification of their subsistence needs, the latter and their "security" needs will remain more prepotent in them than in women with paid work.[91]

As one might expect, psychologists have conducted much more, and much more conclusive, research on phenomena of expectations, adaptation and social comparison, and relative deprivation. We would do well to take cognizance of such findings and qualify our own expectations accordingly. Here are a number of important ones.

When individuals develop expectations from past experience, and *when* they perceive them to be violated, they often do experience relative deprivation.[92] However, individuals may not experience events in the manner one might expect them to. For example, Marx himself stressed only some of several, quite different, sets of events and experiences, and in some studies the results bear out none of them.[93] If relative deprivation from unfulfilled expectations is far from inevitable, a sense of unfairness and injustice is still less so.[94] Among the further conditions which appear necessary for this more complex event are (a) the individual must *want* the expected event to occur (but, for instance, workers may not in fact want to be promoted and socially mobile); (b) s/he may have to believe that the outcome *could* have been favourable to him/herself and/or that it is *not* likely to be so in the future (whereas many workers are fatalistic and others are naively optimistic);[95] (c) s/he probably must believe that such a favourable outcome *should* have occurred because s/he is *entitled* to it (whereas as we have seen, workers often doubt their own worth as individuals);[96] and (d) if one is to see capitalists in particular as unfair and unjust (and there is a huge jump for individuals to go from particular others to social systems[97]), one must first see them as the *source of*, or at least *responsible for*, the unfavourable outcome (but often the world economy, or even the greediness of one's fellow workers, is blamed instead).[98]

It may well be that the more conditions approximate those of real-life workers, and especially where they function collectively, the more the above requirements are met. For example, it may take long-standing outcomes, traditions, and personal habits to produce a sense of entitlement, and a large and sudden violation of expec-tations and aspirations to effect deep feelings of deprivation and betrayal.[99] Furthermore, even the above, mostly experimental, studies indicate that relative deprivation and injustice become much more likely simply by the addition of unfavourable social compari-son.[100] On the other hand, social comparison itself is anything but inevitable. We have already noted this for real life. Here I shall indicate some of the important considerations arising from labora-tory research.

In most experiments, social comparison and relative deprivation are pretty well assured, not only because others are present, but because the experimenter increases their salience and even *invites* comparison, usually by telling subjects how much they and others received from interaction. There is no question that something like this also occurs in real life, when, for example, union negotiators point to the profits of employers or the incomes of other groups of workers with whom they have traditionally compared themselves. However, when their em-ployers are not immediately present or workers do not know their incomes anyway (in North America, at least, a clear majority of workers are *not* unionized), it is quite another matter.

These problems are compounded when there are multiple others with whom one could compare. Here the experimental evidence is very much in keeping with that in industrial sociology: except perhaps where one is *already* struggling with other workers against one's employers (more of this later), one is likely to prefer comparing oneself with a more *similar* other.[101] This has an understandable motivational basis: by avoiding comparing oneself with seemingly superior individuals one avoids the implication that oneself is unworthy. *In fact*, one may even avoid comparing oneself with *similar* others, at least publicly, in order not to (a) incite *their* envy and/or (b) disrupt interaction with them. This appears to be a particularly difficult problem for women, who have to worry about threatening their husbands as well as their male workmates.[102]

Once individuals *have* compared themselves with others, their conceptions of justice intervene between their comparisons and their sense of relative deprivation and injustice, and as noted in Chapter 7, the principles they use may be those of bourgeois ideology – in the literature of social psychology they are labelled "proportionality" or "equity" – rather than even "equality", let alone "need". This is often true for both male and female factory workers as well as middle class college students. Again, women have the additional impediment of patriarchal ideology: since men are usually considered the main breadwinners while women are at a minimum secondary, or even working just for "pin money", many women workers feel that men *deserve* more income.[103]

If one compares oneself with more than one other and/or with more than one input and outcome from/for the same other, one has difficulty processing all of the information and deciding whether the overall outcome is just or unjust, even if one is a well-educated college student.[104] Downwardly mobile white collar workers may not be aware that they have been so, and other "status inconsistencies" may not cause much concern even when they are attended to. One thinks of the blue collar husband who is not fazed by the white collar job of his wife because she is paid less than he is, or because he feels superior as a man anyway. Indeed, some considerable degree of inequality may actually be *desired* by most blue collar workers, as suggested by Sennett and Cobb.[105] "If there is no inequality," they reason, "how can I compare myself favourably with others?"

In suggesting that the latter reasoning is prevalent among producers now, I do not mean to claim that it is in any way the most typical for all time, let alone "natural". It may not pre-date capitalism, and it seems to depend very much upon individuals having to compete for status and self-esteem under conditions where they are scarce. My point is only that we cannot simply assume, as Marx did, that even in our own time workers will have developed their own system of justice based on the principle of "From each according to his ability, to each according to his need", compared themselves unfavourably with their employers, and felt unjustly deprived.

AGGRESSION AND WITHDRAWAL AS RESPONSES TO DEPRIVATION AND FRUSTRATION

Almost all *"tribal societies"* recognize anger, hostility, aggression, and the need to deal with them collectively. Indeed, anger and/or its presumed sources (e.g., stinginess and arrogance) are often regarded as the worst of "sins", and most foragers deliberately try to avoid it/ them by keeping threats to, and frustration for, others to a minimum.[106] Some socialize children to repress competitiveness and hostility, but the latter come out in dreams and other phantasies anyway.[107] More typically, foragers attempt to control their overt expression and/or consequences.[108] Some such peoples deliberately *provoke* individuals to aggress so that they can both release tension and learn to control their natural responses to it.[109] Although there are some interesting exceptions to the rule that frustration produces aggression among tribal peoples, such exceptions do not appear to discount the importance of frustration–aggression theory (hereafter, FAT) altogether.[110]

Unfortunately, there is little such first-hand information about the *ancient civilizations.* Nevertheless, there is little question that the imagery of FAT and withdrawal or "alienation" is used to describe producers in these societies, and far from having been intended as mere asides, these observations are offered as the most important explanations for such important events as the fall of the Mughal empire.[111] De Ste Croix was later to offer much the same scenario for the fall of the Greek and Roman Empires; that is, peasants, especially in the outer reaches of the empires, had little stake in them and therefore made little effort to defend them.[112]

As for *slavery*, the imagery of FAT is admittedly more explicit in some writers than others, as, for example, when Eugene Genovese claims that "smoldering resentment *had to come out* in other forms besides revolt".[113] However, in addition to these assumptions that only so much frustration can and will be tolerated, and that the tension must be released in one way or another, others very much in evidence are the notions of displacement of aggression upon tools, animals, and fellow slaves; partial expression and catharsis of frustration through work songs, spirituals, stories, and other aspects of their own culture; and compensation through the latter as well as various other activities and feelings, including both conning and being morally superior to their masters.[114] The same is true for the withdrawal of effort and emotional involvement in labour, and resignation in the face of a lack of opportunity to successfully rebel. Interestingly, FAT can be seen in the accounts of contemporary observers of slave revolts in antiquity, and "coming-to-terms" and alienation in the sayings of slaves themselves. For instance, one of the latter was "if you don't like being a slave, you will be miserable; but you won't stop being a slave."[115]

The real issues in this literature are not whether humans can only tolerate so much frustration and will naturally aggress against the presumed source when they have an opportunity to do so, but (a) the likelihood of revolt and the social circumstances which increase or decrease it, in absolute terms, and relative to various other responses to deprivation and frustration; (b) what these other responses typically are; and (c) what are the relationships among various responses. For example, does one substitute for another, or do several occur at once? Or, do they perhaps occur in a sequence? Indeed, can responses be separated from one another in the first place, and if they can, can one then legitimately attribute a single response to a single motive? The answers to these questions are complex and indicate that it is no simple matter to explain the responses of slaves with FAT. Nevertheless, neither do they suggest we should abandon the attempt to do so.

The same qualified use of FAT can be seen in accounts of *feudalism*. Thus, according to Hilton, peasants' acceptance of their "outwardly conferred role" and class consciousness need not have been exclusive, and partial rejection of the former was likely to be expressed through "sluggishness" as well as surliness. Later, Hilton refers to "social tensions which had their outcome in social movements, some on a small and some on a large scale, some peaceful and some violent". These "social tensions" were clearly also both *psychic* and *necessary* for rebellion. However, they were not a *sufficient* condition for the latter. Rather, peasants in the early mass movements of the middle ages often lacked awareness of their own aims, let alone the sources of deprivation. As a consequence, there was much scapegoating; for example, of Jews in Spain, and the Flemish in England. Later, at the time of the rebellion in 1381, peasants had a clearer notion of the actual sources of frustration, and there had been a shift in the balance of power toward tenants. Yet after the failure of specific battles for freedom and an end to villeinage there was a great deal of "resignation".[116]

The aforementioned debate about the decline of feudalism has been about not only absolute versus relative deprivation, but about the relative importance of deprivation from both types exceeding serfs' toleration limits and the opportunity to flee provided by the proximity of towns and cities. Thus for Dobb, "pressure" from lords in the form

of having been "overworked and underfed" "became literally unendurable", such that flight became an act of "sheer desperation",
while for Sweezy, deprivation was only moderate, but the perceived
likelihood of successfully fleeing was *very* high. Dobb countered that if
the latter were in fact the most important factor, why should flight and
rebellion have occurred even in backward areas where there were few
such opportunities?[117]

There is relatively little explicit reference to such models in the
literature on *guilds*. However, we do know that such "social tensions"
existed; that small masters and journeymen often displaced aggression
against alien competitors; and that large masters often felt that such
tensions were dangerous enough to warrant their being expressed and
catharted in public in ritualized ways.[118]

The most popular writers on the *early responses to capitalism* have
sometimes been critical of Marx's specific applications of FAT. For
example, in addition to the aforementioned critique of his accounts of
Luddism, Thompson questions Marx's interpretation of religion as the
mere expression of, and consolation for, suffering, and instead suggests
that it was often a goad for revolt, in part because it provided a sense of
community, collective justice and power. Furthermore, rather than
view crime as a response which was necessarily individualistic and took
away from class conscious, collective protest, Thompson, while agreeing that it was "sub-political", argues that crime was often both
collective and facilitative.[119] However, he and others still interpret
such responses as alternative means for dealing with accumulated
"grievances" which exceeded the limits of producers' tolerance, and
they too often classify many other responses as "pre-political" or
otherwise "primitive".[120]

More fundamental critiques of "volcanic eruptions" after the
"welling up of boundless impulse" have come from others such as the
Tillys, who claim that even the responses of 19th century producers
were rational and consciously political, and as such can be explained
only with a "resource mobilization theory" (RMT) specifying the
claims made "by solidary groups organized around articulated interests". Interestingly enough, the latter is seen as completely consistent with Marx himself in his more rational moments, and with the
accounts of Rudé, Hobsbawm and Thompson as well.[121]

To me, this latter claim is problematic. On the one hand, both Marx
and the later historians were more "guilty" of FAT than the Tillys –
apparently in order to muster them as authorities for their own theory
– make them out to have been, but on the other, the formers' own FAT

was far more sophisticated than the Tillys' caricature. The latter may well apply to such contemporary psychologists and political sociologists as Leonard Berkowitz and Ted Gurr,[122] but in the cases of Marx and Rudé et al. there is usually no neglect of existing "interest groups" and their prior collective organization, and no assumption that their members are *necessarily* unaware of their own interests, or the source of deprivation, or impulsive and "irrational" in their responses, or that collective protest can be completely reduced to the convergence of the latter. But the Tillys themselves can be, and have been, criticized for going too far in the *other* direction; for neglecting the importance of accumulated frustration and responses to it which sometimes are not in fact all that conscious and political, because individuals have not in fact been all that organized beforehand.[123] One of the many strengths of Marx's model is that it includes both types of responses and attempts to specify circumstances under which one type is more likely than the other.

This said, let us return to *contemporary industrial sociology*. Much of the work here amounts to claiming that most workers feel much less deprived and frustrated than Marx expected them to be, primarily because they bring low expectations with them to the workplace, seldom compare themselves with their bosses, but *do* compare themselves with other workers who are unemployed or in still less gratifying jobs. However, according to these researchers workers *do* experience deprivation and frustration, and they *do* sometimes respond to it by rebelling or otherwise "striking out at" others when their limits of tolerance have been reached; for example, when they have been insulted. However, because they have learned that rebellion is not likely to be frequent, very collective, organized, or successful, short of such exceptional circumstances, few respond in this manner. In the case of Nichols et al.'s chemical workers, these few are usually the minority of "politicos" and the "bloody-minded"; in the case of Pollert's tobacco workers, they were a small(er?) proportion of "bitter" workers. Most of the rest have clearly withdrawn. Because, in their own words, "What can you do about it?", they "just get by" or "plod along".[124]

There are some important differences in this literature, not just in the proportion of workers with "short fuses" and the relative frequency of rebellion vis-à-vis withdrawal or "alienation", but in traditions of class consciousness and militancy in different regions of England, industries, and factories, and in the "repressive tolerance" of teachers and managers. There may be some important gender distinctions as well, although the differences between, for instance, Sallie Westwood's hosiery workers (from Leicester?) and Pollert's tobacco workers (Bristol) appear to be as great as those between Beynon's autoworkers (Liverpool) and the chemical workers (from Bristol?) he studied with Nichols and Armstrong. Furthermore, most such differences appear to be explained by, rather than exogenous to, Marx's FAT. For example, the school and shopfloor cultures described by Willis, Burawoy, Pollert, and Westwood seem to be alternative responses to full-scale, collective rebellion and individualistic withdrawal which are in one sense only "primitive" and "pre-political" reactions, but also relatively collective, active, and creative attempts to compensate for the lack of gratification in school and work activities.[125] The only "bloody-minded" researcher who explicitly claims to reject FAT is Sennett, but again he is not successful, in that his point is not that workers are not frustrated, angry, and inclined to aggress, or, alternatively, to retreat when they feel powerless to do otherwise, but that their doubts about their own worth lead them to be "ambivalent about their *right* to be angry" and, often, to blame *themselves* for their plight.[126]

Ironically, but not as surprising as it might seem to the uninitiated, given the "cognitive revolution" in *psychology*, FAT has come under the closest and most critical scrutiny there. Here I have relied heavily upon two critical reviews from the mid-1970s – those of James Tedeschi and Michael Billig – and added other studies where appropriate. The following convergences with, and qualifications to, Marx's FAT appear warranted.

First, frustration is neither a necessary nor a sufficient condition for aggression. One may aggress simply in order to coerce another, without being frustrated,[127] and one may be highly frustrated but still not aggress against a frustrator. Certain additional conditions appear to be necessary, and others greatly increase or decrease the likelihood of aggression. Some psychologists claim that one is unlikely to *ever* aggress against a frustrator much more powerful than oneself, but we know this is *not* the case, that it depends upon whether one feels one can "get away with it", and, as Marx claimed, and as we shall see later in this chapter, the "strength in numbers" which comes from being in a group is often sufficient for this. Some claim others' having blocked one from reaching a goal is not enough. Rather, there must be a direct attack, or perhaps even an insult. Others maintain that the frustrator must be seen to have *intended* to frustrate, harm, and/or derogate oneself. We do know that the latter at least greatly increase the *likelihood* of aggression after frustration,[128] and we have already seen that this applies to factory workers.

Secondly, although there may well be such a phenomenon as a tolerance threshold,[129] most individuals are probably much more tolerant of frustration than Marx and others have assumed, and much less "naturally" prone to aggress even after their thresholds have been exceeded. Again, these findings are consistent with those of the aforementioned industrial sociologists.

Thirdly, aggression may or may not be primarily expressive. Certainly, it has yet to be shown that it *never* is. However, there seems little question that *it is more likely to be primarily instrumental*,[130] as suggested by the Tillys for the case of collective violence. However, as noted earlier, this does not refute *Marx's* FAT, which appears to be more general than either cruder FATs or the Tilleys' RMT. If we examine the above sociological studies, we should presumably conclude that there are individual differences in the function of aggression as well as tolerance of frustration, with the bloody-minded perhaps being more expressive, and the political more instrumental.

Fourthly, displacement of aggression and alternatives to aggression clearly occur, as does the substitution of one for another. On the other hand, these alternatives and this process of substitution are not automatic, even when aggression against the frustrator is blocked.[131] The same can be said for workers: as we shall see shortly, there is usually, but not always, an inverse relationship between direct, collective aggression against employers and each other (indicating displacement), and between the former and resignation, withdrawal, and compensation (the latter being, in part, "sublimation").

Fifthly and finally, while the evidence for "catharsis" – the dissipation of frustration after aggression or an alternative response – is far from completely lacking, it is mixed.[132] However, such a notion is post-Freud and was not presumed by Marx.

Clearly, the kind of FAT used by Marx and his followers does not fare all that poorly in the above review. To say that it requires much careful qualification, and that collective protest cannot be reduced to it, is one thing; to claim that the importance of the processes postulated by it is negligible is another. The latter conclusion seems to have been resisted even by some of FAT's harshest psychological critics, such as Michael Billig.[133]

WHAT WE NOW KNOW ABOUT KNOWLEDGE

Here we stray from the specifically historical comparative methodology utilized thus far. This is not because there are no studies of the knowledge and mythology of peoples with pre-capitalist economies, including some inspired by Marx's theorizing. Nor, of course, is Marx's theory of knowledge lacking in comparative hypotheses. Here one need only recall his claim that "The Roman slave was held by fetters; the wage-labourer is bound to his owner by invisible threads", or that, unlike the serf, the worker is not aware of the exploitation of his labour because necessary and surplus labour coincide.[134] However, to my knowledge the former studies have seldom if ever been guided by the particular hypotheses of interest to us here, and we have no, or very few, means of testing the latter, cross-mode hypotheses, since we do not know what ancient slaves and medieval serfs actually knew about the sources of their deprivation and frustration. It is because contemporary sociologists have entertained Marx's hypotheses about how the truth of capitalism is or is not revealed to workers, or at least told us what workers appear to know about its operation, that I have concentrated upon their research here.

Let us begin by recalling the psychologic behind Marx's claims regarding the effects of the nature of social reality upon producers' knowledge of it. For one thing, when several different social processes occur simultaneously, (a) they often overlap, such that one "hides" another, and/or (b) there is, or appears to be, equifinality, such that even when several different social processes are distinguished from each other, the most central and important may not be recognized as such. For another, *what* gets recognized, and recognized as *most central* and *important*, is likely to be that which is the most *immediate, concrete*, perhaps also recent, but certainly *personal*. Let us see whether, and how, this psychologic has proven to be popular and useful. I shall begin with the problem of overlap.

In the first place, managers tend to not only come from an upper middle class family, but to be much more highly educated than blue collar workers. They also often appear to have more technical expertise. As a consequence, contemporary English researchers claim, many workers tend to attribute managers' much greater control over production and higher income and status to their education and presumed expertise rather than their privileged family background. Furthermore, in Burawoy's study, American workers tended to assume that *profit* was *also* a reward their employers deserved for risking "their" capital and expending more effort than others.[135] In fact, even most British workers see maintaining profitability as in the interest of all classes – as a functional requirement of the enterprise as a whole, yet the responsibility of, and reward for, management alone.[136] Conversely, the lesser control, income, and status of workers is usually seen as equally functional and meritocratic, or, at least, workers are highly ambivalent about their own responsibility and entitlement.[137]

Secondly, while workers' own lack of education and the nature of their current employment are objectively and heavily constrained by *their* class background, this is often not apparent to them because these processes are overlain with others, and especially those which appear to involve choices. Thus they may feel that they *chose* not to get more education, and that their tie with their employer is a free and equal contract which gives them the choice to leave or stay. Peter Armstrong and his associates in particular have found that such presumptions tend to legitimate owners' and managers' control over production and distribution, and illegitimate workers'.[138]

Of course, these generalizations require some qualification. For example, for a host of reasons, including the traditionally higher proportion of immigrants who *did* "choose"(?) to go there, North American workers may be more susceptible than Europeans to such illusions of choice.[139] Similarly, because management may have established "internal" labour markets and states and let machines and production quotas take over much of the control of production from "forepeople", workers in oligopolistic firms may feel they have more choice than do those in more competitive circumstances. Moreover, because control over production and income appears to result more from individual ability and effort than from the direct intervention of management, individual machine operators may be less likely than others to see capitalist relations of production as they truly are.[140]

Thirdly, because workers' lack of control often overlaps with the manual, strenuous nature of work itself, which appears to require strength and endurance, it is often the latter rather than the former which is most in focus for male labourers. As we saw earlier, this has had important consequences, in that it has often led the latter to not only accept a lack of control and drudgery, but to do so *willingly*. In fact, Nichols and Armstrong suggest that workers are often prepared to go along with *decreases* in control and *increases* in drudgery as long as they are introduced in such a way that they do not directly challenge workers' male identity![141]

Fourthly, the others with whom workers struggle for control, income, and status may be not simply owners and/or managers, but (a) of another sex and/or race or ethnicity, and/or (b) other workers of the same sex and race or ethnicity. As a consequence, the more immediate and visible competitors may appear to be the latter rather than the former. Thus many women labourers regard their bosses primarily as *men* rather than members or representatives of the capitalist class, and "their" unions as not really theirs at all, but the domain of men. Furthermore, where women workers have collectively resisted managerial control, they have often done so with the myths and stereotypes of gender instead of class relations.[142] That men often regard "fellow" female labourers as their prime enemy is also well-established.[143]

Fifthly and finally with regard to the problem of overlapping processes, both the exercise of managerial control and workers' resistance to it are likely to be informal and interpersonal as well as the opposite, such that the former, being the most immediate, concrete, and personal, are likely to be seen as the more central. Certainly, if not always the exercise of managerial control, then at least workers' resistance to it, is typically seen as exceptional. This may be particularly the case when managers are men and workers are women,[144] but it is far from only so, in that most managers deliberately cultivate personalized rule, and while workers may respond rebelliously, and even collectively, they usually do so informally, such that the individual and informal appear typical. For example, "restriction of output" and sabotage are likely to be seen as the result of the voluntary choices of the bloody-minded and not managerial control.[145]

As for the effects on workers' consciousness of equifinality without much overlap, only Willis's analysis provides us with several different examples. Thus, he suggests, in school working class youth receive information which all points toward the repetitive and meaningless nature of work. Nevertheless, specific occupations, jobs, and work contexts seem to be very different, such that the *capitalist* nature of the context and its responsibility for the repetitiveness and meaninglessness of work is not immediately apparent. Rather, at best the problem is seen to lie in the inherent nature of work itself. Parallel processes occur with regard to exploitation, in that to the extent that it is recognized at all, it is attributed to a combination of chance, fate, or luck (that is, *some individuals* are in a position to exploit, while others are not) and human nature in general ('*everybody* is too greedy' and all-too-prepared to exploit others if given the chance).[146]

Besides problems arising directly from the simultaneous occurrence of several, quite different, social processes, Marx's theory of knowledge points to these others concerning the nature of social reality: the compartmentalization, and therefore segmentation in thought, of basically *similar* social processes; and the illusion that any one set of events or processes are natural and legitimate, which arises either because they have been repetitive and relatively stable, and/or institutionalized. Let us take up each in turn.

Nichols and Armstrong emphasize the importance of workers' working in different plants and on separate shifts. Similarly, profit and wage bargaining occurred on the level of industry and nation rather than on the shopfloor. Politics was compartmentalized from economics, as was a worker's everyday life more generally. This fragmentation is said to be reflected in workers' "ideologies": they saw little possibility of controlling wages, and they could be class conscious with regard to industry but not the official political system, or vice versa. Also, to paraphrase the researchers themselves, since their *immediate* experience did not suggest its own remedy, workers tended to reach for clichés to explain social reality.[147] Beynon stresses that most of his autoworkers were "factory" rather than "class" conscious, and that while the interaction and consciousness of shop stewards did transcend the shopfloor, most stewards were avowedly anti-political.[148] According to Willis, even though conflict in school was based on class, parallel to that on the shopfloor, and partially an instance of intended "anticipatory socialization" for the latter, it tended to be viewed as an island in a sea of peaceful social democracy.[149]

Parallel processes occur with regard to how female workers experience class and gender. Thus since managers are likely to all be male, and all one's "fellow" workers female, in the consciousness of women workers class conflict tends to become compartmentalized within gender, such that it becomes difficult to make wider connections.[150] The separation of factory and home appears to have several different effects. On the one hand, the connections are there objectively; that is, home life is conditioned by domination and exploitation at work, and the latter is aided and abetted by the former. As we saw earlier, the content of shopfloor culture also tends to be heavily gender-specific. On the other hand, the two spheres are often *experienced* as *separate*, with the home usually seen as an escape from work, and sometimes the reverse. Alternatively, to the extent they are seen as connected, class domination–exploitation at work is more likely to be seen as an extension of gender domination–exploitation at home than the reverse.[151]

Perhaps the most obvious case of repetition and stability producing the illusion of naturalness and legitimacy is owners' and managers' control over production and distribution, but most writers also stress the *atypicalness* of *workers'* control. Some claim it hardly occurs at all. Others maintain that it is actually frequent; for example, as an outcome of workers' constant struggle to maintain or establish "custom and practice".[152] However, many of the latter would admit that such struggles are seldom if ever offensive, and still others would say that neither defensive nor offensive attempts at control occur often enough for them to be seen as natural and legitimate. Thus some researchers document changes in knowledge with strikes and other major job actions, but they also note that both such actions and changes in knowledge are likely to be short-lived.[153] In an interesting variation of this process, it is often precisely because unions have been *successful* in keeping management to its part of a contract – that is, in *preventing* change – that workers regard them as doing nothing, and therefore useless and illegitimate![154]

Finally, Armstrong et al. in particular have stressed the importance of institutionalization. Thus the success of management's control is attributed by them as much to their superior opportunity to appeal to institutionalized legitimations as to the proverbial "carrot and stick"; that is, workers have seldom been able to justify their resistance by resorting to the former. Custom and practice is often insufficient to establish legitimacy unless it is also formally recognized by management. This problem is said to have (a) affected how workers explain management's and their own actions; (b) prevented many workers from even *recognizing* their *own* control over production; and (c) limited what they see as even *possible*, let alone natural and justified, action.[155]

If we turn now to those aspects of Marx's theory of knowledge which deal with the particular vantage points of individuals, we can see that Marx's argument is one of "selective perception" and learning. Two subprocesses can be distinguished: what is partial is either individuals' (a) *past experience* – primarily, they do not have an alternative basis with which to compare current social processes or stages of development, or (b) *present interest* – particularly, whether they do or do not have a substantial stake in the *status quo*. The first is more of a perceptual effect as such, while the latter is also motivational, in that besides simply seeing or interpreting reality differently, individuals also do or do not seek out, deny, and/or forget various aspects of reality, depending upon what they do or do not *want* to. Sometimes past experience and the fulfillment of present wishes work in the same direction to make workers more class conscious, as Marx usually assumed. However, as we can now see, they are just as likely to counteract each other.

Take migrants like Marx himself. If we consider only past experience, those who move from less to more developed capitalist regions should be more knowledgeable about the workings of capitalism. There is indeed some evidence for this, beginning with Trotsky's observation that Russian factory workers who had moved from the countryside were often more class conscious than others, and moving on into present times in the research of John Leggett and the Bristol group.[156] Nonetheless, immigrants and migrants are also likely to have experienced both an increase in their standard of living and a desire to rationalize their having moved, such that while they may be more likely than natives to have experienced a change, the latter may be seen as good and legitimate rather than something that needs to be resisted.

Parallel processes appear to occur with age: older workers are obviously more likely to have seen profound changes in the nature of work and work relations, but they too are likely to have seen much worse times, and evidence for their having "come-to-terms" with things they felt they could not change is numerous.[157] A typical concomitant of the latter is a lowering of their aspirations for – or their *interest in* – what they originally (presumably) wished for. Nichols and Armstrong make some observations which illustrate how far individual workers can go in selectively remembering the past and, thereby, justifying their own actions – or inaction – in the present. Thus workers who correctly complain that the workers with whom they worked in the past were much more militant may be rationalizing their own subservience to capital by projecting it onto others.[158]

Finally, much the same can be said for "vertical social mobility", including *downward* mobility. While Marx himself assumed that the petty bourgeoisie who lost their property would both experience more of a change and lose their interest in selectively perceiving in favour of the *status quo* of developed capitalism, current evidence indicates that many individuals are not even *aware* that they *have* been downwardly mobile, and that here too, when they *are* aware of it, facing up to it and blaming the system rather than various scapegoats may be more than they can bear.[159]

Certainly, as the above suggests, Marx was anything but wrong in expecting partial interests, including those in and against the *status quo*, to bias perception, learning, and retention. Thus on average workers appear to know more about the class system upon which capitalism is based than do either forepeople and supervisors or higher management and owners.[160] There is even evidence for the effects of *changes* in interest from natural experiments. Thus Seymour Lieberman found that workers who were promoted to foremen became much more pro-management and anti-union, while those who were elected union stewards showed changes in the reverse direction.[161] This evidence is very much in line with research by psychologists on other sectors of the population; research which indicates, if not always selective *perception*, then at least selective learning, retention, and action on the basis of the original perception. But selective perception *per se* has been demonstrated, including by class. In the classic study here, working class boys judged coins to be larger than did middle class boys.[162]

On the other hand, at least two important qualifications seem warranted. One is that the vantage points and interests of workers are often much more partial than that of class, or even occupation. Thus as the Bristol group in particular have found, how workers have viewed, and now wish to view, social reality depends greatly upon not only the area of a country they have come from and their age, but whether or not their parents are or were unionists and the class or occupation of their spouse, kin, and neighbours.[163] This extends not only to their views of labour/management relations, official politics, and social and private life, but to the very same, small-scale events on the shop-floor![164] The other qualification is that the effects of praxis may often counteract those of passive interest. Thus having to rule others may give capitalists and managers an interest in discovering what "really" makes capitalist industry "tick", while having few opportunities to consciously act on their own class's interest may make workers *less* knowledgeable. Here there is also no dearth of evidence from experimental social psychology.[165]

To conclude our evaluation of Marx's theory of knowledge, let us proceed to his claims concerning the effects of praxis. Recall that the overall thrust is that individuals are likely to learn more about reality when they are actively attempting to modify it in their own interests, when they are in effect experimenting with it, than when they are viewing it more passively, with or without an "interest" in it. At least four conditions presumably increase workers' knowledge about capitalism: (1) when they are at least actively *resisting* management's control; (2) when they are on the *offensive* to gain *more* control over, and/or return for, their labour; (3) when they are doing so *collectively* rather than individually, because then they are likely to have (a) a greater effect upon reality and (b) the benefits of brainstorming as well as social support; and (4) when, in acting, they do so in a conscious and strategically sophisticated way. One might expect these circumstances to be cumulative; that is, each successive condition is a stage which includes the previous ones, and the more conditions are met, the more enlightening praxis should be. A corollary of this reasoning is that information is gained not just from workers' *own* attempts at, and actual modifications of, reality, but from *management's*, and the state's, *resistance* to such attempts.

My own reading of the evidence has led me to these conclusions about the validity of these hypotheses. First, what information we have indicates that, with some qualification, the hypotheses are reasonable ones. Secondly, however, *none* of the four conditions – and especially those having to do with collective and highly class conscious action – occur all that frequently. As a consequence, even according to Marx's own assumptions about how knowledge is gained, workers should not be gaining all that much "good" knowledge about the workings of capitalist relations of production. Thirdly, furthermore, when workers *have* had the higher forms of praxis, the beneficial results have often been offset by those from other processes. Most importantly, workers often encounter *so much* resistance that they lose their struggles, and the overall result is demoralization rather than, or at least in addition to, a gain in knowledge about reality. Alternatively, as mentioned earlier, rather than "coming down hard", management frequently exercises its control and handles workers' resistance relatively carefully and gently, such that the *class* character of domination and exploitation – indeed, perhaps the latter themselves – is (are) not immediately apparent. I shall now attempt to document these conclusions.

As for Condition 1, resistance to managerial control may not in fact raise workers' consciousness very much unless it is undertaken collectively (Condition 3). As for the latter, there are lots of case studies indicating that "job actions" – particularly strikes – make workers more aware of class domination and exploitation than do times where there is not so much active and collective resistance.[166] Nevertheless, single, one-day strikes do not often gather much speed and make much of an impact on workers' consciousness, and some researchers claim the same is true of longer and more bitter ones.[167] Still others have pointed to an important, counteracting by-product of the latter: strikes can become *so very* long and drawn out that the "troops" become "war weary".[168] Almost all of these researchers agree that most workers' actions, whether or not they are collective, are defensive rather than offensive. As some of them put it, few workers have been out to "extend the frontier of control".[169] Most also concur that the consciousness which has guided workers' actions has been one of "factory" and not "class", and that women workers have been still less likely to see themselves as agents of *any* kind.[170] Where industrial sociologists disagree is about how frequent and collective such *defensive* reactions are.

Thus Nichols and Armstrong can be seen to agree with the above hypotheses, in that they criticize Goldthorpe et al. for not linking the apparent lack of class consciousness among the autoworkers they studied to the absence of any strikes up to the time of the study. They then practise what they preach for their own chemical workers, many of whom had in fact *never* been on strike. But this is precisely where they part company with Marx: *most* British workers, they suggest, seldom strike; many *never* do so, or at least not very often.[171] In the case of their chemical workers, there were few job actions short of striking either. Much of the latter is attributed to the way in which industrial relations had been structured in the industry, to the earlier-mentioned fact that most collective bargaining occurs at the industrial and national levels, with little left over for the shopfloor. The rest is explained by demoralization from past defeats. Indeed, these workers were not even able to get good shop stewards. Interestingly, the few incidents they describe where workers were successful in getting managers to back down were small-scale reactions to being insulted, and there workers tended to attribute their success to their manliness rather than class solidarity![172]

On the other hand, some researchers (including Armstrong in a later study) conclude that forms of resistance other than strikes are both ubiquitous and, often, consciousness-raising.[173] However, most would probably fall somewhere between the two extremes, arguing that such actions are more or less frequent, and more or less enhancing for class consciousness, depending upon a host of mediating conditions. I suspect that the discrepancies may be a function not just of which industries and plants were researched, but which actions were looked for and how they were looked at. For example, Nichols and Armstrong interviewed their chemical workers (whom they admit are relatively privileged) outside of the worksite and did not observe them on the latter (?), whereas Armstrong et al., Edwards and Scullion, Willis, and Westwood did observe their workers participatively. Furthermore, having been on the shopfloor, the latter were better able to observe and ask workers about small-scale actions.

But we should not blow such disputes among sociologists out of proportion. Almost all of them claim that most workers' actions are defensive, and that there have been few "explosions" of working class consciousness. Most would further admit that defeat and demoralization have been common, and probably more so than success and explosions in confidence.[174] Finally, just as both sides appear to have retained Marx's general principles of knowledge acquisition while rejecting many of his "initial conditions" or specific forecasts, they have done so with regard to the actions of management. Thus in the chemical plants management not only usually couched their orders in personal and pleasant terms so as not to provoke resistance, but actually encouraged unionism as a still more subtle form of control![175] Although encouraging unionism appears to have been an exception in other studies, personalizing control was not.[176]

GROUPING AND ITS EFFECTS

The initial research by social psychologists on intergroup relations was undoubtedly guided by assumptions similar to Marx's. Thus the Sherifs and their colleagues randomly assigned children into two experimental groups, one of which was given more privileges than the other by the experimenters. In spite of the fact that the members of "ingroups" were initially strangers, individuals came to strongly identify themselves with their ingroup and express a great deal of hostility toward the outgroup.[177] Few now take issue with the importance of such shared interests in "objective", "material" outcomes for group formation (see Proposition A1, Chapter 7). Indeed, even those who have offered alternatives to "realistic conflict" theories of intergroup relations concede that such processes are fundamental to most real-life intergroup conflict. However, as with frustration–aggression theory, many now question whether conflicts of material interest are either necessary or sufficient. This has been especially true of the late Henri Tajfel and his students at Bristol, who have counterposed more cognitively-oriented theories of social "categorization" and "identity".[178]

Their position is based upon two arguments. First, they have conducted "minimal group" experiments where subjects have been shown to identify with, and favour, the ingroup, and compete with, and discriminate against, outgroups even where both objective interests and actual interaction are lacking. Indeed, subjects have often been willing to sacrifice material rewards in order to maintain or enhance status distinctions between their own group and an outgroup, and thereby maintain or enhance their own self-esteem. Secondly, even where objective interests have been present and have figured prominently in group formation and Intergroup (IG) conflict, their effects appear to have been mediated by the categorization of others into groups and identification of oneself with one or another.[179]

This work raises interesting and important issues vis-à-vis Marx's theorizing, but it is not clear that it refutes it. For one thing, as we saw in Chapter 7, Marx himself recognized the importance of status relations among groups, and he cannot accurately be accused of having reduced IG conflict to material inequalities alone. For another, given his theory of a need hierarchy, we might well expect group identification and status differences to predominate where subsistence and middle-level needs are already met. The latter condition was obviously met in both the minimal group experiments and real life groups studied by the Bristol psychology group. Finally, given Proposition A2, it can be argued that Marx also recognized that objective interests *need not* eventuate in group, and especially class, formation and conflict. Rather, individuals must indeed first identify themselves as a class, however crudely. However, they may instead identify themselves only as individuals, or as subgroups.

Here too, the research of the Bristol group appears to complement rather than refute Marx. Thus far from being ubiquitous, identification with, and enhancement of the status of, an ingroup is not likely to occur, even if there is severe deprivation, where (a) intergroup inequality is regarded as legitimate and/or stable, and (b) there is observable social mobility into the privileged outgroup.[180] Again, Marx himself often (but perhaps not often enough) took both factors into account (see Chapter 7). Furthermore, where there are subgroups within an "under"class, individuals may identify more with one or another subgroup than the underclass as a whole, and strive to maintain or enhance differences among the former and not to narrow the gap between the privileged class and the underclass as a whole. Just as historians have noted this tendency among artisans and other craftspeople, so Rupert Brown of the Bristol group has documented it for groups of workers who were anything but very objectively different.[181]

As noted earlier, Marx believed that such intra-class conflicts among workers could and would be overcome through at least three processes: by their being brought together and treated as a single group by capital, the actual interaction which is likely to result from this, and the development of "superordinate goals" – especially having to defend themselves against capital. The importance of these countervailing forces is clear in the literature of social psychology, although it is equally obvious that such presumptions now require careful qualification. Thus being labelled and otherwise treated as a group by the experimenter is the *only* basis for group formation in the "minimal group" experiments, although one suspects that even here the researchers are tapping into long-standing habits. On the other hand, Brown's field study indicates that such treatment from a third party is far from always sufficient, for there the three groups of workers insisted on maintaining their petty differences in spite of concerted efforts by management to have them bargain collectively rather than as separate subgroups. The evidence for the second countervailing force – interaction between subgroups – is also mixed. For some time researchers assumed, with Marx, that contact, at least where the subgroups are fairly equal, reduces hostility and facilitates solidarity. However, it has now been recognized that group identification and intergroup competition often lead to social distance, even where subgroups are equal, such that in spite of physical contact, social interaction is either minimized or simply reinforces the original, hostile intergroup relations.[182]

Marx's idea that having to actively struggle against a common enemy would bring subgroups together and increase solidarity among them tested positively in the Sherifs' "Robbers' Cave" experiments. Here the two groups in conflict were pitted against a rival camp in a day of games. Yet the Sherifs themselves cautioned that this common struggle appeared to redirect rather than completely reduce intergroup hostility, and that even this redirection was temporary. Interestingly enough, the circumstances which were far more effective in reducing hostility did not include the existence and active threat of a third party at all. Rather, they involved the necessity, and actuality, of working together to repair the camp's water system and free a food truck from mud.[183] While these circumstances bear some similarity to those faced by different groups of workers during economic crises, we also know they often lead such groups to try to "save their own skins" until it is too late to coalesce.

As if the latter were not enough to squelch Marx's optimism, the Sherifs themselves have qualified even the latter, their most effective means for reducing intergroup hostility. To wit, in order to maintain the latter and enhance solidarity there probably need to be *repeated* opportunities for common cause.[184] But what happens when the economic crisis or other external threat abates? Worse, what happens if repeated attempts at intergroup cooperation repeatedly fail, for example, if the employer(s) almost always win(s)? What little experimental evidence we have suggests that, in keeping with Marx's claim, failure *need not* scuttle a coalition, especially if there is no long history of intergroup animosity. *However*, where the latter condition is *not* met, groups are likely to scapegoat each other.[185] This appears to occur even where Marx believed it would not – that is, where subgroups are relatively similar,[186] but it is especially problematic where they are not. Even physical differences – not just sexual and racial, but different colour labcoats (!) – may be sufficient to cause groups which have cooperated to revert to hostile relations. In fact, the mere anticipation of recreating intergroup distinctions after cooperation may itself increase the likelihood of future hostility.[187]

Finally, with regard to "superordinate goals", it bears repeating from Chapter 7 that if groups of workers can, and sometimes do, coalesce *against* employers and/or to avert the depriving effects of an economic or other crisis, they can and do also coalesce *with* their employers, against competing firms, foreign or otherwise, and to lessen the effects, often presumed to be mutual to employers and workers, of other crises not so directly tied to such competition. Thus we have the spectre of Marxist sociologists marvelling at employers' encouraging their workers to demonstrate in the streets against Thatcher's economic policies.[188] We also have experimental evidence that when privileged groups expect to have to face the underprivileged, rather than necessarily "close ranks" and express hostility toward the latter outgroup, they sometimes play down intergroup differences, and even become magnanimous in order to placate them.[189] Admittedly, management is seldom magnanimous to labour in times of economic crises, but it is folly to fail to recognize that capital as well as labour can effectively play the game of coalescing under superordinant goals, whether real or illusory.

Collectively, the above qualifications cast doubt on the validity of Proposition A4, which stipulates that ways of group formation can often substitute for, or at least inexorably lead to, the will to do so. Thus homogeneity and contact – what Marx referred to as "universal discourse", are probably *not* enough to produce coalitions among workers, let alone an entire, united, solidary class "for itself". To the contrary, as we have just seen, homogeneity and contact may actually *exacerbate*, particularly long-standing, intergroup hostilities. Certainly, ways cannot *substitute* for wills. The will may in fact come from the emergence of a severe external threat, but it is unlikely to sustain cooperation in the absence of continued interdependence and organizational links.

As for the capacity of groups and intergroup relations to transform individuals and inter-individual ("personal") relations, one can find much more support from contemporary psychology. Again, however, we are forced to greatly modify the generality of Marx's assumptions.

Proposition B1 has two major thrusts. On one hand, group interaction, and especially intergroup conflict, is supposed to make individuals more aware of their own, existing needs and deprivation *as individuals*. Presumably, these include higher-order needs for variety and self-expression and development as well as affiliation and meaningful social interaction. On the other, these same processes are presumed to create *new* wants and aspirations, and therefore also new deprivations.

The latter insight in particular has turned out to be a profound one. Thus once individuals *do* identify with a group, they often develop a new "need" to maintain or enhance the status of that *group*, and not just themselves as individuals, relative to that of *other* groups.[190] Indeed, as we have already seen, like workers who are willing to lose income to preserve their union, individual subjects in experiments are often willing to sacrifice their own material interests in order to maintain or enhance the status of their group as a whole. Furthermore, partly as a consequence of their having developed such new "needs", individual members of a group are likely to feel deprived even when their own individual needs and wants are not directly so, provided that the needs of *other* group members are. As Walter Runciman put it in trying to account for certain phenomena with regard to English workers, such individuals' social comparisons and relative deprivations are "fraternalistic" rather than "egoistic". This distinction has subsequently been emphasized by social psychologists studying both experimentally-created and natural groups; from black and white American workers, to Hindus and Moslems in India, to French and English Canadians.[191] However, both this insight and the previous claim regarding increased awareness of pre-existing individual needs, wants, and deprivations require careful qualification.

In the first place, in general, as with inter-individual comparisons, if there are several different groups with which individuals could compare themselves, the other group with which members of a low status group compare and attempt to maintain or narrow any differences is more likely to be one of *similar* than dissimilar status; in other words, another group of low or intermediate, rather than high, status.[192]

Group identification, and particularly intergroup struggle, appear to statistically increase the likelihood of the choice of a dissimilar relative to a similar comparison group, but this likelihood usually remains less than that for a similar group in absolute terms. Certainly, an increase in the likelihood of choosing a dissimilar group, and unquestionably a *reversal* of the more typical difference, depends upon the existence of more specific circumstances which are often not met. To wit, the relationship of inequality between groups must be seen as *unstable*; that is, capable of, and likely to, change. More importantly, it must be seen as *illegitimate*,[193] and this, of course, is likely to require either (a) a violation of the ruling ideas of morality and justice by the ruling class/ group and/or (b) a very *different* system of morality and justice on the part of the low status group.

As it happens, the latter does occur on occasion, even in laboratory experiments. Thus low status groups sometimes create criteria for status which are quite different from – perhaps the complete reverse of – those of high groups, as when workers maintain that "The rich are not happy or moral", or blacks that "Black is beautiful".[194] However, there is a serious "chicken-and-egg" problem here. Specifically, all of the above processes presuppose that individual "social" mobility is blocked and/or that low status individuals have *already* formed them- selves as a group and competed *as a group* with high status individuals. Yet we have seen how these conditions have seldom been met for Western workers. For example, in Sennett and Cobb's study they were found to be functioning mainly as individuals, and applying bourgeois standards of individual success and worth to each other.

But let us assume that workers or other low status individuals *have* identified themselves, and interacted, as a group. Does this mean that they will then become more aware of their own individual, higher-order needs and deprivations? Perhaps. There is no dearth of examples where this has occurred, not just in Reich's "consciousness-raising" groups of women and youth in the 30s, but in those of women, men, and gays in the 60s and beyond. Nevertheless, there is reason to believe that group formation by low status individuals is neither necessary nor sufficient for such enlightenment, nor even that the latter is a typical consequence when additional circumstances occur. Instead, group identification, interaction, and particularly intergroup struggle are more likely to (a) reduce individual variability within the in- as well as the out-group, and therefore also (b) individual mem ers' awareness of their own individual needs, aspirations, and depri- vations.[195] Such pressures toward objective uniformity and subjective stereotyping appear to be functional for group formation and conflict, whether directly for loyalty and presenting a "united front", etc., or indirectly by justifying the group's interests and actions to others and members themselves through the biasing of perception and rationalizing of reasoning.[196]

Again, to give credit where it is due, Marx was correct that much, and perhaps most, of the latter biasing is toward justifying and protecting the *status quo* for privileged groups, and de-legitimating and altering it for the underprivileged.[197] On the other hand, as in real life, the privileged are far from always so strategically stupid as to play up intergroup differences and thereby risk the perception of illegitimacy and envious comparison on the part of the underprivileged. For example, in experiments by Van Knippenberg, members of high status groups were actually *less* biased than those of low status groups, apparently because they wanted to placate the latter.[198] Furthermore, in terms of the development of group members *as individuals* – that is, their individuation – high status individuals have often been more developed, not necessarily because they put less pressure upon each other, but because high status groups have more resources with which individual members can distinguish and develop themselves, and because others are more likely to recognize individuality and autonomy in high than low status individuals. Moreover, as Erika Apfelbaum has suggested, regarding and treating the members of low status groups as if they are not individuated – as lacking in ability, effort, morality, or whatever – is a frequent, and frequently effective, strategy of divide and conquer on the part of ruling groups.[199] It takes very well-organized and class conscious groups of workers indeed to counteract the latter tendencies. Unquestionably, the development and recognition of the individuality and autonomy of members of low status groups are not "natural" consequences of mere association, or even class struggle.

Proposition B2 goes further, in that intergroup struggle is supposed to develop awareness not only of one's own needs, but that both specific other groups and systems of inequality in general are the most central barriers to need gratification. Presumably, to evaluate this proposition we should ask whether existing groups of workers in struggle are more knowledgeable than workers thinking and acting individually, and whether groups more generally are better problem solvers than individuals.

On the first count, there does seem to be affirmative evidence. Thus Beynon attributes the greater sophistication of his stewards to the fact that they are well-organized and interact beyond, as well as in, the factory; and Willis of his 'lads' because, unlike conformist 'ear oles', they resist and experiment with social reality collectively.[200] Edwards and Scullion suggest that intergroup struggle was not necessary for their clothing workers to be aware that management was the major source of their own deprivation and frustration, but that its absence meant that they tended not to link their own responses of individual withdrawal to these other events.[201] Cavendish recounts an event where, after struggling against management collectively, the women in her factory actually proposed reducing differentials between the highest and lowest paid workers,[202] and so on. But we should be careful here, not only because such intergroup struggle is far from as common as Marx and others have claimed, but also because its consequences are often far from as straightforward. For instance, after noting that group discussion of the effects of collective action may promote knowledge seeking, even after defeat (more of this shortly), Pollert cautions that the answers workers come up with are often "stock" rather than new. Here it also makes sense to recall Mann's suggestion that the outcome of workers' struggles is likely to mirror its initial goals: if all workers demand is job security and higher income, then even successful intergroup struggle may well only reinforce workers' assumptions that they are simply exchanging their labour for a living wage.[203]

The upshot of the above is that interclass struggle by workers may well, but *need not*, make them especially aware that capitalist relations of production are at the root of their problems. The same should be said for groups more generally. Groups are often *different* decision-makers from individuals. For example, they frequently take more, and almost as frequently less, risks than do individuals. They are also *better* problem solvers for many types of problems. On the other hand, this does not hold for *all* problems. On some, groups tend to be less effective than individuals, and sometimes the more complex and/or time-consuming the problem, the less better groups are relative to individuals.[204] It may well be that discovering the "deep structure" beneath the surface of labour/management relations is of the latter type, and that it helps to have an individual like Marx present.

Finally, recall that Marx went still further and claimed that some outcomes of intergroup struggle – *failures* – are more informative than others. Is *this* the case? His own reasoning – that until workers organize and actively threaten their employers, they are not likely to experience the latter's and the state's active, collective intervention – is not faulty in and of itself. However, as mentioned in Chapter 7, it does not take into account several likely counteracting effects. On the side of knowledge alone, it is easier to realize and repeat what one has done if one has succeeded than it is to discover what one did *not* do right and should do in the future if one has failed. Although the evidence for this proposition pertains to individuals, there is no reason to believe that it does not also hold for groups. On the side of motivation, one has the additional problem of demoralization after defeat, and therefore a decrease in interest in either continued knowledge-seeking or any other form of group activity. Whether defeat might have other, more positive by-products is taken up later in this section.

According to Proposition B3, interaction and intergroup struggle give workers and other low status individuals another, very specific experience: the "gut feeling" and awareness that they have the strength to *remove* the barriers which interaction and struggle have also helped them see. If we are to believe many of the aforementioned industrial sociologists, this proposition does apply to workers. In fact, Edwards and Scullion imply that without collective experimentation, workers may not even be aware that collective responses to deprivation and frustration are *theoretically* possible![205] However, as suggested earlier, belief in collective strength does seem to depend very much upon whether or not past collective experimentation has succeeded. Trying and failing *collectively* may well be more demoralizing than either doing so individually, or doing *nothing* individually *or* collectively. This is in effect what Nichols and Armstrong claim happened with their chemical workers; that is, they had tried the route of collective struggle on the shopfloor and failed. Other studies in this tradition also indicate demoralization after defeat.[206] Some claim the longer term effects were increased knowledge and a return to optimism,[207] but others do not.

To my knowledge, experimental social psychologists have not tested this proposition directly. However, they have done so indirectly through their use, in effect, of Proposition B4, the "Contingency Hypothesis", which states that individuals functioning *as groups* are much more likely to rebel and otherwise directly aggress against barriers than are individuals functioning *as individuals*, who are in turn more likely to displace aggression, withdraw, and/or compensate. Thus in general, individuals tend to be more aggressive in groups than when they are alone, and the processes typically used to explain the connection all stress either or both group members' belief in their greater strength as a collectivity and/or the lesser likelihood of their individual actions or persons being observable, and/or held responsible.[208] Furthermore, when low status individuals identify themselves as a group, intergroup competition and conflict tends to increase relative to individual mobility as a strategy for dealing with deprivation and frustration. This experimental evidence is complimented by field data indicating that group formation and struggle also lessen individual withdrawal and self-derogation.[209] Finally, critics of Tajfel et al.'s minimal group experiments have suggested that some of their major findings are artifacts of the distribution of power tacitly built into them. To wit, low status group members only discriminate in favour of the ingroup because experimenters have given them the resources and power to do so, whereas in experiments whose conditions are more real-life-like – that is, where third parties do not intervene so directly – low status members are not free to, and do not, discriminate against high status outgroups anywhere near as much.[210]

The latter and other experimental findings point to the need to qualify the Contingency Hypothesis. In particular, even ingroup cohesion, to say nothing of mere ingroup identification, may be insufficient to produce either depreciation of, and hostility toward, a high status outgroup or such various more proximate, and perhaps necessary, conditions for rebellion, as an active threat from the high status outgroup or the collective strength to alter its monopoly on material resources and communal power. Furthermore, the turn away from displacing aggression upon other members of the low status group appears to be much more likely in well-established and organized than in *ad hoc* and less organized groups.[211] This may go a long way toward explaining why temporary coalitions of workers and community groups so often fail. Nevertheless, where these various additional conditions are met, the Contingency Hypothesis does appear to hold.

Perhaps the best test is a "natural experiment" by Edwards and Scullion. In two clothing factories, tight managerial control led not only to a great deal of deprivation and frustration, but also little room for shopfloor organization. Presumably as a consequence, workers tended to respond by withdrawing individually, by changing jobs or being absent a lot. In turn, the latter reinforced tight managerial control. However, in a majority of four engineering plants studied, substantial managerial control and deprivation and frustration were accompanied by a great deal more shopfloor organization. Here workers responded both individually and collectively, but there were many fewer individual and many more collective responses than there were in the clothing factories. The authors themselves see shopfloor organization in the latter as having allowed and channelled expressions of frustration and instrumental attempts to reduce it in a collective, and often rebellious, direction. In keeping with the FAT interpretation offered here, in a continuous process fibre factory, where there was both less managerial control and more workers' control for the latters' protection than there was in the clothing factories, there was in turn *both* less deprivation and frustration (apparently) *and* less conflict of either the individual or collective kind.[212]

To complete our evaluation of Marx's underlying social psychological theory of intergroup relations, let us consider the propositions in section C of Chapter 7.

The first part of Proposition C1 appears to be unproblematic; that is, *anything* which increases the salience of group membership tends to increase ingroup identification and loyalty, and negative identification with, and hostility toward, an outgroup; and active intergroup conflict is probably one of the more effective sources of group salience.[213] And Marx was unquestionably correct that loyalty to a group can take precedence over narrow, short-term self-interest. We have already seen at least two sets of strong evidence for this in the experimental literature, in that group members can and do feel deprived and moved to action even when their own individual needs are not deprived, and they are often willing to sacrifice individual material gain in order to maintain or enhance the status of their group. However, the second part relating to group cohesion and organization needs to be made more conditional. That *successful* struggle furthers ingroup cohesion and organization, at least in the form of internal differentiation, is well-established,[214] but matters are more complicated when the outcome is failure.

For one thing, failure is clearly less likely to produce cohesion than success. For another, in order for failure *not* to *decrease* cohesion, other, very specific conditions appear to be necessary. One is that individuals have *already* committed themselves to the group; another is that the circumstances leading to failure are either obviously external to the ingroup or ambiguous, for otherwise members are likely to see each other as barriers to their own need gratification, and group membership as depriving.[215] A final caveat: internal differentiation by status and power may improve the external success of the group, but it may also create frustration and alienation for, and factions among, the rank-and-file,[216] such that gains on one set of dimensions are wiped out by losses on another.

Whether explicit political programs and procedures for arriving at them are necessary for the long-term success of classes (Proposition C2) is also not so straightforward a question as it might seem. To the extent that they provide superordinate goals which are otherwise lacking, or the only effective means for achieving them, the proposition becomes almost a truism. However, we now know that (a) the formalization and institutionalization of ingroup processes can have the above-mentioned effect of frustrating and alienating the rank-and-file, such that the means subvert the end, and that (b) while social movements with very diffuse goals have their problems, those with very *specific* ones also have difficulty continuing when such goals are achieved as well as when they are not. It is for such reasons that many contemporary groups for social change have come to emphasize process as much as, or more than, specific political programs, and de-centralized decision-making and consensus rather than hierarchy and competitive voting procedures, both of which tend to require losers as well as winners.[217]

If one poses the problem as one of ideology rather than explicit political programs and procedures, one can probably achieve greater consensus on the validity of the proposition. After all, a group which does not develop *its own* collective interpretations of, and justifications for, its existence and performance is unlikely to be externally or internally successful. Most of the evidence in the studies examined here deals with the latter, converse conditions, and is therefore not fully comparative, yet it is persuasive. For example, Marty Patchen discovered that oil refinery workers did not feel relatively deprived when they compared themselves to professionals, because they thought that the latters' investments in their work were higher.[218] In other words, they lacked their own, working class standards. The fullest study demonstrating how workers usually lack the ideological tools to fight management effectively, and especially to "extend the frontier of control", is that of Peter Armstrong and his associates.[219] However, there are many other examples in the studies reviewed here, including those on women, who, as noted earlier, often undercut their own attempts to resist managerial control because they interpret them as anti-male rather than anti-capitalist.

In Chapter 7 I suggested that Marx had not had the benefit of much research on leadership, but it would be inaccurate and unfair to claim that his own assumptions about it were necessarily off-base. Thus the power of working class leaders, whether opportunist or otherwise, has been demonstrated manyfold since Marx's own time, and the same is true for their capacity to mislead workers for religious, nationalistic, and even fascistic purposes. Furthermore, while it should be said that Marx underestimated workers' tolerance for self-serving and otherwise misguided leaders, even in unions – those "guerilla" organizations most responsible for assuring the gratification of workers' most basic needs – the generality of his claim that rank-and-file workers will eventually throw off such leaders is borne out even by laboratory research, where subjects generally depose leaders when their groups fail, or at least when they have used up their "idiosyncratic credit".[220]

As for the last proposition of Chapter 7 (C4), which proposes that a particularly well-organized and class conscious rank-and-file may compensate for poor or opportunist leaders, or the converse, I know of no substantial amount of relevant data, whether systematically gathered or otherwise. However, it might be worthwhile sifting through the perennial debates between Marxists and anarchists, since the former have often dismissed the latter as Utopian because they have denied the necessity for strong, centralized leadership, while the latter have accused the former of substituting themselves for rank-and-file workers. For example, Marxists have often alleged that the anarchist brigades in the Spanish Civil War were incompetent, while anarchists have countered that had the rank-and-file organizations of Russian workers, soldiers, and sailors not been suppressed by the Bolshevik party, Soviet Russia might still be run by Soviets.[221]

I shall not take sides here on either the alleged facts or the actual conclusions. However, as suggested in Chapter 7, I suspect that *both* sides may be largely correct; that successful intergroup struggle, and especially long-term control of social movements and institutions "from below", require *both* a well-organized and class conscious "mass" *and* an effective and non-opportunist leadership. Certainly, a cursory perusal of the studies by industrial sociologists relied upon here indicates that the workers who seem to be most militant and successful in defending themselves against management are those who also have effective leaders. However, the latter tend to be not full-time, high level union officials or party leaders from outside the factory, but shop stewards and other low level union personnel who tend to be (a) elected from the shopfloor, (b) organized *beyond* it, but (c) nevertheless not beholden to, and therefore compromised by, either management or high level, full-time, union officials.[222] The record is strewn with tales of workers having to battle their own unions as well as management,[223] and as such it is far from an encouraging one. Yet the fact that groups of workers continue to struggle on both fronts, with occasional success, is reason for hope.

NOTES

1. Bicchieri, op. cit., pp. 412–18, 439–40. Christian and Gardiner, op. cit., pp. 3–4. Lee, 1979, op. cit., p. 435. Richard Preston, "The development of self-control in the Eastern Cree life cycle", pp. 83–92 in K. Ishwaren (ed.), *Childhood and Adolescence in Canada* (Toronto: McGraw-Hill Ryerson, 1979) p. 87. J. J. Honigman, in Helm, op. cit., p. 737. Leacock and Lee, pp. 7–8, 12–13; Briggs, pp. 113–15, 123–4; Turnbull, pp. 138–9; Brian Morris, "The family, group structuring and trade among South Indian hunters-gatherers", pp. 180–2, all in Leacock and Lee, op. cit. Damas, 1984, op. cit., pp. 412–18, 439–40.
2. Steward, 1938, op. cit., pp. 1, 45–6, 257; "Causal factors and processes in the evolution of pre-farming societies", pp. 321–34 in Lee and DeVore, op. cit. Marvin Harris, *Cultural Materialism* (New York: Random House, 1979).
3. Steward, 1965, op. cit., pp. 360, 411; Gardiner, op. cit., pp. 425–6; Helm, op.cit., p. 193; Lee, 1979, op. cit., pp. 24, 244, 458–60; Damas, 1984, op. cit., p. 192.
4. Sahlins, 1974, op. cit.; Lee, 1979, op. cit., pp. 446–7.
5. Ibid., p. 460. Briggs, op. cit., p. 115.
6. E.g., Lee, 1979, op. cit., p. 456; Helm, op. cit., p. 193.
7. Sahlins, 1974, op. cit.
8. E.g., see Alastair Clayre, *Work and Play* (New York: Harper and Row, 1974).
9. See Note 5, Chapter 8.
10. Steward, 1938, op. cit., pp. 1, 45–6, 231, 257; 1946/8, op. cit., pp. 100, 156, 263, 339, 463. Balikci, in Lee and DeVore, op. cit., p. 82. Clastres, in Bicchieri, 1972, op. cit., pp. 152–3.
11. Sahlins, 1974, op. cit., p. 214. See also Leacock and Lee, op. cit., p. 77, and Damas, 1984, op. cit., pp. 490–2.
12. See Note 9, above.
13. Biardeau, op. cit., p. 83; Dumont, 1965, op. cit., pp. 85–90; Carter, op. cit., pp. 98, 124.
14. Raju, op. cit., pp. 265, 277–8, 281, 306–7, 313, 317; Chan, op. cit., pp. 178–85, 205–6, 216–17.
15. Raju, op. cit., pp. 242, 249, 306–7. For a clear example of this reasoning, see the *Bagavadgita*, Chapter 3, Verse 62. There the reader is warned that contemplation leads to attachment, attachment to desire, and desire to anger. Therefore, one should not contemplate and desire, so that one can avoid frustration and anger. Obviously, here deprivation and frustration are assumed to be inevitable.
16. D. D. Kossambi, *The Culture and Civilization of Ancient India in Historical Outline* (New Delhi: Vikas (Vani Educational), 1986) pp. 145, 173.
17. Kossambi, 1965, op. cit., pp. 64–5, 85; Rostovtzeff, op. cit., pp. 289, 316–21; Wittfogel, op. cit., pp. 294–5; Habib, op. cit., p. 330.
18. On the earlier periods, see, for example, Wittfogel, op. cit., pp. 16–17, 137, 142–3, and Note 27, Chapter 8. For the contemporary situation, see especially Lannoy, op. cit., pp. 93, 97, 101.

19. E.g., Raju, op. cit., pp. 364–5; Wild, op. cit., pp. 101, 106.
20. On the first point, see ibid., p. 95; on the second, Finley, 1973, op. cit., pp. 151–2.
21. Wild, op. cit., pp. 108–10, 114; Finley, 1964, op. cit., p. 154.
22. Clayre, op. cit., pp. 157–60.
23. De Ste Croix, op. cit., pp. 200; 180.
24. E.g., S. Stuckey, p. 255, 262–3, in A. J. Lane, op. cit.; Genovese, 1976, op. cit., pp. 140–9, 650; Patterson, 1982, op. cit., p. 94.
25. Ibid., p. 207; Genovese, 1976, op. cit., pp. 303, 313.
26. Stampp, op. cit.; Genovese, 1976, op. cit., pp. 137–8, 619; Patterson, 1967, op. cit., p. 260; 1982, op. cit., pp. 172–3.
27. E.g., Fredrickson and Lasch, op. cit., pp. 225, 234–5, 242–3; Patterson, 1977, op. cit., pp. 415–16.
28. Finley, 1973, op. cit., pp. 63, 68, 83; Wiedemann, op. cit., pp. 12, 200, 209; E. E. Thorpe, pp. 36–7, in A. J. Lane, op. cit.; Patterson, 1967, op. cit., pp. 261, 273–8; 1977, op. cit., pp. 415–16; Genovese, 1976, op. cit., pp. 392–3, 592, 648–9.
29. Bloch, 1961, op. cit., p. 149; 1966, op. cit., p. 270; Hilton, 1966, op. cit., pp. 50, 138; 1975, op. cit., pp. 21–2; 1977, op. cit., 72. 156, 224.
30. Hilton, 1977, op. cit., p. 77, 84, 87–8, 114–15, 118–19.
31. Bloch, 1966, op. cit., pp. 148, 181, 184; Hilton, 1966, op. cit., p. 127.
32. Hilton, 1977, op. cit., pp. 51–3.
33. Bloch, 1961, op. cit., pp. 249, 276; Hilton, 1966, op. cit., pp. 125, 136, 161, 166; 1977, op. cit., pp. 32–7, 40–1, 64, 116, 145, 154, 161–2, 166–7, 174–5.
34. Dobb, 1947, op. cit., pp. 42–6. See also Hilton, 1966, op. cit., p. 123.
35. Sweezy, 1978, op. cit., p. 43.
36. Dobb, 1947, op. cit., p. 70; 1978, op. cit., pp. 60–1.
37. E.g., Pirenne, 1963, op. cit., p. 128; Black, op. cit., p. 184; Unwin, 1957, op. cit., p. 63.
38. Clark and Slack, op. cit., p. 16.
39. E.g., Rörig, op. cit., pp. 156–9.
40. Pirenne, 1936, op. cit., p. 185; Dobb, 1963, op. cit., pp. 90–3.
41. C. R. Dobson, *Masters and Journeymen* (London: Croom Helm, 1980) pp. 114, 149.
42. E.g., Pirenne, 1936, op. cit., pp. 207–8; Unwin, 1957, op. cit., pp. 47–9.
43. E.g., Unwin, 1957, op. cit., p. 210; Hilton, 1977, op. cit., pp. 190–1.
44. E. P. Thompson, 1963, op. cit., pp. 63–6, 446.
45. Ibid., pp. 202–3, 211–12, 241, 261–2, 303–7, 311, 318, 544.
46. E.g., see Runciman, op. cit., p. 76.
47. E.g., E. Wight Bakke, *Citizens Without Work* (New Haven: Yale University Press, 1969).
48. *White Collar* (New York: Oxford University Press, 1956) pp. 227–8, 297; 215, 219. On the latter point, see also Clayre, op. cit.
49. Mills, op. cit., pp. 227–8; 221–4.
50. Fred H. Blum, *Toward a Democratic Work Process* (New York: Harper and Row, 1953).
51. Blauner, op. cit., pp. 23, 26, 121–2, 174; 29, 87.
52. Goldthorpe et al., op. cit., pp. 59–60, 82, 181–2.

53. Nichols and Armstrong, op. cit., p. 149.
54. E.g., see Arthur Kornhauser's *The Mental Health of the Industrial Worker* (New York: Wiley, 1965) pp. 159–62, 269–71. He found that older workers tended to be less dissatisfied with the very same working conditions. According to him, the longer one is on the job and the less one feels one can find another, the more likely one is to "come-to-terms" with one's situation by lowering one's aspirations.
55. Mann, op. cit., pp. 25–30; 32–3.
56. Nichols and Armstrong, op. cit., pp. 20, 80, 149, 151, 153, 157–8, 164, 201–2.
57. Beynon, op. cit., pp. 90–4, 113, 153; Nichols and Armstrong, op. cit., pp. 47–9, 60–1, 64, 71–2, 82, 90, 131–9, 204; Nichols and Beynon, op. cit., pp. 22–3, 27–8, 185.
58. Beynon, op. cit., pp. 99–100; Nichols and Armstrong, op. cit., pp. 56–7.
59. Michael Burawoy, *Manufacturing Consent* (Chicago: University of Chicago Press, 1980) pp. 132–5, 200; Willis, op. cit., p. 179.
60. Burawoy, 1980, op. cit., pp. 66–7, 84; Willis, op. cit., pp. 39, 73–5, 95, 102, 150.
61. E.g., see Studs Terkel's *Working* (New York: Pantheon, 1972) and Barbara Garson's *All the Live Long Day* (Harmondsworth: Penguin, 1977).
62. Burawoy, 1980, op. cit., pp. 66–7, 84; Willis, op. cit., pp. 103–4.
63. This should already be evident for the case of Willis, who also prophesies that the "ear 'oles" who accept their teachers' promise of social mobility and interesting work may well subsequently experience their work as more depriving than do "lads" who identify themselves more closely with the working class (op. cit., p. 110). In the case of Burawoy, much of machine operators' pleasure came from favourable social comparison with workers who were less successful in "making out".
64. E.g., Wilhelm Reich, *The Mass Psychology of Fascism* (New York: Simon and Schuster (Touchstone), 1970) Chapter 10, and pp. 191–200. Herbert Marcuse, *Eros and Civilization* (New York: Random House (Vintage), 1962). See especially the appendix.
65. Interestingly, however, most of those who have researched the matter imply that it is much more a matter of the sexually liberated having *already* been politically liberal than that their sexual liberality led them to become liberal in other ways. For example, see Ira L. Reiss, Ronald E. Anderson, and G. C. Sponaugle, "A multivariate model of the determinants of extramarital sexual permissiveness", *Journal of Marriage and the Family*, vol. 42 (May 1980), pp. 395–419.
66. *Escape From Freedom* (New York: Avon, 1965). [1941] Jean-Paul Sartre, *Search for a Method* (New York: Random House (Vintage), 1962).
67. *Political Ideology* (Glencoe, Ill.: Free Press, 1959) Chapter 4.
68. Sennett and Cobb, op. cit., pp. 5–7, 18–22, 53, 163–9, 211–12, 251; 119–20.
69. Ibid., pp. 28–9. Sennett also admits to having put words in the mouths of his interviewees when he felt they couldn't quite articulate what they themselves had in mind (pp. 42–3). However, Nichols and Beynon

(op. cit., pp. 193–8) also allude to similar processes among English workers.

70. Ibid., pp. 73–4.
71. *More Than A Labour of Love* (Toronto: Women's Press, 1980).
72. E.g., for the first claim, see Ann Oakley's *The Sociology of Housework* (New York: Pantheon, 1974); for the second, a secondary analysis of a national sample of the Canadian labour force by Owen Adams and myself and reported in my *Social Psychology* . . . , op. cit., pp. 222–5. The third finding is in Terrence H. White, "Autonomy in work: Are women any different?" pp. 213–26 in Marylee Stephenson (ed.), *Women in Canada* (Toronto: New Press, 1973).
73. *Girls, Wives, Factory Lives* (London: Macmillan, 1981) pp. 73–4, 86–7, 121.
74. Ibid., pp. 101, 125, 130–1.
75. Ruth Cavendish, *Women on the Line* (London: Routledge and Kegan Paul, 1983) pp. 19, 24, 31–6, 40, 90–6. Sallie Westwood, *All Day, Every Day* (London: Pluto Press, 1984) pp. 20, 43, 89–91, 102. Charlene Gannage, *Double Day, Double Bind: Women garment workers* (Toronto: Women's Press, 1986) pp. 66, 107, 126.
76. Cavendish, op. cit., pp. 97–8; 38, 50, 161.
77. E.g., Cavendish, op. cit., pp. 13, 55, 159; Gannage, op. cit., pp. 44, 89, 117, 122, 146–7.
78. Pollert, op. cit., pp. 20, 91, 104–6, 109; Cavendish, op. cit., pp. 38, 50–2, 72; Gannage, op. cit., p. 124.
79. Pollert, op. cit., pp. 82, 120–1; Gannage, op. cit., pp. 81–2, 91; Cavendish, op. cit., pp. 59–66. As to whether women wage labourers also compare their jobs and income with those of *men*, and, if so, experience relative deprivation, there is no easy answer, since in the studies examined here, two researchers conclude either that women do relatively little comparing with men or/and that if they do, they do not usually experience intense relative deprivation anyway, while two others conclude the opposite. See Pollert, op. cit., pp. 84–6, 99, 111–13, 135, and Gannage, op. cit., pp. 23–4, 100, 105–6, versus Cavendish, op. cit., pp. 79–80, 131, 164 and Westwood, op. cit., pp. 41–2, 59–60.
80. E.g., see the critical review by Gerald R. Salancik and Jeffrey Pfeffer, "An examination of need-satisfaction models of job attitudes", *Administrative Science Quarterly*, vol. 22 (September 1977), pp. 427–56.
81. Ibid., pp. 436, 441–2.
82. Arthur N. Turner and Paul R. Lawrence, *Industrial Jobs and the Worker* (Boston: Harvard University, 1965) pp. 36–8, 44–8, 113.
83. Ibid., pp. 124–8; 117; 125.
84. Ibid., pp. 122–3. For Charles L. Hulin and Milton R. Blood, see their "Job enlargement, individual differences, and worker responses", *Psychological Bulletin*, 1968, vol. 69 (1), pp. 41–55.
85. See Note 153, Chapter 8.
86. *Industrial Democracy: The sociology of participation* (London: Constable, 1968) p. 123. See also D. V. Nightingale, op. cit.
87. E.g., see Michael Maccoby's *The Games-man* (New York: Bantam, 1978) pp. 234, 238, 240–8.

88. For the first type, see, e.g., Soper, op. cit., pp. 15–17, 88–9. Interestingly, she does not seem to be aware that her criticisms of the concept of a need hierarchy are also criticisms of *Marx's* theory of needs. For the second, in addition to Salancik and Pfeffer, op. cit., see the review by Mahmoud A. Wahba and Lawrence G. Bidwell, "Maslow reconsidered: A review of research on the need hierarchy theory", *Organizational Behaviour and Human Performance*, vol. 15 (April 1976), pp. 212–40.

89. Ibid., pp. 235–6.

90. E.g., Frank Friedlander, "Importance of work versus nonwork among socially and occupationally stratified groups", *Journal of Applied Psychology*, vol. 50 (December 1966), pp. 437–41. W. W. Ronan, "Relative importance of job characteristics", *Journal of Applied Psychology*, vol. 54 (June 1970), pp. 192–200.

91. "Need fulfillment in the career development of women", *Journal of Vocational Behavior*, vol. 20 (February 1982), pp. 53–66.

92. Thomas Cook, Faye Crosby, and Karen M. Hennigan, "The construct validity of relative deprivation", pp. 307–33 in Jerry M. Suls and Richard L. Miller (eds), *Social Comparison Processes* (Washington: Wiley (Hemisphere), 1977) p. 323. William Austin, Neil C. McGinn, and Charles Susmilch, "Internal standards revisited: Effects of social comparisons and expectancies on judgments of fairness and satisfaction", *Journal of Experimental Social Psychology*, 1980, 16, pp. 426–41. Lawrence A. Messé and Barbara L. Watts, "Complex nature of the sense of fairness: Internal standards and social comparison as bases for reward evaluations", *Journal of Personality and Social Psychology*, vol. 45 (July 1983), pp. 84–93.

93. E.g., see Marylee C. Taylor, "Improved conditions, rising expectations, and dissatisfaction: A test of the past/present relative deprivation hypothesis", *Social Psychology Quarterly*, vol. 45 (March 1982), pp. 24–33.

94. Austin et al., op. cit.; Messé and Watts, op. cit.

95. Cook et al., op. cit. Morty Bernstein and Faye Crosby, "An empirical test of relative deprivation theory", *Journal of Experimental Social Psychology*, vol. 16, pp. 442–56. Faye Crosby, *Relative Deprivation and Working Women* (New York: Oxford University Press, 1982). Robert Folger, David Rosenfield, Karen Rheaume, and Chris Martin, "Relative deprivation and referent cognitions", *Journal of Experimental Social Psychology*, (1983) vol. 19 pp. 172–84.

96. Cook et al., op. cit., pp. 323–4; Bernstein and Crosby, op. cit., p. 453.

97. William Austin, "Equity theory and social comparison processes", pp. 279–305 in Suls and Miller, op. cit. pp. 290, 294.

98. Mary Kristine Ute and Robert F. Kidd, "Equity and attribution", pp. 63–93 in Gerold Mikula (ed.), *Justice and Social Interaction* (New York: Springer-Verlag, 1980).

99. In addition to the material in Chapter 8, see William Austin and Elaine Hatfield, "Equity theory, power, and social justice", pp. 25–61 in Mikula, op. cit., p. 33. Also John Urry, *Reference Groups and the Theory of Revolution* (London: Routledge and Kegan Paul, 1973) p. 127.

100. Bernstein and Crosby, op. cit.; Austin et al., op. cit.; Messé and Watts,

op. cit.

101. E.g., see Charles L. Gruder, "Choice of comparison persons in evaluating oneself", pp. 21–41 in Suls and Miller, op. cit.
102. Ibid. See also Philip Brickman and Ronnie Janoff Bulman, "Pleasure and pain in social comparison", pp. 149–86 in the same source (pp. 149, 159–61), and Thomas Ashby Wills, "Downward comparison principles in social psychology", *Psychological Bulletin*, 1981, vol. 90 (2), pp. 245–71; p. 265. Some of this research is on blue collar workers. E.g., see Austin's (op. cit., p. 292) description of Patchen's study. On the last problem, see, e.g., Pollert, op. cit., p. 172.
103. Ibid., pp. 84–5, 99, 135, 208; Gannage, op. cit., pp. 100, 105–6.
104. Austin, op. cit., p. 283.
105. Op. cit., pp. 65, 75. On the former point, see John H. Goldthorpe, *Social Mobility and Class Structure in Britain* (Oxford: Clarendon, 1980), p. 230.

Aggression and withdrawal as responses to frustration

106. Helm, op. cit., p. 194; Lee, 1979, op. cit. The latter, for example, is true of the Mbuti pigmies studied by Turnbull, 1982, op. cit., pp. 133–4.
107. E.g., the Paliyans of India. See Gardner, op. cit., p. 431.
108. E.g., the Kalahari bushpeople deliberately distract children with the prospect of more pleasant activities (Briggs, op. cit., p. 126); the Paliyans avoid alcohol (Gardner, op. cit., p. 431).
109. Thus adults as well as children are teased and ridiculed until they "erupt" and cathart. Among other common ritualized ways of expressing and catharting are public fist fights and 'song duels' among male Eskimo (Damas, 1984, op. cit., pp. 425, 615), and tugs-of-war between male and female pigmies (Turnbull, 1982, op. cit., pp. 142–3).
110. For instance, Clayton Robarchek ("Frustration, aggression, and the nonviolent Semai", *American Ethnologist*, vol. 4 (November 1977) pp. 762–79) claims that a tribe of primitive agriculturalists on the Malay Peninsula almost never respond to frustration with anger and aggression. Instead, frustration invokes *fear* and a host of magical rituals to dissipate it or avoid frustration in the first place. For example, the Semai try to avoid putting others in the position where they would be deprived, insulted, etc. Robarchek suggests that while arousal in general is a natural response to frustration, aggression as such is not. Rather, it is much more conditional, depending upon past learning, among other circumstances.
111. Karl Wittfogel, *Oriental Despotism* (New Haven: Yale University Press, 1973) pp. 137, 142–3, 156–7, 331, 421. Kossambi, 1965, op.cit., pp. 151, 195. Habib, op. cit., pp. 330, 351.
112. De Ste Croix, op. cit., pp. 481–2, 485–6, 489, 503.
113. Genovese, 1976, op. cit., p. 588. See also pp. 125, 132, 140–3, 148–9, 587–660, and 1965, op. cit., pp. 54–5, 74; 1971, op. cit., pp. 125–7. For others' imagery of this nature, see Stampp, op. cit., p. 91; Wiedemann, op. cit., pp. 10–12; Bryce-Laporte, op. cit., pp. 274–6; and Patterson, 1982, op. cit., pp. 172–3.

114. E.g., see Bryce-Laporte, op. cit., pp. 274–6, 479; Stuckey, op. cit.
115. Genovese, 1965, op. cit., pp. 43–4; Wiedemann, op. cit., pp. 77, 200–1.
116. Hilton, 1975, op. cit., pp. 14–15, 21–2; 1977, op. cit., pp. 19, 157, 235; 109, 125, 197; 161; 232.
117. Dobb, 1978, op. cit., pp. 42–3, 46; Sweezy, op. cit.; Dobb, 1978, op. cit.
118. E.g., Unwin, 1973, op. cit., pp. 247–8; C. Phythian-Adams, pp. 68–9 in Clark and Slack, op. cit.
119. Thompson, 1963, op. cit., Chapter 11; pp. 59–60.
120. Ibid., pp. 198–203, 303–7. See also Hobsbawm, 1959, op. cit., p. 23, and even Barrington Moore (*Injustice: The social bases of obedience and revolt* (White Plains, N.Y.: M. E. Sharpe, 1978) pp. 156, 161–5, 169), who claims not to like such a model.
121. The Tillys, op. cit., pp. 2, 271–3, 278–9.
122. E.g., see Billig's critical review (op. cit.) of the work of Leonard Berkowitz. For Ted Gurr, see his *Why Men Rebel* (Princeton: Princeton University Press, 1970).
123. E.g., Keith Webb, Ekkart Zimmerman, Michael Marsh, Anne-Marie Aish, Christina Mironesco, Christopher Mitchell, Leonardo Morlino, and James Walston, "Etiology and outcomes of protest: New European perspectives", *American Behavioral Scientist*, vol. 26 (January/February 1983), pp. 311–33. Pp. 312, 315–18. David Snyder, "Collective violence: A research agenda and some strategic considerations", *Journal of Conflict Resolution*, vol. 22 (September 1978), pp. 499–534. See especially pp. 502–7.
124. Nichols and Armstrong, op. cit., pp. 51, 61, 64–9, 71–3. See also Paul Edwards and Hugh Scullion, *The Social Organization of Industrial Conflict* (Oxford: Blackwell, 1982) pp. 58, 65, 79–80, 89–90, 173, 230. Pollert, op. cit., pp. 120–5, 130.
125. See Notes 62, 74 and 75.
126. Sennett and Cobb, op. cit., pp. 24, 73, 79, 95–7, 114–18, 159, 186.
127. James T. Tedeschi, R. Bob Smith and Robert C. Brown, "A reinterpretation of research on aggression", *Psychological Bulletin*, vol. 81 (August 1974), pp. 540–62. See especially pp. 541–4. Billig, op. cit., Chapter 5.
128. E.g., see the review by Leonard Berkowitz, "Whatever happened to the frustration-aggression hypothesis?", *American Behavioral Scientist*, vol. 21 (May–June 1978), pp. 691–708.
129. Ibid., pp. 694–5.
130. E.g., see Tedeschi et al., op. cit., and Billig, op. cit.
131. E.g., see Billig, op. cit., pp. 131–5. But for some contrary evidence, see David S. Holmes, "Aggression, displacement, and guilt", *Journal of Personality and Social Psychology*, 1972, vol. 21 (3), pp. 296–301. On the relationship between aggression and other responses, see, e.g., Paul Babiak, "Locus of control as a moderator of the relationship between worker frustration and aggression, escape, avoidance, stress and fixation", *Dissertation Abstracts*, vol. 43 (June 1983), pp. 4184–5B.
132. Berkowitz, op. cit.; Billig, op. cit.
133. Billig, op. cit., pp. 151–2.

What we now know about knowledge

134. *Capital 1*, p. 538.
135. Nichols and Armstrong, op. cit., pp. 56–7, 168, 198; Nichols and Beynon, op. cit., p. 189; Armstrong et al., op. cit., p. 61; Burawoy, op. cit., pp. 28–9.
136. Armstrong et al., op. cit., pp. 67, 73–80.
137. See especially Sennett and Cobb, op. cit., pp. 66, 72, 79, 96, 158–9, 170–1, 182. Also Cavendish, op. cit., pp. 43, 48.
138. Sennett and Cobb, op. cit. Nichols and Armstrong, op. cit., pp. 168–9; Nichols and Beynon, op. cit., p. 189; Willis, op. cit., pp. 120–1, 131, 172. Armstrong et al., op. cit., pp. 71–3.
139. For example, compare Sennett and Cobb's results and analysis to those of the English researchers cited above.
140. Burawoy, op. cit., pp. 70, 92, 100, 167, 182, 186; 84. Gannage, op. cit., pp. 122, 128 suggests that the women garment workers she studied were *particularly* likely to experience the latter.
141. Willis, op. cit.; Nichols and Armstrong, op. cit., pp. 60–1.
142. E.g., respectively, Pollert, op. cit., pp. 87–8; Westwood, op. cit., p. 101.
143. Nichols and Armstrong, op. cit., pp. 96–7.
144. Pollert, op. cit.
145. Willis, op. cit., pp. 59, 166–8. Nichols and Armstrong, op. cit., pp. 69–70, 76–7. See also Armstrong et al., op. cit.
146. Willis, op. cit., pp. 163, 165.
147. Nichols and Armstrong, op. cit., pp. 28; 15–16, 30, 112; 19–20; 48, 141.
148. Benyon, op. cit., pp. 86–7. See also Edwards and Scullion, op. cit., p. 222.
149. Willis, op. cit., p. 169.
150. Pollert, op. cit., pp. 87–8.
151. Cavendish, op. cit., pp. 70–1; Gannage, op. cit., pp. 23–4.
152. For the first position, see especially Nichols and Armstrong, op. cit., pp. 151, 180, 202, 208; for the second, Armstrong et al., op. cit., p. 194, and Willis, op. cit., pp. 99, 132–3, 145–6, 162–3.
153. On the first point, see particularly Armstrong et al., op. cit., pp. 39–40, 51, 121, 128; on the second, Pollert, op. cit., pp. 199, 210, and Cavendish, op. cit., pp. 141, 145, 147, 153.
154. Burawoy, op. cit., pp. 112–13. See also Cavendish, op. cit., p. 156.
155. Armstrong et al., op. cit. For claim (b), see especially Kusterer, op. cit. Of claim (c), Edwards and Scullion (op. cit., pp. 162–4) discovered that most of their workers were not even aware that collective resistance was a possibility.
156. Trotsky's observation as well as more systematic evidence is contained in John Leggett's *Class, Race and Labor: Working class consciousness in Detroit* (New York: Oxford University Press, 1968) pp. 71–3. Otherwise see Nichols and Armstrong, op. cit., pp. 130–4.
157. E.g., see Kornhauser, op. cit.
158. Nichols and Armstrong, op. cit., pp. 130–4.
159. See Note 105.
160. E.g., Armstrong et al., op.cit., pp. 117–18.

161. "The effects of changes in roles on the attitudes of role occupants", *Human Relations*, 1956, vol. 9, pp. 385–402.
162. J. S. Bruner and C. D. Goodman, "Value and need as organizing factors in perception", *Journal of Abnormal and Social Psychology*, 1947, vol. 42, pp. 33–44. However, the findings of this study have not always been completely replicated. For example, see Donald D. Dorfman and Robert B. Zajonc, "Some effects of sound, background brightness, and economic status on the perceived size of coins and discs". Ibid., 1963, vol. 66, pp. 87–90.
163. E.g., Nichols and Armstrong, op. cit.; Nichols and Beynon, op. cit.
164. Cavendish, op. cit., p. 45.
165. At least, those who have to act on their knowledge tend to look at *more* aspects of something and *organize* it more than do those who are less active. See the description of the work of Robert Zajonc and his associates in my *Social Psychology . . .* , op. cit., p. 168.
166. E.g., ibid., pp. 143–4; Beynon, op. cit., pp. 270, 284–5; Armstrong et al., op. cit., p. 194; Pollert, op. cit., pp. 199, 204, 210, 225–6; Cavendish, op. cit., pp. 65, 147.
167. E.g., Edwards and Scullion, op. cit., p. 281.
168. Beynon, op. cit., p. 310.
169. Ibid., pp. 317–18. See also Note 153.
170. E.g., Edwards and Scullion, op. cit., p. 96.
171. Op. cit., pp. 151; 180, 208; 202.
172. Nichols and Beynon, op. cit., p. 160; Nichols and Armstrong, op. cit., p. 61.
173. Armstrong et al., op. cit., pp. 16–20, 49, 88, 182; Edwards and Scullion, op. cit., pp. 108–9, 128–9, 132–3, 245, 274–7, 281; Willis, op. cit., pp. 99, 132–3, 145–6, 162–3; Westwood, op. cit.
174. Beynon, op. cit., pp. 202, 210–11; Nichols and Armstrong, op. cit., pp. 71–3, 113, 211; Nichols and Beynon, op. cit., pp. 145, 160; Armstrong et al., op. cit., pp. 111, 200, 225–6; Pollert, op. cit., pp. 225–6.
175. Nichols and Armstrong, op. cit., p. 68; Nichols and Beynon, op. cit., pp. 109, 113.
176. E.g., see Armstrong et al., op. cit., pp. 23–4; Edwards and Scullion, op. cit., pp. 173–4, 285; Burawoy, op. cit., p. 167; Westwood, op. cit., p. 17.

Grouping and its effects

177. Mustafer Sherif and Carolyn Sherif, *Groups in Harmony and Tension* (New York: Harper, 1953).
178. Henri Tajfel and John C. Turner, "An integrative theory of intergroup conflict", pp. 33–47 in William G. Austin and Stephen Worchel (eds), *The Social Psychology of Intergroup Relations* (Monterey: Brooks/ Cole, 1979) p. 34. Henri Tajfel, "Social psychology of intergroup relations", *Annual Review of Psychology*, vol. 33, 1982, pp. 1–39. P. 31.
179. Tajfel and Turner, op. cit., pp. 34, 38, 42; Tajfel, op. cit., p. 31; John Turner, "Social identification and psychological group formation", pp. 518–38 in Henri Tajfel (ed.), *The Social Dimension* (Cambridge: Cambridge University Press, 1984. Volume 2).

180. Tajfel and Turner, op. cit.; Donald M. Taylor and David J. McKirnan, "A five-stage model of intergroup relations", *British Journal of Social Psychology*, vol. 23 (November 1984), pp. 291–300.

181. E.g., see Thompson, 1963, op. cit., pp. 244, 310. Rupert Brown, "Divided we fall: An analysis of relations between sections of a factory workforce", pp. 395–429 in Henri Tajfel (ed.), *Differentiation Between Social Groups* (London: Academic Press, 1978). See also the following studies by industrial sociologists: Nichols and Armstrong, op. cit.; Edwards and Scullion, op. cit., pp. 160–1, 185, 216, 219; Pollert, op. cit., pp. 150, 155, 181; Cavendish, op. cit., pp. 28, 61; Gannage, op. cit., p. 49.

182. Mustafer Sherif, "Superordinate goals in the reduction of intergroup conflict: An experimental evaluation", pp. 257–61 in Austin and Worchel, op. cit., p. 261. Stephen Worchel, "Cooperation and the reduction of intergroup conflict: Some determining factors." Ibid., pp. 262–73; p. 263.

183. Ibid., pp. 264, 267.

184. Sherif, op. cit., p. 258.

185. Worchel, op. cit., p. 269. See also Cavendish, op. cit., p. 156, for a real-life case with workers. Perhaps one of the most striking examples of late is that of the "Solidarity" movement in British Columbia in 1983–4.

186. See especially Brown, 1978, op. cit.

187. Worchel, op. cit., pp. 271, 273.

188. Westwood, op. cit., p. 64. See also Gannage, op. cit., p. 125.

189. Ad F. M. Van Knippenberg, "Intergroup differences in group perceptions", pp. 560–78 in Tajfel, 1984, op. cit. Tajfel himself recognized this counter-trend to his own theory, in both this work (p. 701) and an earlier one (1982, op. cit., p. 18).

190. Tajfel et al., op. cit.

191. Runciman, op. cit., p. 40. Reed D. Vanneman and Thomas F. Pettigrew, "Race and relative deprivation in the urban United States", *Race*, vol. 13 (April 1972), pp. 461–86. Iain Walker and Thomas F. Pettigrew, "Relative deprivation theory: An overview and conceptual critique", *British Journal of Social Psychology*, vol. 23 (November 1984), pp. 301–10. Rama Charan Tripathi and Rashmi Srivastava, "Relative deprivation and intergroup attitudes", *European Journal of Social Psychology*, vol. 11 (July–September 1981), pp. 313–18. Serge Guimond and Lise Dubé-Simard, "Relative deprivation theory and the Quebec nationalist movement", *Journal of Personality and Social Psychology*, vol. 44 (3), 1983, pp. 526–35.

192. Brown, op. cit. For the experimental evidence, see Rupert J. Brown and John C. Turner, "Interpersonal and intergroup behaviour", pp. 33–65 in John C. Turner and Howard Giles (eds), *Intergroup Behaviour* (Oxford: Blackwell, 1981). Rupert J. Brown, "The role of similarity in intergroup relations", pp. 603–45 in Tajfel, 1984, op. cit.

193. Tajfel, 1978, op. cit., pp. 15–16; John C. Turner and Rupert J. Brown, "Social status, cognitive alternatives, and intergroup relations", ibid., pp. 201–34; John C. Turner, "Social comparison, similarity, and in-group favoritism", ibid., pp. 235–50; Brown and Turner, 1981, op. cit.;

Tajfel, 1982, op. cit., pp. 25–6; Brown, 1984, op. cit.

194. See Tajfel and Turner, op. cit., who refer to this as group "creativity".

195. Tajfel, 1978, op. cit.; Brown and Turner, 1981, op. cit., p. 39; Turner, 1981, op. cit., pp. 79–80; Tajfel, 1982, op. cit., pp. 13–14, 21–2; Turner, 1984, op. cit., pp. 528–9.

196. Henri Tajfel, "Social stereotypes and social groups", pp. 144–67 in Turner and Giles, op. cit. "Intergroup relations, social myths and social justice in social psychology", pp. 695–715 in Tajfel, 1984, op. cit.

197. Ibid., pp. 698–701. See also Tajfel, 1982, op. cit., pp. 19–20.

198. Van Knippenberg, op. cit.

199. E.g., see Tajfel, 1984, op. cit., p. 700. Apfelbaum, "Relations of domination and movements for liberation: An analysis of power between groups", pp. 188–204 in Austin and Worchel, op. cit., pp. 197–8.

200. Beynon, op. cit., pp. 74, 197, 206, 240; Willis, op. cit.

201. Edwards and Scullion, op. cit., pp. 90–1.

202. Cavendish, op. cit., p. 150.

203. Pollert, op. cit., p. 217 and p. 37, respectively.

204. E.g., see Marvin E. Shaw, *Group Dynamics*, 3rd Edition (New York: McGraw-Hill, 1981) pp. 68–79; 57–68, 77–9. James H. Davis, *Group Performance* (Reading, Mass.: Addison-Wesley, 1969) Chapter 3. Shaw, op. cit., pp. 57–68, 77–9.

205. E.g., Cavendish, op. cit., pp. 57, 155; Westwood, op. cit., p. 67. Edwards and Scullion, op. cit., pp. 162–3.

206. E.g., see my *Social Psychology as Political Economy*, op. cit., p. 197. Nichols and Armstrong, op. cit., pp. 72, 113. Pollert, op. cit., p. 205; Cavendish, op. cit., pp. 151–2; Gannage, op. cit., pp. 150, 184–5.

207. Cavendish, op. cit., p. 155.

208. See Brown and Turner, op. cit., pp. 42–3; Tajfel, 1982, op. cit., p. 15. Philip G. Zimbardo, "Individuation, reason and order versus deindividuation, impulse and chaos", pp. 237–307 in W. J. Arnold and D. Levine (eds), *Nebraska Symposium on Motivation* (Lincoln: University of Nebraska Press, 1970). L. Mann, J. W. Newton, and J. M. Innes, "A test between deindividuation and emergent norm theories of crowd aggression", *Journal of Personality and Social Psychology*, vol. 42, 1982, pp. 260–72. S. Prentice-Dunn and R. W. Rogers, "Effects of public and private self-awareness on deindividuation and aggression", *Journal of Personality and Social Psychology*, vol. 43, 1982, pp. 505–13.

209. Tajfel, 1978, op. cit.; Tajfel and Turner, op. cit., pp. 43–6; Taylor and McKirnan, op. cit. For the latter, for example, when members of a community in Massachusetts organized, the incidence of mental illness decreased dramatically. See William Ryan's "Preventive services in the social context: Power, pathology, and prevention", *Proceedings of the Mental Health Institute*, (May–June 1969), pp. 49–58 (Boulder, Col.: Western Interstate Commission for Higher Education).

210. Sik Hung Ng, "Social psychology and political economy", pp. 624–45 in Tajfel 1984, op. cit., pp. 636–9. Miles Hewstone and Joseph M. F. Jaspers, "Social dimensions of attribution", ibid., pp. 379–404. See p. 398. Itesh Sachdev and Richard Y. Bourhis, "Social categorization and power differentials in group relations", *European Journal of Social*

Psychology, vol. 15, 1985, pp. 415–34. "Status differentials and intergroup behaviour". Forthcoming in the same journal.

211. Kenneth L. Dion, "Intergroup conflict and intragroup cohesiveness", pp. 211–24 in Austin and Worchel, op. cit., pp. 220–2.

212. Op. cit., pp. 158, 171, 275–6; 262–4. However, Edwards and Scullion themselves are not completely comfortable with a FAT interpretation. Thus according to them, individual responses do not simply take energy away from the collective, nor are either the result of a rational choice of one or another from a 'toolbox' of possible responses (pp. 162–4, 274–7). On the other hand, they do describe workers' responses as either or both expressions of frustration or attempts at relief from it (pp. 14, 101). Furthermore, individual and collective responses *did* seem to substitute for each other when one or another was blocked, although, as we would expect from FAT, this did not always occur consciously (pp. 158, 171, 276).

213. Tajfel and Turner, op. cit.; Brown and Turner, op. cit.; Turner, 1984, op. cit.

214. E.g., see Dion, op. cit.

215. Ibid., pp. 217–19. Turner, 1981, op. cit., pp. 90–3; 1984, op. cit., pp. 534–5. John Turner, M. A. Hogg, P. J. Turner, and P. M. Smith, "Failure and defeat as determinants of group cohesiveness", *British Journal of Social Psychology*, vol. 23 (June 1984), pp. 97–111.

216. E.g., see Robert F. Bales, "Task roles and social roles in problem-solving groups", pp. 437–47 in Eleanor E. Maccoby. Theodore M. Newcomb, and Eugene L. Hartley (eds), *Readings in Social Psychology* (New York: Holt, Rinehart and Winston, 1958) 3rd Edition. Also Blumberg, op. cit.

217. E.g., see Luther Gerlach and Virginia Hine, *People, Power, Change* (New York: Bobbs-Merrill, 1970) pp. 65–7, 111. Also Blumberg, op. cit., pp. 74, 78, 119.

218. *The Choice of Wage Comparisons* (Englewood Cliffs, N.J.: Prentice-Hall, 1961). See also Vanneman and Pettigrew, op. cit., pp. 464–5; Armstrong et al., op. cit.

219. Armstrong et al., op.cit.

220. Robert L. Hamblin, "Leadership and crises", *Sociometry*, vol. 21, 1958, pp. 322–35. E. P. Hollander, "Conformity, status, and idiosyncrasy credit", *Psychological Review*, vol. 65, 1958, pp. 117–27. For an example of this from industrial sociology, see Cavendish, op. cit., p. 153.

221. E.g., the latter is implied by Victor Serge, an eventual Trotskyist (?) with anarcho-syndicalist sympathies, who managed to live through the aftermath of the Russian Revolution without suffering the fate of so many others of such sympathies. See his *Memoirs of a Revolutionary, 1901–41* (Oxford: Oxford University Press, 1963). David Mandel (*The Petrograd Workers and the Fall of the Old Regime* (London: Macmillan, 1983)) makes a good case that large sections of the Petrograd working class were far in advance of many members of the Bolshevik party in that, for example, they recognized the necessity for workers themselves to control their factories. However, the Civil War and its most serious by-product, starvation, was to remove this natural check on Bolshevik political leaders.

222. E.g., see Beynon, op. cit.
223. E.g., Nichols and Armstrong, op. cit.; Pollert, op. cit., pp. 138–9, 181–3; Cavendish, op. cit., pp. 137, 150–3; Westwood, op. cit., pp. 69, 79, 85–7; Gannage, op. cit., pp. 125, 148–51.

10 Conclusion

A currently popular joke takes this form: someone returns to his or her residence after doing an errand and announces: "I have good news and bad news." The good news is usually *very* good (for example, the messenger has just won a lottery), but then the bad news is usually equally as bad (s/he has subsequently lost the money gambling, or down a sewer). In some respects my overall evaluation of Marx's theories of human nature takes this form, except that the bad news is not always as bad as the good is good, and the process of evaluation is not intended to be, nor, hopefully, will be taken as, a joke.

The first bit of good news has been dealt with extensively in the general Introduction and Parts I through III, and will not be expanded upon here. It is this: despite the protestations of Marx's fans and critics alike, and sometimes Marx himself, Marx's theorizing does not lack anthropological and psychological assumptions about human nature. In fact, such assumptions are far more numerous, systematic, and central to the rest of his theorizing than has hitherto been recognized. The *bad* news here is that both Marx and his followers have been much less *aware*, and critical, of such premises than they should have been. As a result, some of these notions have been implausible and/or contradictory. A prime example of the first is Marx's claim that workers gain far more insight into the workings of capitalism after failing to protect and enhance their interests than they do by succeeding (see Chapters 7 and 9). An instance of the second is his having predicted both that the gratification of lower-order needs will automatically lead workers to concern themselves with those of a higher order and that deprivation of the latter leads to "regression" to the former (see Chapter 4).

Another piece of good news is Marx's method for theorizing about human nature. Contrary to most interpretations, he was not opposed to making generalizations about it, and in fact made many of them, often explicitly. However, he stressed that such generalizations cannot legitimately be made from "arm-chair" speculation, or even systematic observation of individuals in only one form of society, historical epoch, or class. Rather, they require *comparative, historical* research. Furthermore, in contrast to those who have viewed such general features of human nature as pre-existent, or "outside of history", Marx saw them as inevitably "confounded" with historically-specific circumstances.

299

Because of this, generalizations about human nature can seldom if ever be used on their own. But there is bad news here as well, in that Marx did not always practise what he preached. Indeed, after lambasting classical political economy and Hegelian philosophy for having imposed the characteristics of individuals in their own societies and classes upon those in all, he sometimes hypocritically did much the same himself. Perhaps the worst cases entail his unacknowledged acceptance of Victorian prejudices about foragers and Asians.

As for the generalizations themselves, those concerning "human nature as modified in each historical epoch", while not totally original – Marx's debt to Hegel's *Philosophy of History* was huge, and much too little noted by himself – are, as with so much of the rest of his work, at least an original *synthesis* of previous theorizing which has provoked a unique line of theory and research on the changing parameters of the social and the individual, on the "social construction" of individuality, sexuality, and so on. Yet as we have seen in the Introduction to Part IV and Chapter 8, these generalizations are far from unproblematic. Nor is this simply a matter of Marx's modes of production and representative individuals having been too "ideal-typical". Were we to criticize Marx on this score by noting, for example, that the "Asiatic mode of production" was neither the only mode in early Asian civilizations nor characteristic only of Asian peoples, or that feudalism had many different faces, even among Western European peoples in medieval times, his disciples might well defend him on the grounds that he himself expected such variations, and was in fact aware of some of those we have just mentioned.

No, the problems with Marx's conception of human nature "as modified in each historical epoch" run much deeper than this, to the Hegelian-derived model itself. "History" does not appear to have begun without either "individuals" (individuation) or "history" (historic agency), in that, as we have seen, "tribal" peoples have not in fact totally lacked either. Nor, as we have also noted, can the transformations in individuation and agency which have occurred through "history" be completely reduced to changes in dominant modes of production, considering, for instance, that the relative lack of individuation and free and historic agency in Asian societies has long outlived their Asiatic mode of production, and that the substantial increases in individuation and agency during the "Renaissance" appear to have pre-dated the dominance of the capitalist mode of production. Clearly, such facts point to the need to treat "superstructural" circumstances much more seriously than Marx usually did.

Nevertheless, Marx's theories of individuation and agency raise many questions, and provide many answers, which other theories have not. Thus as suggested in Chapter 8, although the changes in individuality and autonomy during the Renaissance cannot be reduced to the freeing of labour from feudal and guild restrictions, it would be difficult indeed to explain them at all adequately *without* invoking the latter. Similarly, Marx may have exaggerated the de-individuating effects of belonging to the capitalist class, and the individuating effects of class conscious interaction among workers; yet his insight that the dominance of the capitalist mode means much more a change in the form of domination and exploitation, and therefore also individuation and agency, than in their lessening, is a profound one. For these reasons alone, we would be well-advised to continue to start from, and revise, Marx's theories than to dispense with them altogether.

Knowing, as we do, that Marx has so often been wrongly construed as not having *had* theories of "human nature in general", the fact that most of the latter are *both* very similar to those currently in use *and*, apparently, somewhat better supported by evidence than are his theories of human nature as modified in each historical epoch, which are far more unique, is a major irony of the present work. This message clearly contains good news. To wit, Marx's theories of needs and wants, relative deprivation, frustration–aggression, knowledge-acquisition, and intergroup relations have proven highly useful, and, in many cases, perhaps indispensable, to the work of contemporary social science. However, there is not-so-good news here as well, because certain of Marx's generalizations about human nature – most notably the need hierarchy and the assumption that humans can tolerate relatively little deprivation and frustration – have yet to be (in the case of the first), or have never been (in the case of the second), well-corroborated by the facts, and at a minimum require serious qualification.

If there is one paramount lesson to be learned from this enterprise, it is probably this one: Marx and most of his followers have been far too little cognizant and critical of their assumptions about human nature, and if we wish to make his theories more effective we must rectify this. The present work is intended as a step in this direction.

Index

Abrams, P., 41nn.
Abramsky, C., 162n.
accumulation of capital, 28, 74n.
acquisitiveness, 28, 89, 235–6, 240, 249
action (social) analysis, 19–20, 25–8, 31–2
activity, need for, 84, 88, 235
Adams, O., 288n.
Adams, R. McC., 167, 176–7nn.
adaptation level, 90–3, 101, 103, 122, 141, 238, 242–5, 251–2, 254, 260, 267
affiliation, need for, 84, 88, 90, 97, 102, 141, 235
agency, 1, 15–16, 19, 21–5, 31, 33, 37nn., 46, 49, whole of Chapter 3, 80, 124–7, 165, 169, 172, much of Chapter 8, 300–1
  distinctions among "representative", "free", and "historic", 15
alienation, 3–4, 18–19, 21, 28–9, 35, 54, 62, 68, 73n., 85, 92–4, 97–8, 104, 106, 126, 136, 152, 162, 214–15, 237, 246–7, 252, 257, 260, 279–81
Allport, F., 37n.
Althusser, L., 1, 8nn., 13, 33, 37–8nn., 41nn., 81n., 139n.
Anderson, P., 16, 37–40, 52–4nn., 176n., 207–8, 224n., 226n., 229n.
antiquity (classical), 46–9, 53, 65–6, 168, 185, 239–40
Apfelbaum, E., 278, 295n.
Aptdecker, H., 196, 226n.
Archibald, W. P., 38–40nn., 110n., 176n., 221n., 226n., 230n., 232n., 293n., 295n.
"aristocracies of labour", 138, 160n.
Aristotle, 121, 225–6
Armstrong(s), Pat and Hugh, 231n.
Armstrong, Peter, 231–2nn., 247, 250, 261, 264, 266–8, 271, 280, 283, 287nn., 291–7nn.

Arnold, W. J., 295n.
Asiatic mode of production, social formation, 21, 47, 64–5, 73n., 166–8, 172, 176, 187–90, 237–9, 300
aspiration level, or level of aspiration, 92, 96n., 101, 238, 240, 244–7, 250–1, 268, 287nn.
"atomization", "fragmentation", or "individualization" of individuals, 5, 28, 34–6, 37n., 52, 68, 71, 79, 98, 123, 128, 139, 150–1, 197
Auboyer, J., 178n.
Austin, W., 289–90nn., 293n., 294–6nn.
automation, 54–5, 72, 118, 171, 215, 218
Avineri, S., 20, 74n., 110n., 176n.
avoidance conditioning, 149

Babiak, P., 291n.
Bakke, E. W., 286n.
Bakunin, M. A., 157
Bales, R. F., 296n.
Balikci, A., 285nn.
Bandura, A., 252
Baran, P., 178n.
Barnett, S. et al., 224n.
Barrett, M., 231n.
Barry, H. et al., 222n.
Baudrillard, J., 179n.
Bauer, B., 38n.
begging, vagabondage, robbery, thievery, and other "deviant" or criminal responses to deprivation and frustration, 51, 70, 101, 150–1, 259
Bell, D., 178n.
Berger, P., 125, 130nn.
Berkowitz, L., 260, 291nn.
Bernstein, M., 289nn.
Betz, E., 254, 289n.
Beynon, H., 231–2nn., 247, 261, 266, 278, 287–8nn., 295–7nn.
Bhadra, B., 176–7n.
Biardeau, M., 223n., 285n.

303

Bicchieri, M. G., 222–3nn., 285n.
Bidwell, L. G., 289nn.
Billig, M., 41nn., 110n., 261–2, 291nn.
Black, A., 178n., 205, 228nn., 286n.
Blanqui, A., 157–8
Blauner, R., 231n., 246, 286n.
Bloch, Marc, 170, 177–8nn., 199, 227–8nn., 286nn.
Bloch, Maurice, 221n.
Blood, M. R., 252–3
Bluestone, B., 178n.
Blum, F. H., 286n.
Blumberg, P., 253, 296nn.
Bologh, R. Wallach, 18, 32n., 73n.
Bottomore, T., 39n.
"bourgeois", or "classical", political economy, 13, 16–17, 22, 27, 35, 41n., 62, 79, 84, 124, 137, 300
Bourhis, R. Y., 295–6n.
Boyce, M., 223n.
"brainstorming", 147, 269
Braudel, F., 178n.
Braverman, H., 231n.
Brickman, P., 290n.
Briggs, J., 285nn., 290n.
Brook, E., 231n.
Brown, R., 273–4, 294–5nn.
Bruner, J. S., 293n.
Bryce-Laporte, R. S., 226n., 290–1nn.
Bulman, R. J., 290n.
Bulmer, M., 231n.
Burawoy, M., 178n., 230n., 247, 250, 261, 263, 287nn., 292–3nn.

Caesar, J., 169
Calhoun, C., 229n.
Campbell, J., 223n.
capitalist mode, and/or relations, of production, 21, 50–3, 57n., 101, 117–18, 121, 124, 248, 264
dominance of, 101
Carnoy, M., 162n.
Carter, A. T., 224nn., 285n.
Carver, T., 94–5nn.
catharsis, 258–9, 262, 290n.
Cavendish, R., 251, 279, 288nn., 292nn., 294–7nn.

centralization of capital, 71, 129, 145, 217
Chan, W.-T., 223n., 285n.
Chandra, B., 223n.
Chang, K., 177n.
Chartism, 211–12
Childe, V. G., 167, 177nn., 190, 223–4nn.
Christian, 221–3nn., 285n.
circulation, process and/or sphere of, 52–3, 70
city-state, 47, 135, 137
Clark, P., 228nn., 286n.
Clarke, H. D. et al., 232n.
class-consciousness, 1, 3, 63–4, 68, 71, 99, 118, 146, 200–1, 210–11, 216, 258–60, 266–7, 270–1, 278, 284, 301
"negative" class-consciousness, 200
"class-for-itself", 133–6, 147, 154–5, 209, 211, 275
class formation, 5, 118, 125, 129, 133–40, 154, 211–12
"classical" definition of truth, 113, 129n.
Clastres, P., 285n.
Clayre, A., 285–6nn.
Cobb, J., 232n., 249, 256, 277, 287nn., 291–2nn.
"cognitive (social) categorization, differentiation, and/or identity", 153, 272, 295n.
Cohen, G. A., 7, 9n., 23, 39nn.
Cohen, J., 13, 37n., 40n.
Cohen, M. et al., 161n.
Collins, H., 162n.
commodity, commodity production, 30, 33, 35, 53
commodity exchange relations, 35, 50, 56, 114–15, 121, 144, 146, 181, 190–1, 193–4, 200, 279
communal property, 46–8, 73n., 137, 166–8, 186, 220
communism, communist mode of production, 21, 54–6, 62
prerequisites for, 62, 72, 103, 171
"comparison level of alternatives", 91–2, 95n.

compensation, compensatory gratification, 106–8, 247, 252, 261–2, 280
concentration of capital, 71, 101, 129, 145, 217
"constructivism", constructivist" conception of knowledge, 113, 129n.
"contingency hypothesis", 150–2, 197, 260–2, 277, 280–2
Cook T. et al., 289nn.
corporations, "joint-stock" companies, 117, 138
"cottage", or "putting-out", system, 170, 208, 210
crafts, and/or grouping by, 19, 31, 48–9, 136, 143, 170, 194
craftsmanship as an ideal, value, 202–5, 240, 245
crises, 70–2, 102, 107, 109, 118, 129, 274–5
Crosby, F., 289nn.
Currie, K., 176n.

Damas, D., 222–3nn., 285nn., 290n.
Darley, J., 161n.
David, P. A. et al., 225n.
Davis, H. H., 231n.
Davis, J. H., 161n., 295n.
Dawe, A., 20–1, 39n., 73n., 179n.
"deferential" working class community, 215–16
"de-industrialization", 171, 219
de-skilling process, 215
    see also proletarianization
de Ste Croix, G. E. M., 225–7nn., 257, 286n., 290n.
Deutsch, M., 96n.
DeVore, I., 221–2nn., 285nn.
dialectic(al) (ian), 19, 45, 166
"diffusion of responsibility", 161n., 295n.
Dion, K. L., 296nn.
displacement of aggression, 105–6, 109, 210, 219, 257–9, 261–2, 275, 281
division of labour, 29, 32, 34, 39n., 46, 48, 52, 54–6, 65, 98, 102, 134, 145, 156, 170, 181–6, 190, 193, 208

    see also gender, sex relations
Dobb, M., 178n., 208, 227n., 229–30nn., 242–3, 258, 286nn., 291n.
Dobson, C. R., 286n.
Dollard, J. et al., 110n.
dominance of, dominant, modes of production, 24, 121–2, 165, 169, 172, 300–1
Dorfman, D. D., 293n.
Dubé-Simard, L., 294n.
Dumont, L., 3, 8n., 13, 37n., 224nn., 285n.
Durkheim, E., 22, 39n., 57nn., 73n.

Easton, L., 56n.
"ecological fallacy", 23
Edwards, P., 271, 279–81, 291–5nn.
Edwards, R., 231nn.
"effective" wants and/or demands, 1, 33, 93–4
ego psychology, 248–9
"egoistic" versus "fraternal" social comparison, 141–3, 146, 249, 255–6, 276
Elkins, S., 196, 226n.
Elliott, D., 233n.
Elster, J., 3, 8n., 13, 16, 20, 37n., 39–40nn.
embourgeoisement, 216
emergent processes, 15, 22–3, 28–31, 35, 71–2, 135, 141, 147, 155, 244–9, 254–6, 271–84
enclosure system, 230n.
Engels, F., 1, 37n., 103, 134, 155, 160n., 207, 224n., 229n.
Engerman, S. L., 225n.
epistemology, 20, 80
equality
    degree of, 50, 52, 70–1, 145
    principle of, 143–5, 235, 237, 256, 273, 277
equifinality, 263, 265
"equity", or "proportionality", principle, 142, 256
equivalence, equivalents, 29–30, 50, 91, 115, 142, 144
    see also universal equivalent
ethics, justice, and/or morality

(especially different systems of, by caste, class, etc.), 5, 85, 143–5, 173, 238, 244, 254–6, 259, 277
ethnic, and/or race, relations, 56, 69, 105–6, 115, 127, 136, 143, 166, 264–5, 275
see also racism
exchange, exchange relations, 29–30, 46, 53, 56, 57n., 68, 115, 146, 166, 182–6, 202
see also commodity exchange relations
exchange-value, 56, 114–15, 118
existentialism, vii, 130–1n., 244, 248–9
expressive, or "intrinsic", orientation, 87, 107, 135, 238, 240, 245, 262
"extrinsic", or "instrumental", orientation, 35, 106–7, 135, 240, 247, 251, 262

"factory consciousness", 266, 271
factory system, 208, 244
"false needs", 141
feminism, 173–4, 179n.
see also sexism
Festinger, L., 95n., 161n.
fetishism, 73, 173
feudal mode of production, feudalism, 24, 46, 49, 67–8, 117, 143, 150, 154, 167, 169–70, 173, 181, 197–201, 205, 227nn., 241–3, 258, 300–1
Feuerbach, L., 14, 17, 25–6, 37–8nn.
Finley, M. I., 7, 169, 177n., 190, 224–6nn., 286nn.
Finn, D., 231n.
fixation, psychic process of, 38n., 87–8, 122–3, 291n.
Fogel, R. W., 225n.
Folger, R. et al., 289n.
foraging, or hunting and gathering, mode of production, social formation, 172–3, 181–6, 222–3nn., 235–7, 257, 300
forces of production, 47, 55
form of political control, 46–7, 51, 70, 181, 184–7, 193

Foucault, M., 39n.
"fraternal" versus "egoistic" social comparison
see "egoistic"
freedom, liberty
degree of, 2, 22, 50–3, 70–1, 100, 126, 193, 244, 246
principle of, 126, 145, 240–2, 258
Fredrickson, G. M., 226n.
Freud, S., 130n., 248–9, 262
Freudianism, neo-Freudianism, vii, 2, 6–7, 244, 248
Fried, M. F., 221nn.
Friedlander, F., 289n.
Friedman, A., 231n.
Fromm, E., 249, 287n.
frustration-aggression, process and theory of, 3, 6, 62–4, 100–9, 110n., 174, 210, 239, 252–67, 280–1, 285n., 290nn., 296n., 301
functionalism, functionalist, 8n., 20, 22–3, 27–8
functions, "latent" versus "manifest", 23

Gallie, D., 231n.
Gannage, C., 288nn., 290n., 292nn., 294–7nn.
Gans, H., 232n.
Gardiner, P., 221–3nn., 290nn.
Garson, B., 287n.
gender, sex relations, 56, 65, 69, 106–8, 127, 134, 136, 143, 173, 183–4, 247, 256, 264–6, 271, 275, 300
see also sexism, feminism
Genovese, E. D., 7, 225–6nn., 257–8, 286nn., 290–1nn.
Geras, Norman, 8n., 40n.
Gerlach, L., 296n.
Germanic mode of production, social formation, 47–9, 66–7, 168–9, 172, 186–7
Giddens, A., 21, 39–40nn.
Giles, H., 294–5nn.
Gilmour, R. S., 232n.
Gold, D. et al., 162n.
Goldthorpe, J. H., 231–2nn., 246, 271, 286n., 290n.

Goodman, C. D., 293n.
Gordon, D. et al., 231n.
Gorz, A., 232n.
Gough, K., 222n
Gould, C., 38n., 54–5, 58nn.
Gramsci, A., 159
Greenblatt, S., 228–9nn.
Gruder, C. L., 290n.
guild mode of production, guild-system, 19, 46, 49–50, 67–8, 135, 137, 150, 170, 201–5, 228nn., 243, 259, 301
Guimond, S., 294n.
Gupta, D., 224n.
Gurr, T., 260, 291n.
Gutman, H. G., 225nn.

Habermas, J., 179n.
Habib, I., 223n., 285n., 290n.
Hamblin, R. L., 296n.
Hamilton, A., 221n.
Hannan, M. T., 39n.
Harris, M., 235–6, 285n.
Harrison, B., 178n.
Hatfield, E., 289n.
Hegel, G. F., 5, 29, 62, 73n., 144, 162n., 166, 169, 172, 300
Hegelianism, 4–5, 14, 17, 38n., 56n., 79, 104, 119, 140, 300
  see also "Left", or "Young", Hegelians
Heller, A., 8n., 33, 41n., 74n., 89, 95n., 206, 228n.
Helm, J., 221–3nn., 285n., 290n.
Helson, H., 95n.
Hewstone, M., 295n.
hierarchy, hierarchical social relations, 143, 184, 189–90, 198, 205, 224nn., 237, 283
Hill, C., 208, 227–9nn.
Hilton, R., 7, 227nn., 258, 286nn., 291n.
Hine, V., 296n.
"historic" agency, social change, or "history" in the strictest sense, 14–15, 37n., 61–5, much of Chapter 3, 133, 169, 172, 300
historical materialism, materialist, 14, 25, 32

Hobhouse, L. T. et al., 221n.
Hobsbawm, E., 259, 291n.
Hoggart, R., 232n.
Hollander, E. P., 296n.
Holmes, D. S., 291n.
Honigman, J. J., 285n.
Hulin, C. L., 252–3, 288nn.
humanism, humanist, 1, 16–17, 25–6, 207
Hunter, J., 232n.
hunting and gathering mode of production, social formation
  see foraging

identification with others, or a group, 85, 99, 127, 153–4, 272–4, 277, 281–2, 293n.
  "negative" identification, 153, 282
ideology, 1–2, 17, 25, 35–6, 41–2n., 51, 113, 121, 124, 127–8, 134, 138, 142, 152, 175, 200, 207, 238, 256, 266, 283
  "immiseration", 71, 74n., 122, 145, 214, 259, 296n.
Inden, R. B., 224n.
individualism, practice and/or principle of, 143, 199, 224n., 235, 237
individuation, 15–16, 45–6 (definition and sources of), most of the rest of Chapter 2, 63–4 (consequences of), 65–8, 125–6, 165, 169, 172–5, most of Chapter 8, 278, 295n., 300–1
  *de*individuation, 161n., 295n., 301
  "ingroup" versus "outgroup" relations, 58n., 153, 273–84
"instrumental" functioning of the state, 155
instrumental learning, 99
"instrumental" orientation toward labour, others, products, etc.
  see "extrinsic" orientation
"interactive", or "multiplicative", conceptions of causality, 140, 157–8, 275–6, 284
interest(s), 1, 15–16, 34, 41n., 46, 50, 64, 68–71, 73n., 98, 122–3, 134–7, 142, 147, 152–7, 201, 215, 217,

225n., 232n., 260, 263, 267–9, 272, 278, 280, 282, 299
"internal" labour market, state (to a corporation), 264
"intrinsic" orientation toward labour, others, products, etc.
see "expressive" orientation
irrigation, 166–7, 176–7nn., 184
Israel, J., 13, 37n.

Jaggar, A. M., 179nn., 231n.
Jaspers, J. M. F., 295n.
Jessop, R., 162n.
"job enlargement" or "enrichment", 253, 288n.
Johnson, L. C., 178n.
Jones, D., 230n.
"juridical", or formal-legal, individuality, personality, 52–3, 193–4, 202
"jurisdictional" disputes, 210
justice, injustice
see ethics, etc.

Kamenka, E., 229n.
Kaplan, H. R., 230n.
Kay, G., 160n., 230n.
Keddie, V., 232n.
Kelley, H., 95n.
Kern, H., 231n.
Kidd, R. F., 289n.
kinship, 173, 200, 217, 224n.
knowledge, 34–6, 62, 66, 71, 80–1, 104–5, 109, all of Chapter 6, 148, 256
Kolakowski, L., 129n.
Kornhauser, A., 287n., 292n.
Kosambi, D. D., 223–4nn., 285nn., 290n.
Kovel, J., 190, 224nn.
Krader, L., 177n., 179n.
Krauss, R., 96n.
Kusterer, K., 231n., 292n.

labour-power, 33, 69, 115, 118, 124, 144–5, 247
Labreche, J., 230n.
Lamb, R. B., 232n.
Lane, A. J., 226nn.

Lane, R., 249, 287n.
language, 26, 40n., 127, 173, 175, 179n.
Lannoy, R., 224n., 285n.
Lasch, C., 226n., 286n.
Latané, B., 161n.
Law of Effect, 97
Law of Value, 29, 40n., 121, 144
Lawrence, P. R., 252–3, 288nn.
laws, legal systems, 52–3, 68–9, 116–17, 181, 184–7, 193–4, 198–203, 226n.
Laxer, R., 178n.
Leacock, E., 177n., 221–3nn., 285nn.
leadership, 134, 144, 152, 156–9, 186–7
"Least Effort" principle, 235
Lee, R., 172, 177n., 221–3nn., 285nn., 290n.
"Left", or "Young", Hegelians, 14, 17, 38n.
Leggett, J., 268, 292n.
LeGoff, J., 206, 228–9nn.
Lenin, N. I., 159
Lenski(s), G. and J., 221–3nn.
levels of analysis, 3, 19–22, 152
Levine, D., 295n.
Lewin, K., 96n.
Lichtheim, 160n., 230n.
Lieberman, S., 269
Lockwood, D., 231nn.
logical positivism, 166
Luckmann, T., 125, 130nn.
Luddism, Luddites, 210, 218, 259
Lukács, G., 1, 8n., 13, 38n., 41nn., 130n., 140, 160n., 162n.
Luxton, M., 250, 288n.

Maccoby, E. E. et al., 296n.
Maccoby, M., 288n.
Macfarlane, A., 227n.
Maine, H., 166
Mallet, S., 231n.
Mandel, D., 296n.
Mandel, E., 221n., 230n.
Mann, L. et al., 295n.
Mann, M., 214, 232n., 246–7, 279, 287n.
Mantoux, P., 178n., 229–30nn.

manufacturing system, 170, 208
manumission, 193–5, 240
Marcuse, H., 287n.
Markus, G., 18, 38n.
Martines, L., 228nn., 229nn.
Maslow, A., 253–4
"master" or "proof" piece, 170, 203
McCarney, J., 159–60nn.
McKirnan, D. J., 294–5nn.
McLellan, D., 94–5nn., 110n.,
    160–1nn.
McMurtry, J., 8n., 81n., 100, 110n.
mechanization, 52, 116, 118, 143,
    147, 170, 208–10, 215
mediation, 21–3, 113, 123, 127
Meissner, M. et al., 231n.
Menzies, H., 178n.
Mepham, J., 41–2nn., 124, 127
mercantilism, 51, 205, 209
Merton, R., 23, 39n.
Messé, L.A., 289nn.
methodological holism, 13–15
methodological individualism, 1, 3,
    13–15, 20, 27
Mézáros, I., 8n., 18, 38nn., 41n.
Mikula, G., 289nn.
Miller, R. L., 289nn.
Mills, C. W., 162n., 245–6, 286nn.
mobility, social, 102, 114, 122, 136,
    143, 145, 150, 194, 202–3, 217, 238,
    254, 256, 268, 273, 277, 281, 287n.,
    290n.
Molina, V., 8n., 16, 34n., 41–2nn.
Moore, B., 161n., 291n.
morality
    see ethics, etc.
Morris, B., 285n.
Morris, C., 228n.
Mowrer, O. H., 161n.
mystification, and/or
    de-mystification, 50, 70–1, 114–15,
    121, 124–8, 263–6, 279

Naqvi, S., 176n.
national differences, in
    ability of current working classes to
    strike a "better deal" from their
    employers and states, 213, 229n.
    feudalism, 198–9

guild-systems, 202–3
    slavery, 194–7
    socialist nature of early working
        class movements, 211–13
    timing of, and struggle for, the
        ascendancy of the bourgeoisie,
        209
nationalism, nation-state, 166, 283–4
"natural" individual, and/or
    individuality, as opposed to
    "juridical" or formal-legal, 52–3
    see also "juridical"
"natural", or "spontaneous", events,
    processes, modes of production
    and/or social formations, as
    opposed to "voluntary" ones, 15,
    22–4, 28–36, 39n., 41nn., 52, 74n.,
    120, 125
"natural rights", 103, 144, 211
Neale, R. S., 209, 229nn.
needs, 1–2, 17, 30, 32–3, 36, 37–8n.,
    61–3, 68, 71, 73n., 79, 81, most of
    Chapter 4, 119, 122, 126, 133, 141,
    145, 235–7, 278, 288–9nn., 293n.,
    301
need hierarchy, 3–4, 85–8, 94, 107,
    122, 174, 235–6, 239–43, 248–9,
    253–4, 273, 276, 288n., 301
Newman, K. S., 221–2nn.
Ng, S. H., 295n.
Nichols, T., 231–2nn., 247, 250,
    260–1, 264, 266, 268, 271, 280,
    287–8nn., 291–7nn.
Nicolas, R. W., 224n.
Nicolaus, M., 95n.
Nightingale, D. V., 230n., 288n.
Nightingale, M., 232n.
Nisbet, R., 39n.
Noble, D., 233n.
nurturance, 84–6, 174, 249, 254

Oakley, A., 288n.
"objective teleology", 23, 29
O'Connor, J., 232n.
Ollman, B., 6, 8n., 16, 18, 37n., 41n.,
    79, 81n., 95n., 100, 110n.
ontology, 18, 38n., 299
"open-" versus "enclosed-field"
    systems, 199

operant conditioning, 99
organic, organicism, 20, 28, 119, 128
"Original Affluent Society" thesis,
182
Ostor, A. et al., 224nn.
ownership
see property, forms of; communal
property; private property

Palliser, D. M., 228nn.
Parekh, B., 159n.
Paris Commune, 158
Parsons, T., 23, 58n.
participation of workers in decision-
making, "participative
management", 213, 219, 253,
288n.
"particularism", as opposed to
"universalism", in social relations,
56, 58n.
pastoralism, pastoral mode of
production, 19, 65
patriarchy, patriarchal relations, 46,
174, 256
Patterson, O., 177n., 193, 225–6nn.,
286nn., 290n.
Perkin, H., 178n., 209, 212, 229–
30nn.
"personification", 16, 29, 98
Pettigrew, T. F., 294n., 296n.
Pfeffer, J., 252, 288–9nn.
phenomenolog(ists) (ology), 128,
130–1n.
Phillips, U. B., 195–6, 226n.
Phythian-Adams, C., 291n.
Pirenne, H., 178nn., 201–5, 228nn.,
286nn.
Plamenatz, J., 6, 8–9n., 142, 160n.
Pollert, A., 250, 260–1, 279, 288nn.,
291–7nn.
populism, populist movements, 210
"post-industrial society", 171, 219
praxis, 1, 26, 63, 71, 113, 119, 123–9,
149, 269–70
Prentice-Dunn, S., 295n.
Preston, R., 285n.
primitive accumulation of capital
see accumulation

private property, ownership, 48, 69,
98, 135–7, 166–8, 181, 186, 191,
194, 202, 222n., 237
"privatized" working class
community, 215–16
"productivism", 173–4, 179n., 182,
186
productivity deals, 219
productivity of labour, 54–5, 68, 86,
118, 160n., 230n.
profit-sharing, 213
proletarianization, 98, 109, 118, 122,
136, 210–11, 215
property, forms and ownership of,
46, 73n., 116, 168–9, 177n., 190,
220
Proudhon, P.-J., 144
"public" versus "private" relations,
spheres, and/or individuals, 16, 53
psychological reductionism, 3, 18–20,
22–3, 36

racism, 172–3, 195–6
Rader, M., 6, 8–9n.
Radhakrishnan, S., 223–4nn.
Raju, P. T., 223–4nn., 285–6nn.
Ramsey, H., 230n.
rationalism, rationality, and/or
*ir*rationality, 2, 4, 6, 16, 31, 87, 99,
104, 145
rebellion, riot, 67, 94, 104–6, 135,
241–2, 244, 258, 260
"reflectionism", "reflectionist"
conception of knowledge, 119
regression, defence mechanism of,
91, 106–7, 262, 299
Reich, W., 248, 277, 287n.
reification, 124
reinforcement, processes/principles
of, 97–100, 148–9
Reiss, I. L. et al., 287n.
"relative autonomy", of individuals
or the state, 155, 213, 217, 239
relative deprivation, 4, 71–2, 83, 141–
3, 176, 218, 235, 238–45, 250, 254–
6, 258, 276, 288–9nn., 294n., 301
religion, 26, 38n., 63, 73n., 134, 168,
173–5, 181–2, 185, 200–3, 206–7,
224n., 237, 248, 259, 283–4

Buddhist, Confucian, Hindu, Muslim, Zoroastrian, 188–9, 238
Puritan, 201
Protestant Reformation, 207–8, 229n.
Renaissance, 205–8, 245, 300–1
repression, defence mechanism of, 41n., 106–7, 122–3, 130n., 248, 250, 268
"repressive tolerance", 260
reproduction of social relations, 22–3, 26–7, 34, 46, 49, 61–2, 66, 117–18, 125
reserve army of labour, 217–18
"Resource Mobilization Theory", 259
revolt, revolution, 24, 30–1, 36, 41n., 63, 68, 74n., 91, 94, 103–4, 106, 108–9, 120, 137, 140, 144, 150–2, 195–6, 202, 204, 208, 211–12, 241, 259
Rinehart, J., 230n.
"rising expectations", process/ principle of, 91–2, 241–3, 289n.
Robarchek, C., 290n.
Roberts, K. et al., 231n.
Rogers, R. W., 208n.
Ronan, W. W., 289n.
Rörig, F., 205, 228n., 286n.
Rostovtzeff, M., 177–8nn., 223n., 285n.
Rudé, G., 229nn., 259–60
Rudwick, B. M., 226nn.
Runciman, W., 232n., 276, 286n., 294n.
Ryan, W., 295n.

sabotage, 24, 69, 151, 210, 265
Sachdev, I., 295–6n.
Sahlins, M., 179n., 221–2nn., 236, 285nn.
Salancik, G., 252, 288–9nn.
Samuel, R., 178nn., 229n.
Sartre, J.-P., 249, 287n.
scarcity, 47, 54–5, 86–8, 90, 93–4, 182, 235–8, 244–5, 256
Schaff, A., 8n.
Schumann, M., 231n.
Scullion, H., 271, 279–81, 291–5

secondary reinforcement, 98
Seeman, M., 162n.
"segmented" labour markets, 214
selection (social), chance and/or natural, 23, 29, 31
selective perception, 122–3, 267–9, 278
"self-activity", 88, 90, 97, 102, 235, 247, 250
"self-actualization", development and/or expression, need for, 86, 97, 100, 107–8, 142, 235–9, 246–7, 250, 254
Seligman, M., 161n.
Sengupta, N., 177n.
Sennett, R., 232n., 249, 256, 261, 277, 287nn., 291–2nn.
Serge, V., 296n.
Sève, L., 81n., 106
Sewell, W. H., 178n., 229n.
sexism, 168n., 173–4, 179n., 231nn., 247, 250–1, 256, 265
sexual activity, need for, 83–4, 87, 106–7, 173–4, 248
Shaw, M. E., 295n.
Sherif(s), M. and C., 272, 274, 293–4nn.
Sinha, D. P., 222n.
Slack, P., 228nn., 286n.
slave mode of production, slavery, 49, 67, 169–70, 181, 191, 193–7, 225nn., 240–1, 257
Smart, B., 21, 39n.
Smith, A., 38nn., 99
Smith, D., 230n.
Snyder, D., 291n.
social comparison, level and/or process, 3, 71, 91–2, 103, 141–3, 146, 217–18, 235–9, 251, 254–6, 260, 276–8, 287–8nn., 290nn., 294n.
see also "egoistic" versus "fraternal" comparison
"social individual", 14, 54–5
"social intercourse", 141, 276
social mobility
see mobility, social
socialization of labour, 22, 36, 62, 115, 118, 145

socially necessary labour, 54, 88, 115, 118, 263
"social needs", 84–7
sociological reductionism, 13, 19
Soper, K., 33, 38n., 89, 93, 95nn., 289n.
Srivastava, R., 294n.
Stampp, K., 196, 286n., 290n.
state, 48, 66, 71, 99, 116–18, 120, 137–8, 155–6, 166–7, 191, 213, 217–18, 238, 270, 279
state capitalism, 160n., 171
status, 87, 142–3, 169, 184, 189, 194, 201–3, 206, 240, 243–4, 249, 256, 264, 273, 276–7, 282, 294n.
status inconsistency, 256
Stedman Jones, G., 229n.
Stephenson, M., 231n., 288n.
Steward, J., 221–3nn., 235–6, 285nn.
Stirner, M., 17, 38n., 87, 106
Stone, L., 227n.
"strength in numbers", process/ principle, 147–9, 280–1
structuralism, structuralist, 1, 16–17, 23–5, 31, 41n., 128
Stuckey, S., 286n., 291n.
sublimation, 262
subsistence, subsistence labour and/ or needs, 47, 70–1, 83–8, 133, 142, 182–5, 212, 223n., 234–45, 248–50, 254, 273
Suls, J. M., 289nn.
"superordinant(ate)" goals or interests, 137–8, 274–5, 283, 294n.
surplus, surplus labour, 47–9, 55, 65, 70, 114–15, 118, 167, 181–4, 222n., 236–8, 263
surplus value, 29–30, 40n., 52, 116, 124, 142, 230n.
Svejmar, J., 230n.
Sweezy, P., 178n., 243, 259, 286n., 291n.
symbolic interactionism(ist), vii, 130–1n.
systematization, systemic, 20–2, 24–7, 31–6, 71, 140

Tacitus, P. C., 169

Tajfel, H., 272, 281, 293–6nn.
"taking the role of" others, 85, 95n., 127
Tannenbaum, A., 37n.
Taylor, D. M., 294–5nn.
Taylor, M. C., 289n.
technology, technological change/ innovation, 47, 65, 68–9, 160n., 166–9, 181, 209, 219–20, 232n., 235–6, 246
technological determinism, 33, 183
Tedeschi, J. et al., 261, 291nn.
Terkel, S., 287n.
Thibaut, J., 95n.
Thomas, D. et al., 160–1n.
Thompson, E. A., 177n., 223nn.
Thompson, E. P., 7, 8n., 13, 16, 20, 27, 37nn., 210–11, 216, 229–32nn., 244, 259, 286nn., 291n., 294n.
Thorndike, E. L., 109n.
Thorner, D., 176n.
Thorpe, E. E., 286n.
threshold of tolerance for frustration, 102–3, 108, 176, 257–62, 301
Ticktin, H., 160n., 178n.
Tilly(s), C., L. and R., 211, 229n.
"totality", 13–14, 26, 140
Touraine, A., 178n.
"traditional" working class, versus "deferential" and "privatized", communities, 215–16
Traugott, M., 229n.
"tribal" societies, 173, 181–7, 257, 300
tribute, tributary or "pre-bendal" relations of production, 45, 65, 166–8, 188, 239
Tripathi, R. C., 294n.
Trotsky, L., 268, 292n.
Tucker, D. R. T., 3, 8n., 13, 37n.
Turnbull, C., 186, 222n., 285n., 290nn.
Turner, A. N., 252–3, 288nn.
Turner, B., 176n.
Turner, J. C., 293–6nn.
Turner, R., 41n.

Udy, S., 221n.
uneven development, 215

universal class, 64, 70, 74n.
universal equivalent, 91
   see also equivalence; exchange;
   commodity exchange relations
"universalism(istic)", as opposed to
   "particularism(istic)", 56
universal suffrage, 103, 147, 211
Unwin, G., 178nn., 202–5, 228nn.,
   286nn., 291n.
Urry, J., 289n.
use-value, 114–15, 118
Ute, M. K., 289n.
Utopian socialism(ists), 4, 139, 157,
   207

Vanneman, R. D., 294nn., 296n.
Van Knippenberg, Ad F. M., 278,
   294–5nn.
variety, need for, 84, 88, 97, 235–7,
   247, 250
Vincent, D., 179n., 230n.

wage-labour, 35, 101–3, 197–8, 205,
   210, 223n.
Wagner, A., 99
Wahba, M. A., 289nn.
Wainwright, H., 233n.

Walker, I., 294n.
Watts, B. L., 289nn.
Webb, K. et al., 291n.
Weber, M., 189
Wells, D., 230n.
Westwood, S., 261, 271, 288nn.,
   292–4nn., 297n.
White, T. H., 288n.
Wiedemann, T., 225–6nn., 290–1nn.
Wild, J., 224n., 286nn.
Williams, R., 179n.
Willis, P., 232n., 247, 250, 261,
   265–6, 271, 279, 287nn., 292–5nn.
Willis, T. A., 290n.
Wilmott, P., 231n.
Wittfogel, K., 285nn., 290n.
Wood, A., 161n.
Wood, S., 230–1nn.
Worchel, S., 293–6nn.
"working class authoritarianism",
   216, 249

Young, M., 231n.

Zajonc, R., 293n.
Zimbardo, P. G., 295n.

GPSR Compliance

The European Union's (EU) General Product Safety Regulation (GPSR) is a set of rules that requires consumer products to be safe and our obligations to ensure this.

If you have any concerns about our products, you can contact us on ProductSafety@springernature.com

In case Publisher is established outside the EU, the EU authorized representative is:

Springer Nature Customer Service Center GmbH
Europaplatz 3
69115 Heidelberg, Germany

The manufacturer's authorised representative in the EU is Springer
Nature Customer Service Centre GmbH, Europaplatz 3, 69115 Heidelberg,
Germany. If you have any concerns regarding our products, please
contact ProductSafety@springernature.com

Printed and bound by CPI Group (UK) Ltd, Croydon, CR0 4YY

22/04/2026

02095150-0001